Russian Theatre in Practice

RELATED TITLES

Christoph Schlingensief: Staging Chaos, Performing Politics and Theatrical Phantasmagoria
Anna Teresa Scheer
ISBN 9781350001053

Brecht on Theatre
Bertolt Brecht
ISBN 9781350068902

Brecht on Performance: Messingkauf and Modelbooks
Bertolt Brecht
ISBN 9781350077065

The Great European Stage Directors Set 1: Volumes 1–4: Pre-1950
Anthology edited by Simon Shepherd
ISBN 9781474254113

The Great European Stage Directors Set 2: Volumes 5–8: Post-1950
Anthology edited by Simon Shepherd
ISBN 9781474254168

Russian Theatre in Practice

The Director's Guide

Edited by Amy Skinner

methuen | drama
LONDON · NEW YORK · OXFORD · NEW DELHI · SYDNEY

METHUEN DRAMA
Bloomsbury Publishing Plc
50 Bedford Square, London, WC1B 3DP, UK
1385 Broadway, New York, NY 10018, USA

BLOOMSBURY, METHUEN DRAMA and the Methuen Drama
logo are trademarks of Bloomsbury Publishing Plc

First published in Great Britain 2019

Copyright © Amy Skinner and contributors, 2019

Amy Skinner and contributors have asserted their right under the
Copyright, Designs and Patents Act, 1988, to be identified as the authors of this work.

Cover design by Hugh Cowling

All rights reserved. No part of this publication may be reproduced or transmitted in any form or by any means, electronic or mechanical, including photocopying, recording, or any information storage or retrieval system, without prior permission in writing from the publishers.

Bloomsbury Publishing Plc does not have any control over, or responsibility for, any third-party websites referred to or in this book. All internet addresses given in this book were correct at the time of going to press. The author and publisher regret any inconvenience caused if addresses have changed or sites have ceased to exist, but can accept no responsibility for any such changes.

A catalogue record for this book is available from the British Library.

A catalog record for this book is available from the Library of Congress.

ISBN: HB: 978-1-4742-8442-4
PB: 978-1-4742-8441-7
ePDF: 978-1-4742-8444-8
eBook: 978-1-4742-8443-1

Series: Performance Books

Typeset by Integra Software Services Pvt. Ltd.

To find out more about our authors and books visit www.bloomsbury.com
and sign up for our newsletters.

For Christopher, with love.

CONTENTS

List of Illustrations ix
Notes on Contributors xi
Note on Transliteration and Russian Terms xv

Introduction *Amy Skinner* 1

1 Innovative Practices: Stanislavsky Directs Chekhov and Gorky *Maria Shevtsova* 13

2 Vsevolod Meyerhold: Creating an Interdisciplinary Mise-en-scène *Amy Skinner* 27

3 Nina Simonovich-Efimova: Theatre as Living Sculpture in Motion *Dassia N. Posner* 43

4 Yevgeny Vakhtangov: The Future Head of the Russian Theatre *Andrei Malaev-Babel* 61

5 Alexander Tairov: Theatricalizing the Theatre *Claire Warden* 79

6 Michael Chekhov: Directing an Actors' Theatre *Tom Cornford* 95

7 Alexandra Remizova: A Dialogue with Time *Andrei Malaev-Babel* 109

8 Natalia Sats: A Soviet Life in the Theatre *Manon van de Water* 127

9 Mar Sulimov's School of Directing: A Case Study
   of the Production *Shoo, Death, Shoo!*
   Sergei Tcherkasski 141

10 Anatoly Efros's Principles of Acting and Directing:
   Psychological Truth, Active Analysis, Adaptations –
   'Zigzags' and Thematic Modernity *James Thomas* 161

11 Oleg Efremov: The Heir to Stanislavsky
   Jesse Gardiner 179

12 Interviews with Genrietta Ianovskaia
   Manon van de Water 193

Conclusion *Amy Skinner* 209

Postscript: Where to Next? *Amy Skinner* 217

Notes 223
Bibliography 253
Index 263

LIST OF ILLUSTRATIONS

2.1   *The Second Army Commander*, State Meyerhold Theatre (1929) 38
2.2   *Roar China*, Meyerhold Theatre (1926) 40
3.1   Nina Simonovich-Efimova with Big Petrushka (1930) 44
3.2   The Efimovs' travelling show booth (n.d.) 53
3.3   Nina Simonovich-Efimova, shadow scene from *The Stolen Sun* (n.d.) 53
3.4   Nina Simonovich-Efimova, the witches of *Macbeth* (1931). 59
4.1   Yevgeny Vakhtangov, 1918 62
4.2   Alexandra Remizova as Zelima and Yuri Zavadsky as Calaf in *Princess Turandot*, 1922 65
4.3   Actors' parade at the start of *Princess Turandot*, 1922 75
7.1   Alexandra Remizova, 1950s 110
7.2   Yuliya Borisova as Anisya and Nikolai Bubnov as Zazypkin in *Gold*, 1955 119
7.3   Remizova in rehearsal, 1950s 124
8.1   Natalia Sats and Sergey Prokofiev during a rehearsal of *Peter and the Wolf* in 1936 129
8.2   The building of the Moscow State Children's Musical Theatre, supervised by Sats 138
9.1   Mar Sulimov in rehearsals for *Shoo, Death, Shoo!* (LGITMiK, 1983) 142
9.2   Andrius and Barber Finkelstein. *Shoo, Death, Shoo!* (LGITMiK, 1984) 145
9.3   Andrius and Cow. *Shoo, Death, Shoo!* (LGITMiK, 1984) 154
9.4   Mother and Father. *Shoo, Death, Shoo!* (LGITMiK, 1984) 157
10.1 Anatoly Efros 162
11.1 Svetlana Mizeri and Oleg Efremov in *Alive Forever* at the Sovremennik Theatre Studio, 1956 181

11.2 *Five Evenings* by Aleksandr Volodin at the Sovremennik Theatre Studio, 1959 190
12.1 *Dog's Heart*, 1987 198
12.2 *The Storm*, 1997 203
12.3 *The Balding Cupid*, 2016 207

NOTES ON CONTRIBUTORS

Tom Cornford is Lecturer in Theatre and Performance at the Royal Central School of Speech and Drama, University of London, and also works as a director and dramaturg in theatre and contemporary dance. He is the author of articles about acting, directing and dramaturgy for journals including *Theatre, Dance and Performance Training*, *New Theatre Quarterly*, *The Journal of Contemporary Drama in English*, *Shakespeare Bulletin* and *Shakespeare Studies*, as well as contributions to edited collections including a long essay with Roberta Barker on the director Tyrone Guthrie in *The Great European Stage Directors*, Vol. 3 (Methuen Drama, 2018). Current projects include a special issue of the journal *Contemporary Theatre Review*, co-edited with Caridad Svich, on the director Katie Mitchell, as well as two forthcoming books: a monograph, *Theatre Studios: A History of Ensemble Theatre-Making* (2019), and an edited collection, *Michael Chekhov in the Twenty-First Century: New Pathways*, with Cass Fleming (Methuen Drama, forthcoming). Tom was the winner, in 2017, of the David Bradby Award for Early Career Research in European Theatre and, in 2018, of the Society of Theatre Research's Stephen Joseph Award. He serves on the editorial board of the journal *Studies in Theatre and Performance*.

Jesse Gardiner is Lecturer in Russian at the University of St Andrews, where he teaches Russian language, literature and culture from the nineteenth to the twenty-first century. He works primarily on twentieth-century Russian theatre and drama, Soviet cultural history, Socialist Realism and critical theory. He received his PhD from the University of Nottingham, writing his thesis on Soviet theatre during the Khrushchev Thaw. He has published articles on Bertolt Brecht's reception in Russia (2015) and the theory of 'conflictlessness' in post-war Soviet drama (2018). He is currently working on a monograph titled *Return of the Avant-Garde: Soviet Theatre during the Thaw*, which interprets the revival of Russian avant-garde theatre in the 1950s and 1960s as a disruption of aesthetic norms and hierarchies. He is also a theatre director and incorporates theatre practice into his teaching and stages Russian plays with his students.

Andrei Malaev-Babel is Professor of Theatre and Head of Acting at the Florida State University/Asolo Conservatory for Actor Training. He served as the producing artistic director for the Stanislavsky Theater Studio, an award-winning company in Washington, DC, where he was nominated for a Helen Hayes Award as an Outstanding Director. Malaev-Babel's reputation as one of the leading experts on Russian theatre and acting techniques has brought him special engagements and commissions from institutions such as Stanford University, the Smithsonian Institution, the World Bank, Russian State Institute of Performing Arts (St Petersburg), the Latin American Film Festival and Teatro Escola Macunaíma (Brazil), and the Odessa Philharmonic (Ukraine). He is an author, editor and contributor to several books on key figures of Russian theatre such as Yevgeny Vakhtangov, Michael Chekhov and Nikolai Demidov. He serves on the board of the Michael Chekhov Association in NYC and on the advisory board of Rose Bruford College's Stanislavski Centre. He is also a member of the International Scientific Committee for *Arti Dello Spettacolo-Performing Arts* (Italy). Andrei Malaev-Babel is a graduate of the Vakhtangov Theater Institute in Moscow, Russia. He trained and worked under Alexandra Remizova, co-founder of the Vakhtangov Theatre, Stanislavsky's student and Vakhtangov's protégé.

Dassia N. Posner is Associate Professor of Theatre and Slavic Languages and Literatures at Northwestern University and the director of the Interdisciplinary PhD in Theatre and Drama. Her books include *The Routledge Companion to Puppetry and Material Performance* (2014), co-edited with Claudia Orenstein and John Bell, and *The Director's Prism: E. T. A. Hoffmann and the Russian Theatrical Avant-Garde* (2016), in which she analyses the vivid directorial work of Vsevolod Meyerhold, Alexander Tairov and Sergei Eisenstein. The companion website to *The Director's Prism*, which features over a hundred fully annotated archival Russian theatre sources, can be accessed at www.fulcrum.org/northwestern. Posner is also a puppeteer and a dramaturg; recent dramaturgy projects include *Grand Concourse, Russian Transport* and *Three Sisters* at Steppenwolf Theatre Company.

Maria Shevtsova is Professor of Drama and Theatre Arts at Goldsmiths, University of London. She is Doctor honoris causa of the University of Craiova and a consultant to the International Shakespeare Festival of that city. Author of more than 140 articles and chapters in collected volumes, her books include *Dodin and the Maly Drama Theatre: Process to Performance* (2004), *Fifty Key Theatre Directors* (2005, co-ed.), *Robert Wilson* (2007), *Directors/Directing: Conversations on Theatre* (2009, interviews), *Sociology of Theatre and Performance* (2009), which assembles three decades of her pioneering work in the field, and *The Cambridge Introduction to Theatre Directing* (2013, co-authored). Her book *Rediscovering Stanislavsky* is forthcoming. Her publications have been translated into twelve languages. She has held extended seminars at such institutions as the Academy of Theatre Arts in St Petersburg and the Grotowski Institute in Wroclaw and has extensive international multimedia appearances and lectures internationally at universities, theatre schools (Moscow) and theatre festivals on contemporary European theatre, including Russian theatre, and the sociology of the theatre. She is co-editor of *New Theatre Quarterly* and on the editorial team of *Stanislavsky Studies* and *Critical Stages*, the online journal of the International Association of Theatre Critics.

Amy Skinner is Lecturer in Drama and Theatre Practice in the School of Arts at the University of Hull. Her research interests include Russian and early Soviet theatre, theatre direction and scenography, and interdisciplinary connections between theatre, fine art and early twentieth-century physics. She is also a theatre director and designer, specializing in contemporary stagings of multi-lingual texts and plays in translation. Her work on Vsevolod Meyerhold includes contributions to *The Great European Stage Directors, Vol. 2: Meyerhold, Piscator and Brecht* (Methuen Drama, 2018), *Encountering Ensemble* (Methuen Drama, 2013), *Russians in Britain* (2012), as well as her monograph *Meyerhold and the Cubists* (2015). She has also written on other aspects of Russian and Soviet theatre, including Socialist Realism and the theatre of Nikolai Okhlopkov (2017) and stage design during the Perestroika era (in *The Routledge Companion to Scenography*, 2017).

Sergei Tcherkasski is a theatre director and Head of the Acting Studio at the Russian State Institute of Performing Arts (former St Petersburg Theatre Arts Academy, founded in 1779). He has directed more than three dozen productions; two of them – *Dangerous Liaisons* and *Great Catherine* – ran in St Petersburg for twelve and sixteen years, respectively. He is an internationally known expert on actor training and the Stanislavsky System. He has led workshops for actors and directors in forty major theatre schools in seventeen countries and has directed at, among others, RADA (London), NIDA (Sydney) and NTI (US).

Tcherkasski's books include *Stanislavsky and Yoga* (2016; also in three other languages), *Sulimov's School of Directing* (2013) and *Valentine Smyshlyaev – Actor, Director and Teacher* (2004). These books form a kind of trilogy representing Tcherkasski's professional family tree which grows from Stanislavsky to Smyshlyaev (member of the MAT First Studio, director of *Hamlet* with M. Chekhov) and then to Sulimov (one of the leading Russian teachers of directing).

His most recent book, *Acting: Stanislavsky – Boleslavsky – Strasberg. History, Theory and Practice* (2016), received the Russian National Prize for the Best Theatre Book 2016 and the International Stanislavsky Prize 2017.

James Thomas is Professor of Theatre in the Maggie Allesee Department of Theatre and Dance at Wayne State University in Detroit. He received his BA from St Ambrose College, MA from Villanova University and PhD from the University of Texas at Austin. He is the author of *Script Analysis for Actors, Directors, and Designers*, now preparing its sixth edition. Supported by the Murray Jackson Creative Scholar in the Arts Award, his book, *A Director's Guide to Stanislavsky's Active Analysis*, was published by Bloomsbury in 2016. He has translated the books of the Russian director Anatoly Efros, and his translation of the rehearsal journals for Efros's groundbreaking production of Anton Chekhov's play, *The Seagull*, will be published later this year. He is presently translating Inna Solovyova's biography of Vladimir Nemirovich-Danchenko.

Claire Warden is Senior Lecturer in English and Drama at Loughborough University. Her research focuses on modernism, theatre history, performance practice and physical culture. She is the author of three monographs, including the British Academy-funded *Migrating Modernist Performance: British Theatrical Travels through Russia* (2016).

Manon van de Water is the Vilas-Phipps Distinguished Achievement Professor; Chair of the Department of German, Nordic, and Slavic; and Director of Theatre for Youth at the University of Wisconsin-Madison. She is the author of *Moscow Theatres for Young People: A Cultural History of Ideological Coercion and Artistic Innovation, 1917–2000* (2006); *Dutch Theatre for Children* (2008/2009); and *Theatre, Youth, and Culture: A Critical and Historical Exploration* (2012), for which she received the 2013 American Alliance for Theatre and Education (AATE) Distinguished Book Award. She has also edited several scholarly anthologies for the International Theatre for Young Audiences Research Network (ITYARN.org), including *TYA, Culture, Society: International Essays in Theatre for Young Audiences* (2012, published in Spanish 2012), and co-authored a text book *Drama and Education: Performance Methodologies for Teaching and Learning* (2015, published in Chinese 2018). In 2017 she received the AATE Judith Kase-Cooper Honorary Research Award for lifetime achievement. Van de Water's current research project is a biography of Natalia Sats. Support for the research on the two chapters in this volume was provided by the Vilas Trust Estate at the University of Wisconsin–Madison.

NOTE ON TRANSLITERATION AND RUSSIAN TERMS

There exist a number of systems for the Romanization of the Russian (Cyrillic) alphabet, and, as a result, there is some inconsistency in how Russian words, names and terms are written in the English language. For the sake of clarity and to enable the reader to cross-reference as easily as possible, in the main body of this text, the most common spellings of names and terms have been used. Particularly significant terms have been standardized, even if they are not in common usage in English; the most notable example being the Russian term '*rezhissyor*', meaning 'director', which appears in this form throughout. Otherwise, I have tried to retain the spelling preferences of the chapters' authors. Where there is any inconsistency in common spellings which might cause confusion, Roxane Permar's translation of Konstantin Rudnitsky's volume *Russian and Soviet Theatre* has been used as a spelling authority.[1] Spellings of the names of directors included in the volume appear in the form preferred by the chapter's author. All quotations of extant translations retain spellings used by the original author. For ease of reading, diacritics have been omitted in the main text and endnotes, but are included in references and the bibliography.

In Russia, during the Soviet era in particular, the use of acronyms was very common. These referred to government departments, policies, theatre schools and theatre companies. In this volume, acronyms are defined at their first usage and given in both their Russian and English forms. Thereafter, only the acronym is used.

Introduction

Amy Skinner

> [N]ot for nostalgic conversation about the theatre of the past,
> nor for grim judgement of the theatre of today,
> but for inspired guidance to the theatre of the future.
> DAVID CHAMBERS[1]

The quotation which I have borrowed to begin this introduction refers in its original context to the work of Vsevolod Meyerhold; it could, however, equally be applied to any of the directors discussed in this volume. Indeed, the belief that these practitioners can act as inspiration for future theatre makers is a guiding principle behind this project, whose basic premise is that the leading figures of twentieth-century Russian theatre have much to say to contemporary directors and students of directing. This volume is an invitation to engage with these directors, whose practice not only shaped Russian theatre, but whose influence has been felt, directly or indirectly, across the world. Although the book contains historical material and analyses of productions which, in some instances, took place over a century ago, the aim is not to prompt nostalgia for a theatre-past. Neither is it to facilitate a comparison between the theatre of Russia and the Soviet Union and today's Western theatre which finds either one lacking by the other's standards. Instead, as Chambers observes, the goal is to find ways in which these practitioners speak to contemporary theatre, the challenges they issue to our practice and the approaches they suggest which expand the resources available to today's theatre directors. In this introduction, I intend to explore why I believe the Russian theatre is uniquely placed to do just that. The embodied experience of theatre making is at the heart of this volume, in both the analysis and the practical exercises, and I hope that, as you engage with these practitioners, you will have opportunities to explore their work in practice, use their tools in your own rehearsals and, as Stanislavsky exhorted, employ their practice to start '[making] up something that works for you'.[2]

Why Russian theatre?

It is difficult to overestimate the international significance of twentieth-century Russian theatre. The early 1900s saw the rise of both Stanislavsky's systematized realism and Meyerhold's avant-garde rebellions, practitioners whose legacy is keenly felt in today's theatre practice. In his introduction to *A History of Russian Theatre*, Robert Leach notes that his volume is 'founded on the premise that developments in contemporary theatre practice probably owe more to what happened in Russia than to any other country'.[3] Leach associates this lineage firstly with Stanislavsky's pervasive influence, arguably firmly established, and with the, to his mind, 'more surprising' influence of Meyerhold.[4] Indeed, Stanislavsky's very overt and acknowledged legacy and Meyerhold's more meandering and complex influence certainly suggest a range of responses to the better-known Russian theatre makers in the West, and this is reflected in the relative amounts of material available on the two directors. Although we should also be wary of framing Stanislavsky and Meyerhold as polar opposites (a perspective which neither director endorsed), the contrasts between their approaches prompt Leach to note that:

> [It] is arguable that the two main streams of twentieth-century theatre practice flow from the work of Stanislavsky and Meyerhold, who bestride the modern theatre like colossi.[5]

It is these 'colossi' with which this volume begins, a deliberate act of framing which forefronts the significant influence of both men on the development of theatre practice not only in Russia, but also in the West. As Stanislavsky and Meyerhold epitomize, the role of the stage director was established and developed in Russia as nowhere else, and the nation's theatre emerged as a space of aesthetic experimentation, political discourse and cultural dialogue. Names as diverse as Peter Brook, Ewan McColl, Katie Mitchell, Declan Donnellan and Peter Sellars acknowledge the significance of Russian theatre in the development of their own practice.[6] It is clear that, in their influence on contemporary theatre directing in Britain and America, Russia's twentieth-century theatre directors still demand our attention.

Beyond Stanislavsky and Meyerhold lies a diverse field of directors whose work is perhaps underestimated in the English-language version of the Russian canon. Of the directors included in this book, there are many whose names might be familiar to readers, and others whose profile is much less developed outside of Russia. What is particularly important to note is that the Russian contribution to international theatre is far more diverse than the Stanislavsky–Meyerhold (false) binary would suggest, and that this was already apparent in the earliest writing in English on the subject. The rehearsals recorded by Norris Houghton and André van Gyseghem, for example, include a range of productions beyond the stages of the Moscow Art Theatre (MAT) and the State Meyerhold Theatre (GosTIM).[7] These names may not have gained the same traction in Western theatre, but their practice has much to offer to today's theatre makers, grappling as they were with the same challenges in sociopolitical circumstance, the same cultural history and the same theatrical heritage. This volume aims to go some way towards redressing this disparity, by presenting these directors alongside their better-known counterparts, and by emphasizing the lines of influence between the varied practitioners.

Although it is important to establish the degree of influence that Russian theatre practice has had on contemporary theatre worldwide, it is equally necessary to consider why this influence is so profound, and what elements of Russian theatre history make it so appealing as a training ground for today's directors. These reasons are, of course, manifold, but I would like to begin this volume by suggesting three elements of Russian theatre which have helped to establish its status for anyone interested in the art of theatre directing. These are: how the Russian theatre responds to context; how the value of theatre is constructed in Russian practice; and how working models facilitate specific ways of engaging with theatre from theoretical and practical perspectives. These elements connect all of the directors discussed here; they also suggest some challenges for contemporary directors in terms of how we theorize and conceptualize our own practice.

Responding to context: Theatre, politics and government

When Stanislavsky and Nemirovich-Danchenko founded the MAT in 1898, Russia was a country under the autocratic rule of a tsarist system. Less than twenty years later, in the wake of one failed and two successful Revolutions, the Bolshevik party had seized power under the leadership of Vladimir Lenin and the country was in the grip of a Civil War. Throughout the twentieth century, Russia remained a nexus of political and cultural change which significantly shaped theatre practice. The construction of theatre's role and purpose during the Soviet era was vital in shaping the creative choices of the directors addressed in this book. On one level, they were responding to their unique sociopolitical context; on another, they were working within (and sometimes against) a complex bureaucratic and ideological structure which directly targeted all artistic practices. From its initiation, the arts policies of the Soviet Union influenced the processes, content and form of theatre in twentieth-century Russia. As some understanding of the history of Soviet Russia from the perspective of the arts is essential in engaging with the directors in this volume, a short summary of the key moments follows.[8]

Revolutionary theatre

In the words of Soviet historian Nikolai Gorchakov, the Bolsheviks 'assign[ed] a role to the theatre', actively pursuing theatre makers as potential contributors to the enactment of the Soviet Revolution.[9] It is important to remember that the events of October 1917 were only the beginnings of a Revolution, and, as the dust settled, the onus was on the new Bolshevik government to develop a Soviet mind-set among the Russian people. The communicative potential of theatre for a government faced with a largely illiterate and geographically scattered population was reflected in the propaganda trains and living newspaper performances used to spread Bolshevik news after 1917.

Not all professional theatre makers were immediately enamoured with Bolshevism, and many initially played their cards close to their chests. Edward Braun notes that:

> In November 1917 the Bolsheviks transferred all theatres to state control and [Anatoly] Lunacharsky [the People's Commissar for Enlightenment ...] invited a hundred and twenty leading artists to a conference to discuss the reorganisation of the arts. Only five accepted the invitation, and they included Blok, Mayakovsky and Meyerhold.[10]

The reluctance of the remaining 115 artists to affiliate with the new regime is clear; however, those who were willing to associate with Bolshevism did so vocally and with gusto: both Mayakovsky and Meyerhold claimed 1917 was their 'second birth'.[11] Theatrical form was also encountering a rebirth, with influences from the Russian and European avant-garde meeting a new zeal for socially and politically engaged performance. Konstantin Rudnitsky cites the organization Proletkult (*Proletarskaya Kultura*, or Proletarian Culture), whose goals included a complete re-making of cultural approaches:

> 'New art,' [Proletkult] maintained, 'only arises with the development of new forms. A new form of theatre is not possible as long as the stalls and the stage, the actor and the spectator, the author of the play, all elements of the old theatre still exist, even if the author has written the most Revolutionary play and the most exclusively proletarian public has filled the stalls.'[12]

What these aims highlight is the emerging division between form and content as markers of Soviet credibility in art: for the Proletkult, the ultimate indication of proletarian culture was the destruction of any formal element belonging to the pre-revolutionary theatre. The organization's influence, however, was brief: by 1920, it was clear that they had fallen out of favour, and that Lenin and Lunacharsky were not willing to support the complete destruction of old culture in favour of the new forms that Proletkult advocated. As such, alongside avant-garde experimentation, the former Imperial Theatres continued to operate (under the title 'Academic'), and the MAT in particular was offered ideological support. The early Soviet theatre, then, was strikingly diverse in its form.

Stalin, Socialist Realism and the Purges

In 1924, Lenin's death sparked a three-year power struggle for succession between Joseph Stalin and Leon Trotsky. Stalin ultimately emerged successful, and over the twenty-six years of his leadership strove to tighten government control over the arts. Stalin's desire to modernize the Soviet Union was reflected in his move towards Five Year Plans – rapid industrialization and collectivization of farming, leading to grain requisition and mass starvation in the countryside. These economic choices influenced Soviet playwriting in particular: the complex dramaturgy of the so-called NEP satires produced in the mid-to-late 1920s by Nikolai Erdman and his contemporaries left their writers open to criticism in an increasingly constrictive system of Soviet censorship.[13] Erdman's play *The Suicide* was a case in point, banned before its opening night. From 1934, government grip on the arts increased with the announcement of Socialist Realism as the approved style for Soviet culture at the First Soviet Writers' Congress. Blending realism with romanticism, Socialist Realism advocated a highly ideologically inflected approach to theatre making. In reality, the Socialist Realist diktat was clearer in terms of its ideological stance than its stylistic requirements, indicating the purposes of art as overtly pro-Soviet, but giving little detail of how this should be achieved. Marc Slonim observes that:

> Theoretically, the formula of socialist realism was contradictory and vague since it confused such different concepts as aesthetic method, artistic intention, requirements of a school, and political demands. But in practice it became an inviolable table of the Communist credo, and it required political conformity and traditional form.[14]

The need to comply with Socialist Realist doctrine, combined with the vagaries of what compliance meant in practice, resulted in a comprehensive curbing of innovation and experimentation in playwriting and performance. The threat of misinterpreting the requirements of form and content resulted in formulaic play texts which imitated any lauded work, leading to a series of low-quality, but acceptable, performances. In the context of Stalin's Purges, which included the surveillance, arrest, torture and trial of those suspected of anti-Soviet activity, the consequences associated with non-compliance to the Socialist Realist mode were severe, and the purging of Russia's artists and theatre makers led to the exile or execution of many significant figures, Meyerhold amongst them.

Thaw, stagnation, *glasnost* and *perestroika*

After Stalin's death in 1953, Nikita Khrushchev initiated a sustained period of de-Stalinization, beginning with his Secret Speech (1956), which denounced the atrocities of the Stalin era and began to dismantle the Cult of Personality surrounding the former leader. The period of relaxed control that followed was known as the Thaw (taken from the title of Ilya Ehrenburg's 1954 novel), and included a lessening of censorship and a number of posthumous pardons for victims of the Purges. Under Leonid Brezhnev, Russia saw a return to reactionary policies and a slowing of economic growth, leading to what is now called the Era of Stagnation. During these years, as Birgit Beumers suggests, reactionary cultural policies led to theatrical stagnation paralleling the political *zastoi*.[15] The brief tenures of Yury Andropov and Konstantin Chernenko did little to reverse this stagnation, and it was under the leadership of Mikhail Gorbachev that Russia saw its most substantial political reform. In 1985, Gorbachev introduced a policy of *perestroika*, meaning 'rebuilding' and referring to social, economic and political restructuring. This was followed in 1986 by *glasnost* (openness), which encouraged more open debate and transparency in the USSR. The intention was the reformation of the Soviet system; the result, however, was its destruction. Between 1990 and 1991, Soviet Russia began to collapse, and on 25 December 1991, Gorbachev resigned as President of the USSR. His successor, Yeltsin, would take charge of a Russia that was no longer a Soviet state.

Interestingly, the removal of the Soviet system was arguably as problematic for theatres as its censorship had been. Anatoly Smeliansky notes that the 'transcendent' potential of the Soviet theatre, shaped by years of censorship and repression which had led to innovative and metaphorical stage practices, had 'in circumstances of relative freedom […] lost its special significance'.[16] In other words, the post-Soviet theatre was left in a position where it had to invent a new mode of communication, a new theatrical language for a new – and, as Smeliansky notes, unprecedented – era.

'Elemental processes': The value of theatre

The unprecedented nature of twentieth-century Russian politics is perhaps one of the reasons for the significance of its theatre directors. These practitioners were responding to the problematics of staging theatre in a previously unrealized political context, where theatre as an art form has been afforded particular significance. Viktor Shklovsky noted in 1920 that:

> All Russia is acting, some kind of elemental process is taking place where the living fabric of life is being transformed into the theatrical.[17]

The transformative potential of theatre, what Shklovsky calls the 'elemental process', allowed performance to function as a tool for processing the myriad sociopolitical changes in Russia between 1900 and 1991. As much as the government sought to develop a way to turn theatre towards the Soviet project, Russia's directors sought to understand how and why theatre functioned as a medium. They were, in effect, working out how the 'elemental process' came into being. An engagement with the theatricality of theatre – that is, with the unique functioning of theatre as an art form – is a fundamental concern for the directors addressed in this volume. There is a fascination with the question of 'realism' and the relationship between theatre and everyday life – known in Russian as *byt*. Although finding different expressions, the way in which theatre forms a relationship with the world outside the auditorium is a fundamental concern for each of the directors addressed here. Realism emerges, in this Russian context, as a nuanced and inflected term, which illustrates the nature of the relationship between reality and the stage, from the naturalism of the early MAT to the Fantastic Realism of Vakhtangov or the Socialist Realism enforced from the 1930s.

Working models

Russia's directors understood theatre as a medium which occurred at the nexus of art forms. In her chapter on Konstantin Stanislavsky, Maria Shevtsova describes it as a 'unique, separate but not autonomous art'; that is, a practice which exists at the meeting point between other art forms, yet is still distinct from them. This uniqueness is seen in the working models employed by many of the directors in this volume. There are many references to collaboration, to how the director works with other practitioners to achieve their goals. These collaborators include, but are not restricted to, writers, designers and, of course, actors. How the final performance is shaped, how the ensemble is constructed and how the director forms the working company are all key concerns which a number of the directors addressed here consider. Some authors here have turned to the hyphen to describe a director's approach, emphasizing the interaction between directing and other theatrical practices. These hyphenated directors are operating in a space of transition between different approaches, for example, as director-actors (Shevtsova on Stanislavsky), director-puppeteers (Posner on Simonovich-Efimova) or director-pedagogues (Malaev-Babel on Remizova).

The hyphenated term allows for an inflected reading of a director where a specific priority needs to be highlighted and enables the reader to consider the broader significance of other practices in their influence on the craft of directing.

In addition, many of the directors here combine their professional practice on productions with laboratory work and teaching. In a number of instances, pedagogy plays a large part in their working lives, running studios or training programmes. These usually involve the professional development of actors or other directors, although in her chapter on Alexander Tairov, Claire Warden also notes the director's desire for a children's theatre school. Many directors also produced theoretical treatises, lectures or essays on their own productions, now invaluable archive documents that supplement understanding of their practice and which form the basis of the chapters here. The idea of the director as working in the mode of theorist and teacher, as well as in the rehearsal room, suggests the need for a holistic approach to Russia's theatre makers which should be borne in mind when reading about these directors and their practices.

The directors

This volume features chapters on twelve Russian directors. The number of potential practitioners for inclusion was vast and led to a process of selection which is inevitably flawed. Many other names could – and perhaps should – have found a place here; those which have been included were chosen partly because of their significance as individuals in the Russian canon, but also because of their inter-relatedness, and the potential they offer the reader to trace relationships and practices throughout the volume, comparing directorial approaches with similar roots and sources.[18] Relationships between teachers and pupils, affiliates and friends, those who embrace or reject one another's key tenets, are all thematic in this volume, and these echoes can be seen across chapters. Two additional concerns were taken into consideration: firstly, the inclusion of a variety of aesthetics which reflects the diversity of theatre making in the Soviet Union (for example, the desire to include practitioners who work with different audiences – adults, children, youth – and with different aesthetic modes – puppetry, for example). Finally, it was particularly important to include female directors, and to acknowledge within this book the significant contribution of female theatre artists to the development of Soviet and post-Soviet theatre. As such, although this book starts with Stanislavsky as an acknowledgement of his status, it ends with Genrietta Ianovskaia, whose work has been crucial in contemporary Russian theatre making.[19]

Maria Shevtsova's chapter on Stanislavsky offers a new and detailed perspective on the director's approach to play texts as staged texts, realizing what she calls the 'scenic potential' of the works. The significance of Chekhov and Gorky in the development of the MAT's innovative aesthetic is made particularly clear, and the examples from Stanislavsky's director's scores allow the reader a unique insight into how his directorial work functioned in practice. The influence of Stanislavsky is apparent throughout the chapters which follow, and key tenets of his practice return, in modified and adapted forms, in the work of other practitioners. References to objectives, tasks and supertasks, bits (or *kuski*), experiencing (or *perezhivanie*), Active Analysis and physical action emerge throughout this volume, indicating the centrality of Stanislavsky's thinking to the development of modern Russian theatre practice. As a counterpart, in the second chapter, I introduce Meyerhold's directing practice, focusing on his work on the mise-en-scène as a unique communicative tool in performance, and suggesting ways that his approach can be adapted for today's practitioners.

In Chapter 3, Dassia Posner introduces the work of director-puppeteer Nina Simonovich-Efimova. Framing her puppet work as a 'small theatrical revolution that still reverberates today', Posner offers a history of Efimova's contribution to theatre making through her work with young audiences and her engagement with puppetry as a genuinely popular theatre form. Her definition of the director as a 'synthetic visual and movement artist who creates, responds to, and performs with objects' suggests a significantly different and highly inter-disciplinary reading of directing practice. The first female director considered in this volume, Simonovich-Efimova is an example, in Posner's words, of women artists' willingness to '[immerse] themselves in historically marginalized art forms', and use these practices to 'straddle popular and elite culture'. Much overlooked in comparison to their male counterparts, as Posner argues, these directors made a vital contribution to the development of Russian theatre directing.

Andrei Malaev-Babel's work on Yevgeny Vakhtangov positions the director's relationship to realism as foundational in creating his Fantastic Realist aesthetic. The importance of what Malaev-Babel calls 'the "Stanislavskian" law of inner justification' demonstrates Vakhtangov's innovative approach to truth in performance, highlighting how this justification was less based on the creation of character and more on the actor's truth as 'master-creator'. By unpacking Vakhtangov's emphasis on the subconscious and his grasp of the production as synthesis, Malaev-Babel illustrates the solutions that the director offered to the 'essential dilemmas of the contemporary theatre'. For Claire Warden, Alexander Tairov has been largely marginalized in English-language work on the Russian canon, as a result of his 'perceived trickiness' as a director. Focusing on five aspects of his directing work (collaboration, characterization, constructivism, actor-audience relationship and promotion of Western plays), Warden seeks to engage directly with this trickiness to paint a portrait of a director whose practice was dynamic, innovative and deeply embedded in collaboration.

In Chapter 6, Tom Cornford considers Michael Chekhov's contribution to theatre directing. As a practitioner who worked in Russia, the United

Kingdom and the United States, Chekhov's internationality brings a new angle to this volume. As Cornford argues, Chekhov is best known for his approaches to actor training, and his directorial practice has been seen as secondary to the methodologies which he developed for the actor. Cornford suggests instead that the focus on a director's output of productions is a form of fetishization that leads to commodification of the director as *auteur*. By focusing on Chekhov's development of the ensemble company, he suggests an alternative understanding of the director, where the actor is placed at the centre of the theatrical experience. In Chapter 7, Andrei Malaev-Babel addresses the career of Alexandra Remizova, closely contextualizing her work against Russian and world events from the 1920s to the 1980s. Identifying her ability to create productions in which classic texts responded to the contemporary moment, Malaev-Babel traces Remizova's unique contribution to the theatre, seen in both her courage as an artist and her 'non-authoritarian and collaborative' approach to rehearsal. Incorporating Remizova's reflections on her practice and case study productions from the 1940s and 1950s, the chapter paints a picture of a director whose 'characteristic qualities [...] were stellar acting ensembles and a carefully elaborated, harmonious composition of characters'.

In Chapter 8, Manon van de Water addresses the work of Natalia Sats, whose commitment to theatre for children, and to the 'aesthetic education' of young people, led to the creation of the first professional theatre by adults for children in the world. Sats's determination to take children's theatre seriously subverts contemporary expectations that the Soviet children's theatre was simply a tool for propaganda. Her innovative approach to theatre for children included 'preparing the audience' through a pre-show talk which introduced not just narrative, but also theatrical conventions and stylistic choices. The role of children's theatre becomes thematic in the later chapters of the book: Anatoly Efros and Genrietta Ianovskaia, are also examples of practitioners who worked in the context of theatre for young audiences. In Chapter 9, Sergei Tcherkasski considers the education of theatre practitioners through his analysis of Mar Sulimov's approach to training directors. Sulimov's own background reflected the legacy of the MAT, training with both Valentin Smyshlyaev (who worked with Stanislavsky) and Ivan Bersenev (who worked with Nemirovich-Danchenko). As a graduate of Sulimov's Studio at LGITMiK, Tcherkasski recounts his experiences of a production process which also functioned as a training ground. His engaging and personal account gives an insight into the experience of working alongside Sulimov in rehearsal, and is enhanced with extensive direct quotation from the director, taken from rehearsal records and his own notes.

In Chapters 10 and 11, emphasis turns towards the theatre of the Thaw era. In Chapter 10, James Thomas explores the work of Anatoly Efros, whose practice combined 'Stanislavsky-based psychological acting, a keen contemporary sensibility, animated staging and modernist production values'. Thomas's chapter guides the reader through Efros's use of Active

Analysis, considering the intersection between mental analysis and the etude, or practical study. The exercises in this chapter offer a step-by-step guide to using Active Analysis in rehearsal, drawing on Efros's methods. In his chapter on Oleg Efremov, Jesse Gardiner demonstrates that the influence of Stanislavsky was no less significant during the *glasnost* and *perestroika* eras. For Gardiner, Efremov was an 'actors' director', whose goal was the revitalization of Stanislavsky's System. With an overview of his tenure as Artistic Director at the Moscow Art Theatre, and a detailed analysis of his adaptation of Stanislavsky's techniques, Gardiner demonstrates how Efremov sought to bring Russia's master back to life for the post-Soviet era.

In the final chapter, Manon van de Water discusses the career and directorial practice of Genrietta Ianovskaia using material gathered in interviews with the director. Through three case studies, including her celebrated production of Ostrovsky's *The Storm*, van de Water discusses Ianovskaia's approach to rehearsal, her work with actors and her collaboration with scenographer Sergei Barkhin to create productions which are visually striking, but also metaphorically rich and populated with complex performances. As van de Water writes, 'Genrietta Ianovskaia is one of the last active directors, trained in the Soviet tradition, to stage productions straddling the old Soviet world, and contemporary Russia'. As such, her work is a fitting end to this volume.

Approaching practice: The exercises

As each director here demonstrates, the heart of directing is the embodied and communal practice which takes place in the rehearsal room. The chapters in this volume contain 'In Practice' boxes, with exercises which are intended to give the reader some practical ways to approach aspects of the director's work in the classroom or rehearsal room. Chapter authors have been given the freedom to use these boxes as they see fit: in some instances, they contain quotations from the directors or samples of their written work; others explore the director's work in the rehearsal room, or offer contemporary adaptations of their directing exercises. Not every director in this volume left written guidance on their practice, but each exercise included here is either taken directly from the director's archive or has been devised in response to archive material by the chapter's author. What they all have in common is that they offer an opportunity to put these directors' ideas into action. Of course, the diversity and scope of even an individual practitioner's aesthetic mean that these can only offer a snapshot into their practice as a starting point, and further sources of information on each director are offered in the postscript at the end of this volume. It is my hope, however, that the combination of these chapters with the 'ways in' provided by the exercises will allow readers an opportunity to experience the potential of twentieth-century Russian theatre directing, in all its innovation and complexity, within the context of their own rehearsals.

1

Innovative Practices: Stanislavsky Directs Chekhov and Gorky

Maria Shevtsova

Stanislavsky was an amateur, although anything but a novice, when Vladimir Nemirovich-Danchenko contacted him to discuss the possibility of founding a new type of theatre.[1] He had a considerable number of acting and directing achievements behind him with the Society of Art and Literature, which he had established in Moscow in 1888.[2] Nemirovich-Danchenko was an esteemed playwright whose now forgotten *The Worth of Life* won the prestigious Griboyedov prize in 1896 over *The Seagull* by his friend Anton Chekhov; and while he prided himself on being a literary man, he was also a teacher of acting at the Moscow Philharmonic School. As is well known, the Moscow Art Theatre (MAT) was born from their eighteen-hour deliberations in 1897 on what, exactly, they would expect of a new professional theatre without the clichés, posturing and rhetoric dominating professional Russian theatre practice.[3]

Two opposing approaches to directing

Nemirovich-Danchenko had persuaded Chekhov to allow the Art Theatre to stage *The Seagull* after its humiliating flop at the Aleksandrinsky Theatre in St Petersburg. In fact, its failure was due to a misunderstanding in that the play had been billed for a benefit and, since such occasions generally anticipated lightness of tone, it was performed as an outright comedy.

This did not sit well with Chekhov's subtle composition, and the actors overacted, caught in their uncertainty as to what kind of play it was and how it was to be performed. Chekhov was loath to repeat the experience, especially in a fledgling venture like the Art Theatre, despite Nemirovich-Danchenko's reassurances as to *The Seagull*'s literary merits, on the one hand, and Stanislavsky's experience as a director, on the other. *The Seagull* was the last production of the Art Theatre's first season in 1898, and its novelty was evident. The play was of an unclassifiable genre, and the stage work was nothing like anything audiences had seen before. Irrespective of the production's various weaknesses – including Stanislavsky's and Maria Roksanova's performances as Trigorin and Nina Zarechnaya – the actors were less forced and more natural, and they worked towards a harmonious whole in which the stage design and all other scenic elements were integrated.

Uncle Vanya (1899), followed by *The Three Sisters* (1901) and *The Cherry Orchard* (1904), both of which Chekhov wrote especially for the Art Theatre, obliged Stanislavsky and the actors to work in unaccustomed ways even more. Chekhov's story lines were not clear-cut; links between causes, effects and consequences were tenuous; and dialogue appeared fragmented – at times inconsequential and, at others, simply disconnected. His revolutionary dramaturgy relied on mood rather than event, on impression and association rather than firmly etched action, on the ambiguity of emotions rather than explicit passions. Furthermore, its social and historical markers were allusive, and so a far cry from the accurately detailed *Tsar Fyodor Ioannich* by Alexei Tolstoy, which inaugurated the Art Theatre, or the no less explicit *The Sunken Bell*, reprised from Stanislavsky's earlier production of Gerhart Hauptmann's play for his Society to close the MAT's first season. It is small wonder that, faced with Chekhov's innovations in *The Seagull* for the very first time, Stanislavsky did not know by which end to begin.[4]

It is not that Stanislavsky's theatre experience had deserted him but that it was challenged, and his initial bewilderment fed Nemirovich-Danchenko's belief that Stanislavsky had little knowledge of literature. Indeed, this was the assumption on which the two men had agreed their division of labour for the MAT, which was to cause friction in the near future: Nemirovich was in charge of literary decisions – the choice and interpretation of plays and discussion of them with the company – and, in the event of Stanislavsky's disagreement, he had the veto on them; Stanislavsky had the upper hand on matters of staging, on which he had a corresponding veto. In actual practice, their blueprint did not work out quite so neatly, especially as Nemirovich-Danchenko began to overstep the boundaries of his remit.

Stanislavsky had gone along with Nemirovich-Danchenko's assessment of his alleged literary deficit, but his production plan for *The Seagull*, as later for the remaining plays of the Chekhov quartet, showed a fine instinct for textual analysis when it was to be put to use on the stage. Nemirovich-Danchenko was suitably impressed, writing to Chekhov that the blocking was 'very bold';[5] later, he extolled Stanislavsky's 'fiery and highly gifted imagination'.[6] In the meantime, when rehearsing the play while Stanislavsky continued to work on the 'score' – the term Stanislavsky used rather than 'plan' – he tempered anything that might interfere with the half tones he deemed to be quintessentially Chekhovian.

The Seagull, then, was an initiation into a dimension that *Uncle Vanya*, *The Three Sisters* and *The Cherry Orchard* were to expand but which Stanislavsky had not previously encountered; that, in fact, no one at the MAT had met before, not even Nemirovich-Danchenko who may well have seen the literary value of *The Seagull* immediately (as he was to see it in all of Chekhov's plays, with marked reservations about *The Cherry Orchard*) but whose full scenic potential he had not grasped, unlike Stanislavsky who had, and quickly, while he was writing the score. In other words, embedded in the MAT's deep engagement with Chekhov were two opposing directorial approaches that would soon encompass Maxim Gorky's very first plays *The Petty Bourgeois* (*Meshchanye*) and *The Lower Depths*, both mounted in 1902.[7] By the end of the Chekhov and Gorky period – Chekhov died in 1904, while the last MAT Gorky première was *Children of the Sun* in 1905 – the divergence between the two directorial approaches was more than clear.

Their divergence can be put simply. Stanislavsky's premises were those of an actor-director while Nemirovich-Danchenko's, for all his hands-on work with the MAT actors as a director, were those of a writer-director for whom the word as such, the author's word, pre-empted and determined staging. As a consequence, the author's word had priority over any scenic needs perceived by a director or, for that matter, by an actor. Stanislavsky's croaking frogs during Treplev's play within the play in *The Seagull*, for instance, or the scraping sound of a mouse during Masha and Vershinin's unspoken avowals of love in *The Three Sisters* irritated Nemirovich-Danchenko beyond measure: they were Stanislavsky's fanciful additions to the author's texts – 'caprices' was Nemirovich-Danchenko's word. For Stanislavsky, by contrast, invented details like these, much like cuts in dialogue or repetitions of phrases, were devised by and for the theatre, which had to be identified by its integrity as a unique, separate but not autonomous, art.[8]

This did not mean that Stanislavsky downgraded the text and its precisions and complexities as such. On the contrary, as his scores show, he paid close attention to dramatic texts, developing his scenic vision from them. What Stanislavsky's approach indicates is his concern with the non-said beneath and beyond the words on the page (he was to call it the 'subtext') and how this could be communicated through body language – stance, gesture, movement – and through sound, light, colour and other sonic and visual means. The latter group also materialized the words on the page by denoting (or only implying) time, place, situations, circumstances and social conditions, all of which provided more than a stage setting: they suggested the feeling, atmosphere and innuendos of the not-said and, too, of the not-done, like the invisible love affair between Masha and Vershinin. The strongest outward sign of their love was the sound of 'tram-tam-tam', made joyfully in Stanislavsky's production. Stanislavsky's appeal to the sensory expression of meanings that were generated by performance, however excessive this expression may have been (Chekhov famously derided the abundant sound effects of *The Cherry Orchard*), was always motivated by his sense – a sixth sense – of the stage.

In the case of *Uncle Vanya*, both Stanislavsky and Nemirovich-Danchenko put the production before their differences. Stanislavsky's actor-and-performance perspective and Nemirovich-Danchenko's author-oriented one converged in *Uncle Vanya,* creating such a unison of mood and tone not only between the actors' performances but also between them and the entire stage composition that even Aleksandr Kugel, the MAT's harshest critic, barely found fault with it.[9]

Stanislavsky had contributed to the success of *Uncle Vanya* by his sterling performance of Astrov, but he had also resorted to his 'caprices' by writing vignettes into the production that were not to be found in Chekhov's text. Take this one, for example. When Serebryakov and his wife prepare to leave the estate in Act IV, he kisses everyone including his wife, forgetting that she was going with him. No sooner does he realize his mistake than he waves it away with his hand. Stanislavsky saw possibilities for humour in a situation that, in the closing scene of Act III, was fraught with tension, and he had suggested these actions to the actor in the role. As Marianna Stroyeva observes, embroidered moments such as these had introduced a comic tone not obvious in *The Seagull*, and this brought a new awareness that Chekhov's characters were capable of stoic resistance against their suffering instead of submitting to it.[10] Stanislavsky's insight allowed him to heighten the resilience and hope filtering through Sonya's closing speech.

Stanislavsky's and Nemirovich-Danchenko's respective positions on directing throw into relief the seminal practices of the MAT's Chekhov-Gorky period and just how much they had overturned the theatre conventions of their time; and they were to affect world theatre throughout the twentieth and twenty-first centuries. These two factors – the one internal to the MAT's definition of itself in Russia and the other external in its inspiration, impact and influence outside Russia – need to be recalled since, having made history, the MAT's pioneering actions for the modern era can all too easily subside into history and be taken for granted or forgotten.

What were these innovative practices? First of all, the MAT established the principle of a theatre's close artistic collaboration with writers. This new theatre understood that it could not sustain its claims to newness without contemporary material; nor could its box office survive on classics alone. It found a contemporary playwright in Chekhov, as it was to do in Gorky, a popular prose writer whom Chekhov had convinced to write plays for the company. Second, the MAT fostered its relationship with these writers to ensure that it received a succession of fresh scripts capable of encouraging the company's creative growth – a model that the MAT attempted to maintain during the turbulent 1920s and 1930s, with mixed results. Chekhov quickly became the house playwright, which the MAT hoped Gorky would also do (this did not eventuate), and the bond between the company and its dramatist, who wrote parts in *The Three Sisters* and *The Cherry Orchard* with specific actors in mind, had a twofold effect: it stimulated the MAT's commitment to ensemble acting, as well as its efforts to perform in that seamless, free flow which, in several years to come, Stanislavsky would define as 'organic'. Gorky's plays for the MAT, although of a different character to Chekhov's by their plebeian milieu and front-on depiction of social reality, as Gorky knew it, sustained these goals.

The third innovative practice, then, of the Chekhov–Gorky years concerns acting. A new theatre required new actors, and Stanislavsky looked to the development of the MAT actors as he questioned his own way of acting while he came to grips with the vanguard drama of his day. The process for Stanislavsky, as he went from Astrov among the intelligentsia of *Uncle Vanya* to Satin among the disenfranchised, the poor, the outcast and the homeless of *The Lower Depths*, was one of learning how to embody the everyday life (*byt*) appropriate to given protagonists and endow them with believable emotion. The everyday was peculiar to the new drama – also in other countries of Europe, Henrik Ibsen's version being particularly familiar to Stanislavsky – and the theatrical 'tricks' that, to Stanislavsky's mind, were nothing but cheap tricks were wholly inadequate for the unassuming tasks of truthfulness set for the stage when everyday life appeared on it.

It is from Stanislavsky's search for a transparent theatre that emerged the fourth decisive practice – that of the modern director, the orchestrator-conductor who pulled all the strands of a production together, as in a symphony, necessarily involving all the players at work. Stanislavsky had garnered his directorial experience at the Society for Art and Literature, largely in the tyrannical style of Ludwig Chronegk, who had commanded the company of the Duke of Saxe-Meiningen.[11] His vision of the MAT as an ensemble company called such antecedents into question. Furthermore, his encounter with Chekhov's and Gorky's plays gradually forced him to reassess the very nature and purpose of his production plans, which, essentially, told actors what to do and when to do it. He began to ascribe to the director the role of equal responsibility, above all with actors, for the work they generated together. And this reversed the old prototype of the potent individual who, alone, made and answered for a production.

Meanwhile, Nemirovich-Danchenko had learned how to write production plans from Stanislavsky, and he was convinced that they were indispensable. But Stanislavsky rebelled – openly in 1903 during rehearsals of Ibsen's *The Pillars of Society*, which followed Nemirovich-Danchenko's plan. He argued that he did not want the 'tone and tempi of the whole act' to fill the actors' heads before they went on to the stage and that some plays, at least, could do without decisions being made by a director beforehand.[12] The actor in Stanislavsky had already 'intuitively felt', when he wrote his own production plans, that they 'constrained an actor's creativity because everything was given in advance'.[13] In 1905, he came into conflict once again over production plans, as much with himself as with Nemirovich-Danchenko, and let the problem drag on until 1908, after which he generally wrote only notes and reflections of varying length on the productions he had in mind or which he already had in hand with the actors. Crucially, the actual directing developed in conjunction with the actors on their feet, playing. This was the basis of his method of *etudes*, which Stanislavsky developed continually over the years for actors, finely connecting it to the processes of directing for directors, especially in the 1930s through his Method of Physical Action.

It took Stanislavsky his confrontations with Nemirovich-Danchenko to turn himself into a new type of director, but, until then, he followed the straightforward procedures that they had adopted. While Stanislavsky was busy writing production plans, Nemirovich-Danchenko rehearsed the acts he had already received, anticipating the next ones to appear. Stanislavsky, when freed from acting, also took rehearsals, readjusting scenes that his partner, when in disagreement with him, had adjusted. This arrangement meant that the distribution of rehearsals was uneven: for instance, in December 1898, shortly before the opening night, Nemirovich-Danchenko ran fifteen rehearsals for *The Seagull* while Stanislavsky only had nine.[14] There had been preparatory rehearsals in the summer, and there were coaching sessions with individual actors, as happened when Nemirovich-Danchenko monitored Stanislavsky in the role of Astrov to make sure that, having played Trigorin tepidly, he did not repeat his mistake. None of Stanislavsky's chorus of critics, least of all Chekhov, who disliked his interpretation of Trigorin, appeared to have considered that Stanislavsky had taken the character's own words about his lack of will to the letter. Ironically, he had paid *too* much attention to Chekhov's literary precisions. He was to learn as a director-actor, with the accent now falling on 'director', that, call it 'mirror-performance' – a listless character played listlessly – was not necessarily viable theatrically.

The two men's direction by relay was pragmatic, but it was not tuned in collaboratively, as it was originally meant to be, precisely because of the discord between them regarding directing. However, what Stanislavsky had lost in Nemirovich-Danchenko, he had gained in his designer Viktor Simov, his veritable production collaborator throughout these intensive years of discovery. It was with Simov that he showed part of the lake in *The Seagull*, opposing Chekhov's opening stage direction, where the lake is out of sight. Again, he and Simov rejected Chekhov's symmetrically placed shrubbery and generally symmetrical view, choosing, instead, a multilayered design that suggested the simultaneous occurrence of disparate actions in which the spectators of the play within the play could have their back to the audience and, at the same time, could appear to be an extension of that audience while being actors on a stage. Laurence Senelick comments with amusement on the 'crude daubs of Simov's landscape' and cites Chekhov's quip about the lake ('Well, it's wet').[15] Even so, Simov's design facilitated the work of the actors in a daring scene that exposed Chekhov and the MAT to an audience that was testing both of them.

Stanislavsky's continuing collaboration with Simov was the fifth innovatory practice of the MAT's early years, foreshadowing the cooperative director-and-designer model of the theatre of the future. In Russia, that model was to be taken to a higher level by Vsevolod Meyerhold, Treplev in *The Seagull* and Tuzenbach in *The Three Sisters*. Meyerhold, it could be said, was a born director. Stanislavsky, by contrast, learned to be a director and did so through being an actor: he saw directing with the eyes of an actor; he directed actors through his intimate knowledge of acting and actors. This may go some way to explaining why he never trained directors formally but only 'trained' them by example as he guided them as actors, passing to them the practice of theatre through his practice, as a grand master does to his pupils in instrumental music or the martial arts.

Scores: *The Seagull* and *The Cherry Orchard*

The example below from the score of *The Seagull* shows how Stanislavsky visualized the play in performance: visualization made his scores imaginative extrapolations from plays rather than mere illustrations of them.[16] Stanislavsky places Chekhov's text beside his own adumbrations, in parallel, on separate but adjacent pages. Here they are placed in adjacent columns. Numbers are in bold to facilitate cross-referencing for the reader.[17]

The extract comes from towards the end of Act III, when Arkadina and Trigorin are about to depart. In the preceding piece of dialogue, Trigorin had entreated her to stay another day and then rapturously declared his love for Nina. After a short exchange, Arkadina asserts, 'You are the last page of my life!' and goes down on her knees to him. This is what follows.

Chekhov's text	Stanislavsky
TRIGORIN: **106** Someone may come in! (*Helps her to get up.*)	**106.** Trigorin tries to free himself from her embrace, but Arkadina holds onto him more firmly than ever.
ARKADINA: **107** Let them come. I'm not ashamed of my love for you! (*Kisses his hands.*) My dearest treasure, why do such a desperate thing? You want to behave like a madman, but I don't want you to. I won't let you… (*Laughs.*) **108** You're mine – mine!… This forehead is mine, these eyes are mine, this lovely silky hair is mine!… You're all mine. Oh, you're so gifted, so clever. You're the greatest of all our modern writers. You're Russia's only hope… You have so much sincerity. Simplicity, freshness, healthy humour… With one stroke of your pen you can express what is most significant and typical of any person and place. Your characters are wonderfully alive. One can't read you without delight. You think I'm exaggerating? Flattering you? **109** Well, look into my eyes!… Please, please!… Do I look as if I'm telling you lies? Well, you see! I alone know how to appreciate you, I alone am telling you the truth! Oh my darling, my precious darling!… **110** You will come with me, won't you? You won't leave me, will you?	**107.** Speaks in the tone with the sort of pathos usually employed in melodrama.

108. Trigorin collapses helplessly in a chair. Arkadina drives home her advantage with still greater force. Trigorin sits like a dummy, without even attempting to defend himself.

109. Arkadina flings herself on her knees before him, holding up her face to him to force him to look at her.

110. Searches for Trigorin's eyes. Arkadina has now turned completely with her back to the audience, while Trigorin, sitting in a chair, faces the audience. |
| TRIGORIN: I have no will of my own… I never had one… Listless, flabby, always submissive. No! No woman can possibly care for a man like me! Take me away with you, carry me off, only for heaven's sake don't let me out of your sight for a single moment! **111** | **111.** Arkadina throws herself on his neck, a long kiss, then she gets up. |
| ARKADINA (*to herself*): **112** Now he's mine! (*Cheerfully, as though nothing had happened.*) **113** But of course if you like, you can stay. I'll go by myself and you can join me later. In a week perhaps. Why, indeed, should you be in such a hurry? | **112.** Arkadina (as I see it) having got up, passes her hand through his hair, i.e. tousles his hair, and while doing so, she says in an aside, 'Now he's mine'.
113. Gazes at him triumphantly from above and holds out her hand to him to be kissed. |
| TRIGORIN: **114** No, we had better go together. | **114.** Trigorin shakes his head silently, staring motionlessly in front of him: he has now entirely gone to pieces.[18] |

First – a warning. All the exclamation marks in this extract, all *thirteen* of them, have been inserted by the translator, which suggests that he has taken Stanislavsky's 'melodrama' above literally, allowing punctuation to imply that the scene is melodramatic. Moreover, the translator has deleted Chekhov's only exclamation mark ('One can't read you without delight!'), which 'justifies', in Stanislavsky's sense of the word to actors, Arkadina's disclaimer to Trigorin that she is flattering him. Apart from justifying Arkadina's words and emotions, the exclamation mark draws attention to her sincere admiration for Trigorin's talent: the dialogue in Russian, which is far more sober because it is without exclamation marks, allows this interpretation. Then, to boot, the translator adds the line, 'Please, please!' (with an exclamation mark), which does not exist in Chekhov's text but which, again, slants the scene towards melodrama and imposes the translator's view on the reader. The suspension points above are Chekhov's.

Such problems of prejudicial translation aside, Stanislavsky's visualized body language for Arkadina and Trigorin (Stanislavsky's glossaries 109–11) echoes the exaggerations not only of melodrama but also of the farces he had enjoyed performing as a youth, before his ten years with the Society. Stanislavsky further accentuates this perspective by his shift of sequence at 112, when he turns Arkadina's 'Now he's mine' (the Russian without an exclamation mark) into 'an aside'– an old melodramatic trick. In this way, he counters Chekhov's '*to herself*', which indicates that Arkadina makes a quiet comment under her breath. In addition, Stanislavsky's invented intimate gesture for Arkadina (she 'tousles his hair'), while she utters her aside, brings down her great emotional crescendo.

This very same moment clinches the image built up of her as a manipulative woman: note 'triumphantly' and how she gazes, in a position of domination, 'from above'. Yet, at the same time, her manipulative manoeuvres go hand in glove with her genuine love for Trigorin. The physicality of the scene also shows a collapsed Trigorin. Observe how Stanislavsky implies Trigorin's traumatic sense of loss, expressed 'silently', inwardly, 'entirely in pieces'. Stanislavsky sees whatever may be melodramatic, comic or farcical about Arkadina in relation to a serious crisis worthy of high drama. With this drama – deadly, by the end of his score – he creates a melodic baseline for his entire composition.

There are no records to show how far the actual production deviated from the envisaged one on paper, but it is certain that, in rehearsals, both Nemirovich-Danchenko and Stanislavsky adjusted playing according to how it worked among living actors in real time.[19]

Stanislavsky may initially have been unsure of *The Seagull*, but he had no qualms whatsoever about *The Cherry Orchard*. For various reasons, Nemirovich-Danchenko left him to direct it virtually on his own. Rehearsals, however, did not come easily, especially those of Act II, which seemed to

STANISLAVSKY IN PRACTICE

Keep in mind that Stanislavsky subsequently repudiated production plans. The purpose here is to go through the discipline of writing one so as to gather your thoughts as you stimulate your imagination by visualization. How you, as a director, share your intuitions, guesses and ideas with your actors depends on how you work with them and how they shape and share their own visualizations with the acting group. The aim is not to imitate Stanislavsky but to take some cues of perception and method from him so that you are observing Stanislavsky and learning skills from him, as did the directors and directors-to-be by his side.

It would be interesting to start with the selected extract before you choose your own. The questions below may be useful prompts. Chekhov's suspension points are mini-pauses, consonant with the gaps he marks by the word 'pause'. It is well known that Stanislavsky sought musicality in outer *and* inner action and that he composed tempi-rhythms by amalgamating the silence of pauses – counted precisely throughout *The Seagull* in seconds, each having its own duration – with spoken and other sounds. The whole, in its musicality, functioned like a score (hence this term for his production plans).

1. Write the score of suspension points in Arkadina's speech, articulating her inner states of being. Can her love for Trigorin be heard together with – in counterpoint with? in tension with? in contradiction with? – her determination to win him? How would your notation of her varied emotions form (musical) themes for this scene and for your envisaged production as a whole?

2. What are the dynamics between Arkadina and Trigorin? Is the actor obliged to be guided by Trigorin's account of himself as 'flabby' and always submissive? Stanislavsky was attacked for playing Trigorin in a 'flabby' way. What kind of Trigorin would not collapse in his chair? How would you direct your actor to 'go entirely to pieces' differently from Stanislavsky's solution?

3. The extract goes into a diminuendo at Chekhov's stage direction, which says 'a pause'. During this pause, which allows Trigorin and Arkadina to calm down, Trigorin writes something in his notebook. Dialogue resumes for a few more lines. It shifts gear when Shamrayev enters, announcing that he has provided horses for the carriage. Chekhov's stage direction right here is sparse, but Stanislavsky, by contrast, imagines the hustle and bustle of a crowd of servants gathering at the bottom of the stairs: Yakov brings down the last suitcases, the servants begin to line up, and so on.

> Direct this shift with less motion and noise, perhaps with none at all. How and why does your alternative change the atmosphere of the preceding 'bits' (*kuski* – Stanislavsky's habitual term), where Trigorin is first in 'pieces' and then pulls himself together by writing a note? Does your alternative affect the sequence that starts with Trigorin's 'Someone may come in'? That 'someone' could have been Sharayev.

be monotonous, devoid of any action that could excite spectators. Yet the company must have found their cue to the second act in Stanislavsky's long account of its landscape – titled 'mood' in his production plan – given how lyrically one critic, a regular at the MAT, spoke of there being 'something wonderful, aromatic, charming, musical and thoughtful about this marvelous picture of a summer evening'.[20]

Below is the shortest of fragments from Act II. The sun is about to set on this 'summer evening'. Charlotta, Yepikhodov and Dunyasha have gone off, one by one. Enter Ranyevskaya, Gayev and Lopakhin. Yasha is told to leave shortly before this fragment. Lopakhin tells Ranyevskaya to lease her cherry orchard for 'summer cottages… and you will be saved'. He has told her this 'every day'.

Note Stanislavsky's extrapolations from Chekhov for charting movement, which provide a meticulous choreography for Lopakhin.

Chekhov's text	Stanislavsky
RANYEVSKAYA: 46 Summer cottages and summer people – forgive me but that is common. GAYEV: 47 I completely agree with you. LOPHAKIN: 48 I will weep, or scream, or have a fainting fit… 49 I can't stand it any more…You have worn me out (*to Gayev*) 50 You're an old woman! 51	46. Uncertain, timid. 47. Quickly and confidently. He is even happy. 48. He spits uncouthly on the ground in despair. Here his peasant origins are suddenly evident. He is standing on his knees, pulls at his hair, beats his breast, his voice even chokes. In short, this is some sort of very powerful but ridiculous display of temperament. 49. Gets up quickly, throws his head back nervously. Goes and picks up his hat (where he was sitting, that is, to the left of Gayev). 50. Has picked up his hat. 51. Walks across.
GAYEV: 52.Who? LOPHAKIN: You. You're an old woman. 53 (*starts to go.*) 54	52. He is now going to be hurt. 53. Even more harshly, having stopped by Gayev's right side. 54. Goes off.[21]

STANISLAVSKY IN PRACTICE

1. Stanislavsky elaborates Chekhov's description of setting considerably for the sake of 'mood'. Visualize your setting (and discuss with your designer) so that it is not just a static backdrop against which the actors sit (as they all do at specific moments during this short 'bit') but is an environment to help them to act, and their characters to interact with each other.

2. Direct this fragment, keeping in mind Chekhov's reminder to Stanislavsky that Lopakhin had 'fine hands' (Trofimov's words in Act IV).

Gorky: Focus on *The Lower Depths*

Lopakhin, upwardly mobile, is closer, in terms of social origins, to Gorky's characters than to Ranyevskaya, and Stanislavsky, on recognizing the great difference of social milieu in *The Petty Bourgeois*, looked for the signs of a different dramaturgical organization to guide his directing. He found several in the openly noisy squabbles and unrestrained violence of the Bessemenov household, as well as in Gorky's affirmative vision of Nil, who, although not gentrified, was definitely not coarse or vulgar. Nil was not socially mobile, nor had he found freedom. He was a presentiment of freedom, of that new human being whom Gorky was to evoke in *The Lower Depths*. Stanislavsky perceived Gorky's sentiment and, in both his score and production, highlighted the good buried in the narrow-minded and mean-spirited majority of Gorky's universe. With this, he did away with evil villains in one stroke, while not quite espousing the 'tramp romanticism' for which Gorky had become known through his prose and was now transposing to his drama.

Such drama was uncommon in the Russian theatre, and Stanislavsky appears to have implemented a new, two-tiered directorial approach for *The Petty Bourgeois*. On one level, he merged the particular and the general: the production foregrounded *this* human being but invoked humanity at large. On the other, secondary level, he indicated, but did not explore, the conflict between contradictory social and moral forces of profound interest to Gorky.[22] Stanislavsky's usual impulse was to soften sharp edges, so he did not delve into Gorky's revolutionary pursuits. The authorities feared otherwise. As a result, when the MAT premiered *The Petty Bourgeois* in St Petersburg, as part of its tour to the city, the police manned the theatre, expecting sedition. Tension was high. Students called for revolution from the gods, but revolution waited for 1905. In any case, Stanislavsky was averse to tendentiousness in art, leaving even the staid critics of Moscow dissatisfied with his focus on *byt*, which, to their mind, was overburdened with picturesque detail at the expense of the play's serious concerns.

The Petty Bourgeois was a critical and public failure. *The Lower Depths*, following nine months later, was a success. However, it suffered from a similar disjunction between social life reduced to the mundane and social life understood as a struggle in which the dispossessed were mired and dehumanized. There was no exit from these conditions other than death (the Actor) or *ex machina* disappearance (Luka); and Gorky saw Luka as a 'swindler'.[23] Neither Stanislavsky nor Nemirovich-Danchenko was prepared to take up Gorky's advocacy of radical social change. As a consequence, neither fully grasped the political drive behind Satin's monologue-like speeches (Stanislavsky played the role), which come in Act IV, after Luka vanishes. Here, waiting for maximum impact towards the end of the act, Gorky provides a revolutionary counterpart to Luka's benevolent humanism, quashing this humanism with its rhetorical power. Gorky's theatrical strategy appealed to Stanislavsky the director as much as the aria-like structure in Act III between two separate voices – first Luka's perorations, then Satin's long replies. Even so, Stanislavsky toned down the debate incipient in this structure, subsuming it under the measured cadences of philosophical reflection.

Gorky's play asks what it is to be human, and several lines of Satin's first would-be monologue respond to the question. Thus, a human being is 'truth', whereas 'a lie justifies the weight that crushed a worker's hand, and it blames the man who is dying of hunger'; and a human being is his/her 'own person, independent, not eating somebody else's bread'.[24] Stanislavsky's parallel commentary in his score notes that Satin is sitting on a table and is 'drunk-inspired. One feels a talented human being – a drunken cabaret orator'. The rest of his commentary pictures an attentive group of people in a calm, rather than inebriated, scene.

Satin's second 'monologue' accelerates the argument of the first. His third is meant to be a climax, a *tour de force* pivoting on three main points: 'a human being is free'; a human being is 'you and me and them... all rolled into one' (my suspension points); a 'hu-man be-ing – it's magnificent! It rings... so proudly! A hu-man be-ing! A human being must be respected! Not pitied, not humiliated with pity'.[25] Stanislavsky's commentary for most of Satin's speech centres on Satin's qualities: he speaks with 'kind feelings'; he is 'sincere'; he 'has a great deal of love, and a sense of the beauty in people. You can feel an artist in him'. Elsewhere in Act IV, when Satin's lines are short, Stanislavsky indicates that he speaks 'affectionately', 'gently' or in a 'good-humoured' way. There is nothing in any of this about grandstanding, let alone political conviction.

The MAT had great difficulty in finding the right 'tone' for *The Lower Depths*, 'tone' having become its mantra with its Chekhov productions.

> **STANISLAVSKY IN PRACTICE**
>
> 1 Stay with Stanislavsky's remarks about Satin and see where they take you and your actors as regards the relation between Luka and Satin and their views.
>
> 2 Modify Stanislavsky's remarks according to your own impressions and observe how your directorial changes affect the way the actors deliver the Luka–Satin debate.

Worse still, 'tone' did not seem to be the right mantra. Gorky's was a fundamentally discordant play with its emphasis on psychological and physical abuse, Satin's seemingly abrupt change of character in Act IV, Luka's preaching to lost souls (Gorky had not presented him as a 'swindler' to the company – rather, the reverse), and the Luka–Satin polemic, which looks like Gorky's afterthought, since he had started out with Satin's defence of the old man to the assembled 'cattle' (Satin's word). It is enough to bedevil any director, let alone one attuned to Chekhov, as Stanislavsky had become. Stanislavsky lovingly wrote Chekhovian-inspired depictions of 'mood' and 'atmosphere' into his score for *The Lower Depths*. But, while the actors used them in rehearsals to help them, they overplayed the protagonists, and Stanislavsky leaned on his 'old methods' of 'intensity, inward tension, etc.,' until Nemirovich-Danchenko pointed out to both the actor *and* the director in Stanislavsky that what was required was a '*lightness* of touch'.[26] Wearing his director's mantle, Nemirovich-Danchenko further advised that the actors needed to 'declare' their lines, rather than go inside their characters, and stand outside them, as if they were commenting on them.[27]

Stanislavsky fully accepted Nemirovich-Danchenko's advice, and, between them, they produced an acclaimed production. Yet Nemirovich-Danchenko's observation about standing outside the characters was acute for another reason. It foreshadowed the idea of *ostraneniye* adopted by Meyerhold, which, in Bertolt Brecht's practice, became *Verfremdungseffekt*. And Brecht's affinity with Gorky is legion. Stanislavsky was not to follow the directorial line of distancing technique, but what he had learned from it was beneficial after 1905 and, again, after 1917 for the tasks he had set for himself and the MAT's ascent to glory.[28]

2

Vsevolod Meyerhold: Creating an Interdisciplinary Mise-en-scène

Amy Skinner

Meyerhold's theatre: Innovation and interdisciplinarity

Vsevolod Emilevich Meyerhold made his name as one of theatre's revolutionaries. His constant desire to overturn existing staging conventions resulted in a diverse and often-shifting aesthetic grounded in experimentation and innovation. His theatrical interests were broad, and his theoretical treatises consider not only the practical elements of the director's craft (his understanding of acting, scenography and text, for example) but also his contributions to questions on theatre's purpose as an art form. At the centre of his aesthetic, and essential in developing his innovative approach, was his commitment to interdisciplinary influence: from the latest discoveries in psychology to the cutting-edge aesthetics of avant-garde painting and sculpture, Meyerhold's theatre was in an ongoing dialogue with the emergent ideas of his era. As a director who considered theatre incomplete until it was viewed by the audience, interdisciplinarity allowed Meyerhold to explore the form and function of theatre's communication with the spectator and to expand the devices available to the director to achieve his creative goals. This chapter considers Meyerhold's interdisciplinary approach in action, exploring how his understanding of fields outside of theatre contributed to his stage direction. By focusing on one field of influence in particular

– the fine, or visual, arts – I explore how these media shaped Meyerhold's understanding of theatrical mise-en-scène in both theory and practice, suggesting that both his approach to staging and his interdisciplinary model offer much to the contemporary theatre director.

Born in Penza, southeast of Moscow, in 1874, Meyerhold began his formal theatrical education at the Philharmonic School under the tutelage of Vladimir Nemirovich-Danchenko in 1896. He continued to work in theatre until accusations of anti-Soviet sentiments led to his arrest, and on 2 February 1940, he was executed by firing squad.[1] His directorial career lasted a total of thirty-seven years: his first experiments as a director took place in the Russian provincial theatre in the autumn of 1902; his final production – a version of Prokofiev's *Semyon Kotko* at the Stanislavsky State Opera Theatre in Moscow – remained unfinished on his arrest in June 1939. From his earliest productions, Meyerhold proved to be a theatrical chameleon: his first professional engagement was as an actor at the Moscow Art Theatre, and, steeped in Stanislavskian naturalism, he started directing by 'imitating' Stanislavsky's style.[2] By 1905, however, he had rejected naturalism in favour of what Edward Braun calls his 'search for new forms', a lifelong quest for a new approach to theatricality.[3] He turned first towards symbolism, then the grotesque and commedia dell'arte in attempts to discover a way of making theatre that would exploit what he saw as the medium's unique potential to engage the spectator.

Despite his extensive output prior to 1917, it is Meyerhold's work during the Soviet era that has received the most attention. Robert Leach considers 1917–1930 to be the director's years of 'triumph', and it was during this period that Meyerhold's desire for formal innovation found new impetus.[4] He saw the Revolution as 'not only destruction, but creation as well', prompting his commitment to developing Russia's new political theatre in which performances would be in active dialogue with current sociopolitical events.[5] It was his belief in the need for theatre to respond to evolving political circumstances which not only assured Meyerhold's place at the forefront of the Russian avant-garde in the 1920s and 1930s but also, ultimately, led to his increasing persecution and eventual arrest, when his constant drive towards theatrical innovation fell afoul of the more culturally conservative Stalin regime.

Meyerhold's drive for innovation meant that his directing practice was never formulaic: his desire for 'new forms' ensured that the staging for each of his productions responded to the unique conditions suggested by the chosen play text and the sociopolitical context. Although his aesthetically diverse practice does offer the contemporary director a range of lessons in staging devices drawn from different theatrical styles, it also raises broader questions about Meyerhold as a director: how did he develop the ability to generate these diverse stagings, and what characterized the intellectual and practical approach to theatre making which he encouraged in himself and in others? It is Meyerhold's development of his theatrical mindset, the way of thinking about theatre that he applied to all of his production practice, that is the focus of this chapter. As much as theatre was the 'main interest in [Meyerhold's] life', his understanding of theatricality was in part shaped by his experiences of other disciplines.[6] This is reflected in the scope of reference seen in his own writing: as well as theatre history, Meyerhold refers to mathematics, psychology, philosophy, sport, literature and the visual arts. It is clear that he considered breadth of knowledge essential for the theatre director. This chapter discusses three elements of visual art influence on Meyerhold's directorial mindset: how the act of looking at artworks was centralized in the director's approach; how the act of making visual art was incorporated into his rehearsal and preparation processes; and finally, how specific visual art techniques found expression in Meyerhold's stage images. However, before turning to the visual arts specifically, it is necessary to consider Meyerhold's conceptualization of the mise-en-scène and how this influenced his approach to staging.

Meyerhold, mise-en-scène and the 'main idea'

In their survey of the rise of the director, David Bradby and David Williams consider Meyerhold's contribution to the development of directing as a craft: whereas before him, the director had been considered 'as merely a privileged spectator arranging and perfecting the performance before it was shown to the public', in Meyerhold's theatre, the director 'must reformulate the author's work in terms of a fresh and living stage idiom'.[7] This understanding of the director's role underwrote Meyerhold's approach to the mise-en-scène, that is, the complex system of visual and aural communication that is enacted through the staging of the play text. For Meyerhold, the play text alone was restricted in its communicative potential: 'How long before they inscribe in the theatrical tables the following law', he writes in 1912, 'words in the theatre are only embellishments on the design of movement?'[8] These 'designs of movement' became the foundation for Meyerhold's mise-en-scène, a sequence of patterns and poses which formed the production's visual score.

In Meyerhold's theatre, the visual elements of the mise-en-scène had an essential role in constructing meaning for the spectator. Like the director, the mise-en-scène sits between the playwright and audience. In Meyerhold's words, it is 'the notes by which the spectator reads the melody'.[9] Patrice Pavis emphasizes the importance of this mediation in his definition of the mise-en-scène as

> [the] performance considered as a system of meaning controlled by a director or collective. It is an abstract, theoretical notion, not a concrete and empirical one. It is the tuning of theatre for the needs of stage and

audience. Mise en scène puts theatre into practice, but does so according to an implicit system of organisation of meaning.[10]

This act of 'put[ting] theatre into practice', with its inherent emphasis on meaning making, highlights how Meyerhold approached the mise-en-scène in his productions. What Pavis calls 'the organisation of meaning' operates in Meyerhold's theatre through the creation of stage imagery which unpacks the production's theme and purpose for the spectator. Meyerhold emphasizes the production's overarching idea more than any play text's specific narrative. In notes taken during early rehearsals for *Thirty-Three Fainting Fits* (1935), Norris Houghton records Meyerhold's comments to the company:

> 'Two things are essential for a play's production, as I have often told you,' Meierhold begins. 'First, we must find the thought of the author; then we must reveal that thought in a theatrical form. This form I call a *jeu de théâtre* and around it I shall build the performance.'[11]

Note how the director turns not to a character or plot device to develop the production's theme but to the author's thought or purpose in writing. In some productions, this amounted to a staging intended to capture the essence of the playwright's entire oeuvre (*The Government Inspector*, 1926, for example); in others, it required detailed historical contextualization (*Don Juan*, 1910). In all instances, it prioritized the writer's place within the written text.

The development of the *jeu* allowed Meyerhold to express this thought as the 'living stage idiom'. Meyerhold's productions were organized around a central idea, which permeated the director's choices and was the foundation stone for the construction of the staging. Meyerhold calls this the 'main idea' and suggests that its centrality to the production should be such that it communicates constantly, although not always consciously, with the spectator. He reflects that

> the ultraviolet rays of a production's main idea must be invisible and penetrate the spectator in such a way that he does not notice them.[12]

Meyerhold's observation indicates that communication between the spectator and the mise-en-scène is both direct and indirect in its function. In constructing the mise-en-scène, the director combines both the manipulation of the elements of staging which are consciously noted by the spectator and those which may not be immediately registered but are still significant in creating the production's 'ultraviolet rays'. Among these is the production's visual score, that is, the construction of a system of visual images according to an underlying structure which facilitated a, partly subconscious, communication with the spectator.

As a result, the development of a visual style for each of his productions was a foundation stone in Meyerhold's practice. Meyerhold was acutely aware of the power of the onstage image and how it can be used to shape the theatrical experience. Discussing the essential skills for a director, he notes:

> The contemporary director must know not only the direct impact of an actor's emotion – he steps to the footlights and brilliantly delivers a soliloquy – but also the complex and peripheral turns of associative imagery.[13]

Meyerhold's emphasis on the role of the actor's emotion perhaps echoes his time with Stanislavsky; but his reference to the use of imagery for impact draws on the visual arts and suggests that director must be skilled in using the stage image to prompt responses in the viewer. Again, Meyerhold appears to highlight the indirectness of the stage image in its communication with the spectator: in his description, the actor trying to create an emotional connection with the auditorium is face to face with the audience, near the footlights, delivering a soliloquy. The effect of imagery, however, is 'complex [...] peripheral' and 'associative': Houghton notes that the visual score for Meyerhold's *Lady of the Camelias* (1934) was 'apparent only on analysis' and that 'one is scarcely conscious of it'.[14] Meyerhold was clearly aware that the spectator engages differently with visual imagery and that the visual score allows the director to engage the viewer in an active and imaginative process. Meyerhold associates the visual with the imaginative as early as 1906 in his essay 'The Naturalistic Theatre and the Theatre of Mood'. Citing Schopenhauer's observations on fine art, he writes that

> a work of art can influence only through the imagination. Therefore, it must constantly stir the imagination. But it must really stir it, not leave it inactive by trying to show everything. To stir the imagination is 'the essential condition of aesthetic activity as well as the basic law of the fine arts'.[15]

The suggestive power of the associative image, be it on the stage or on the canvas, prompts the spectator's imagination into action. The visual score for the production becomes a powerful tool for the director seeking to mediate between the thoughts of the playwright and the experience of the spectator.

Thinking like an artist: The value of 'looking at pictures'

In Meyerhold's theorization of the mise-en-scène, then, it is the indirect and associative communicative power of the image which takes centre stage. In order to ensure that the mise-en-scène functions theatricality, these stage images must express the production's main idea, using their associative quality to enable the viewer to engage imaginatively with the production's content. How these images function in practice, as Schopenhauer notes, is closely associated with how images function in the visual arts. Meyerhold's fascination with the visual arts is clearly documented: he was avidly interested in art history, and associated with the artists of his own era, spending time at their exhibitions and inviting them to produce stage designs for his theatres.[16] However, Meyerhold's work with the visual arts, as his reference to Schopenhauer implies, extended beyond his desire to find designers for his productions. In painting and drawing in particular, he found models for understanding visual communication which were as applicable to the stage as they were to the canvas.

In her survey of his work with his set designers, Alla Mikhailova considers the role of visual artists essential in Meyerhold's development as a director:

> [The] decisive influence on Meyerhold's progress as a stage director was undoubtedly exerted by artist-designers. This may have been due to his keen visual perception: he used to say that vision was his greatest natural endowment, that he was able to see a play in his mind's eye before he could hear it.[17]

That Meyerhold began with the stage image – seeing the play before he heard it – reiterates the significance of the visual elements of his aesthetic. His wide scope of artistic references points indicates, however, that this 'keen visual perception' was not an entirely 'natural endowment': Meyerhold clearly fed his interest in fine art through systematic reading about movements and artists and, most importantly, by studying images. For Meyerhold, an education in the visual arts was essential for a theatre maker, be they designer, actor or director. Houghton notes that 'watching [Meyerhold] work his students can learn about acting and directing and pantomime [...] and something about painting',[18] Gladkov recalls Meyerhold's encouragement to his students to 'look, look at pictures!'[19] and Mikhailova notes that Meyerhold applied the same principles to his own practice: '"Looking at pictures", pondering over them was one of his favourite pastimes.'[20]

Meyerhold's ability to cross-reference stage images with visual source material was noted by Mikhail Kupriyanov, Porfiri Krylov and Nikolai Sokolov, a trio of artists known collectively as the Kukryniksy who designed the first act for his production of Mayakovsky's play *The Bedbug*.[21] They recalled that the director was 'greatly interested in fine arts', noting that 'during the dress rehearsal on the illuminated stage [...] Meyerhold told Mayakovsky: Look, it's like Rembrandt.'[22] Mikhailova confirms that Meyerhold had 'stored in his memory a vast number of works'.[23] In addition, his interest in visual art fuelled his collaborations with visual artists, who frequently acted as designers at his theatre. Again, his stylistic influences were diverse: from World of Art painter Alexander Golovin, who worked with Meyerhold during his pre-revolutionary years at the Imperial Theatres, to his projects with the constructivist artists during the 1920s, Meyerhold intentionally brought those at the forefront of Russian visual art into his theatre buildings.

> **MEYERHOLD IN PRACTICE**
>
> Meyerhold believed that all theatre makers needed an education in the visual arts: the act of directing was underwritten by the act of studying and processing images. As Mikhailova illustrates, he was a vocal advocate for the art of 'looking at pictures' in galleries, exhibitions, published collections and catalogues. This activity was not seen simply as preparation for a specific production but as part of the director's ongoing development as a theatre maker. These exercises draw on Meyerhold's approach to 'looking at pictures' from a director's perspective:
>
> 1 Spend some time in a gallery looking at visual artworks from different eras. Compare the content, form, style and composition of the works: what catches your eye and why? Consider how depth, shape, form and light are manipulated by the artist, and how this affects your experience as a viewer. How is your eye drawn across the canvas, for example?
> 2 Imagine the visual artwork as a theatrical event: how would you turn it into staged action?
> 3 Make a sketch of the artwork. Your emphasis should not be on artistic or technical competence but on how the act of drawing allows you to explore your own engagement with the image.

Directors who draw: The desire for 'double competence'

'Looking at pictures' was important to Meyerhold, but as training for a director, looking alone would not suffice: in addition, he called for directors to develop their own artistic skills. Meyerhold coveted the ability to design his own productions, a goal which Mikhailova calls 'double competence':

> Meyerhold's idol was [Edward] Gordon Craig, who was proficient both as director and designer. Meyerhold, who lacked this double competence, had to solve the painful problem of how to make up for the absence

of professional drawing and painting skill [...] 'None of my plans will be realized on stage in their true dimensions until I become my own decorator' [he wrote].[24]

As Mikhailova explains, the theme of 'double competence' runs through Meyerhold's practice and is particularly reflected in the training programmes he developed for aspiring directors. Discussing the curriculum for his 'Courses of Instruction in the Art of Theatre Production' (1918), she writes:

> [Meyerhold] elaborated a programme of 'co-education' of stage designers and directors, and himself offered a course in 'stage arrangement' (*stsenovedeniye*) and stage directing. In his lectures he insisted that a director had to possess a degree of drawing skill and a command of stage space, so as to be able to provide a general plan of the scenery [...] Future directors and artist-designers attended the same classes and were instructed in the same subjects: stage directing, drawing, model-making, stage engineering, decorative painting, on-stage motion, etc.[25]

The suggested content of Meyerhold's Stage Arrangement lectures indicates that he saw a direct connection between the director's role, the mise-en-scène and the act of drawing or sketching. The two skills on which Meyerhold 'insisted' – 'a degree of drawing skill and a command of stage space' – exist in parallel. The implication is that directors do not draw in order necessarily to produce their own stage designs, but that drawing develops a specific way of thinking about stage space that can only emerge through the constraints of putting pencil to paper. Flavia Loscialpo writes that drawing is

> at once medium and process, performative act and idea, it is sign, symbol and diagram. It is a space of negotiation for both established meaning and what is yet to be known, defined and articulated. It is a medium for analysis, for the acquisition and facilitation of understanding. It is observation tool and recording practice.[26]

Loscialpo emphasizes the multiple functions of drawing not only as a way of generating pictures but also as an act of thinking, processing and documenting ideas. Just as the stage image prompts the spectator into an imaginative process, the act of generating drawn images allows the director to think about their production, considering the implications of their theatrical choices by rendering them in a different medium. Meyerhold advocated drawing during the rehearsal process and in performances, and the Meyerhold collection at RGALI includes extensive numbers of drawings generated by Meyerhold and other artists during his productions. These sketches capture the form of the stage image, as well as the shapes of the performers' bodies and their trajectories across the stage space.

In addition to drawings made for the purpose of rehearsals and planning, Meyerhold also encouraged a group of young artists (Sergei Urusevsky, Victor Vakidin, Vitaly Goryaev and Ivan Bezin) who requested the opportunity to draw during his productions. Olga Feigelman, reflecting on Bezin's drawings made during performances of *The Government Inspector*, notes the benefits of the act of drawing in terms of processing the contents of the production:

> It required much effort, much attention and concentration. In front of the artist there was a constantly moving actor. The tempo and the peculiarity of the actor's movements influenced the manner of drawing. The importance of the artist's creative attempt shouldn't be underestimated as neither the existing descriptions of the acting nor the photographs duplicate the artist's sketches depicting what was going on in front of him.[27]

For Feigelman, the contribution of Bezin's sketches is unique: the constraints of creating the drawings during performance conditions inflected the artist's style and reproduced Meyerhold's production from a new perspective. In his sketches of actor Erast Garin in the role of Khlestakov, for example, the rough outline of the actor's figure demonstrates less about Garin's outward appearance and more about the quality of his movement and characterization. Bezin's use of simultaneous representation, with multiple poses depicted on the same page, builds the impression of the character, and, as Feigelman notes, the drawings 'help to see Khlestakov's style the way that it was created by Meyerhold and realized by Erast Garin'.[28] Neither Meyerhold's rehearsal sketches nor Bezin's drawings of performances rely on life-like representations of the stage space; instead, they are ways of processing the production. The act of drawing reveals the most important elements of the director's work, clarifying the onstage priorities and capturing or shaping the vital visual score.

MEYERHOLD IN PRACTICE

Incorporating drawing into the rehearsal process gives the director new ways of engaging with their production. These exercises are based on acts of drawing similar to those that took place during Meyerhold's rehearsal and production processes.

1. Consider drawing sketches of your scenes as preparation for your rehearsal process. Reflect on the staging that you plan to incorporate. Can your blocking be expressed as shapes or trajectories? Alternatively, rather than drawing positions for the actors prior to a rehearsal, consider drawing after the rehearsal as

a re-constitutive act in which you process the ideas explored and the decisions made.

2. Try to draw a rehearsal as you watch: what do you notice that wasn't apparent before? How can you capture the temporal nature of rehearsal within the confines of the piece of paper?

3. Bezin's sketches of characters from *The Government Inspector* are particularly useful in identifying how physical characteristics are seen on stage. Choose one character from your rehearsal process and draw their movement. What qualities of movement do the images suggest? You could also try this for a pair or group of characters to consider the relationships between each figure. Consider the ways that these sketches could be used in your work with actors.

Adapting visual art techniques: Drawing the stage image

In some productions, the influence of painting on Meyerhold's practice is particularly apparent, seen in references to specific visual sources. Leach, for example, notes allusions to the work of Édouard Manet in *The Lady of the Camelias* (1934) and Diego Velásquez in *The Second Commander* (1929).[29] These examples demonstrate the fruit of Meyerhold's 'looking at pictures': how his knowledge and experience as a viewer of artworks contributed to his stagings. In addition, Meyerhold balanced direct references to individual paintings with broader work on artistic principles. Discussing his production of *Sister Beatrice* (1906), he rejected any reference to particular artists, claiming instead that the stage images were 'produced in the style of Pre-Raphaelite and Early Renaissance painting' and that 'the movements, groupings, properties and costumes were simply a synthesis of the lines and colours found in the primitives'.[30] In his reference to the use of lines, that is, the trajectories drawn or implied on the canvas, Meyerhold indicates his application of a specific visual arts technique in his construction of the mise-en-scène. The remainder of this chapter will focus on the director's use of line on stage, considering three functions of this technique in his theatre: the communication of associative meaning, the development of the compositional schema and the creation of movement within the still image.

Line and associative meaning

Line is a basic structural element in visual art, whose qualities create both form and meaning for the viewer. For Walter Crane, writing in 1900, line in the visual arts is 'a language' that is capable not only of recording natural fact and defining character, but also of conveying the idea of movement and force, of action and repose; and, further, of appealing to our emotions and thoughts by variations and changes in its direction, the degree of its emphasis, and other qualities.[31]

In Meyerhold's mise-en-scène, similar structures are created through the lines formed by the actors' bodies, the stage design (including props and stage furniture) and the effects of light (shadows or visible beams). Each of these elements offers the director a line with which to work; moving, rotating or otherwise manipulating the elements allows the director to control line in a similar way to the painter.

Nick Worrall picks up on the themes of shape and line in his analysis of Meyerhold's production of *The Government Inspector*. Discussing what he calls Meyerhold's 'distorting of outline', he notes the position of one character (the Officer in Transit) in relation to an onstage staircase:

> He sat at the foot of the stairs and slightly to the left, leaning sideways on a small circular table, asleep. In this position, the line of his body, particularly that of the leg, became an exact echo of the odd bend in the line of the stair. This bend was then repeated in the line of the shoulder, leaning sideways, and taken up again in the curve of the tabletop.[32]

In terms of theatrical construction, Meyerhold's use of line is a primary building block for the mise-en-scène. In this sequence, for example, the onstage lines do more than create an interesting visual moment: Worrall notes that 'a strong psychological atmosphere was projected before a word had been spoken'.[33] Through this communication of mood, Meyerhold's use of line contributes to his development of associative imagery in the mise-en-scène. Other uses of line imply a more direct sociopolitical commentary: in the uniformity of the crowd scene 'Interlude War' from *The Second Commander* (1929), for example, the repetition of the horizontal lines of the actors' bodies implies a sense of collective unity echoing communist ideals with the shadow on the back wall implying an extension of the crowd beyond the figures on stage (see Figure 2.1). Here, line allows the director to associate his onstage crowd scene with the ideals of the Soviet Revolution.

Line and compositional schema

The associative meaning of the individual stage image finds a fuller expression in the compositional schema (*kompozitsionnye skhemy*) of the production as a whole. This term is taken from the work of art historian Nikolai Tarabukin, whose detailed analyses of Meyerhold's productions draw on visual art technique. Tarabukin was acutely aware of the difficulties of a purely drawn analysis of a theatrical production, which he claimed could only '[reveal] a number of the most characteristic pictorial elements

FIGURE 2.1 The Second Army Commander, *State Meyerhold Theatre* (1929) © A. A. Bakhrushin State Central Theatre Museum.

[of the staging], but necessarily presented in the static mode'. To capture the 'continuous movement' of the performance, he notes that 'the sheet of paper should be a projection of the stage. The graphics should show the direction (arrow), character (line), tempo (figures) and other actors' movement'.[34]

What Tarabukin proposes is a method for the notation of the stage production which takes into account not just the visual appearance of the stage image at any given moment but also the dynamic, temporal elements of the director's mise-en-scène as these develop throughout the performance. Tarabukin's readings of Meyerhold's plays, rendered as annotated sketches, emphasize the visual construction of the onstage lines and the way in which these lines alter over time. Tarabukin uses these changing spatial structures to uncover visual themes in Meyerhold's work which encapsulate the production's 'main idea', a mise-en-scène which, in Tarabukin's words, 'corresponds to the ideological concept of a production'.[35]

Tarabukin's reading of Meyerhold's production *Woe to Wit* (1928) illustrates this element of the director's practice in action. In his analysis, Tarabukin focuses on the diagonal lines of the stage space and how these relate to sequences played in the horizontal, or front-on, plane:

Throughout the entire play the visual design stays symmetrical. Within this structural balance the action is set on the diagonal, changing its direction depending on changes in the semantic content of the episodes. A dynamic episode is replaced with a static or frontal one, followed, in turn, by a dynamic or diagonal mise-en-scène. This movement between contrasting episodes determines the rhythmic pattern of the production.[36]

It is the alternation of the diagonal and frontal constructions of the mise-en-scène that not only reflects the play's theme but also embeds it with a rhythmic structure. This shifting compositional schema underwrites the production as a whole, highlighting the essential 'main idea' and framing any moments of associative meaning emerging from an individual stage image.

Line and movement

As Tarabukin's rhythmic reading implies, lines lend a dynamism to Meyerhold's stage images. The manipulation of line is a conscious act which allows the artist to control, in part, the viewer's engagement with the canvas: lines direct the viewer's eye through the image, giving structure and shape to the viewing experience. As the eye is drawn through the image, a sense of dynamism or movement can emerge. On the canvas, still lines are not necessarily static and can instead be read as trajectories or implied movements. In Meyerhold's use of line, it is also possible to see similar implied movement and dynamism within the stage image. This is particularly apparent in images which create echoes between the bodies of the performers and the space around them, for example, in the director's frequent use of an extended limb or pointed finger to direct the viewer's eye away from the actor's body and towards another part of the space. This effect is enhanced in the relationship between the actors' bodies and elements of set or stage furniture, where lines are often echoed or deliberately set in conflict. These lines are particularly apparent in the complex, constructivist-influenced stage sets with which Meyerhold experimented in the early 1920s, in *The Magnanimous Cuckold* (1922), *The Death of Tarelkin* (1922) and *Lake Lyul* (1923). Figure 2.2, a photograph from Meyerhold's production of *Roar China!* (1926), serves as an example of how the stage image can be read. Here, the sense of dynamism can be seen in the positions of the ensemble, whose raised arms draw the viewer's eye through the space, mimicking the hustle of an angry crowd. The dynamic poses of the actors' bodies contrast with the stillness of the vertical figure stage left, whose arm points in the opposite direction to the dynamics of the group. As a result, the image is structured around two main lines, encapsulated primarily in the shapes created by the actors' arms: the first runs from the ensemble to the solo figure; the second from the figure back to the ensemble. Through

FIGURE 2.2 Roar China, *Meyerhold Theatre (1926), directed by V. F. Fedorov (student at the State Experimental Workshops GEKTEMAS) with V. E. Meyerhold* © A. A. Bakhrushin State Central Theatre Museum.

the tension between these lines, the image captures a sense of dynamic conflict.

Meyerhold's attitude towards the dynamic line is perhaps seen most clearly in his metaphor of the bridge:

> When you look at a bridge, you seem to see a leap imprinted in metal, that is, a process and not something static. The dynamic tension expressed in the bridge is the main thing, and not the ornamentation that decorates its railings. The same is true of the mise en scène.[37]

In this description of the bridge, Meyerhold highlights a key element of his approach to directing: that the director's role is to create dynamic tension through the lines in the stage image. Through this process, directors can shape the overall impression of the image, rather than focusing on ornamental details which can distract the viewer from the essence of the production. The dynamic lines of the stage space become a form of communication between director and audience through the agency of visual art techniques whose goal is, always, to inform the spectator about the production's 'main idea'.

MEYERHOLD IN PRACTICE

In his detailed use of line and depth in staging, Meyerhold created stage environments which developed and communicated ideas about the production through the application of devices used in the visual arts. These exercises experiment with the use of line, exploring how the visual arts can become part of the 'ultraviolet rays' that communicate a director's ideas about the play to the spectator.

1. Using a short scene with which you and the actors are already familiar, select a moment that seems to encapsulate the significance of this scene to the play text as a whole. Play the scene up to this moment; when the moment arrives, pause in a freeze-frame and then continue with the action. Repeat this until the pause begins to feel like a suspension of the scene, a moment which is potent with potential and movement akin to Meyerhold's bridge that is a 'leap imprinted in metal'.

2. Consider the mise-en-scène at this moment: look at the lines made by the set, stage furniture and actors' bodies. Approach the visual form of the moment consciously and with intention: can you apply Meyerhold's principles of line here? Consider extending and exaggerating lines to draw attention to characters or relationships. Think about how the actor's body relates to the playing space, and how the trajectory of lines can be used to develop these relationships. Remember that the goal is not to create an aesthetically pleasing image but to draw the mise-en-scène so that it communicates the important themes of the scene to the spectator.

The interdisciplinary director

For Tarabukin, the role of form is essentially ideological: the composition of the artwork or the performance is the 'organization of an artistic whole which by its very structure conveys the ideological conception of a production'.[38] Meyerhold's approach to the mise-en-scène demonstrates the complexity of this process in action. The question of ideology – the production's 'main idea' – was central to both Meyerhold's aesthetic and the Soviet attitude towards artmaking. However, the director's emphasis on the formal expression of the ideological led to the accusations of formalism and anti-Soviet practices which eventually resulted in his execution.

Meyerhold's serious and consistent exploration of the ways in which the visual elements of the production can communicate with the spectator, however, offers much of value for contemporary theatre directors. Through the application of ideas and techniques from the visual arts, Meyerhold's mise-en-scène emerges as a vital facet in the director's 'organization of [the] artistic whole', able to suggest indirect and associative meaning for the spectator. Meyerhold's interdisciplinary approach is more than an interest in the visual; it is a way of approaching theatre making which allows the director to expand their creative vocabulary and develop new ways of thinking about how theatre communicates with the audience. Beyond the specific applications of the visual arts, Meyerhold's interdisciplinarity also suggests the value for the theatre director of thinking beyond the theatre's walls, drawing on developments in other disciplines and conceiving of theatre as a truly cross-disciplinary practice. It was his commitment to this mindset that fed Meyerhold's onstage innovation and that ultimately made his theatre one of the most vibrant and relevant of the twentieth century.

3

Nina Simonovich-Efimova: Theatre as Living Sculpture in Motion

Dassia N. Posner

> *The puppet theatre, simply put, has its own laws, and [the puppeteer] is a new kind of actor.*
> – NINA SIMONOVICH-EFIMOVA[1]

In 1930, Russian director, visual artist and puppeteer Nina Iakovlevna Simonovich-Efimova (1877–1948) danced with an unusual partner: a life-sized puppet (Figure 3.1).[2] When she designed it, she made no attempt to mask its puppetness: 'Big Petrushka' had an absurdly long nose, exposed knee joints, a papier-mâché head and body and high-heeled shoes that attached to the puppeteer's feet at the toes. Yet even as this inanimate object celebrated its objectness, it came to life through movement. Simonovich-Efimova's son Adrian later recalled his mother's dance with Petrushka:

> Petrushka takes wide, deep strides, bows deeply to the lady, looks into her face; slowly, with small steps, he leads, holding his head high ... before coming to a stand-still. Of course it is clear that this is a puppet ... but it is also clear that it is he who is leading.[3]

FIGURE 3.1 *Nina Simonovich-Efimova with Big Petrushka (1930). Photo courtesy of the Museum Archive of the Obraztsov State Central Puppet Theatre, Moscow.*

Simonovich-Efimova's understanding of puppets as performance partners brought to life through movement initiated a small theatrical revolution that still reverberates today. For her, all theatre begins with the puppet, a living sculpture in motion. Even in the earliest days of the rise of the director, her definition of directing was radical; for her, a director is a synthetic visual and movement artist who creates, responds to and performs with living objects. Her career was dedicated to establishing an artistic puppet tradition in Russia that would equal the theatre of live actors and expand the possibilities of puppet theatre, aims that were inspired by her 'revolutionary' desire 'to free sculpture from its imposed role of immobility' and to free puppetry from its oft-assumed insignificance.[4]

Simonovich-Efimova and her husband Ivan Efimov, two of the founders of Soviet puppetry, were the first Russian visual artists to become professional puppeteers during the tumultuous period that encompassed the First World War, the October Revolution and the Russian Civil War.[5] As a director, Simonovich-Efimova merged visual art, literature and nineteenth-century Russian fairground performance with experimental ideas about what puppetry could be. She was prolific in multiple areas: she created over three thousand works of visual art;[6] she directed and performed in more than thirty hand, rod and shadow puppet productions between 1916 and 1922 alone; and her 1925 book *Notes of a Petrushka Player* (*Zapiski petrushechnika*), adapted into English in 1935 as *Adventures of a Russian Puppet Theatre*, is the first Russian book to detail the practical aesthetics of puppet theatre.[7] This chapter introduces Simonovich-Efimova's understudied work in the larger context of the early twentieth-century fascination with the puppet, traces the development of her theatre, explores her directorial innovations and nods to her enduring influence on twentieth-century theatre. Practical exercises in this chapter are drawn from or inspired by Simonovich-Efimova's written advice for beginning puppeteers, part of her larger mission to expand the form by cultivating its creators.

The puppet in theory and practice

Simonovich-Efimova's innovations in puppetry theory and practice were part of a much larger fascination across Europe and the United States with the puppet – especially the string marionette. Henryk Jurkowski pinpoints this early twentieth-century phenomenon as the moment when puppetry began to be acknowledged as a legitimate, independent theatrical form:

> It was an unexpected stroke of fortune for puppetry that at the beginning of the twentieth century ... puppet theatre was included in the aesthetics debate, thus establishing its uniquely characteristic features, its essence and its specificity. It seemed that puppetry was at last to attain a stable position among all the subjects of aesthetics and was now to be recognised as a form of theatre with its own laws and functions.[8]

Numerous factors contributed to the Russian branch of this marionette madness, including the early twentieth-century proliferation of miniature theatres and cabarets and an increased nostalgia for folk and popular entertainments during the decline and eventual erasure of the Russian fairground (*balagan*).[9]

Significantly, the rise of the director and the explosion of interest in puppets occurred simultaneously. Several directors discussed in this book – Vsevolod Meyerhold, Natalia Sats, Alexander Tairov and others – were fascinated with puppets, drawing inspiration from theatrical theories – by Edward Gordon Craig, Valery Briusov, Feodor Sologub and others – that centred on the marionette metaphor; from the 'marionette' plays of Maurice Maeterlinck; and from the tales of E. T. A. Hoffmann, who had proposed replacing live actors with puppets a century before in *Strange Sorrows of a Theatre Manager* (1818).[10] A recurrent theme in many such writings was that of the marionette as an ideal actor that yields to the puppeteer's will. This idea became especially popular among directors who attempted to create a unified theatrical vision yet worked with actors whose training and artistic methods clashed with this unity. Craig, for instance, whose 'The Actor and the Übermarionette' was first translated into Russian in 1911, believed the marionette to be an ideal actor specifically because it lacks messy human individuality. By contrast, Meyerhold admired the puppet for its inherent theatricality: because puppet shows 'inevitably fail to resemble exactly what the spectator sees in real life', he wrote, they unlock possibilities for artists and audiences to imagine their own worlds.[11]

Despite the ubiquitous theoretical interest in puppets among Russian directors, artists and writers, surprisingly few used actual puppets. The native puppet traditions – *Petrushka* (fairground and street-corner glove-puppet shows) and *vertep* (itinerant folk nativity shows) – were by then in decline. There never had been widespread professional marionette or rod puppet traditions in Russia. Amateurs and children typically performed Russian shadow shows in parlour settings rather than in theatres, despite the avid Russian cross-cultural interest in French puppetry at cabarets like the Chat Noir.

Most artists and writers who did create puppet performances were women. Simonovich-Efimova was the first Russian visual artist to stage puppet shows before the Revolution, shortly after which she founded the Petrushka Theatre. Although Ivan Efimov helped to design the Petrushka Theatre's puppets and performed in many shows, Simonovich-Efimova was its initiating director, artist, writer, performer, theorist and driving force. Yet she was far from the only woman to experiment with puppets. Visual artist Olga Glebova-Sudeikina created diminutive doll versions of notable Russian theatre personalities. Liubov Iakovleva-Shaporina founded a marionette theatre in Petrograd in 1918. Iulia Slonimskaia, in collaboration with avant-garde artists from the World of Art group, created an opulent marionette show, *The Forces of Love and Magic*, at the St Petersburg cabaret The Players' Rest in 1916 and published a seminal theoretical treatise on the marionette that same year.[12]

Within the larger wave of important women contributors to early twentieth-century art, literature and theatre, Simonovich-Efimova and other female innovators seem to have had fewer qualms than some male counterparts about immersing themselves in historically marginalized art forms – theatre for young audiences and puppet theatre – that they believed provided opportunities to straddle popular and elite culture, theatre for children and for adults, fairground spectacle and fine art. In the age of the rise of the frequently male theatrical director, these women became directors, designers and performers in their own theatres – miniature versions of the artistic worlds pursued by directors who worked in larger, more established venues.

Beginnings

Simonovich-Efimova's theatrical worldview was informed by several converging influences, the most important of which was her family background in art and education. She and her husband began as visual artists: Nina was a painter and Ivan a sculptor. Born into the vibrant culture of the Russian artistic intelligentsia, Simonovich-Efimova was surrounded by prominent artists from childhood. Her aunt Valentina Serova, composer Alexander Serov's wife, was Russia's first professional woman composer. Her older sister Maria Lvova, a sculptor, was also the subject of the famous *Girl in Sunlight* (1888), painted by their first cousin Valentin Serov, Simonovich-Efimova's artistic mentor and one of her teachers at the Moscow School for Painting, Sculpture, and Architecture, from which she graduated in 1911.[13] She also studied in France at the studios of Eugène Carrière (1901–1902) and Henri Matisse (1909–1911).[14] This prolonged exposure to the work of major artists influenced her puppetry in two ways: she viewed the puppet as an ever-moving, ever-changing work of art, and she sought out audiences of fellow artists at her earliest public performances.

Simonovich-Efimova believed deeply that art should serve a beneficial social function, a world view inspired in part by the child-centred educational innovations of her mother, Adeleida Simonovich, founder of the first Russian preschool. It was for the students at her mother's village school that Simonovich-Efimova, in her early teens, first developed *Petrushka* sketches with *guignol* glove puppets her sister had brought from France. After graduating high school in 1896, she began experimenting more seriously with glove-puppet and shadow theatre.[15] Between 1904 and 1906, the year she married Ivan Efimov, she created domestic shadow shows for Serov's children.[16] In Paris (1909–1911), she presented shadow shows at evening gatherings and schools.[17] These domestic and school performances soon led to shows at cabarets and other public venues. In 1914, the Efimovs joined the Moscow Association of Artists, an exhibition society known for fostering 'diverse and controversial trends' in art.[18] Two years later, Simonovich-Efimova was invited to give a puppet show for the association. In this, her first major public performance, she presented *Petrushka* sketches, which were later to become a mainstay of her theatre.

Petrushka and petrushki

Petrushka, 'the Russian *Punch and Judy* show', was probably first brought to Russia by wandering Italian Pulcinella players in the early nineteenth century and adapted to a Russian context on Russian fairgrounds and street corners.[19] This glove-puppet tradition features the hook-nosed hero Petrushka alongside a series of other puppets, most of whom Petrushka kills with his slapstick in varied comical ways. As is the case in many world glove-puppet traditions, Petrushka's shrill 'otherworldly voice' is produced with a swazzle (*pishchik*), a tiny wind instrument held in the puppeteer's mouth.[20] Petrushka players typically performed in a portable booth theatre with curtains and a shallow playboard, a small shelf-like stage framed by the booth's proscenium opening.

Simonovich-Efimova's *Petrushka* played with elements of the popular tradition rather than duplicating them: her show opened with a swazzle (to focus the audience's attention), after which characters instead spoke in rhymed verse; some scenes involve a slapstick (though now it is Petrushka who gets hit); and Petrushka himself is jubilantly mischievous (though no longer violent). Like many other artists of her day, Simonovich-Efimova was convinced that the street and fairground *Petrushka* was stage-worthy but crude, 'a hooligan entertaining hooligan friends' – that *Petrushka* needed 'the artist' to reach its potential.[21] She was not squeamish about violence per se, but she did believe that post-revolutionary child audiences had already been inundated with too much of it from living through prolonged war and famine – and that a more childlike Petrushka could restore the youth and wonder of even the roughest street children.[22]

Simonovich-Efimova therefore altered the story line significantly; *Petrushka Gets Sick*, first published in 1925, features three characters: Petrushka, an Old Lady and a Nurse-Practitioner (based on the Doctor from the popular tradition). The action consists of Petrushka being bitten by fleas, complaining to the Old Lady and shunning the Nurse's disturbing 'cures'. He is the only character to get beaten: the Nurse hits him to find out where it hurts. There is more threat of violence than actual violence: the Nurse's entrance with a wad of cotton on a stick (reminiscent of a slapstick) sends Petrushka under the bed in terror at the prospect of getting a vaccination. When the Nurse proposes to saw off Petrushka's leg, Petrushka immediately plays dead. The moment the Nurse leaves, he jubilantly returns to life.

As a director in the *Petrushka* tradition, Simonovich-Efimova mined Petrushka's range of physical gestures, many of which she describes in the published play's stage directions. In fact, her script contains nearly as many stage directions as spoken words. Her physically precise information for aspiring puppeteers is reflected in the detail in which she describes the mise-en-scène, both of the puppet and of the puppeteer's hand in the puppet.

SIMONOVICH-EFIMOVA IN PRACTICE

Puppet Mise-En-Scène

The following is an extended excerpt from Simonovich-Efimova's *Petrushka Gets Sick*.²³ Note the technical descriptions of physical action. How do stage directions also function as instructions for puppeteers?

> **Nurse-Practitioner:** Where's the patient? Where's the poor thing?
> Oh my! He's all skin and bones.
> (*Walks up to Petrushka and touches him.*)
> He's in such a fever sweat his shirt's soaked through.
> (*Puts hands together, walks away, and then comes back to him.*)
> Tell me where it hurts.
>
> **Petrushka:** (*He sits up suddenly, his back to her.*)
> Forgive me if I sound uncouth.
> It's my belly –
>
> **Nurse-Practitioner:** I was told your tooth!
> Does it hurt here?
> (*She hits him on the head.*)
>
> **Petrushka:** A little higher, lower, to the right, to the left.
> (*Gesture with the centre finger up and down, and with the thumb to the left and right.*)
>
> **Nurse-Practitioner:** I need to listen to your chest.
> Lie on your left shoulder.
> (*Petrushka lies down.*)
> Take a deep breath.
> (*Taps and listens, three or four times; to do this, the performer very quickly taps Petrushka with the middle finger, and quickly places her head on him, first one ear, then the other.*)
> Stick out your tongue ...
>
> **Petrushka:** (*Turns around on the bed, his back toward the audience. The nurse leans over him, facing him, and looks into his mouth.*) Ahhhhhh.
>
> **Nurse-Practitioner:** Your tongue is covered in white bumps.
> Your kidneys are starting to grow lumps.
> If you want to grow old and wise,
> I must have you immunized.

> I have the contraption in my pack.
> Stay put and I'll be right back.
> (*Exits, nodding her head, and returns with a large cotton wad on a stick. Petrushka squeals and hides under the bed.*)

As the scene continues, note, too, the frequent, playful use of rhyme. How is repetition used for comic effect? How do sound and rhyme establish a musical rhythm for the scene?

> **Nurse-Practitioner:** (*Looks under the bed.*) Come out, Petrushka, don't take cover.
> I'll swab your arm one way or other.
>
> **Petrushka:** (*Continues squealing.*)
>
> **Nurse-Practitioner:** Come on, Petrushka, I don't bite.
> Hey kids, this won't hurt him, right?
>
> **Kids:** (*They yell back.*) No! No!
>
> **Nurse-Practitioner:** There, you see.
>
> **Petrushka:** (*Rolls over under the bed, so that now he is looking up at her.*)
> If you want me to get better,
> Then my leg off you must sever,
> Then I'll have no need of socks,
> The single-legged still take walks.
> The leg is now the latest fad,
> And costs a pittance – not so bad!
>
> **Nurse-Practitioner:** I have the contraption in my pack.
> Stay put and I'll be right back. (*She exits.*)
>
> **Petrushka:** (*Claps his hands.*) Oh what a treat, oh what a treat.
> On trams I'll always have a seat. (*Sits on the bed.*)
> I'll scratch my leg one last time.
> Goodbye my le-e-e-g.
> (*Hugs his leg and rocks back and forth on the bed with it.*)
>
> *Nurse-Practitioner enters with a saw.*
>
> **Petrushka:** (*Darting about the stage.*) Kids, yell to her with all your might:
> Petrushka died under the bed tonight.
> (*Climbs under the bed, droops over the playboard, head down, his squeals gradually growing softer. The puppeteer removes her three fingers from his head and hands.*)

> **Nurse-Practitioner:** He's dead? Really?
> (*Drags him out from under the bed by the leg and puts him on the floor to her left, where he droops over again. Raps him on the head three times with the tin saw.*)
> He's truly dead. Now what a shame.
> I'll have to fetch his poor old dame.
> (*She exits.*)
>
> **Petrushka:** (*Immediately sits up on the edge of the playboard.*)
> Here I am, back from the dead.
> I avoided something really bad.
> (*Sings, clapping his hands.*)
> Tram, tram tasty,
> I ate a pastry.
> Tram tram tream,
> Filled with cream.
>
> *The music picks up his tune in rhythm. Petrushka exits, closes the curtains, reappears, and bows to the applause.*

While Simonovich-Efimova experimented with a wide variety of puppets in later years, the *Petrushka* tradition remained central to her practice. For her, the popular tradition and the puppet type were so inseparable that she termed all glove puppets 'petrushki'.

Moving sculpture in a mobile theatre

The positive audience response to Simonovich-Efimova's performance at the Moscow Association of Artists encouraged her to continue developing new work. In 1917, she created new puppets and shows – dramatized fables by Ivan Krylov and *Petrushka* plays – for the Café Pittoresque, a luxurious cabaret decorated by avant-garde artists.[24] As Nekrylova notes, the Krykov fables were 'a purely Efimov find, one that in many ways determined the direction of the theatre and its creative character'.[25] These well-known Russian fables inspired the Efimovs to experiment with combined glove-and-rod puppets in what also became first Russian puppet plays to exclusively feature animal characters.[26]

Simonovich-Efimova gave a wide range of additional performances between 1916 and 1918 at literary cafes and cabarets, including a 1916 shadow show at the Moscow cabaret The Bat and an invited performance in Konstantin Stanislavsky's home. She made the decision to embrace puppetry as a lifelong career, however, in 1918. In the wake of the October Revolution, she found it 'psychologically impossible' to continue easel painting because she felt urgently that art must now serve a social purpose.[27] The Efimovs's response to the Revolution was to use puppetry to bring joy to audiences of peasants, children, workers and artists and to use puppetry as spiritual sustenance during the lean, cold Civil War years.

In 1918, the Petrushka Theatre became itinerant: after building a portable show booth that summer, the Efimovs gave over seventy shows in Moscow and the surrounding area (Figure 3.2). Thus it was that Simonovich-Efimova's understanding of the puppet as a mobile sculpture brought to life through movement translated to mobile art as a way of life. As Nekrylova explains, these itinerant performances

> gave them the opportunity to serve a greater number of people, to penetrate remote, god-forsaken places, to perform before any kind of audience, and most importantly, to perform where the theatre itself, especially puppet theatre, did not go, and often could not go. Mass appeal and accessibility were achieved in actual fact.[28]

The Efimovs performed throughout the Moscow Province and up and down the Volga and Kama Rivers at rural 'schools, in hospitals, in train stations, in workers' clubs, in factories, on playgrounds, and on piers', charging a potato or a bowl of porridge for admission during the worst of the famine years.[29] Simonovich-Efimova later wrote, 'Theatre was just what people in the stormy Revolutionary period very much needed, what they watched with great, greedy eyes. Theatre then was like bread.'[30]

In autumn 1918, the Efimovs were invited by the Moscow branch of TEO, the Theatre Department of Narkompros, to participate in the first professional Soviet theatre-studio for young audiences.[31] They became resident performers at the Theatre of the Moscow Soviet of Workers, Soldier, and Peasant Deputies at 10 Mamonovsky Alley, a puppet theatre-studio under the leadership of Natalia Sats.[32] Here the Efimovs presented glove-puppet and shadow shows in one theatre (Figure 3.3), while a second stage featured marionette plays by various performers. The Efimovs's shadow pieces were based on Russian fairy tales and poems.[33] Simonovich-Efimova adored the aesthetic possibilities of shadow play and felt that shadow theatre is 'more an artist's theatre than an actor's theatre'.[34] The Efimovs first performed at Mamonovsky Alley in October 1918 and gave roughly twenty shows a month for the eight months following.[35] Due to a prolonged firewood shortage, the theatre was entirely unheated.

After eight months, the Mamonovsky Alley Theatre closed, and the Petrushka Theatre permanently became 'a theatre on foot': between 1918 and 1924 alone, the Efimovs played nearly 600 shows in Moscow and surrounding areas.[36] They developed most of their new work between 1916 and the mid-1930s, after which they created few new shows, probably because their unorthodox performance style 'remained outside the stream

FIGURE 3.2 *The Efimovs' travelling show booth (n.d.). From right to left: Ivan Efimov, Adrian Efimov, Nina Simonovich-Efimova and an unidentified fourth puppeteer. Photo courtesy of the Museum Archive of the Obraztsov State Central Puppet Theatre, Moscow.*

FIGURE 3.3 *Nina Simonovich-Efimova, shadow scene from* The Stolen Sun *(n.d.). Photo courtesy of the Museum Archive of the Obraztsov State Central Puppet Theatre, Moscow.*

of [the] formation and development' of Socialist Realism, the only legal style for two decades beginning in 1934.[37]

Theory and practice of a director-puppeteer

Looking back in 1940 on her early performances, Simonovich-Efimova wrote with satisfaction: 'Every show ... was a sermon for what we were doing, and, after five years, puppet "Petrushka theatres" began to appear all over the Soviet Union, first one by one, then by the dozens and hundreds.'[38] Her lifelong goal was simple: to further the art of puppetry however she could. This included expanding the physical vocabulary of puppets, how they were built, for whom they were performed and by whom they were created. She cultivated this expansion by developing practical written resources for aspiring puppeteers.

The earliest formulation of Simonovich-Efimova's theatrical theory was her 1919 article 'About Petrushka' (*O Petrushke*).[39] She also published books and pamphlets on glove, rod and shadow puppets. Her most famous work is *Notes of a Petrushka Player* (hereafter *Notes*), which chronicles her early performances, publishes several plays and drawings, and gives performance, design, and construction advice. Everything Simonovich-Efimova discusses in this book is connected in some way to the greater 'mission of our theatre':

> To show how expressive and subtle Petrushka gestures are, how incredibly many of them there are, how nuanced they are ... Our theatre's concern is *not novelty of plot, not novelty of word or of stageworthiness, but a new concept of Petrushka gesture.*[40]

She maintained that a fuller exploration of the expansive range of puppet movement, design and repertoire was key to puppetry being recognized as a valid, unique discipline.

In *Notes*, Simonovich-Efimova challenges several assumptions of the larger theoretical conversation about the marionette. In particular, she defies the common assumption that the puppet is an automaton, a lifeless being or a submissive, obedient actor. By viewing the puppet as a dead object devoid of spontaneity, Simonovich-Efimova contended, many theatre theorists of her day had limited its potential. The assumption of life, she maintained, provides more expansive possibilities in terms of movement, innovation and repertoire. In her words, 'a puppet show begins when the audience believes in the puppet as a living being'.[41]

For Simonovich-Efimova, the physical contact between the puppeteer's body and the puppet is the primary source of the puppet's life. Like George Sand, with whom she felt a particular artistic kinship, Simonovich-Efimova

SIMONOVICH-EFIMOVA IN PRACTICE

Life

The puppet comes to life for the audience when it is also alive for the puppeteer. Both puppet design and movement are developed in response to the puppet's materials and latent potential for life, its plasticity. The following exercise, inspired by Simonovich-Efimova's *Petrushka Gets Sick*, is an introduction to exploring the life of objects.

- Look carefully at a glove puppet. Experience its colour, its texture, its plasticity. With the puppet on your hand, move it, exploring its range of motion. How does it *want* to move?
- Bring it to life. How does it discover the world, itself, the audience, you?
- Take away that life. Emphasize its lifelessness, its reversion to objectness.
- Bring it to life again. How is its life different the second time?

maintained that glove puppets, which are intimately connected to the puppeteer's hand, are superior to string marionettes, which are operated from a distance.[42] She argues that

> Marionettes are a mechanism, a system of strings, levers, and hooks. They are forced, melancholic. (I am placing the marionette in the worst light in order to contrast her with petrushki.) If she offers a bouquet, the scent of its flowers is mixed with the smell of the sweat of the operator who has slaved over the creation of this act of offering ...
> She is a bourgeois among puppets.
> But Petrushka is a flame; in him is spontaneously poured the inspiration of the artist.
> Because a live human hand is in him! The palm replaces the face ... There is no intermediary in the form of strings and operator.[43]

Simonovich-Efimova believed that the hand (soul) of the puppeteer fills the puppet with life as it fills the puppet itself. By extension, the director-artist-puppeteer should be involved in every phase of puppet theatre creation so that the performance itself can be similarly alive: even the playwright should wear a puppet, 'scrutinize [it] like a living being' and respond to it while composing.[44]

Simonovich-Efimova advocates for the value of glove-puppet theatre by contrasting puppeteers with live actors. Many theorists of her day did not consider the puppeteer when writing about the puppet. Simonovich-Efimova instead focuses on the puppeteer's requisite virtuosity and versatility:

> The face is replaced in the Petrushka theatre by the performer's hands, but this is no worse than a face.
> The pianist also plays with the hands, and sounds emerge, and images appear ...
> The artist who simultaneously has a puppet on each hand plays with the fingers and, like a pianist, gives birth to images.
> The images are not aural, but visual.
> There are as infinitely many of them as there are in music, as infinitely great a number of nuances.[45]

Simonovich-Efimova's likening of the puppeteer to a pianist is not accidental. For her, it was an ethical imperative to pursue a similar level of artistic excellence in the puppet theatre. Her own preparation for the necessary physical and vocal dexterity included immersion in the visual and musical arts and physical training in Lesgaft exercises, 'very complicated combinations of gestures that are implemented from vocal commands rather than from physical demonstration'.[46] She reflects on the value of this early experience:

> I put it to the test now when I perform with and speak for two figures worn on my right and left hands. They react differently to what happens and speak with different voices; it is difficult to believe that their nervous systems come from a single mind. But, after all, a musician also plays different parts with two hands and is concerned with many things at once.[47]

In addition to Lesgaft exercises, she suggests Dalcroze eurhythmics, playing musical instruments, singing and music theory, and juggling as techniques for developing dexterity, precision and the simultaneous performance of independent gestures.

SIMONOVICH-EFIMOVA IN PRACTICE

Technique

The following advice for basic puppetry technique is excerpted from Simonovich-Efimova's *Notes of a Petrushka Player*.[48] Each suggestion can be experimented with individually in the cumulative development of an overall practice.

> *Fundamental requirements*: in the Petrushka [hand puppet] theatre, movements should be very precise, unhurried, and distinct, but all gestures should flow one out of the other.
> Do not make superfluous movements that lack meaning; *do not flap the puppet* (beginners love to do this).
> In dialogue, the figure who is speaking at a given moment is the one who moves; the one who is silent holds some pose or other. [...]

> There should not be a single empty or even remotely uninteresting moment in the play.
> Rule #1: *Puppets must be kept vertical.*
> Rule #2: *They must be held up at full height.*
> Rule #3: *Perform on the downstage plane.*
> Seek out gestures and rehearse roles in front of a mirror. [...]
> Practical *backstage advice*: always put each puppet in the same spot and place light against dark, dark against light. Then you won't waste even an instant when changing the puppet on your hand – this is essential.
> Every puppet is made for a specific hand, *right* or *left*, and it should always be played on that hand. This must be strictly remembered and adhered to.
> You yourself should speak for the puppets with which you perform, as do all folk Petrushka players.
> It is essential that you train yourself to speak and move simultaneously. [...]
> Know your part better than by heart: no name yet exists for the extent of this kind of knowing. You should speak lightly, not only not thinking about what you say, but thinking – attentively thinking – about something entirely different – about how your right wrist is moving just then and what the pinky finger on your left hand is doing. This is how well you need to know it. Then the puppets come to life and become capable of improvisation.
> When a virtuoso plays the violin, the instrument takes on a life and a voice. The same thing happens with puppets. They begin to live independently.

For Simonovich-Efimova, rehearsal, especially in its early stages, is a process of playing with puppets to discover the gestures they want to perform:

> These little actors do not have facial expressions, but they do have effective gestures: they kiss, fight, bow (what's more, their bow can have all the nuances of a bow), they bless each other; they die 'stupendously' (according to the audience), they get frightened; they convey clearly the nature of their good feelings, they tenderly caress, amicably greet one another, heatedly or fervently take offence, become angry, trembling with their whole body or head; they applaud and dance.[49]

When developing shows, Simonovich-Efimova choreographed every movement, often in front of a mirror.[50] Her plays featured compact, expressive action organically derived from the physical capabilities of the puppet.

SIMONOVICH-EFIMOVA IN PRACTICE

Gesture

Inspired by Simonovich-Efimova's 'About Petrushka', the following are prompts for discovering and refining puppet gestures.

- Work in front of a mirror to investigate the full range of a puppet's movement. Use the mirror as a tool for focusing on the puppet from the perspective of an audience member. Pay particular attention to the puppet's materials and design.
- Repeat gestures that work well, exploring variations and nuances as you do.
- Perform multiple gestures in sequence, developing them so that a new gesture grows out of the previous one. Eliminate fussy gestures that lack precise meaning.
- Practise gestures and sequences many times until they can be reproduced instinctively, training as would an athlete, musician or dancer.

Simonovich-Efimova's attentive responsiveness to puppet materials and movement inspired her numerous innovations in puppet design. She experimented tirelessly with expressive costuming and unusual modes of manipulation. She and her husband developed shadow theatre as an art form in Soviet Russia. They designed puppets that could be worn on the head so that more than two characters could appear at once with one puppeteer manipulating them. 'Big Petrushka', introduced at the start of this chapter, was the first of several life-sized puppets in the Petrushka Theatre; their 1934 *Thirteen Writers*, for instance, featured life-sized puppets of famous writers seated around a table. And they actively developed puppetry as a serious form for adult audiences; most notable are their collaborations with the Moscow Satire Theatre (1927, 1933) and their adaptations of *The Enchanted Pear Tree* (from Boccaccio's *Decameron*, 1921) and *Macbeth* (1931).[51]

Macbeth featured numerous design innovations, including a new rod puppet design (patented by Simonovich-Efimova in 1926): the puppeteer's hand was inserted into the body like a glove puppet, but the arms and hands were manipulated on rods attached at the elbow for expressiveness of arm gesture. Macbeth and Lady Macbeth also had 'double profiles': different profiles on the right and left sides of the face so that when the heads were pivoted, they changed expression.[52] The train of Lady Macbeth's dress was attached to Simonovich-Efimova's head so that the fabric itself could express emotion as it danced, was flung in anger or coiled around her like a snake.[53]

FIGURE 3.4 *Nina Simonovich-Efimova, the witches of* Macbeth *(1931). Photo courtesy of the Museum Archive of the Obraztsov State Central Puppet Theatre, Moscow.*

The three witches became a single puppet (Figure 3.4): 'a flat outline of three figures made of thick wire, lightly draped with pieces of grey tulle and soft grey silk. When the witches swarm and twirl, a piece of bright blue tulle twists on the folds of the stuff, like a flame amids[t] the grey shreds of a mist.' When they fly upwards to taunt Macbeth, 'their gigantic transparent shadows on the ceiling and walls of the theatre hall seem to stress their ghost-like nature'.[54]

The legacy of a Petrushka theatre

Over the course of her long career, Simonovich-Efimova reinvented Russian and Soviet puppet theatre by expanding what puppetry can do and be as a performance form. She created an immediate theatre based in popular and folk forms, a theatrical theatre that allows movement to determine action and a responsive theatre in which the director-artist simultaneously controls and is guided by the material world. Her productions sparked a thriving puppet tradition, and her pioneering role in the first Soviet children's puppet theatre provided a base for the later proliferation of Soviet puppet theatres for young audiences.

Simonovich-Efimova's greatest contribution to theatre, though, was her insistence that the puppet's life is a quintessential element of its nature. The miracle of the puppet is that it comes to life anew each time an artist brings it into play. This seems to be a truth that most puppeteers have discovered in their own experiments. But what was quietly radical about Simonovich-Efimova doing so was that it was in such unassuming, yet stubbornly defiant, opposition to the larger conversation in Russia about the marionette and its seeming nature. Her revolutionary insight, that sculpture, motion and belief together equal life, made later, bolder stylistic experiments more possible: once artists assumed the puppet was alive, many felt freer to play with its boundaries in innovative, fantastical ways.

Simonovich-Efimova directly and indirectly laid a theoretical foundation for the concurrent Soviet puppetry of the 1920s and 1930s: Alexandra Exter created cubist marionettes that revelled in their status as visual metaphors;[55] Vladimir Sokolov, who directed the puppet studio at the Kamerny Theatre, used puppets as distillations of images or thoughts, like abstract paintings in motion;[56] and Sergei Obraztsov, one of the Efimovs's early students, redefined puppetry, even using his own bare hands as puppets.[57] Through Simonovich-Efimova's written work and teaching, she directed the future direction of puppetry; her book, plays and articles were published and read in Russia and well beyond. The American interest in her work is documented on the pages of *Puppetry Yearbook* (edited by Paul McPharlin, founder of Puppeteers of America), a major turn-to source for mid-century US puppeteers. Probably the most famous recent example of the ongoing influence of Efimova's thinking is captured in the name of South Africa's Handspring Puppet Company, inspired in part (via Sergei Obraztsov) by Simonovich-Efimova's belief that 'the soul of the puppet lies in the palm of the hand'.[58]

In Simonovich-Efimova's theatre, the invisible soul is made tangible through responsive physical contact with a puppet in motion. In her dances with 'petrushki', she sought not to create the illusion of life but to expand where life can be found. Her theatrical practice similarly invites a rethinking of the common understanding of where the director can be found. There are many reasons why many of the artistic revolutions of the early twentieth century are attributed to male directors; I'll briefly note two that are germane here. One is insufficient recognition of the important artistic contribution of sustained creative collaborators, the mutually generative artistic partnership of Alexander Tairov and Kamerny Theatre lead actress Alisa Koonen being an example in the context of this book. Another is a too-narrow understanding of what a director can be. Simonovich-Efimova's work prompts an expanded definition of directing in which the director-artist-performer-writer is both inside and outside the production, in which an individual does not *lead* but can *be* all of the artists in a unified production, and in which the artist is perpetually present in the here and now of interactive theatrical space, time, material and audience. Her theatrical worldview also allows for a more nuanced perspective on the practice of directors like Meyerhold, who was often accused of viewing actors as puppets. To heed the puppet, after all, is to open a window into the creative possibilities of the material world.

4

Yevgeny Vakhtangov: The Future Head of the Russian Theatre

Andrei Malaev-Babel

One of the purest representatives of the Russian theatrical avant-garde, Yevgeny Vakhtangov (1883–1922) rehearsed his productions through a deeply personal act of creation. For Vakhtangov, the creative act of a theatrical collective was as important as the author's Word – a production's pretext. At the same time, his art was rooted in the 'Stanislavskian' law of inner justification; it's just that the basis by which the art must be justified, according to Vakhtangov, was creativity (creative play), rather than mundane, 'everyday' life. His 'play' was as organic and as truthful as life itself. However, it was freer and bolder than mundane human behaviour, constricted by the goal of survival and safety. Even in everyday life, Vakhtangov sought art, transgressed mundanity by his own act of creative living, based on overcoming life's pettiness. Such life – transformed, beautified and ennobled – became for him a perfect material for rehearsal and performance (Figure 4.1).

Vakhtangov's legacy is of importance to us today as that of a thinker and practitioner, who, through his body of work, proclaimed the primacy of a theatre collective's free and spontaneous creativity. Vakhtangov's concept of theatre artists as improvisers – passionate, imaginative and utterly free in their choice of expressive means – provides the creative atmosphere, the needed oxygen that allows both actor and director to breathe freely onstage. It is relevant as an antidote to the narrow, literal reading of the highly influential method, known as the Stanislavsky System. It also provides

FIGURE 4.1 *Yevgeny Vakhtangov, 1918. Courtesy of Andrei Malaev-Babel.*

an essential 'missing link' between Stanislavsky's techniques and the non-naturalistic theatre schools originated by Stanislavsky's direct collaborators such as Michael Chekhov and Nikolai Demidov.

Last, but not least, Vakhtangov's heritage is needed in the theatre of the future – because of its forward-looking dynamic and its mentality of a ceaseless creative search. Vakhtangov himself once said about his elder colleague, Vsevolod Meyerhold: 'Meyerhold gave roots to the theatres of the future. The future will give him his due.'[1] These words equally apply to Vakhtangov himself.

Vakhtangov's influence

In April 1922, approximately one month before Vakhtangov died in Moscow at the age of 39, Konstantin Stanislavsky gave him his photograph, inscribed 'To the hope of the Russian art, to the future head of the Russian theatre'.[2] Vakhtangov's coffin was lowered into the ground at the Novodevichy Cemetery on 31 May, all speeches said, the grave covered with earth. At that point, Stanislavsky asked to be left alone at the grave. Who was Stanislavsky burying on that day? What else, besides Vakhtangov's body, lay in that grave? What did he lament? The future of the Russian theatre?

Upon Vakhtangov's death, two of the most prominent, and drastically opposing Russian theatrical figures, Stanislavsky and Meyerhold both called Vakhtangov 'a leader', while Nemirovich-Danchenko echoed this sentiment. However, in the decades to come, Stanislavsky reversed his praise of Vakhtangov. That happened, in part, because Vakhtangov's less-than-complimentary private writings on Stanislavsky were published in the mid-1930s, and they personally wounded Stanislavsky. After that, Stanislavsky went on to paint Vakhtangov's legacy as 'outdated', or mix some of his less significant students and followers with the master himself. In the meantime, Stanislavsky's own productions of the 1920s, such as Ostrovsky's *Ardent Heart*, and Beaumarchais's *The Marriage of Figaro* bore a clear resemblance to Vakhtangov's aesthetic. In the opinion of Georgy Tovstonogov, one of Russia's most prominent directors of the second part of the twentieth century, Stanislavsky's 1926 production of Ostrovsky's *Ardent Heart* was his reply to Vakhtangov[3]: 'Having accepted Vakhtangov's challenge, and having inwardly accepted him, Stanislavsky directed a production in the vein of the psychological grotesque.'

Following Stanislavsky's example, many directors, in Russia and abroad, continued their peculiar dialogue with Vakhtangov. In fact, it is difficult to find a significant twentieth-century theatrical personality who did not have something to say on Vakhtangov's concepts, did not study his techniques or did not see his productions. This list includes pivotal theatrical figures such as Gordon Craig, Max Reinhart, Bertolt Brecht, Lee Strasberg, Jerzy Grotowski, Eugenio Barba, David Mamet and many others. One way or another, through agreement or disagreement, direct or indirect influence, Vakhtangov's heritage is present in the works of all these masters of theatre. Even Peter Brook, who denied Vakhtangov's influence, has been compared by Russian critics and theatre professionals – to Vakhtangov, of all other directors. This comparison is justified, if one is to consider Brook's directorial lightness and ease, and the truthfulness of his actors, combined with the symbolism and convention of his theatrical environment and devices.

Vakhtangov's direct students and disciples exhibited extraordinary dedication to their master's heritage. From dozens of Vakhtangov's student collectives (in Russia of the period they were called Studios) came many leading directors, actors and teachers of theatre and film. Their influence and careers spread beyond Russia, into Europe, Israel and the United States. Among them were Michael Chekhov, Richard Boleslavsky, Hannah Rovina and Rouben Mammalian.

Following Vakhtangov's untimely death, most of the members of his own Studio[4] dedicated themselves to the establishment of the State Academic Vakhtangov Theatre in Moscow, one of Russia's key companies – from its inception until today. The Shchukin Institute, affiliated with the Vakhtangov Theatre, has been considered one of the top five theatre schools in Russia for more than nine decades. The longevity of Vakhtangov's final directorial masterpieces is unprecedented. His production of Carlo Gozzi's *Princess Turandot*, staged in 1922, ran for 1,038 performances in its original rendition.[5] Vakhtangov's production of *The Dybbuk*, directed at the Moscow Jewish Habima Studio in 1922, played a crucial role in the establishment of the National Theatre of Israel, the Habima. It was performed in its original rendition for over forty years, bringing to the Habima international fame and admiration of such twentieth-century figures as Albert Einstein, Maxim Gorky, George Bernard Shaw, Rabindranath Tagore and Marc Chagall. Vakhtangov's 1921 performance of Strindberg's *Erick XIV*, directed at the First Studio of the Moscow Art Theatre (MAT) with Michael Chekhov-Erick, became a landmark in the history of Russian theatre.

In his directorial work, as well as in his pedagogical practices and theories, Vakhtangov created working models for some of the major theatrical problems of the contemporary theatre. In his final productions, such as *Erick XIV*, *Dybbuk* and *Turandot*, Vakhtangov creatively interpreted the problem of an actor's improvisational freedom vs. formal discipline, thus paving the way for Jerzy Grotowski. Vakhtangov also anticipated Grotowski's approach to theatrical aspects, such as act and ritual. Several of Vakhtangov's final productions prompted his critics and colleagues, before Antonin Artaud, to speak of cruelty. Vakhtangov was the first to insist on the 'cruelty' of Chekhov's drama and to realize it onstage in his 1920 production of *The Wedding*.[6] He did so more than forty years ahead of the time when the term 'cruel Chekhov' appeared in Russian theatre criticism, inspired by Chekhov productions of the 1960s – those directed by Tovstonogov and Anatoly Efros. All of Vakhtangov's biographers noted his gift for unmasking his characters and permeating the darkest corners of their psyche.[7] According to his first biographer, Nikolai Volkov, Vakhtangov's 'cruel talent' was capable of conveying 'the beauty of ugliness'.[8] A leading contemporary Vakhtangov scholar in Russia, Vladislav Ivanov, suggests that his final masterpieces practically anticipated Artaud's concept of 'cosmic trance'.[9] Michael Chekhov, who, per his own admission, took notes of Vakhtangov's talks and rehearsals, was influenced by Vakhtangov's concept of rhythm and gesture. Yet the influence in this case was mutual, as Vakhtangov arrived at some of his own conclusions studying the work of Michael Chekhov – the actor. Nikolai Demidov developed his technique of 'subconscious perception and subconscious expression' in close dialogue with Vakhtangov.

In one way or another, the problems creative artists of today's theatre experiment with, explore and think about, had all been tackled by Vakhtangov in an unorthodox, creative way. Among them is the theatre's chief problem: the one of finding truth in an environment that is intrinsically based on a lie – marrying the authenticity of an actor's life onstage with glaring theatrical convention. As early as 1923, Pavel Markov had this to say of Vakhtangov's answer to this dilemma in his production of *Princess Turandot*:

> Vakhtangov gave to the theatre the truth about the actor; this truth became the truth of a performance. The actor was asserted as the creative origin of the performance; [...] The character did not absorb the actor; the character's weight did not bend the actor's individuality to its will; the actor – master and histrionic – revealed its simple, but personal essence (large or small, significant or insignificant). This essence was intrinsic and distinctive to him alone. [...] Vakhtangov justified theatre's existence that was on the verge of becoming fruitless, and annihilated its ethical and moral contradictions.[10]

FIGURE 4.2 *Alexandra Remizova as Zelima and Yuri Zavadsky as Calaf in Act III, Scene 6, of* Princess Turandot, *1922. Courtesy of Andrei Malaev-Babel.*

By placing an actor's point of view on character into the foreground, Vakhtangov's *Turandot* foreshadowed the Brechtian device of 'alienation' (Figure 4.2). It did so, however, according to the 'Stanislavskian' principle of inner justification by placing an actor-creator at the centre of a production.

Vakhtangov, the biography

Vakhtangov's biography was full of conflicts and contradictions, fuelled by his time – the age of the Russian Revolution. It featured a childhood with a tyrannical father, who disapproved of his son's theatrical aspirations. At the age of twenty, Vakhtangov left his home in Vladikavkaz (Caucasus) and came to Moscow where he eventually entered the theatre school founded by Adashev, a MAT actor. At the Adashev School, Vakhtangov met his mentor, Leopold Sulerzhitsky, the future head of the First Studio of the MAT. Sulerzhitsky is remembered today as a valued associate of artistic figures such as Lev Tolstoy, Konstantin Stanislavsky and Gordon Craig. He also played a crucial role in the development of an entire generation of Russian actors and directors. Among them are such noted theatrical figures as Michael Chekhov, Richard Boleslavsky and Maria Ouspenskaya.

Admitted by Nemirovich-Danchenko to the MAT in 1911, Vakhtangov quickly attracted the attention of Stanislavsky who, in the same year, entrusted him to teach classes in his 'System' to a group of young MAT actors. One of the students in this group, Michael Chekhov, became Vakhtangov's friend, rival and his creative accomplice. The First Studio of the MAT was formed in 1913 under the leadership of Sulerzhitsky. It was initially meant as an experimental laboratory for the emerging Stanislavsky technique. Vakhtangov's relationship with Stanislavsky developed dramatically. On the one hand, Stanislavsky publicly admitted that Vakhtangov was a better teacher of the System. On the other hand, Stanislavsky grew increasingly jealous of the First Studio's independence, of its desire to produce its own repertoire and of Vakhtangov's independent pursuits as director. Following the death of Sulerzhitsky in December 1916, Vakhtangov became the informal leader of the First Studio of the MAT (future MAT the Second) – a role he kept until his own untimely death.

Throughout the 1910s and early 1920s, Vakhtangov became increasingly popular as a teacher. He was in high demand in Moscow's numerous theatrical institutions. His own Studio (the future State Academic Vakhtangov Theatre in Moscow) was organized in 1913. There Vakhtangov prepared a new generation of Russian directors and actors. At his Studio, Vakhtangov experienced the love and betrayal of his best student disciples, their departures and returns.[11] During the last two talks with his students, Vakhtangov formulated his concept of Fantastic Realism. Surrounded by them, he died three months after the bittersweet directorial triumph of his final masterpieces.

Both tragic and triumphant, this final period of Vakhtangov's short life in art deserves the most attention. In this period, lasting less than a year (from March 1921 to February 1922), Vakhtangov, already hopelessly ill and suffering from excruciating pain, managed to secure himself a place in theatrical history and leave a legacy. During this year, he opened three drastically different productions: Strindberg's *Erick XIV*, An-sky's *The Dybbuk* and Gozzi's *Princess Turandot*. All three productions were seen by Vakhtangov's contemporaries as not just works of theatrical art but as models for resolving some of the essential dilemmas of the contemporary theatre. As a teacher, Vakhtangov continued to collaborate with at least ten theatrical institutions, where he conducted classes and lectures and oversaw the life of Studio collectives as a mentor and spiritual guru. In his final years, Vakhtangov also produced street performances for the masses, organized theatrical enterprises, conducted extensive correspondence and wrote conceptual notes on acting and the art of theatre.

Shortly before his death, Vakhtangov formulated his Method of Fantastic Realism. Several documents on the Vakhtangov method survived. One of them, the so-called All Saints' Notes, outlined several key concepts of the new method but did not give it a name yet. The second document *circa* April 1922, 'Two Final Talks with Students', introduced the actual term 'Fantastic Realism'. While outlining his method, Vakhtangov called for a significant expansion of formal techniques and devices previously utilized by Stanislavskian representational theatre, also known as 'the art of living onstage' and 'the art of experiencing'.

Vakhtangov on the subconscious nature of the creative process (subconscious perception and subconscious expression)

The chief principle of the Stanislavsky technique, expressed through the motto 'to the subconscious through the conscious', did not occupy Vakhtangov's attention for long. Vakhtangov's own way of working was that of an immediate, intuitive grasp of the entirety of the theatrical phenomenon – be it a play, or a character, a form of theatre, or a principle of theatrical technique. Most directors and actors must analyse the object of their study, thus breaking it into elements. They need to study these elements separately, one by one. The rationale behind such a laborious process is that once an artist comprehends every building block individually, he or she will be able to put the blocks back together, thus grasping the entirety of the play, scene or character. Stanislavsky also suggested that an actor, or director, can intellectually analyse the play's circumstances and characters, then 'forget' the results of analysis and trust their creative instinct. Every rehearsal or performance will introduce its inimitable 'complex of accidents', causing a theatre artist to spontaneously express their analytical findings onstage.

In reality, the process of 'recreating the whole' often gets postponed until it is too late, and at times it does not happen at all. A play, a scene or a character, not to mention the creative process itself, being a dynamic, living and complex artistic phenomenon, defies the mechanical exercise of 'dissection'. This is especially true when analytical dissection precedes a creative, synthetic grasp of the whole. When the work begins with analysis, such a beginning can often kill the very soul or essence of a creative object. Vakhtangov's own method allowed him to embrace an object of study in its entirety, bypassing the period of analytical dissection. In other words, his method was one of an instantaneous synthesis. Since every element and detail of a harmonious artistic whole contains in it the spirit and essence of the entire whole, Vakhtangov relied on his creative intuition to shorten significantly the process of study. By the end of his career, a single hint, one aspect or detail of the whole was sufficient for Vakhtangov to immediately grasp its entirety. In March 1921, Vakhtangov wrote, comparing his directorial intuition with Meyerhold's:

> I feel that my intuition is better than Meyerhold's. He needs to study an historic epoch, to grasp its spirit. I, however, from two-three empty hints, for some reason, clearly and vividly feel this spirit. I always, almost unmistakably, can tell in detail the life of the century, society, class, habits, laws, costumes and so on.[12]

Vakhtangov closely observed his own way of working, as well as the work of some of his contemporaries and colleagues who also possessed the gift of immediate intuitive grasp or syntheses. These observations allowed him to formulate the Vakhtangov doctrine. The following quotations from Vakhtangov, although taken from different sources, nevertheless, give us a complete picture of Vakhtangov's views on the nature of creativity:

> Consciousness does not create anything – ever … Only the subconscious does. It has an independent ability to choose material for the creative process, bypassing the conscious mind …
>
> He who consciously feeds his subconscious and expresses the results of its work in a subconscious way – is a talent.
>
> He who subconsciously feeds his subconscious and engages in a subconscious expression – is a genius.[13]
>
> A genius actor is different in the way that he … immediately, at once, embraces the character in its entirety, thus finding himself immediately at its apex.[14] It is from this place that he perceives the details.[15]

To comprehend the true meaning and significance of Vakhtangov's teaching, one should somehow bypass the word 'genius', used by Vakhtangov. Ultimately, Vakhtangov speaks of a method, of a technique a genius actor possesses subconsciously, often without being able to comprehend it. In his daily practice, Vakhtangov strived to discover talent or 'genius' in every one of his collaborators and students. He succeeded in the way that he managed to inspire them to achieve performances that far surpassed their creative abilities, as they were previously known. As one constantly works to surpass one's current capacities, one gradually approaches his genius. An actor's persistent self-demand not to repeat himself in his next work, and constantly work to sharpen and expand his technique, is capable, over a period, to enlarge significantly his creative individuality. This faith in unlimited hidden human resources also united Vakhtangov with other artists of the Russian avant-garde.

Instantaneous grasp of the whole: Synthesis

Vakhtangov practised his doctrine of subconscious perception and expression not just in his personal work but also in work with his colleagues – actors, other directors, designers and composers. When it came to working with actors, Vakhtangov often appealed directly to their creative subconscious by 'inspiring' them with an image, gesture or demonstration that expressed their character's essence.

Sensitive to the creative individuality of the other artist, he never demonstrated the character's essence from the standpoint of his own creative individuality but rather from the standpoint of the creative individuality of the actor. In other words, when demonstrating a character, Vakhtangov would undergo a double transformation. He would transform into an actor who was performing the part. Out of this creative place, he would demonstrate the essence of the part to the actor, as only this actor could play it. One of Vakhtangov's closest disciples, Boris Zakhava, had this to say on the subject:

> Vakhtangov composed his productions in such a way that every member of the collective, even those not participating in a given production, felt it as their own. They could say of each quality in the performance: with this quality Vakhtangov expressed me; he expressed me so truly and so fully, as I could not have done myself.[16]

In his memoir, Michael Chekhov recalls how Vakhtangov demonstrated to him the pattern of the part of Erik (from Strindberg's *Erick XIV*) 'over the course of the whole act of the play – and […] did this in no more than a couple of minutes'. Chekhov wrote:

> After his [Vakhtangov's] demonstration, the whole act in all its details became clear to me, although Vakhtangov had not gone into these at all. He had simply given me the basic structure, the structure of the character's will, within which I could then position all the details and particulars of the role.[17]

Clearly, Vakhtangov's demonstration was born out of his own full grasp of the entirety of the role of Erik – the kind of grasp that is only possible when one observed what Vakhtangov called 'the essence of the role'.

Michael Chekhov, as any other of Vakhtangov's actors, accepted Vakhtangov's instructions and concepts 'as if those ideas were his own'.[18] That couldn't have happened unless Vakhtangov demonstrated to Chekhov his own hidden, subconscious creative intentions. In addition to the ability to permeate the essence of the play, role or a scene, Vakhtangov also could permeate any given actor's hidden creative essence.

Vakhtangov's demonstrations were never of the segment from the actual play. Depending on an individual actor's way of perception, Vakhtangov could demonstrate to them a symbolic gesture expressing the essence of the character as a whole or the scheme of their character's life in a segment of the play. Such was his way of working with Michael Chekhov that inspired the actor to create his technique of Psychological Gesture. To a different actor, however, Vakhtangov would 'demonstrate' by living onstage for a few seconds as their character in a situation that was not featured in the play. By doing so, Vakhtangov ensured that his demonstration could not be copied directly. Instead of concentrating on the details of the demonstration in order to be able to reproduce it later, the actor was encouraged to grasp its soul. In such demonstrations, Vakhtangov appealed to the actor's subconscious, thus planting the 'kernel' of the character directly into the actor's subconscious realm. According to Vakhtangov actors' testimonies, after such demonstrations, they could usually grasp the character as a whole and play it in any given circumstances.

Vakhtangov believed that a theatre artist can achieve an instantaneous grasp of a character using yoga-inspired exercises. This is how Vakhtangov described such techniques to his students in 1915.

VAKHTANGOV IN PRACTICE

Would you be able to perform the following, somewhat strange exercise: would you be able to go behind the curtain as a little devil and, as a little devil, examine everything backstage. This is an

> exercise in intuition. Can you do the following: I see myself sitting in a chair. In a similar way, I can also feel myself as a cat. [Michael] Chekhov, while observing a cat, stopped perceiving who was the cat – him or the cat. Through some power of yours, you guess how the object of your concentration feels at this moment. I can sense your will with my entire being. For a second I somehow transport myself into you. There is a distinction between abnormality and delight here. The latter belongs to the realm of art. I can internally somehow penetrate the essence of the given subject; in other words, I can guess its 'kernel'. This is the principle thing for an actor.[19]

This exercise, while seemingly meant for an actor, is crucial to Vakhtangov's directorial practices; it will be discussed further in connection with Vakhtangov's gift of inwardly merging with an actor, during a rehearsal.

Boris Zakhava left us an excellent description of Vakhtangov's ability to simultaneously merge with several actors onstage, during rehearsal:

> I can't think of a director who had a greater insight into the inner state of an actor than Vakhtangov. I often witnessed Vakhtangov, having watched some performance or rehearsal, retell a stunned and amazed actor a complete trajectory of his human experiences and sensations during his time onstage. Vakhtangov would say:
> At such and such moment you grew scared; then you corrected your course; as you became excited at the things going so well, you then wished you acted even better. That caused you to overact, so you became irritated with yourself; then you gave up, and began to act carelessly, etc.
> Moreover, Vakhtangov could tell this to everyone participating in the performance – not just to one actor. It seemed unfathomable how he could keep so many objects of attention at once, and not to miss even the slightest detail.[20]

To some degree, there was nothing mysterious in Vakhtangov's ability to see into his actors' creative minds. Actors, while in the creative space, often unwittingly betray their hidden, subconscious creative intentions via microscopic, imperceptible movements and gestures. An experienced director can 'read' these miniscule signals or reflexes to determine what the actor actually wants to do in each moment or even how an actor wants to play a given role.

VAKHTANGOV IN PRACTICE

When watching your actors rehearsing a scene, notice how you want them, at certain moments, to move somewhere, or to do something to their partner, or to speak. Sometimes, you guess these impulses by observing merely perceptible microscopic movements, facial expressions or gestures, indicating such an intention; such impulses are rarely followed – they are usually immediately stifled by the actors, who don't even notice them. In other moments, you might experience a strong sense of radiation[21] streaming from an actor into the direction where they really wanted to move but did not. After the scene is over, you share these observations with the actor, as your directorial suggestions, only to hear: 'This is exactly what I wanted to do.' Realize that the reason why you wanted the actor to do something is that they really wanted to do it, and you just read their hidden intentions.

An actor did not fulfil his or her urge out of fear. Perhaps, their intuitive urge contradicted their rational, intellectual understanding of the character – what their character 'would or would not do'. Or else, they thought that a given urge contradicted your directorial concept of the character. Realize that the reason you found their acting less than convincing was that the actors themselves were not 'convinced' – inwardly, instinctually, they wanted to do one thing; at the same time, they were making themselves do another. According to Vakhtangov's formula 'The audience believes everything an actor believes', you could not find that kind of acting convincing.[22] Any kind of acting where the actor goes against what they actually experience in the given moment cannot be convincing for the audience. And, vice versa, whenever an actor submits to their actual experience, this brings them (and their audiences) to the feeling of truth.

Instead of formulating your observations as 'directorial notes', or suggestions, ensure that your actors act upon their creative urges in the future by pointing out those instances when they did or did not follow them and urging them to follow such urges.

During those minutes and seconds leading up to the start of rehearsal, actors find themselves in a hypersensitive state. Unknowingly, they are 'in the presence of the character', beginning to inwardly live the character's life while surrounded by its aura. An inexperienced director can easily 'scare away' this precious state by striving to 'mobilize' an actor for the scene. 'Well, let's begin!' a director exclaims enthusiastically, clapping his or her hands. An actor instinctually mobilizes, shakes off the character (which was present on a deep subconscious level) and proceeds 'to rehearse'. Vakhtangov, who was deeply aware of this phenomenon, gave us the following precious guidance:

VAKHTANGOV IN PRACTICE

The first state an actor experiences onstage is the one he just experienced in life. One needs great courage not to betray this experience. One must surrender entirely to the power of one's artistic nature. It will do all the necessary things. Don't impose any solution upon yourself in advance. The quality to develop in an actor is courage.

No matter what you take from life – everything will apply.[23]

Following Vakhtangov's advice, watch an actor intently (but secretly) during those moments leading up to the rehearsal of his or her scene. When you manage to permeate their mood and psychophysical state, try to match it, when inviting an actor to step into the scene. By doing so, you will ease, if not erase, a sense of transition from pre-rehearsal state to that of rehearsing. Insist that an actor preserves not only the pre-rehearsal mood but also any small businesses or automatic movements you've observed in him or her during those seconds leading up to the scene.

Meyerhold opened his rehearsals for the audiences – his dazzling demonstrations were constantly accompanied by applause. Vakhtangov kept his creative act open only to those initiated. According to Michael Chekhov's testimony, Vakhtangov imagined the house full of audiences when he rehearsed.[24] These imaginary ideal audiences guided Vakhtangov's directorial improvisations. Based on Vakhtangov's technique, Michael Chekhov offered the following exercise to the director.

VAKHTANGOV IN PRACTICE

Having consulted the imaginary audience's big 'heart,' the interpretation of the play by actors and directors will be better guided and more inspired by the audience's 'voice.' The audience is an active co-creator of the performance. It has to be consulted before it is too late, and especially when searching for the super objective of the play.

At first the experiences of your imaginary audience will appear before your mind's eye as a spontaneous, unclarified and general

> impression. But you must draw all the sharp and specific conclusions from it, formulate all the potential thoughts and define all the emotions. A little practice with this experiment should make you adept at it and secure in the feelings that the imaginary audience will not fail you.[25]

The Method of Fantastic Realism

In April 1922, in his final talks with students, Vakhtangov had this to say on his Method of Fantastic Realism: 'A play can be directed naturalistically, or using the method of Fantastic Realism. And the latter will be the strongest, because a sculpture is intelligible to every nation.'[26] At a different point, Vakhtangov called an actor a 'master, who creates textures'.[27]

These two concepts complement each other. When referring to sculpture, Vakhtangov asks theatrical art to acquire expressivity of a symbol, capable of triggering the work of an audience's subconscious – directly, bypassing their intellectual mind. In sculpture, or painting, as well as in the graphic arts, an artist often alternates between different textures, styles and techniques within the scope of the same work. For example, expressionistic style can be mixed with the painterly. An artistic image dictates the richness of expressive means – it often calls a painter to create a complex perspective of painting techniques and styles.

Meanwhile, actors, if they want to remain 'truthful', are limited to a relatively small number of physical, psychological and vocal reactions, 'allowed' to them by 'characterization' or by a 'kernel' of his or her character. If they are to break out of this narrow circle, they will stop being true to life, to the character they portray; the sincerity of their life on stage will be lost. Vakhtangov broke the myth that an actor's emotional sincerity is incompatible with the freedom of formal means. In his final productions, he solved this dilemma by transforming the concept of character creation, as it was understood in his contemporary representational theatre. Instead of demanding of actors to live sincerely and truthfully onstage as their characters, he asked them to live a creative, truthful and inspired life of an artist and master. Such master-creators can be equipped with a variety of expressive means, or textures, and they can create the artistic image of the character onstage mixing elements of realistic and condensed characterization, theatrical grotesque, impressionism, expressionism, constructivism and surrealism. At times, the actor can simply exist onstage unmasked, as his true self – a creative individuality.

Vakhtangov's production of *Princess Turandot* provides an excellent example of the use of multiple acting textures within the same production.

At the top of *Turandot*, the actors of Vakhtangov's Studio introduced themselves to the audience as their own creative selves. In the tradition of commedia dell'arte, Vakhtangov called this opening a 'parade' (Figure 4.3). Instead of wearing their character's costumes, the actors in the parade wore what Vakhtangov referred to as a theatrical uniform. This was not Meyerholdian *prozodezhda* – sack-like grey overalls used for both men and women alike and designed in constructivist style. No, Vakhtangov's male actors wore elegant tails, and his actresses wore evening gowns designed by Nadezhda Lamanova, a leading Moscow fashion designer of the time.

The year was 1922, the fifth year of the proletarian revolution, and the time period was that of 'military communism'. Dressing his actors in tails and evening gowns was a bold move on Vakhtangov's part. And yet it was entirely accepted by the audience. Vakhtangov refused to 'reflect his times' literally. Nevertheless, the pulse of contemporary time did beat in Vakhtangov's *Turandot*. It reflected the essence of the period, its lightning-quick rhythms and futuristic tendencies, rooted in social optimism. However, theatre for Vakhtangov was the world of artistic beauty, and his actor had to look beautiful and elegant.

During the parade, the actors were introduced to the audience by the four classic commedia masks – Tartalia, Pantalone, Brigella and Trufaldino. They wore traditional commedia costumes, were made up in the same style and did not initially pose as Vakhtangov Studio actors. Their acting technique, or texture, contained a slight element of characterization. This characterization,

FIGURE 4.3 *Actors' parade at the start of* Princess Turandot, *1922. Courtesy of Andrei Malaev-Babel.*

however, was executed with such skill, lightness and ease that it never overshadowed the performer. The texture of a commedia mask, as 'worn' by a Vakhtangov actor, was transparent – the actor's individuality could be tangibly sensed through the mask. Most importantly, the characterization was clearly 'fantasized' by the actor. For example, Pantalone, in the good tradition of the commedia, spoke in a dialect; except that it was a very recognizable dialect of the provincial Ryazan region of Russia.

An actor 'juggled' the mask with great virtuosity: characterization could increase, at which point it condensed and bordered on the 'comedic grotesque'. It could also decrease, and finally it could almost disappear. During the performance, an actor playing a mask could 'come out of character' and ask his fellow actor to pick up a set of keys he just dropped on the stage, addressing him by his real name. This style of acting made many of the critics and theatre practitioners proclaim that Vakhtangov foreshadowed Brechtian theatre by making his play a point of view on their characters. A more careful examination of Vakhtangov's character structure in *Turandot* will show that he created a Brechtian effect using the means of his own school – that of experiencing.

To begin with, Vakhtangov actors played actors. They were introduced as such, and when the performance began, they remained their actor-selves at their core. Vakhtangov asked each of his performers to develop a 'character' of the member of the travelling commedia troupe. These actor-characters were elaborated by the actor according to the 'science' of the Stanislavsky System – they had biographies, elaborate relationships with each other and so on. On top of this, each 'Italian actor' played their own character (from Gozzi's *Turandot*) or their specific commedia mask, also as asked by Gozzi. As appropriate for the Italian commedia, they treated their mask with a pinch of irony, while the Vakhtangov actors, in turn, treated their Italian 'colleagues' somewhat ironically. This aspect of the actors' life in the performance was harmonious with the theatrical logic of things and by no means constituted 'playing one's point of view'. The fact that actors had a point of view did not mean that they played it. The audience, however, could receive such an impression. In the meantime, Vakhtangov's actors simply lived creatively onstage, alternating between several different qualities, textures or techniques of acting.

The three layers of the character structure (Vakhtangov Studio actor – commedia troupe member – *Turandot* character or mask) were present in every aspect of the performance. Its artistic tapestry consisted of elements belonging to three different 'realities', and all three harmoniously merged in *Turandot*. The first reality was the one of 1922 Revolutionary Moscow and the Vakhtangov Studio at the Arbat Street. The second was of Italy in the times of commedia dell'arte. The third reality was of a fairy-tale China (the plot of *Princess Turandot* takes place in China). Elements of all three realities were present in the set, music, audience experience and so on.

What made Vakhtangov's *Turandot* a revolutionary production signifying a new method in theatre was the fact that the actors' method of creative living onstage actually included all three of these layers. In the realm of acting, Vakhtangov developed an organic structure that allowed his actors to live truthfully in a fantastic reality. Only this can explain why Stanislavsky, after the opening of *Princess Turandot*, addressed members of the Vakhtangov Studio by saying: 'In the twenty-five-year history of the MAT such victories were few. You found what many theatres sought for long and in vain.'[28]

This was just one of several eternal paradoxes of theatre resolved by Vakhtangov in the final two years of his short creative life. In those cases where Vakhtangov ran out of time to solve a particular problem practically or theoretically, he, at the very least, pointed those who came after him in the direction where they could find such a resolution. One can agree or disagree with his solutions, but knowing them is essential for anyone who seriously approaches the field of theatre.

5

Alexander Tairov: Theatricalizing the Theatre

Claire Warden

Unlike many of his more well-known and celebrated peers, director Alexander Tairov (1885–1950) is often overlooked in theatre historiographies (or at least prominent Anglophone narratives) or else becomes a footnote in studies of Vsevolod Meyerhold or Konstantin Stanislavsky. There are myriad reasons for this neglect; partly it is due to a perceived lack of available archive (although actually more documents and images survive than it might initially appear) and partly to the difficulty in defining his approach and placing his unique body of directorial work in mainstream accounts of twentieth-century Russian theatre.[1] However, he remains a vital figure for these genealogies, making significant and unparalleled advances in areas such as inter-artistic collaboration, actor training, hybrid transnational aesthetic practice and the marrying of contemporary methods and themes with older forms. Throughout his career, Tairov placed great importance on the director whose 'intrinsic role is the coordination and ultimate harmonization of the creativity of the separate individualities'.[2] For Tairov, the director was the arranger of all facets of the theatrical event.

Like Stanislavsky and Meyerhold, Tairov lived through a time of great political, social and artistic upheaval. He began his career in Vera Komissarzhevskaya's theatre (where he met Meyerhold) before touring Russia with the Mobile Theatre and working with the Free Theatre in Moscow. In 1914, he established his own theatre, the Kamerny in Moscow, alongside his wife and lead company actor Alisa Koonen. The connection between the director and his theatre was strong; American head of the Federal

Theatre Project Hallie Flanagan, upon visiting the Moscow theatres in the late 1920s, went so far as to describe the Kamerny as 'not a simple theatre, but a projection of a complex and fascinating personality, that of director, Alexander Tairov'.[3] His directorial style seemed to be 'gentle, humane and undictatorial' but, at least for Flanagan, Tairov and his Kamerny Theatre remained inseparable, one reflecting and revealing the other.[4]

Tairov is equally difficult to define in terms of a movement or style. On the one hand, Tairov rejected the confines of naturalist realism, suggesting that the director working in such a mode 'had *of necessity to stifle* genuine acting creativity'; on the other, he suggested, the director in the stylized theatre 'subjugated the actor to a false principle'.[5] For his part, Stanislavsky criticized Tairov's directing style which treated the actor as 'no more than putty in the hands of the prime mover'.[6] Meyerhold was even less balanced, stating that he 'would sooner agree to be St Basil's neighbor than Tairov's'.[7] Tairov was equally critical of Meyerhold, lamenting his 'poverty of ideas'.[8] Other directors waded into the argument; Yevgeny Vakhtangov, for example, stated that Tairov's 'Kamerny … changes its style annually [and] naturally ends up with vulgarity'.[9] In his *Notes of a Director*, Tairov distances himself from the theatrical conventions of other Russian directors by suggesting that the early days of the Kamerny were 'guided only by *negative* principles', that is, a rejection of other schools or movements.[10] While clear connections can be seen in the theatrical work of Stanislavsky, Vakhtangov, Meyerhold and Tairov, the latter actively sought an entirely different creative route.

If it is difficult to contextualize him theatrically, then it seems doubly complex to understand his work in light of the changing sociopolitical landscape of Soviet Russia. At times, Tairov was regarded as an anti-revolutionary pariah, his aesthetics considered profoundly reactionary and detached from the Bolshevik cause. At others, he was celebrated, eventually even made a People's Artist of the USSR. In a sense, as American visitor Oliver Sayler acknowledged, the Kamerny Theatre came directly out of the war[11] and regularly acknowledged the political revolution in productions such as *The Man Who Was Thursday* (G. K. Chesterton 1923), which critiqued capitalism and, more obviously, the 1933 *The Optimistic Tragedy* (Vsevolod Vishnevsky) which created a much-emulated model for Soviet theatre. In the same year as this latter celebrated production, Tairov proclaimed that theatre should 'strive to solve the problem of dynamic realism, in which content and form ought to be synthetically united by the social feeling and artistic style of our epoch'.[12] Here, in this proto-Soviet explanation of his practice, Tairov purposefully elucidates the interconnection of time and aesthetic.

But, ultimately, his work still often felt out of step with Soviet decrees; unlike Meyerhold, Tairov did survive Stalin's push towards Socialist Realism, but his theatre, though clearly able to adapt to the changing times, came under increasing scrutiny until, in 1949, it was closed entirely leading to Tairov's transfer to the Vakhtangov Theatre as an assistant director, though he never actually staged anything there. Back in 1917, in a pamphlet entitled *Proclamation of an Artist*, Tairov concluded: 'Art is for all those in whose souls there is either a conscious or unconscious thirst for beauty.'[13] While his practice changed and developed with time, and came under significant pressure from the Soviet authorities, Tairov's 'thirst for beauty' seemed to be the driving characteristic of his entire theatrical oeuvre, a trait that, unsurprisingly, led to tensions with the government. Commissar for People's Enlightenment Anatoly Lunacharsky summed up the typical Bolshevik government response to Tairov's work in 1924 when, during a debate on contemporary theatre, he acknowledged the successes of the Kamerny, founded in a time when there were few important and interesting subjects to address in the theatre: 'When there are no enthralling plays, then at least let there be coloratura.'[14] However, by 1924, for Lunacharsky at least, important subjects of collectivism, class warfare and political freedom could at last appear on the stage and 'coloratura [or "beauty", as Tairov suggests above] can be developed as an auxiliary' only.[15] The tension between Tairov's concern for beauty and the government's commitment to didactic theatre is clear.

This chapter uses Tairov's perceived trickiness as a catalyst, unpacking his directorial work through five intertwined concepts: collaboration, characterization, constructivism, the relationship between stage and audience, and his unparalleled promotion of Western plays. Through these ideas, the chapter seeks to ascertain 'the director's singularity', presenting Tairov as a unique presence in the history of the Russian stage.[16]

Collaboration: Directors, actors, composers, choreographers and designers

Tairov proposed the director as a 'helmsman of the theatre; he pilots the ship of the theatrical production, avoiding shoals and reefs'.[17] For this boating analogy to work, of course, Tairov needed people in his ship. Yes, the director governed the process, but collaboration really created the work: after all, he said, 'The art of the theatre is a collective art.'[18] The Kamerny benefitted enormously from cross-disciplinary collaborations, with Tairov relying on the expertise of others. The most obvious example of this spirit of collaboration was the contribution of co-founder and lead actor Alisa Koonen. Koonen trained with Stanislavsky before setting up the Kamerny with Tairov, and she remained the company's lead actor throughout Tairov's directorship. Tairov considered the actor to be the most important presence in the theatre; this 'master-actor' was to be carefully trained and in total control of her own material (the body). The prominence of Koonen in the organizational structure of the Kamerny theatre surely encouraged this actor-focused approach. Konstantin Rudnitsky goes further, saying that 'Alisa Koonen was the first actress who managed to preserve within the integrated structure of directorial theatre all the rights the old theatrical system had granted the heroine.'[19]

So, for all the innovations of the Kamerny, Koonen, in some ways, adopted the role of traditional female 'star' protagonist. Nowhere was this clearer than in Tairov's 1917 version of Oscar Wilde's *Salome*, a production that Laurence Senelick confirms was significant in the general progression of the Kamerny Theatre and its artists:

> It acted as a second birth of Aleksandr Tairov's theatre, established Aleksandra Ekster as a major scene-designer, confirmed the Kamerny in its impulse towards 'cubist' productions, and set Alisa Koonen at the head of Russian actresses.[20]

Koonen played the title role in a sensual, visceral way and certainly commanded the stage. But Sayler's first-hand description of her performance brings further nuance:

> *Salome* at the Kamerny is not a one-role play, except as Wilde himself made it so. Nevertheless, Koonen's picture of the princess is such a masterpiece in impassioned action that she towers far above the rest of the cast.[21]

Here, Sayler recognized both Koonen's star quality and the importance of ensemble. Tairov acknowledged the value of both in his ambitions for a new drama school for children from which 'the most gifted would become heroes and heroines, leading men and leading ladies. The rest would form that indispensable *corps-de-théâtre* of my dreams, without which genuine scenic art is altogether unthinkable'.[22] It would seem that *Salome* relied on both elements.

Salome was also notable due to its innovative set design, another area for significant collaboration. Tairov employed avant-garde painter Ekster to create the scene. Breaking through the tradition of static painted backdrops, Exter used dynamic, kinetic materials of various colours and shapes.[23] Tairov criticized both the realistic visual illusions created by naturalism and the geometric, painterly designs of the stylized theatre. His rejection of both was based, once again, on his commitment to the actor – that three-dimensional focus that was so often (as he thought) either held captive by inflexible mimesis or else presented as an afterthought by directors more interested in scenic pictures. Tairov maintained that 'in the production of *Salome* I took the first steps on the path to a solution of the *problems of dynamic transformation of scenic atmosphere*'.[24] The desire for a dynamic stage led to a number of other collaborations with designers and visual artists, including Alexander Vesnin who produced the playing space for *Phaedra* (Valery Briusov 1922). For this production, Tairov spent much of his free time away from rehearsals in the model shop with Vesnin, a dedication that illustrates his expansive, multifaceted view of the director's role.[25] The result – shaped planes which combined in different patterns during the play – visually embodied Tairov's commitment to the kinaesthetic, imaginative stage space.[26] In the second half of the 1920s, Tairov turned to the Stenberg Brothers, Vladimir and Georgy, to create sets which enabled the actors to operate 'in a variety of positions, relating to each other and to the audience vertically, horizontally, and diagonally'.[27] So their set for Tairov's *Desire under the Elms* (Eugene O'Neill 1926), for example, included a series of four-sided geometric shapes, connected with a series of steps. Only a symbolist suggestion of a tree stands outside this structure, indistinctly connoting the isolated New England farm.[28] Although critical of the performance, Walter Benjamin, who attended *Desire under the Elms* in December 1926, did note the fascinating way that the actors moved across and over this set, suggesting that the innate kinaesthetic character of the design 'accelerated the dynamism' of the whole piece.[29]

TAIROV IN PRACTICE

Tairov remained committed to synthesizing the stage and producing a space that enabled his newly trained actor to perform. In *Notes of a Director*, he describes the following task:

> First execute a series of movements which one can perform on the level expanse of the floor. Then place on the floor even so much as a stool, using it as a new plane, as a second area for the development of your movement, and you will see how your gesture is enriched, how many new plastic possibilities.[30]

Once this experiment has been completed with a stool, other objects and planes can be brought into the sequence to provide, in Tairov's words, 'absolutely inexhaustible possibilities for gesture and form'.[31]

While Tairov understood the importance of the director as instigator, driver and conductor, then, he remained entirely committed to a collaborative theatre, inviting actors and designers to contribute significantly to the process. He sums up his response to collaborative processes thus:

No, the theatre is a collective art and it must be accepted as such. Unity, without which of course any work of art is unthinkable, is born as the result of the marriage of a whole line of wills, merging at last into a single, monolithic work of scenic art.[32]

There is a real sense of harmony here, a determination that, in the end, the various characters involved in the process could successfully combine to create one piece of art. To return to Tairov's analogy, the director might pilot the ship, but the ship needed to be populated with multitalented, theatre-focused artists in order to fully realize a successful work of art.

Characterization: From ancient Greece to Soviet Russia

In this collaborative directorial practice, Tairov placed special emphasis on the figure of the actor. The actor (and indeed human presence on the stage more generally) was a particularly fraught topic in early twentieth-century theatre. In response to this polygonal understanding of the twentieth-century actor, Edward Gordon Craig, for example, advocated the *Übermarionette*, a figure that could overcome the quirks and irritations of the human actor, freeing him/her of the 'emotion [that] *possesses* him' that means that actors do not present a 'work of art' but a 'series of accidental confessions'.[33] Tairov wholeheartedly disagreed with Craig, rejecting the marionette in favour of another new archetype: 'the living actor, the actor-creator, the actor-master'.[34] He disagreed equally vehemently with his Russian contemporaries, denying both the synthetic representational characters of Meyerhold and the emotion-driven naturalist mirrors of Stanislavsky. His vision for the actor was unique – neither, as he saw it, a 'slave to the writer' as in the Moscow Art Theatre nor a 'slave to the artist-designer' as on Meyerhold's stage.[35] Instead, Tairov wanted a 'polymath master performer', an independent and highly trained artist who, nevertheless, voluntarily subjected him/herself to the orchestration of the director.[36] In order to develop skilled actors, Tairov established an in-house training programme in the early 1920s with classes in gymnastics and acrobatics, as well as voice and theatre history. Tairov committed to freeing his actors from the trappings of the stage: props, costumes and unhelpful sets. This was clear from Tairov's earliest work; in his 1914 opening production *Sakuntala* by Kalidasa (for which he found 'oriental' inspiration from the British Museum in London), Tairov used body paint for his actors rather than costumes to enable as much bodily freedom as possible. He defined the actor musically as an 'enchanted Stradivarius', a sensitive, beautiful and harmonious instrument.[37]

TAIROV IN PRACTICE

Tairov's actors were highly trained using fencing, ballet, gymnastics and acrobatics. But he also used more accessible methods that enabled actors to discover rhythm and develop physical dexterity and discipline. In developing the external technique, Tairov encouraged his actors to try juggling. Attempt this action, considering some of Tairov's most enduring concepts such as the ideas of fantastical play, clowning and rhythm. Firstly, simply attempt to retain an ongoing rhythm with the three balls. Speed up the rhythm and then slow it down, understanding how this change in tempo makes a difference to the tone or atmosphere. During this exercise, inevitably balls will be dropped; errors will be made. Think about how these 'failures' encourage a spirit of buffoonery, risk and play. The voice was another aspect of this external technique. Speak aloud the following extract from *Famira Kifared* using different intonations, stresses and rhythms:

Long have I watched Admet's herds,
Admet's herds.
O, delirium.
Are you, Kifared, one who
Abandons your friends?
O, delirium
Having tuned the flute,
Invest it with
Your own lustre.[38]

Although Tairov acknowledged that the audience did not understand a word of this sequence, nonetheless, he noticed that the rapt spectators gave full attention to the actor simply because of the rhythms of the work spoken in a clear, musical way.[39] Just as with the juggling task, play with the tone, tempos and rhythms of the extract.

His understanding of this new actor was based in a range of different sources, and, perhaps paradoxically, like many modernist theatre makers looked back to established or ancient forms. One of Tairov's primary influences was the ancient Greek stage. He remained fascinated by the diametrically opposed theatrical concepts of tragedy and comedy, and Apollo and Dionysus (that is order and chaos),[40] coexisting facets of human experience that defined the ancient world and continue to define the modern world too.[41] His collaborative set designs, while (often) clearly modernist with platforms, symbolist gesture and cubist geometry, equally reflected the blank spaces and spatial simplicity (the ekkyklema and skene) of the Hellenic tradition. However, this harking back to ancient modes clearly influenced the acting styles too. In *Phaedra*, for example, Tairov used not only cubist sets (designed by Vesnin) but also movements, gestures and poses that nodded to an ancient Hellenistic art.[42] It combined three distinct eras/places: Greek myth, seventeenth-century court drama (it was originally written by Jean Racine after all, translated by Briusov) and, as Tairov put it in a lecture to the Kamerny Troupe in 1931, 'the heavy step of our revolutionary period in this country'.[43]

In addition, he found other recognized character models in the Italian tradition of the commedia dell'arte.[44] Commedia similarly resonated with Meyerhold, of course, but whereas Meyerhold's actors seemed, to Tairov at least, to be subordinated to polemic, Tairov used commedia to free his actors and, indeed, to free the imagination of his audience. His 1920 *Princess Brambilla* (based on a novelette by E. T. A. Hoffman) used these tropes to particular effect. Hoffman's work is a satire, a tale ultimately reflecting on the reformation of the theatre. It used a number of techniques, motifs and objects from commedia, including masks, puppets and phantasmagorical movement. The actors created a sense of dynamism on the stage by manipulating portable screens and banners; in the carnival scenes, the actors donned capes to accentuate the freedom of movement.[45] *Princess Brambilla* celebrated commedia techniques but did not simply revel in theatrical history; rather Dassia Posner reads it as 'timely in its message of hope for the future; in its declaration of the power of art; in the need for art to survive in the most difficult of economic circumstances'.[46] By presenting this celebratory, commedia-infused fantasy in 1920, Tairov seemed to be saying something broader about the need for aesthetic beauty in times of sociopolitical upheaval. As Torda suggests, 'Tairov's special contribution lies in his sophisticated, ballet-oriented approach, transcending the banalities of ordinary life.'[47]

Despite the emblematic characters found in these traditions, Tairov remained committed to encouraging emotion in his actors. He wanted neither the marionettes of the synthetic theatre nor the psychological restrictions of naturalism. Instead, emotion should be real but imaginatively beautiful, emanating from 'the magical land of fantasy'.[48] The way to discover such emotion, said Tairov, lies in improvisation and in the real experiences of the actor on the stage.

Constructivism: Structure, architecture and musical rhythm

As for many other Russian directors of the period, the change in characterization necessitated a transformation in the playing space. Tairov explained the connection as follows:

> The body of the actor is *three dimensional*, therefore the actor can express himself only volumetrically. Hence it is necessary to give action space to

the actor commensurate with his tasks at hand and to provide him with an appropriate stage ambience.⁴⁹

Tairov went on to say that the stage artist 'must focus his attention on the floor of the stage, having broken away from his fascination with the backdrop'.⁵⁰ The floor is where actors move and interact. The backdrop, by contrast, is a two-dimensional interloper, made strangely inert and incongruous as soon as the actor appears. Such spatial and formal questions would appear to suggest some connection with the prominent constructivist mode. But the parallel is not a neat fit, of course. Georgii Kovalenko describes Tairov's practice as 'a variant of constructivist stage design'.⁵¹ Despite his unwavering focus on beauty, abstruse stage politics and position of the audience (of which more in a moment), Tairov's ideas about stage design often resembled those of Meyerhold.

But ultimately they represented a decidedly variant model. Defining Tairov's response to twentieth-century scenographic changes is challenging, as illustrated by professor of comparative literature Horst Frenz who, entirely legitimately, moves between the labels 'futurist, cubist, or post-impressionistic'.⁵² It seemed just as confusing for Tairov's contemporaries; Flanagan referred to Tairov's style as a 'geometry of the soul',⁵³ thereby conflating two prominent Russian modes – Meyerhold's stylization and Stanislavsky's emotional realism – into one highly complex term. It is also important to note, as with all aspects of Tairov's practice, that his vision for the stage changed and developed throughout his career. Julia Listengarten narrates this progression as moving from 'the romantic extravagancies of cubofuturist design to the austere geometrical lines of structural realism'.⁵⁴

Despite tensions, at times, Meyerhold's and Tairov's design decisions did often look remarkably similar. In 1923, for example, Viktor Shestakov designed the 'Western' cityscape for Meyerhold's *Lake Lyul*, a critique of capitalist urbanism.⁵⁵ Tairov's version of Chesterton's *The Man Who Was Thursday*, a thriller about anarchists and policemen in London, also appeared in 1923 with a set designed by Vesnin. In a similar way to Meyerhold and Shestakov, Tairov and Vesnin presented a clear political message.⁵⁶ The set directly attacked the capitalist system.⁵⁷ It was a congested space of constructions, advertisements, bourgeois characters in evening wear and flashing lights.⁵⁸ Again, while often understood as apolitical, or at least more committed to aesthetics than politics, Tairov's theatre exhibits here a real desire to engage with the contemporaneous political scene, even if (due to the crowded nature of the stage and the rather sluggish action) the realization of this vision did not perhaps function as successfully as Meyerhold's/Shestakov's for *Lake Lyul*.

Tairov's production seemed such a departure from Chesterton's original text; certainly the author disliked this version. However, Tairov's response reveals a broader issue about the importance (or otherwise) he placed on the play text. In his critique of *The Man Who Was Thursday*, Lucas Harriman refers to it as a 'betrayal'; this is, says Harriman, not necessarily a criticism, for 'betrayal' in this sense is a 'revelatory rather than merely treacherous factor'.⁵⁹ This analysis of the place of the text in *The Man Who Was Thursday* seems equally relevant for almost every production Tairov undertook. The text, or 'literature' as Tairov described it, should be understood as *'material necessary to it at the present stage of its development'*.[60] The writer (Tairov preferred 'poet') becomes a 'helpmate', part of the collaborative team I have already discussed, rather than a dictator of meaning.[61]

If music was a key motif for Tairov's characterization, it became just as important for his sets. So his spaces were not specifically playgrounds or factories as in Meyerhold's theatre but rather keyboards on which his musical actors could play new, innovative tunes. His description of the steps (designed by Exter) in his 1916 *Famira Kifared* (by Innokenty Annensky) illustrates the following point:

> The decision depends entirely on your rhythmic intent ... if you wish to attach a solemn, liturgical character to the action of the descent, you will construct the steps so that the intervals between them are everywhere the same. They will correspond rhythmically to 1/4 or 1/8 time, in this way giving to the movement of the actress an even and uninterrupted, flowing rhythm.[62]

The set – in this case the positioning of steps – enabled the rhythm of the entire performance.

His 1922 version of Charles Lecoq's operetta *Giroflé-Girolfa* further illustrated the importance of music as a structural device. Obviously music was a key facet of the production, and yet Tairov argued that 'we do not want to pour out feelings in arias, duets, and choruses'; rather the stage composition had a musical quality, an 'acoustical significance' as Tairov put it.[63] The simple design – stripped down costumes which gave the actors permission to move effectively, the basic structures[64] – enabled the entire space to act as a piece of music, an organic and fluid symphony. With music created by Henri Forterre and choreography by Antonia Shalomytova, *Giroflé-Girolfa* represented a truly synthesized theatrical experiment.

TAIROV IN PRACTICE

Music was a vital element in Tairov's directorial practice. The actors were trained in the same way as eminent musicians, sets became acoustic and plays had secret musical tunes to be uncovered. It is worth exploring the multiple levels of Tairov's interest in music (a) by first identifying the physical rhythms of work by composers such as Beethoven and Chopin, as Tairov did (b) by using a similar process to find what Tairov referred to as the 'rhythmic beat of the play' – use Wilde's *Salome* to complete this task, as Tairov suggested that he felt the 'rhythmic and contrapuntal patterns' most acutely when he approached this play,[65] and (c) by considering the musicality of space, for example, the way that walking up and down different sets of stairs changes the rhythm of the action.

Stage and the audience: Engaging spectators/distancing the audience

One of the central aims of 1920s Soviet art in general seemed to be the reduction of the distance between the stage and the audience. Meyerhold imagined everyone in the auditorium to be workers for the Revolution, from the actors on the stage to the people in the audience. In essence, he envisaged a united space. The touring agitprop groups likewise committed to taking theatre to uninitiated new audiences, producing short scripts on outdoor platforms, in factories or on train carriages. Ultimately Soviet theatre (whether the experimental constructivism of Meyerhold, the later hyper-realism of Nikolai Okhlopkov or the more conservative-minded Socialist Realist plays celebrating the heroic workers) focused on reducing the gap between the audience and the stage accentuated by the presence of the proscenium.

While Tairov's practice can be read as constructivist, he differed considerably from his compatriots in his opinions about the audience. Tairov rejected the vogue for communal stage action, productions in which the audience might play an active, onstage role. The fashion, he felt, was a regression. Rather, the audience must 'remain a spectator, not a participant'.[66] This might appear to be a rather restrictive, elitist view of the audience–actor relationship. However, Tairov had another vision:

> The spectator need not actively participate in the performance, but he must view it *creatively*, and if, on the wings of a fantasy awakened in him by the art of the theatre, he is carried beyond its walls into the wondrous land of Urdar, then I wish him a delighted *bon voyage*.[67]

So, while the spectator fulfils a more detached role than in, say, Meyerhold's theatre, the aim is to encourage the audience's sense of wonderment and beauty. This was neither agitprop municipality nor naturalist realist estrangement (though neither of these descriptions are really entirely accurate, of course) but a sense of encouraging a more creative and visionary audience response. This did not mean that Tairov's actors never acknowledged the audience directly (in *Giroflé-Girofla*, for example, the performers flirted and joked with the audience during the dances and songs),[68] but rather that the work of art was created before the audience interacted with it.

This conviction was at odds with prevailing Bolshevik opinions of art. It was the primary reason that Tairov's theatre came under almost constant attack by the authorities who accused him of focusing on theatricality rather than furthering a political message. Lunacharsky recognized the technical brilliance of Tairov's work yet declared that 'almost all of Comrade Tairov's productions are distorted by affectation'.[69] However, in 1934, Tairov produced a play that seemed to baulk against his entire canon and paved the way for a new Socialist Realist theatre: Vsevolod Vishnevsky's *The Optimistic Tragedy*. Vishnevsky's play tells the tale of a woman commissar who is sent on board a Red Navy ship to restore order. She shoots two soldiers who attempted to rape her and subsequently solves the issues on board. However, she is accidentally killed at the end and the optimism is transformed into tragedy.[70] Tairov described this tragedy in a classical Greek way, despite dedicating it to the Red Army. He acknowledged two moments of catharsis that he wanted to accentuate in production: the oath taken by those on board the ship who finally recognize the worth of the Revolution and the death of the commissar who 'perishes as a seed, cast into the earth to become the origin of a new life'.[71] Both of these cathartic moments address the audience; the oath is clearly an affirmation of a general commitment to the Revolution, and the commissar's death encourages the audience to be part of the new life. Koonen recalled the response of the audience:

> The spectators greeted it with exceptional enthusiasm. During the action they would jump up, shout 'Hoorah!' and applaud. The atmosphere in the auditorium, of course, jumped across the footlights to the stage, the performance went with great élan.[72]

Ultimately the Bolshevik authorities celebrated this play precisely because it spoke directly to the audience in a political way.

In 1946 during the Zhdanov purge, the Central Committee of the Communist Party accused Tairov and the Kamerny of 'aloofness from contemporary life' and a 'flight from Soviet reality'.[73] Despite *The Optimistic Tragedy*, in the eyes of communist officialdom, Tairov was a 'cosmopolite', more interested in creating spectacle, emotion and theatricality than putting the stage at the service of the Revolution. The rejection of Tairov was also reflective of an increasing antisemitism, where 'cosmopolite' was also well-known code for 'Jewish'. Notwithstanding Tairov's ability to adapt to changes in Russian social and artistic life, he was ultimately also a rather awkward presence for those intent on creating more overtly political work. The accusation that he was, in the words of a 1949 article in *Soviet Art*, a 'consistent sycophant of the reactionary culture of the West' remained one of the Bolshevik administration's primary allegations levelled at Tairov and his company.[74]

Anglophone theatre: O'Neill, Treadwell, Chesterton and Wilde

More than any other Russian director of the period, Tairov showed an interest in theatre out with Russia. He led his company on three tours during the twenties, and some of the major figures of twentieth-century theatre art admired the productions shown during Tairov's time in Continental Europe, including Jean Cocteau, Ferdnand Léger and Sergei Diaghilev.[75] He also produced a range of challenging plays from outside Russia, including George Bernard Shaw's *St Joan* (1924) and the first version of Bertolt Brecht's *The Threepenny Opera* to appear outside Germany (1930). The scripts he chose were wide-ranging and, in keeping with his more general commitment to elevate theatre above the script, directed without particular concern for textual authenticity or fidelity. In 1933, just before his triumphant production of *The Optimistic Tragedy*, Tairov directed a play from America: Sophie Treadwell's expressionistic *Machinal*. This play theatricalizes a real-life story of a woman who murders her husband after dutifully following the expectations placed on her (marriage, home, babies). Her eventual execution for the crime is often read as a personal tragedy, in keeping with the expressionist model of focusing on a protagonist alienated from the world around him/her. Tairov's *Machinal* created a more expansive critique of the capitalist system (specifically the *American* capitalist system) that oppresses young women.[76] 'Tairov took for the basis of his production,' said Boris Golubovsky, 'an image – everything is "machinal," everything is the same'.[77] The stage set with its giant skyscrapers and identical characters sitting at typewriters exemplified a far broader analysis of capitalism, with the central character a victim of the system. In a way, this approach resembled Tairov's directorial work on his 1945 version of J. B. Priestley's *An Inspector Calls*, another play from outside Russia. Priestley was unable to find a British home for this play and so turned to Russia instead. Its devastating critique of the moral and ethical bankruptcy of the English bourgeoisie, and its focus on the inescapable predicaments of those further down the social ladder, would certainly have appealed to a Soviet audience. Once again, the tragedy of an individual, in this case Eva Smith who commits suicide before the play begins due to abuse and poverty, exemplifies broader political ideas. Tairov's directorial choices added to this impression:

> The manorial dining room of the Birlings is transformed under our gaze into a ... court-room. The table standing in the middle of the room is almost an executioner's block and the four chairs arranged at the sides, the defendants' benches.[78]

Under Tairov's directorship *An Inspector Calls* becomes a tribunal play, a direct criticism of Western capitalism.

His most famous interpretations of Anglophone scripts, however, were his versions of American Eugene O'Neill's plays: *The Hairy Ape* (1926), *Desire under the Elms* (1926) and *All God's Chillun Got Wings* (1928). Tairov's landmark productions transformed O'Neill's scripts into more theatrical, visual spectacles. Take *The Hairy Ape* with a set designed by the Stenberg Brothers. This play focuses on Yank, a stoker who, alienated from the bourgeois, capitalist-driven world in 1920s New York, is eventually killed by the one animal he begins to feel empathy with, the ape in the zoo. The opening set divided the light-filled bourgeois world on the deck from the darkness of the mechanized world below, thereby visually rendering the two sides of American capitalist experience.[79] Tairov chose to dress the nightmarish bourgeois characters in grotesque masks as they walked along Fifth Avenue. After O'Neill saw the play in Paris, he wrote an open letter to Tairov saying that it 'in every way delighted me because they rang so true to the spirit of my work ... a theatre of creative imagination has always been my ideal'.[80] Tairov appeared to have freed *The Hairy Ape* from the shackles of realism or even expressionism and, concurrently, from the notion of the play text as the ultimate source of meaning. These O'Neill plays also marked a definite change in Tairov's aesthetic, moving from indistinct symbolism to a more substantial, solid, place-oriented, society-focused art that would eventually culminate in *The Optimistic Tragedy*.[81]

TAIROV IN PRACTICE

Tairov also remained committed to encouraging the actor's internal technique. Improvisation was a key element in uncovering this. He described his improvisatory practice as uniting the methods of the naturalist stage (which focuses on the stage object rather than the auditorium) and the stylized theatre (which is concerned with the auditorium rather than the stage). In order to expose what Tairov means here, improvise a short scenario with a partner (this could be anything, but it might be worth using one of Tairov's productions as a catalyst – any of the O'Neill plays work very well for this). Firstly, improvise the scene by focusing only on the objects and people in the stage space; secondly, improvise the scene focusing only on the auditorium. Finally, attempt to unite these approaches (as Tairov advocated) by focusing on both at the same time: the 'mastery of the dual object'.[82]

Conclusion: The winding steps of theatre making

Georgy Yakulov designed the set for *Princess Brambilla* as a 'whimsically, steeply spiralling staircase ... intended to provide for the rhythms of carnival movement – light, rapid, and fluid'.[83] In a sense, this set design visually sums up Tairov's directorial practice. It is inherently fantastical and imaginative; it relies on collaborative effort; it has a distinct rhythm and linearity, and yet it is not too geometrical and solid; it uses colour to encourage the imaginative response of the audience; and it is brought to life by the live actors who are encouraged to interact with it as a pianist plays the keys. It is also winding, emblematic of Tairov's constantly changing aesthetic, which responded to both his developing understanding of the stage and the pressures from political sources. Ultimately Tairov's legacy lies in his imaginative response to the difficult business of producing theatre. His vision for, in his words, the 'theatricalization of the theatre' remained his driving ambition, leading to a legacy of work that is as fantastically inventive as it is grounded in a collaborative, actor-led process.[84]

6

Michael Chekhov: Directing an Actors' Theatre

Tom Cornford

A director displaced and overlooked

Michael Chekhov is not usually considered to be one of the Russian theatre's great directors, and he is commonly omitted from lists that include his contemporaries Meyerhold, Tairov and Vakhtangov.[1] There are three principal reasons for this. First, Chekhov was known during his life mostly as an actor, rather than a director. Second, he left Russia in 1928 as a result of political differences with the Soviet regime, and, thereafter, almost all of his directing was conducted in a foreign language, limiting the range of plays he felt able to undertake. Third, Chekhov did not create a string of productions that transformed the understanding of theatre and its possibilities during his lifetime. Indeed, in contrast to his widely celebrated performances, much of Chekhov's work as a director did not even achieve critical acclaim.

My argument here, however, is that although these reasons not to consider Chekhov a 'great director' may seem logical and compelling, they also represent a limited and limiting conception of the practice of directing. There has been an understandable tendency in writing about directors to fetishize individual productions of which there are good historical records and thus to depict directors as *auteur*-like creators of artistic products that are easily delineated and easily commodified. Chekhov did create some such productions, which have already received scholarly attention, but they were not the primary focus of his directorial endeavours.[2] Instead, he was much more deeply engaged with the development of ensemble companies and with the elaboration of the creative processes by which their work would be made. We are fortunate that, although there is very limited material available to Anglophone scholars about Chekhov's productions, there is a wealth of information relating to his directorial processes in the Michael Chekhov Theatre Studio Deirdre Hurst du Prey Archive.[3] This collection, which consists mainly of typed transcripts of Chekhov's classes and rehearsals, reminds us of a paradox of directing: the director's activity predates the performance texts it generates and thus any attempt to read directorial intention from a performance is necessarily speculative. By contrast, directors are usually clearly visible in rehearsal, shaping and organizing the activities by which a production is created. This is the work upon which the archival materials recorded and collected by Chekhov's assistant Deirdre Hurst du Prey primarily concentrate and which will also be the primary focus of this chapter.

Chekhov's career in the theatre

Where Chekhov is remembered today, he is remembered principally as a theorist of actor-training, and he did indeed dedicate a great amount of his working life to the study and teaching of acting.[4] However, as this biographical sketch will demonstrate, Chekhov's work with actors and actors-in-training was always, until the very last period of his working life, enfolded within attempts to foster ensemble companies. Therefore, a more complete account of Chekhov's contribution to the theatre must see his work in actor training not as an end in itself but as a means to the end of creating both companies and productions. These aims are, by definition, those of a director.

Chekhov studied acting first at the Suvorin Theatre School in St Petersburg, graduating into the Suvorin Theatre's Company. Soon afterwards, he was invited by Konstantin Stanislavsky to join the company of the Moscow Art Theatre. In 1912, he was one of the first among the company's actors to sign up for Stanislavsky's First Studio, where he began what he later called 'prying behind the curtain of the Creative Process'.[5] Only six years later, in 1918, Chekhov began a studio of his own in Moscow, where he taught a version of his teacher's System. By 1924, however, when Chekhov became the director of the Second Moscow Art Theatre (as the First Studio had become), he was already developing approaches of his own: 'I was able to develop my methods of acting and directing and formulate them into a definite technique', he wrote (note that this technique incorporated both acting and directing).[6] However, the ideas that formed the basis of Chekhov's technique at this time proved quickly to be unacceptable to the authorities. Whereas the Soviet government insisted upon the materialist doctrine of Socialist Realism, Chekhov was exploring the spiritual ideas of Rudolf Steiner and the Anthroposophists.[7] He was therefore identified as part of the General Political Agency's campaign against exponents of religious ideology,[8] received a letter from Narkrompos (the Ministry governing education and culture) telling him to stop spreading his ideas, and was threatened with arrest.[9] As a consequence, he left Russia speedily in 1928 and would never return.

There followed a period of self-imposed exile in Europe in which Chekhov worked initially, because of the pressing need to earn a living, as an actor. Writing to his former colleagues at the Second Moscow Art Theatre from Germany in 1928, however, he declared that 'it is impossible for me to stay in the theatre just as an actor who merely plays a number of roles [...] Only *the idea of a new theatre in general, a new theatre art* can fascinate me and stimulate my creative work'.[10] Consequently, in 1930, Chekhov was directing again, firstly creating a production of *Twelfth Night* with the Jewish Habima Theatre[11] and then working on *Hamlet* with a group of Russian émigré actors. By the end of 1930, he was in Paris, where the following year he formed *Le Théâtre Tchekoff* and an associated school of acting with his friend and colleague Georgette Boner. The Paris initiative collapsed in 1932 due to a lack of funds, and Chekhov travelled to Riga, Latvia, and Kaunas, Lithuania, where he acted, directed and taught in leading theatres until a military coup in Latvia in the spring of 1934 forced him to leave.

Chekhov's consistent attempts to capitalize upon his status as an actor to develop projects focused on the creation of 'a new theatre art' finally bore fruit in 1936 in the form of the Chekhov Theatre Studio at Dartington Hall. Dartington had been established in 1925 by an American heiress, Dorothy Whitney Elmhirst, and her husband, Leonard Elmhirst. It was conceived as an experiment in regenerating agriculture, rural industries and crafts, as well as education and the arts. In 1935, Dorothy Elmhirst's daughter, Beatrice Straight, who was intent upon a career in the theatre, travelled to New York with her friend Deirdre Hurst to seek out teachers of acting to come to Dartington. They saw Chekhov playing Khlestakov in *The Government Inspector*, were astonished by his performance and arranged classes with him. Soon afterwards, a contract was drawn up for Chekhov to run a theatre school at Dartington.[12]

Chekhov's plan for the Dartington Studio was to develop a company of actors who would go on to work professionally while continually training as an ensemble. After two years of training as a group in Devon, however, the spread of fascism in Europe and the isolation of their rural location caused Chekhov to decide to move the Studio to the United States. It took up residence in Ridgefield, Connecticut, in December 1938. While in Connecticut, Chekhov and his colleagues decided to shift the Studio's emphasis from teaching and performances closed to the public to the creation of new productions. The first of these, an adaptation of Dostoyevsky's *The Possessed*, scripted by Chekhov's colleague George Shdanoff, opened at the Lyceum Theatre on Broadway in October 1939. It received mixed responses and closed soon afterwards. Chekhov and his company then spent 1940 and 1941 rehearsing and touring productions of plays Chekhov had worked on previously: *King Lear, Twelfth Night* and *The Cricket on the Hearth*, as well as a new play for children: *Troublemaker-Doublemaker* by Chekhov and Arnold Sundgaard. In 1942, Chekhov also staged an opera, Mussorgsky's *Sorochinsky Fair*, in New York, designed by his long-term collaborator Mstislav Dobuzhinsky.

There is a discernible pattern in Chekhov's career of being displaced, then settling and becoming established, before quickly being displaced again. America proved no exception. In 1942, when the Studio's male actors were drafted into military service following America's decision to join the war, it was forced to close. Chekhov moved to Hollywood with the support of his friend, the composer Rachmaninov. There, in 1946, he directed his last production, *The Government Inspector*, with actors from the Hollywood Theatre Laboratory at the Las Palmas Theatre.[13] He remained in Hollywood, working as an actor and teaching acting, until his death in 1955. After Chekhov's death, a few of his former colleagues and students tried to sustain the life of his artistic technique and were most successful in doing so by teaching his approaches to acting. Taught in these contexts, Chekhov's technique inevitably became seen as a set of exercises for actors rather than the foundation of the 'new theatre art' that he had envisaged. It is therefore a central contention of this chapter that Chekhov's period teaching acting in Hollywood is best considered as a post-script to his working life, and that to consider him primarily as a theorist of actor-training is to give that phase of his work a prominence that Chekhov would not have considered justified. If we are to develop a more complete understanding of his contribution to the theatre, and of his potential as a theorist of performance, we must see Michael Chekhov as both an actor and director.

The actor is the theatre

To see Chekhov as a director does not, however, require us to diminish his contribution to the study of acting, since his conception of directing places the work of the actor at the heart of the theatre and all its creative processes. Accordingly, the class and rehearsal notes transcribed by Deirdre Hurst du Prey during the period of the Chekhov Theatre Studio (1936–1942) were collected under the title 'The Actor is the Theatre', quoting Chekhov:

> I think the theatre consists of the actor and that is all. Nobody else is important in the theatre, from my point of view. If the actor is not there, then there is no theatre. All that the director, the author, the designer will do will not make a theatre.[14]

This statement (which was not intended for publication) may be easily misconstrued as a deliberate devaluing of the work of non-actors in the creation of a production, but this would take it out of context. Chekhov required that his students did not only act; he also asked them to write, design and direct performances. His own work was likewise deeply invested in all aspects of theatre. This statement should therefore be understood to mean that the actor is the only person who embodies the art of the theatre, and therefore theatre can only be made through her work. Chekhov does not deny that director, author and designer make vital contributions, but he warns that, without a deep understanding of the actor, their work will come to nothing.

Chekhov's approach to the actor's artistry is based upon some fundamental concepts that also underpin his notion of directing. I have chosen four that seem particularly relevant to his practice as a director: the idea of polarity, the dialogue between imagination and incorporation, the use of gesture as a means of exploring and communicating the content of a performance, and the vital importance of atmosphere to a performance's capacity to communicate with an audience. The principle of polarity, as we will see, governed much of Chekhov's directorial thinking. A polarity is any opposition of forces or ideas that are mutually antagonistic but also inseparably connected to each other. A spine, for example, is an embodiment of polarity as it stretches in two directions simultaneously. Chekhov often spoke of the spine of a play and insisted that 'the beginning and the end ... should be, polar in principle'.[15] This approach was borrowed by Chekhov from Stanislavsky's co-director of the Moscow Art Theatre, Vladimir Nemirovich-Danchenko, whose thinking was responsible, according to Chekhov, for the capacity of the Art Theatre's productions to express 'oneness, wholeness, completeness' in their interpretation of a play.[16]

Chekhov believed that the root of all artistic practice was 'a deeply-rooted and often unconscious desire for transformation'.[17] His technique seeks to develop this desire into a skill by means of exercises which combine imagination and incorporation. One such exercise is known as the Imaginary Body. It asks actors to picture the body of their character and then to 'step into this body [...] so that your actual body and your imaginary body will meet in the same space'.[18] I have argued elsewhere that this is merely 'one example of an archetypal pattern in Chekhov's approach, in which an "invisible body" is created as a means of exploring and expressing the intangible'.[19] Chekhov's use of gesture is a further example of the dialogue between imagination and incorporation in his technique. He told his students at Dartington that the 'spiritual content' of the 'desires ... feelings ... ideas' found in a play 'must be expressed by the motions or gestures of the human body'.[20] We will see throughout Chekhov's directing that he uses gesture as a means of exploring and communicating all aspects of a play: not only the movements of its characters but its ideas, its psychological action and the atmospheres it conjures.

CHEKHOV IN PRACTICE

Ask your actors to decide what they are trying to do to the other characters in a scene. Ask them to think about this in terms of direction in space. Are they raising the other character(s) up or crushing them? Dispersing them or gathering them? Making an offer to them or tricking them and taking things from them? Ask them to convert this spatial dynamic into a gesture. Then ask what quality this gesture might have. Is it rough or gentle? Sudden or gradual? Spontaneous or carefully planned? Ask them to create gestures with a clear direction and quality to express their sequence of actions in a scene. By exploring characters' objectives as gestures, you will develop your capacity to experience the action of a scene as simultaneously physical and psychological and to retain that embodied experience while performing.

Of the ideas that sit at the heart of Chekhov's technique, perhaps none is more significant for directing, however, than atmosphere. Chekhov believed that 'the atmosphere is what we, as the audience, have to feel. If you attend a performance which does not touch your soul or feeling, that performance is dead'.[21] He gave the example of the first scene of Gogol's *The Government Inspector* to explain this concept of a dead performance:

> Blandly stated, the scene consists of the bribing officials absorbed in discussions of escape from punishment which they expect with the arrival of the Inspector from Petersburg. Endow it with atmosphere and ... you will perceive the content of the same scene as one of impending catastrophe, conspiracy, depression and almost 'mystical' horror.[22]

For Chekhov, then, analysing the action of a scene alone is not enough; we must also attend closely to the feeling of the space within which the action happens and how the two relate to each other. Despite their apparently subjective and personal nature, however, Chekhov considered such atmospheres to be objective, calling them 'a feeling which does not belong to anybody [...] which lives in the space in the room'.[23] Because of this, and their capacity, in

CHEKHOV IN PRACTICE

Choose a whole play or an extract from it. Consider the opening atmosphere of your chosen section. Where and when does it take place? What kinds of things happen? What is the feeling of this place and time and of these events? Is it placid, violent, hysterical, threatening, joyous? How can you communicate that atmosphere? What colour might

> it be? What physical qualities would it have? What would it feel like to exist within it? Now think of a moment when the atmosphere definitively shifts. How does it change? How can you express this new atmosphere? Divide your space in some way and ask your actors to begin by exploring the first atmosphere in one part of the space, and then to move, when they feel it is right to do so, into the second atmosphere, paying particular attention to the transition. Ask them to practise this transition a number of times in both directions. Then begin to add a little action or text either side of the transition and ask them to explore different ways of achieving the transition using the text, for example taking it at different speeds or different characters moving into the new atmosphere at different times. Do not rehearse the whole scene or try to stage it in any way; just concentrate on the moments where the atmosphere changes.

Chekhov's view, to transform the ability of a performance to communicate directly and powerfully with its audience, they are definitively the preserve of the director. The following section will feature all of these techniques, charting their emergence and development in Chekhov's directorial practice.

Chekhov's productions: Directing through acting

Chekhov's directorial vision is best understood from the perspective of the actor, whose experience of performance he described thus:

> When I am standing on the stage, the stage itself, the music, my partner's body, the lights, my partner's speech, my speech – are all parts of the large and very complicated rhythmical body of our theatre.[24]

Here, the actor's body becomes a metaphor for an entire performance. If 'the actor is the theatre', then, for Chekhov, the theatre is also an actor. This aspect of Chekhov's thinking dates back at least as far as his 1924 *Hamlet*, his first production as Director of the Second Moscow Art Theatre, in which he also played the leading role. Chekhov saw Hamlet as 'the visible embodiment of the victory of the spirit of light over the spirit of darkness' (which he considered to be the play's subject). He therefore chose to play the part himself, leading the production by embodying its central ideas, and handed the directing of rehearsals over to his colleagues Alexander Cheban, Valentin Smyshlyaev and Vladimir Tatarinov, who worked under his artistic leadership. We can also see the principle of the actor functioning as a microcosm of the theatre in Chekhov's interpretation of *King Lear*, of which he considered the guiding idea to be that 'the value of things changes in the light of the spiritual or in the dark of the material'.²⁵ This fundamental opposition was also embodied, for Chekhov, by the play's central figure who was, for him, two Lears: 'one ... an empty, spiritless body, the other ... a bodiless spirit'.²⁶

It is no accident that Chekhov interpreted *Hamlet* and *King Lear* so similarly. His reading of both plays was strongly influenced by his study of Anthroposophy, based on the teachings of the spiritual philosopher Rudolf Steiner. Steiner aimed to 'lift human beings beyond the sense-perceptible world into the spiritual realm' so that his followers would become able to see beyond physical appearances and 'move from the figure we perceive to the actual being'.²⁷ Chekhov's co-director Smyshlyaev described Hamlet's journey from darkness to light in similar terms to Steiner's, as 'protesting, heroic, ... fighting for the affirmation of what makes up the essence of his life'.²⁸

Chekhov had developed his understanding of the spine of a play and its organic relation to the action of its central character(s) with his close friend, the actor and director Yevgeny Vakhtangov. Vakhtangov directed Chekhov in the title role of Strindberg's *Erik XIV* in 1921. Chekhov recalled asking 'many questions, trying to penetrate the very heart of the character', when Vakhtangov suddenly shouted, 'That is your Erik. Look! I am now within a magic circle and cannot break through it!' gesturing to show Chekhov these actions.²⁹ Chekhov recalled that, at this moment, 'the destiny, the endless suffering, the obstinacy, and the weakness of Erik XIV's character became clear to me'.³⁰ But the movement also expressed a wider pattern in Vakhtangov's production, which polarized the play's two worlds: the dead world of the courtiers and the living world of the ordinary people (to which Erik tries, in vain, to escape, hence the gesture of failing to break the 'magic circle'). Thus, Vakhtangov's gesture for Chekhov's portrayal of Erik expressed both the essence of his character and the guiding idea of the whole production. In other words, it made no distinction between the actor imagining the character and the director interpreting the play: they were as two sides of the same coin.

Chekhov's 1924 *Hamlet* reiterated the pattern of his and Vakhtangov's *Erik XIV* by creating two worlds within the play to contextualize the central idea of the eponymous hero's spiritual triumph over the 'forces of darkness'. Those forces were represented, of course, by Claudius who was seen as 'conservative, obstructing all that is holy and heroic [...] trying to hold back everything that is striving forward'.³¹ Alma Law explains that the whole production was divided according to this polarity with 'the guards and soldiers ... Horatio, the Players and Ophelia' with Hamlet, Claudius supported by 'the courtiers, headed by Polonius', and Laertes and Gertrude caught between the two.³² This separation of the characters into three groups represents a further compositional principle of Chekhov's work: triplicity. This idea, that everything has three phases: an opening, a development or transition, and a conclusion, is clearly related to the notion of polarity, since you cannot have two opposed states or positions without a transitional space between them. We can see this in the tripartite structure for *Hamlet*'s 'tragedy of Humanity undergoing a cataclysm' described by Valentin Smyshlyaev: '(i) the presentiment and premonition of this cataclysm, (ii) the struggle with and the realization of the mission received [...] at the moment of the encounter with the Spirit, and (iii) solace through death'.[33]

It is important to note that, although Chekhov tends to refer to his compositional principles in universalist terms, they often underpinned selective interpretations. His treatment of Ophelia in this production of *Hamlet* is a case in point. Chekhov described her in rehearsals as 'the part of Hamlet's soul which is in the hands of the earth', which hinders him 'with earthly love' and must be rejected as 'the first step along Hamlet's thorny path', in an act of 'victorious wisdom' in which Hamlet takes 'an angel from Ophelia's soul and carries it away with him'.[34] This denial of Ophelia's subjectivity and the heroic presentation of Hamlet's abuse of her represent a deeply patriarchal reading of the play. However, we do not have to accept this decision to learn from Chekhov's approach. The lesson for directors, in other words, lies not in Chekhov's particular interpretation but in the dramaturgical rigour of his technique, which commits to a clearly defined reading of the play and deliberately reshapes its action and relationships accordingly.

Chekhov saw rehearsal as an authorial process. He argued that if the 'new theatre ... is to have vitality, [it] must write its own plays',[35] and he created his own plays in rehearsal predominantly through a process of adapting or appropriating classic works such as *Hamlet* and novels by Dickens and Dostoyevsky. He would have agreed with Julie Sanders that

> we need to view [...] adaptation and appropriation from a vantage point that sees them as actively creating a new cultural and aesthetic product [...] that stands alongside the texts that have provided inspiration, and [...] enriches rather than 'robs' them.[36]

We can see this principle at work in Chekhov's production of *The Possessed*, scripted during rehearsals by his colleague George Shdanoff.[37] The novel was written in an attempt to illuminate the crises that followed the collapse of the feudal system in Russia, but Chekhov and Shdanoff's version uses it to explore the rise of fascism and communism in Europe through the polarity of the characters of Verkhovensky, a violent revolutionary, and Stavrogin, who rejects violence but refuses to commit to any other creed.

This adaptation clearly emerged from Chekhov's belief that 'for some of the social problems besetting the modern world the theatre can offer at least a means of study and possibly a solution' and represents his commitment to 'present personal problems, not as an end in themselves, but in their relation to the social background'.[38] Chekhov's directorial engagement with the challenge and opportunity of using the theatre as a space for social and political debate would, however, go no further, and the ensemble that created *The Possessed* would never get beyond its infancy as a group, when their work failed to communicate successfully with its Broadway critics and audiences.[39] We are, however, left, as I have observed, with detailed records of the means by which they developed productions in rehearsal. Some of these are familiar as the acting exercises that have achieved canonical status among teachers and students of Chekhov's technique. Others are less well known, partly because they relate more obviously to directing. In the final section of this chapter, then, I will focus on one such key technique: the Four Brothers.

Directing with Michael Chekhov's technique: The Four Brothers

Chekhov believed that, as he put it, 'in every true piece of art you will always find four qualities which the artist has put into his creation: Ease, Form, Beauty and Entirety'.[40] He called these qualities the Four Brothers. 'Ease' refers to the flowing, natural feeling that Chekhov believed a work of art should have. 'Form' refers to the necessity for a work of art to have a clear structure that expresses its main ideas. Chekhov also believed that, even when its content is horrifying, a work of art should have the quality of 'Beauty'. Finally, 'Entirety' refers to the feeling of wholeness or completeness that a work of art should have; it shouldn't feel as though something is missing or that it is overloaded.

The Feeling of Form

Chekhov believed that 'everything must have a form for us – inner or outer actions both must have form'.[41] This observation is essential to the work of the director, who is responsible for defining the form of a production, but Chekhov does not see that task as a simple, or even a singular, activity. Instead, he offers multiple, simultaneous possibilities for articulating form. The most fundamental of these forms were production scores developed in rehearsal and following the principles of polarity and triplicity. Here is an example from Chekhov's direction of Janis Rainis's play *The Golden Steed*, based on a Latvian folk tale:

> The mission of the evil group is to push Antin down, pushing him gradually slowly, but surely, until he is defeated. That is the dynamic of the scene ... The good group has three gestures: 1. Toward the mountain. 2. To protect the good people. 3. To gently push the evil forces away. The whole scene is a composition of these movements. This is the scaffolding.[42]

Chekhov uses gesture here, as Vakhtangov had in rehearsals for *Erik XIV*, as a means of embodying and articulating the dynamic of a play or scene or a character's action. Where another director might express these actions in more abstract, psychological terms (the evil group wants to defeat Antin, the good group wants to create peace), Chekhov uses gesture as a means of physically experiencing the form of the play. He used the same technique to express the atmosphere of a scene, as in his class notes for a scene from a play called *The Deluge*, which simply list its atmospheres: 'Business', 'Thunderstorm', 'Fear (legato)', 'Panic (staccato)', 'Pause (legato)'.[43] Such sequences of atmosphere, which Chekhov encouraged his students to explore physically, were blended with gestures for a play's action to generate an embodied score for its performance.

The Feeling of Ease

Chekhov continually reminded his students that exercises should be performed with the Feeling of Ease. All art, Chekhov believed, must retain a quality of ease, especially when its content is painful or violent. He believed that ease enabled spectators to appreciate art as art, without being caught up in its content as though it were real life. Ease is also essential to the capacity for spontaneity and improvisation, in both rehearsals and performances, that Chekhov believed was essential. He argued that the actor must always be able to improvise, even within a highly structured production:

> The given lines and the business are the firm bases upon which the actor must and can develop his improvisations. How he speaks the lines and how he fulfils the business are the open gates to a vast field of improvisation.[44]

It is important to note, however, that by 'improvisation' Chekhov does not simply mean doing whatever you want. The Feeling of Ease is closely associated, in Chekhov's technique, with the movement quality of flowing. Like a body in water, ease is supported by and cannot help but be responsive to the movements of its enfolding medium. Thus, Chekhov suggests that developing the capacity for improvisation requires both the support of some 'firm bases' and the freedom to explore the 'vast field' of possibilities that lies between them. This polarity can be found within both of the following exercises.

CHEKHOV IN PRACTICE

Begin by selecting a beginning and an ending. Choose the start of a scene and its end, or two other polarized pieces of action. Be very specific about what the actor(s) must do. Ask the actor to improvise a series of transitions to get from one to the other. Then ask her to repeat

> it and improvise a different journey with exactly the same beginning and ending. As the scene is repeated, begin to add in more fixed points of action or lines of text. Ask the actor to continue to improvise new journeys between the given pieces of business. Continue to add fixed moments within the action of the scene and continue to ask the actor to improvise new transitions between them. Thus, the exercise shifts from improvising between a fixed beginning and ending to a series of improvisations between fixed points within a scene so that you are creating a staging that has both a clear form and the quality of ease as the actors continually find new ways of repeating the same sequence of actions.

The Feeling of Beauty

Chekhov is insistent that art, whatever its subject matter, must be created with the Feeling of Beauty. This is not quite the same as saying that it must be beautiful, in the sense of complying with whatever current aesthetically conservative taste dictates. Instead, Chekhov asked his students to work always 'with the beauty which rises from *within* you'.[45] The simplest way to understand this is to think about an actor doing what Chekhov calls 'radiating' their performance. 'Sincerely and convincingly imagine that you are sending out rays', he instructs, and 'a sense of the actual existence of your inner being will be the result'.[46]

The Feeling of Entirety

Finally, Chekhov suggests that everything, from the smallest action to a full production, should be conceived as a whole and retain the experience of this greater oneness. This idea of Entirety underpins Chekhov's compositional principles, which aim to enable artists to construct complex but self-consistent works in which all of the elements interrelate satisfyingly to generate one clearly articulated whole. We have seen it, for example, in his ideas about the polarities governing *Hamlet* and *King Lear*.

> ### CHEKHOV IN PRACTICE
>
> At any stage in the production process, go and stand at one end of a large space, cleared of any furniture or other items. Imagine that the play is a landscape, stretching out from its beginning, where you are standing, to its end at the far side of the space. Picture yourself above it, looking down as though flying over it. Travel at any speed and in any

direction over the landscape of the play, noticing important features: climaxes, changes in atmosphere, significant events or the trajectories of particular characters. Notice what you picked up on and what was not clear to you, which parts of the landscape were rich and complex, and which less detailed. Ask yourself what relationships you noticed between different areas of the play and how these could be made clearer for an audience. Ask yourself if the details are extraneous and distracting or if they contribute positively to the larger form of the play. Repeat in the opposite direction, from end to beginning, and ask the same questions.

Conclusion: The theatre of the future

Through all his acting and directing exercises, we can see Chekhov developing the practical means to develop what he called 'a new kind of conversation' between theatre makers, enabling them to articulate and explore a performance's structure, its atmospheres, its characters' actions, and so on with a common vocabulary founded on, but not limited to, the art of the actor.[47] If anything, this approach is even more relevant to today's theatre than it was to that of Chekhov's time. With the expansion of technological possibilities in the last half a century, collaboration between substantial teams of creative artists from different disciplines has become the norm in today's theatre. Furthermore, the practice of adapting existing texts for the stage or creating entirely new material through a collaborative process, often known as devising, has become increasingly common since the 1960s. Both of these changes have made Chekhov's ideal of a shared technique developed by collaborating artists both more possible and more significant than it must have seemed in the 1930s, when the collaborative creation of performances was extremely unusual.

However, in the contemporary theatre, directors commonly have more power to establish the vocabulary of a production's working processes than they did in the European and Anglophone theatres that Chekhov encountered in the 1930s and 1940s, which were run solely as commercial enterprises (sometimes with philanthropic support), meaning that they typically had short rehearsal periods and limited production budgets. Chekhov's technique shows us numerous ways in which the possibilities of our contemporary situation can be more fully exploited, and conversations between theatre makers made more imaginative, more thorough and more challenging. Thus, in spite of his limited success in creating the 'Theatre of the Future' about which he thought and spoke so much during his lifetime, Chekhov's approach to directing may yet enable subsequent generations to articulate and develop future theatres of their own.

7

Alexandra Remizova: A Dialogue with Time

Andrei Malaev-Babel

Alexandra Remizova (1903–1989) stands out among other twentieth-century Russian-Soviet directors. The directorial profession has been traditionally considered 'a man's job' in Russia. Moreover, no female director, except Remizova, rose to the top of her profession during the first half of the twentieth century (Figure 7.1).[1] Fortunately, this status quo changed, although not dramatically, in the second half of the century.

Remizova's directorial style and methods also differed from many of her colleagues – male or female. Remizova was a director-coach, or director-pedagogue, who knew how to work with actors. She had the courage to trust them and give them creative freedom. She also differed from her contemporaries in her distrust towards rigid directorial conception and analysis, with its lengthy directorial explications of the play, its characters and so on. She did not tire her casts with laborious analytical table work and preferred to make discoveries 'on one's feet' in rehearsal. Her rehearsal techniques were non-authoritarian and collaborative.

This does not mean that Remizova's productions lacked a directorial hand or were deprived of a strong sense of style and of the author. A competent and creative interpreter of a playwright's work, Remizova, similar to her teacher Yevgeny Vakhtangov, possessed a gift for *mobilizing and inspiring her actors' independent creativity*. Thus, her productions interpreted the world of the author, her own time and the world around by instigating every cast member's inimitable creative individuality and by evoking the ensemble's collective creativity. Among the characteristic qualities of

FIGURE 7.1 *Alexandra Remizova, 1950s. Courtesy of Andrei Malaev-Babel.*

Remizova's directorial style were stellar acting ensembles and a carefully elaborated, harmonious composition of characters. These creative means concentrated the audience exclusively on the story, leading to the seeming invisibility of the director.

Above all, Remizova's productions were marked by an extreme sensitivity towards her time. She possessed a cunning ability to choose a play, classical or contemporary, that would resonate with contemporary audiences in a powerful way, while revealing essential aspects of the current time. Most of her highly successful productions were based on plays that were considered 'difficult' or 'unstageable', and often failed, when approached by other directors. A forward-thinking projection into the future ensured the longevity of Remizova's directorial masterpieces. Many of them survived in the Vakhtangov Theatre's repertoire for decades,[2] while Remizova's independent directorial career stretched for over half a century. Her key productions coincided with pivotal events in the history of twentieth-century Russia and those of the world.

Biography

Aleksandra Isaakovna Remizova (Kabakova) was born in Tbilisi, Georgia, in 1903, to the family of an army doctor. She spent her youth in Georgia, primarily in the village of Akhalkalaki, where her father was stationed. She later moved with her family to St Petersburg and then to the Ukrainian city of Kharkov.

Remizova was accepted into the Third Studio of the Moscow Art Theatre (MAT) (also known as the Vakhtangov Studio) by Vakhtangov himself in 1919. After viewing a performance of the First Studio of the MAT in Kharkov, Remizova made the potentially deadly journey through Civil War–torn Russia to Moscow to audition for the Vakhtangov Studio. On arrival, she was told that Vakhtangov had accepted her: she was to start attending classes immediately. The trip from Kharkov to Moscow was Remizova's audition. As far as Vakhtangov was concerned, she passed the most important test. He believed that people ready to risk their life for a chance to study theatre automatically belonged to the field.

In her second year of training at the Vakhtangov Studio in Moscow, Vakhtangov entrusted Remizova with the supporting role of Zelima in his final, most celebrated, production of *Princess Turandot*, going against the MAT rules precluding a student from participating in a production prior to their third year of training. Remizova performed in all three productions Vakhtangov directed at his own studio. In addition to *Turandot*, she was also part of the cast of Maeterlinck's *The Miracle of St. Anthony* and Chekhov's *The Wedding*. According to Remizova's verbal memoir, Vakhtangov also 'blessed' her for her future directorial career. As young as Remizova was at the time, her studio mates often solicited her advice and critique on monologues and scenes they prepared for Vakhtangov's review. During one such rehearsal, Remizova sat in the director's seat, at the front of the house, while her peers onstage shared their work. Midway through the rehearsal, Vakhtangov silently appeared and sat in the last row, assuming a humble pose. Remizova must have felt his presence, as she turned around to him. Horrified to have taken his place, she wanted to get up, but Vakhtangov made a half-joking gesture of apology for having interrupted her 'process' and silently begged her to continue. Until the end of her life, Remizova considered this her masterteacher's blessing.

After Vakhtangov's death in 1922, Remizova continued her career as a Vakhtangov Theatre character actress, creating several important roles in the theatre's repertoire such as Périchole (*Mérimée's Comedies*, 1924), Madame Tokarchuk (Lev Slavin's *Intervention*, 1933) and Coralie (Balzac's *La Comédie humaine*, 1934). By the mid-1930s, however, Remizova had firmly established herself as a director and pedagogue. She had been teaching at the Vakhtangov Studio's School since 1925 (until 1983). From the late 1920s, she served as a pedagogue at Yuri Zavadsky's and Ruben Simonov's studios, among many others.

In 1934, Remizova coached actors for the noted Russian theatre director and designer, Nikolai Akimov, in his Leningrad Music Hall inaugural production of Eugene Labiche's comedy *Doit-on le dire? (Should we tell?)*.[3] In 1936, at Akimov's Leningrad Comedy Theatre, Remizova directed her first independent production, *The Marriage* – an early Soviet comedy by Aleksey Simukov. Remizova had to wait another five years, however, for her Vakhtangov Theatre directorial debut. Although she had been co-directing with other company members since 1936, her independent directorial debut on the Vakhatngov stage took place in 1941, when she staged Hauptmann's *Before Sunset*.

Throughout most of the war (beginning in 1942), Remizova remained the unofficial head of the Vakhtangov Theatre's Frontline Branch – a semi-independent company, comprising the Vakhtangov company members, and formed to create and perform a specially produced repertoire for the active troops, on the frontline. Consequently, Remizova spent the war among the active army – rather than, like most of her company, in safe Siberian evacuation and then back in Moscow. By going to the frontline, she fulfilled her long-time dream. When Russia joined the First World War in 1914, Remizova, who was eleven at the time, attempted to run off to war. She was, of course, turned around by adults and restored home to her family. With the Vakhtangov Frontline Branch, Remizova entered Berlin in 1945, alongside the Soviet Army. For her service and bravery during the war, she was awarded one of her country's highest military decorations – the Order of the Red Star.

Immediately after the war, Remizova proposed to preserve the Frontline Branch as a semi-independent collective, an affiliate company, which was to operate under the Vakhtangov Theatre umbrella. Surprisingly, the Vakhtangov administration, including its artistic director Ruben Simonov, agreed, but several leading actors inside the Frontline Branch felt uneasy about separating from the 'mothership', and the plan of creating the affiliate company was buried. If these plans had come to a fruition, Remizova would have become the first female artistic director in the history of the Soviet drama theatre. Nevertheless, Remizova did not skip a beat, and – for the next forty years – she continued to direct on the Vakhtangov mainstage, and she actively worked in Russian television and radio. Her most successful productions of that period include Arthur Miller's *All My Sons* (1948), Victor Hugo's *Les Miserables* (1950), Mamin-Sibiryak's *Gold*

(1955), Dostoyevsky's *The Idiot* (1958), Chekhov's *Platonov* (Moscow premiere) (1960), Fredro's *Ladies and Hussars* (1960), Malyugin's *My Mocking Happiness* (based on Anton Chekhov's correspondence) (1965), Shaw's *The Millionairess* (1964) and Ostrovsky's *Enough Stupidity in Every Wise Man* (1968).

As a professor at the Vakhtangov Theatre Institute (also known as the Shchukin School), Remizova trained several generations of Russian actors. Among those who owe their breakthroughs and/or key roles to Remizova are Yuri Yakovlev (1928–2013), Yuliya Borisova (born 1925) and Mikhail Ulyanov (1927–2007). All her key productions, except one, were filmed for Soviet television – an honour and fortune only a few Russian directors enjoyed.

Motivating forces behind Remizova's key productions

Remizova's directorial individuality was formed by the events leading to Russia's entrance into the Second World War, also known as the time of Stalin's Great Purges. It was followed by the period between 1941 and 1945, when the Soviet Army, together with its Western allies, fought the war against fascism. Deeply connected with her tragic time, Remizova saw the world divided by conflict between material values and other values – those that money cannot measure. Among them were not only human decency, friendship, selfless love and self-sacrifice, but also cultural treasures – fruits of wisdom and beauty accumulated by humanity throughout its history. Ironically, the Soviet state proclaimed that in socialist society, this conflict cannot exist as the Soviet society supposedly neither supported nor allowed an accumulation of wealth by individuals. Communist ideology considers money as a temporary means – something to be eliminated entirely in the future. Nevertheless, Remizova continued to explore the conflict between the material and the spiritual in her productions, throughout her entire career. By doing so, she strived to awaken the collective conscious of the nation and to bring its attention to the true values and riches – non-material, humanistic and cultural. Her approach to both art and life was entirely idealistic.

By travelling with the Soviet Army during its march into Europe, at the end of the Second World War, Remizova became a participant in one of the chief events that prepared the collapse of the Soviet Union. Although it was to happen some forty years later, and two years after Remizova's death, the roots of the USSR's demise can be found in the events of the mid-1940s. It was at that time that the Soviet 'victors' witnessed the prosperity of 'the defeated' and became exposed to the life enjoyed in capitalist Western civilization. From that point on, they could no longer go back to the ascetic Soviet ideology prescribing its citizens to live in semi-poverty, while securing the future of Communism.

Another aspect of Remizova's art was prepared by her experience of the war. Many of the Russians who came back home from the frontline had difficulty adjusting to peaceful life. It was lacking the emotional adrenalin of balancing on the threshold of life and death. Soviet war veterans needed to find applications for their wartime passions, in the time of peace, which drove them to extremes in everything they undertook – be it personal life, the pursuit of love and happiness, or the pursuit of prosperity. Families were broken; new families formed; the level of organized crime was on the rise, and so were levels of domestic and other kinds of violence. To further fuel the situation, firearms (illegal in the Soviet Union for private use) were readily available after the war.

It was logical that, when planning for the inaugural production for the Vakhtangov Theatre's Affiliate Company, Remizova chose to adapt for the stage Dostoyevsky's *The Idiot*. Dostoyevsky's characters, possessed by all-consuming passions, presented the perfect material, for Remizova, to develop further the themes of her Vakhtangov directorial debut — Hauptmann's *Before Sunset*. Once the prospect of a new company was abandoned, Remizova tabled the idea, only to return to it in 1958.

1940s

Before Sunset

Before Sunset (1941) established Remizova as a serious independent director. It also revealed her specific creative theme – a through-line of her directorial career. In *Before Sunset*, Hauptmann told the story of the influential publisher Matthias Clausen, an ageing widower, whose family drove him to suicide over his relationship with a young woman, Inken, who shared his idealistic beliefs and aspirations. While the play was often interpreted as romantic melodrama, Remizova, on the contrary, portrayed Clausen (played by Osvald Glazunov) as a thinker and humanist, who outlived his time. The Germany of Goethe and Lessing, represented in the play by the character of Clausen, was juxtaposed in her production against the cynical ideology of 'new men', as represented by the Clausen family. In her production, Remizova defined the war between Clausen and his children as a conflict between classical European culture with its humanistic ideals, on one side, and the materialistic ideology of *nouveau riche* Nazis, on the other. No direct references to the Nazi regime or politics are present in Hauptmann's drama. Remizova, however, significantly reworked its text, aiming to condense the social background of the play by emphasizing the role of the family and especially that of Clausen's son-in-law Klamroth.

In Hauptmann's play, Klamroth mobilized his relatives to proclaim Clausen insane and put him in the family's custody, which would give Klamroth control over Clausen's publishing business. In Remizova's production, Klamroth appeared as a personification of the new breed of German bourgeoisie. Moreover, both Remizova and Leonid Shikhmatov, who played Klamroth, clearly marked him as a member of the Nazi party. That and other allusions to Nazi Germany, introduced by Remizova, managed to distract the attention of the strict Soviet censorship from the production's nearer target.

From the rich Vakhtangov troupe, Remizova chose two actors who could elaborate the portraits of inwardly significant and intellectually superior individuals. Both Glazunov and Tsitsiliya Mansurova, who played Clausen and Inken, kept no illusions about the real face of the Soviet regime, and both consequentially suffered from it. Glazunov's Clausen had no illusions about the utter hopelessness of his course. An astute thinker, he clearly saw what was going on in his country. The suicide he committed at the end of the play was motivated by that clear vision, and it appeared as an obvious choice from the start. The Clausen of Remizova's 1941 production was doomed *in advance*, precisely because of his superior intellect, deep inner content and the outstanding nature of his individuality. Mansurova played Inken as Clausen's intellectual equal, who shared his lofty beliefs and ideals. These spiritual commonalities, rather than romantic or sexual attraction, constituted the basis of their union, as portrayed in Remizova's production.

In this interpretation, both Remizova and her actors awoke dangerous allusions. Outstanding people and significant personalities were as doomed in the Soviet Union in the time of purges as they were in Hitler's Germany. As Remizova began to rehearse *Before Sunset*, a new wave of Stalin's repressions brought their overall toll to over half a million innocent people; among them were theatre director Vsevolod Meyerhold, author Isaac Babel and journalist Mikhail Koltsov.

Like millions of people in the Soviet Union, Remizova's family was not spared. Her uncle, who shared an apartment with her, was taken in the middle of the night. The next day, Remizova collected her belongings and left the apartment, never to come back. She could not bring herself to stay in the flat, tainted by tragedy. After that incident, none of Remizova's apartments had a functioning door buzzer; it was not until the 1970s that she could bring herself to hear that sound again.[4]

It is not a coincidence that rehearsals for the post-war revival of *After Sunset* began in 1953, the year of Stalin's death. A production that, in 1941, marked the national tragedy of the purges, and the threat of fascist ideology, now sounded as a requiem for the fallen victims and a hopeful hymn to a more humane future.

REMIZOVA IN PRACTICE

The production of *After Sunset* presented the challenge of portraying characters of a different nationality to that of the actors. In 1959, Remizova had this to say about her experience of solving this problem: 'Take *After Sunset*, as an example. What feedback do we receive on it from Germans in the audience? They say that they are quite fond of this performance. However, when we asked one German director if our actors are convincing as Germans, his answer was no: "Your way of tackling questions of human relationships is too profound and painful. We treat them differently."'[5]

This and other experiences helped Remizova develop certain principles of working on a 'foreign play'. She shared these in an unpublished interview *circa* 1959, kept in her family archive:

'What kind of work lies ahead of directors, as they approach so-called foreign plays?'

'Firstly, they must consider a national character – what kind of people populate a given country, and their temperament?'

'By temperament we imply the given people's perception of the world. Suppose, you approach a play by a "northern" author, such as George Bernard Shaw. As directors and actors, we need to consider the English people's manner of moving, speaking; how they think and react. ... When approaching a play by an Italian playwright, we consider an incredibly lively temperament of Italian people: their quick speech, rich with gesticulation. People from the north of France speak differently than those from its South.'[6]

'National character is often defined by the predominant religion. I feel that Russian and Greek people are somewhat similar, chiefly because they are united by a common religious denomination. When you see, in the movies, how Greek people, especially women, approach their icons, you are reminded of Russian villages.
... No Italian vivacity, but rather certain slowness, tranquility, thoughtfulness and even somberness. As if they are filled with centuries-old melancholy.'[7]

When working on a 'foreign' play, Remizova used to study numerous paintings and photographs, and read books on the history of the country where it is set, and its contemporary life. She also listened to music by national composers, paying special attention to folk music.

1950s

Les Miserables

In 1948, Remizova staged the Russian premiere of Arthur Miller's *All My Sons*. The production was banned shortly after its premiere – the same year the Soviet government started its anti-Semitic 'campaign against cosmopolitanism'. Several ecstatic reviews were literally halted by two critics who must have received an assignment from the state to launch a campaign against Remizova and her production. The official charge was based on the fact that Remizova produced an American author, who was not 'progressive enough', in the light of the current party policy; however, her Jewish nationality played a role in the political hunt that eventually led to the banning of her production. All critics, including those who charged Remizova with political blindness, considered her *All My Sons* a superb piece of psychological realism and therefore even more politically dangerous. Remizova and her actors were severely criticized for portraying an 'ideological enemy' (the Americans) with too much depth and psychological nuance, thus causing the audience to sympathize with them. Such a political charge could have easily put an end to Remizova's career. Moreover, it could have caused the closing of the Vakhtangov Theatre. Thankfully, the Vakhtangov Theatre's artistic director, Ruben Simonov, was a clever politician, who knew how to preserve not only his company but its valuable players. He did not fire Remizova, as was expected of him, but instead made sure that she 'laid low' for two years so that her name in the headlines would not trigger official sanctions.

By the end of 1950, the incident with Miller's play had been sufficiently forgotten, allowing Remizova to premiere an adaptation of Victor Hugo's *Les Miserables*. It was met by mostly favourable reviews.[8] Yet several critics reproached the director for her peculiar treatment of the revolutionary theme. *Vechernyaya Moskva* critic P. Ivanov asked: 'What kind of revolutionary game are they playing – these fancily dressed, bombastically declaiming youth, fighting at the barricades in their show-white silk shirts?'[9] Other critics echoed, reproaching Remizova, who, having at her disposal close to a hundred Vakhtangov troupe actors, only used a handful of them in all 'mob scenes' connected with the revolutionary uprising.

This criticism was entirely justified. The revolutionaries appeared as the least natural characters in Remizova's *Les Miserables*, and the theme of revolution, per se, played an insignificant part in her production. In doing so, Remizova followed Hugo's original plan, as expressed in his first preface to the novel:

> The book [...] is the march from evil to good, from injustice to justice, from the false to the true, from night to day, from appetite to conscience, from rottenness to life, from brutality to duty, from Hell to Heaven, from

nothingness to God. Starting point: matter; goal: the soul. Hydra at the beginning, angel at the end.[10]

In fulfilling the author's plan, Remizova made some original choices. In the first part of her production, 'negative' characters significantly overshadowed the so-called positive. The main character of Jean Valjean was treated as merely a decorative ornament, a catalyst or the means to provoke and expose the diabolical 'appetite' and 'rottenness' of characters such as Inspector Javert and innkeeper Thenardier.

In Remizova's *Les Miserables*, Andrei Abrikosov's Jean Valjean was incapable of bringing light into the lives of simple folk, good or bad, who kept following their own hellish destiny. Fantine (Mansurova) appeared from the start as doomed and driven to semi-madness. Having saved Fantine from the clutches of Inspector Javert, Remizova's Valjean seemed to have only prolonged her agony, ultimately sacrificing the poor woman's happiness, and her very life, to his own 'noble' ideals. Javert was painted by Remizova as a tragic victim, whose life had been shattered – first, by the imaginary crime he committed against his 'superior', Valjean, and then by his inability to restore Valjean to penal servitude.

One of the highest tragic moments of Remizova's performance came at the end of its first act. In the act's finale, innkeeper Thenardier (Alexander Grave), who just sold his adopted daughter Cosette to Valjean, realized that he could have extorted a much greater sum from his sudden 'benefactor'. When Thenardier guessed that the ransom for Cosette could have taken care of him and his family for good, his *utter agony* transformed the final moment of Act I into a scene of tragic dimensions. Grave's Thenardier, at that moment, rose to the extent of a tragic grotesque: both in terms of the depth of his inhumane greed and the extent of the tragic suffering of a human being, whose very existence was defined and justified by money. The final accord of the first act, therefore, was that of the deepest fall into the depth of Hell.

In the second act, Remizova deceived the Soviet critic's expectations. She failed to introduce Revolution and revolutionaries as 'conscience' and 'duty', leading the world into its future heaven on earth. Cosette (Yelena Korovina) and Marius Pontmercy (Vyacheslav Dugin) were painted by the director as hopelessly naive. Remizova's focus and sympathies remained with those less sophisticated, but truly selfless individuals, who forsook themselves for the happiness of others – namely, with Thenardier's elder daughter, Eponine, and his unloved son, Gavroche. Vicious and wild, Eponine's passionate personality favourably contrasted with that of the 'rosy' Cosette, while Gavroche's true dedication to the cause of *les miserables* overshadowed the rhetorical devotion of the young revolutionaries, including that of Marius. It was those two, who won the sympathies of the audience and the critics of Remizova's production, while the role of Eponine nurtured the talent of the Vakhtangov Theatre's future number-one female star, Yuliya Borisova.

Gold

The most fruitful period in Remizova's career was between 1954 and 1972. During these seventeen years, Remizova revived and/or staged most of her defining productions, thus sustaining her reputation as one of Russia's most significant twentieth-century directors. In 1955, she staged Mamin-Sibiryak's *Gold*, a rarely produced play about the life of Uralian gold industry entrepreneurs. In this production, Remizova uncovered two immense acting talents of the Russian stage. The role of Anisya established Yuliya Borisova as one of the Vakhtangov Theatre's greatest artistic forces – a status she enjoys until this day. Nikolai Gritsenko, who played her father, Molokov, revealed his genius of a tragic-comic actor, capable of bold eccentricity and chameleon-like transformations (Figure 7.2).

FIGURE 7.2 *Yuliya Borisova as Anisya and Nikolai Bubnov as Zazypkin in* Gold, *1955. Courtesy of Andrei Malaev-Babel.*

In Remizova's *Gold*, an older merchant, Zasypkin (Nikolai Bubnov), is brought to ruin his competitor, Molokov. He then took further advantage of Molokov's financial ruin by marrying his young daughter, Anisya. What followed was the free fall to moral and physical ruin of a passionate and bright young woman, who sold herself to an older man. Remizova's production could have easily turned melodramatic or moralistic, or else, it could have amounted to a faithful painting of the everyday life of late nineteenth-century Russian gold-mine owners. Instead, the director was interested in the exploration of passions: not only passion for money, in the first place, but also love-passions, including that of an older man towards a younger woman.

In Remizova's rendition of *Gold*, a passion for the possession of riches was projected onto the character's love passions. It was as if the atmosphere of insatiable hunger for gold poisoned and distorted the very nature of love, turning an archetypally selfless feeling into that based on the destruction of self and others. This was seen in Anisya's love for her old husband's foster-son Vassily, Vassily's own love towards his foster-father's daughter Lena, Vassily's passion for Anisya, and finally, old Zasypkin's passion for his young wife: unable to possess her heart, he would destroy her, and himself, at the end of the play.

Remizova's production was reviewed by several leading Russian theatre critics; of most interest to us is Aleksandr Matskin's review, entitled 'Justification of Grotesque'. The very mention of the 'grotesque' was unsafe at the time, as it was associated with the so-called formalist theatre and its leader Vsevolod Meyerhold. Vakhtangov also 'toyed' with the grotesque. For this, he was reprimanded by his teacher Konstantin Stanislavsky. Stanislavsky's rendition of a dialogue between the two directors, on the grotesque, was published in the Soviet Union two years prior to the premiere of *Gold*; it is mentioned in Matskin's review. In it, Stanislavsky charges Vakhtangov with superficial understanding of the grotesque and thus with the betrayal of their common ideals of truth. At the same time, Stanislavsky considered the grotesque a powerful, *if not superior*, means of theatrical expression – on the condition that it served to externally justify 'all-exhaustive, to the point of exaggeration, internal content' of a character or a play.[11] According to Matskin, Remizova's production 'lived up to the spirit of Stanislavsky's requirements, and to the Vakhtangov Theatre's genuine traditions'.[12] He pointed towards the 'stark deepening' of *Gold*'s actorly and directorial pallet, and he credited Remizova and her actors with significantly expanding the characters of the play. Matskin wrote: 'Everything in this production grew up in size [in comparison with the play]: same people, but larger; same personalities, except more vividly defined. Vakhtangovites offered deeper interpretation of the play, having excavated in each of the characters their concealed potentiality.'[13]

Remizova's performance of *Gold* survived in the Vakhtangov Theatre repertoire for over two decades, and it was filmed by Soviet Television in

1977. The film version reveals further deepening of the production and of its characters. Matskin's 1955 review, for example, pointed to the acute sober-mindedness of Anisya, whose chief motivation was revenge on her husband and his affiliates, whom she despised for their narrow-mindedness and greed. Even her love for Vassily, according to Matskin, 'is the means of revenge, first and foremost'.[14] Anisya of 1977, as interpreted by the same actress, did not give up her revenge. And yet, she also loved Vassily (Vyacheslav Shalevich) as a kindred spirit, who was also lonely and lost in the world, driven by gold. Both the longevity of Remizova's productions, and their gradual deepening, could be attributed to the director's habit of not abandoning her creations after their opening nights. She was present at almost every performance, carefully watching from the artistic director's box. Moreover, she called regular pick-up rehearsals of her productions, thus ensuring their growth and increasing success with audiences.

REMIZOVA IN PRACTICE

The production of *Gold* was one of the finest examples of Remizova's ability to chip away naturalistic details such as insignificant characteristics of everyday life, societal customs, morals and manners, while concentrating on the essential and eternal aspects of a play. Consider the following advice for her fellow directors, shared by Remizova in 1959: 'I believe that directors, when staging a play, must concern themselves with bringing to light the play's grand idea, while casting aside trifles and details of everyday life; otherwise, they can swallow these directors, like quagmire.'[15]

The Idiot

In 1958, Remizova fulfilled her post-war dream of bringing to the stage Dostoyevsky's *The Idiot*. The period between 1956 and 1958 was a pivotal point in the history of the Soviet Union. The historic 20th Congress of the Communist Party saw the new leader Nikita Khrushchev deliver a report on Stalin's personality cult and mass purges. An immediate backlash within the party leadership, against Khrushchev's policy on Stalin, led to attempts to dismiss him from leadership. They were successfully overcome by 1957. By 1958, Khrushchev secured ultimate power by acquiring both of the highest leadership positions in the country. The so-called thaw in the Soviet Union was on the rise. Simultaneously, 1958 signified the time when Khrushchev's false feeling of security drove him to pioneer policies that eventually led to his dismissal in 1964 and prepared the period of political and economic stagnation in the Soviet Union, as well as the height of the Cold War.

It was at this time that Remizova commissioned a new adaptation of *The Idiot* by one of the most anti-establishment Soviet authors Yuri Olesha, actively collaborating with him on the adaptation. Critical reception of Remizova's *The Idiot* was mixed. One of the leading Dostoyevsky scholars of the period Leonid Grossman called the performance 'the greatest artistic event', 'a performance of genuine philosophical depth and tragic force'.[16] In contrast, Nikolai Berkovsky bluntly denied the artistic value of Remizova's production.[17] Not discouraged by the mixed critical reception, Remizova and her actors continued to refine their work. By the mid-1970s, Remizova's *The Idiot* survived over 200 performances and became one of the hottest tickets in town, almost impossible to acquire.

In *The Idiot*, as interpreted by Olesha and Remizova, a saintly man, Prince Lev Myshkin, returns to Russia, having spent several years in a Swiss mental institution, where he was treated for epilepsy. In his motherland, the harmony of Myshkin's spiritual world is tested by the material ugliness of the society surrounding him. Unwittingly, he finds himself entangled in two tempestuous love triangles, involving a kept woman, Nastasya Filippovna. A series of catastrophic events follow, pouncing at the divine world of Myshkin's 'truly beautiful soul'.[18]

Nikolai Gritsenko's portrayal of Prince Myshkin was deprived of any traces of pathology.[19] At Remizova's insistence, Gritsenko played Myshkin as 'transparent and genuine, his countenance attractive and noble', with a gaze 'bright and kind', 'his movements tranquil and soft, large beautiful hands trustingly reaching toward people'.[20] According to Golovashenko, Myshkin's epileptic fit, as played by Gritsenko, was triggered by 'extreme emotional agitation', due to the 'tragic force of his passionate plea for betterment, addressed to the society he rejected'.[21]

Myshkin's seeming isolation from the society, and even from reality, in Remizova's performance was actually triggered by intense inner work undertaken by Gritsenko at every second of his life onstage.[22] This deep inner work did not cease even during the scene of Myshkin's insanity, at the play's finale. According to Golovashenko, 'Despite the relapse of his illness, he remains burdened by the cruel comprehension of his surrounding reality, and he is tortured by it.'[23]

In Remizova's finest traditions, the society surrounding Myshkin and Nastasya Filippovna was elaborated in her production with painstaking concreteness. The 'cruel and greedy world of the newest Baal', as Grossman called it, quoting Dostoyevsky, 'was represented in [Remizova's] *The Idiot* by a gallery of figures, as characteristic as they were revolting'.[24]

Like Gritsenko, Yuliya Borisova appeared a wholehearted advocate of her character, Nastasya Filippovna. She stressed her heroine's inner and outer purity, and her work was marked by the same level of inner intensity as that by Gritsenko. According to Chebotarskaya, Borisova's

> Nastasya Filippovna exists in a constant state of internal strain. Even when outwardly calm and still, her arms dropped, or when looking aside, immersed in thought, her soul is in endless torment. Greedily she peers into each interlocutor, as if striving to understand what's hidden underneath their words, trying to peer ahead, to guess what might happen in the next moment.[25]

This incessant gaze, peered into the future, full of fear and expectation, coupled with deep inner work striving to understand the nature of men at

REMIZOVA IN PRACTICE

In working with Gritsenko on the character of Prince Myshkin, Remizova wholeheartedly accepted the actor's numerous character 'sketches', even though they had nothing to do with Myshkin as he finally appeared in the production. Nevertheless, Remizova never told the actor that his suggestions contradicted her directorial plan. On the contrary, she applauded his initiatives, proclaiming every next sketch better than the previous. In doing so, she allowed Gritsenko to 'work out of his system' all his preliminary drafts for the role, thus clearing the way for his unique Myshkin.

Some of the very rare practical advice Remizova would give to a young director was: 'Don't be in a hurry to solidify blockings.' Perhaps, the chief reason why her actors surpassed themselves in her productions, revealing their true creative talent, or even genius, was that she trusted them. She never shot down their practical suggestions, offered onstage, in rehearsals, while discouraging theoretic discussions of characters or play. By exhibiting such trust in the actors, Remizova inspired their creativity. Her own directorial choices were solidified at the very end of a rehearsal process, and they were made with the actors' creativity in mind. Even when suggesting something to an actor, she did so while considering that actor's individuality. Like her teacher, Vakhtangov, she transformed into the given actor and, out of his or her individuality, then transformed into a role. Her rare demonstrations were given either from that perspective, or else, they expressed the very essence of what she suggested without prescribing to the actor how to execute her suggestion (Figure 7.3).

FIGURE 7.3 *Remizova in rehearsal, 1950s. Courtesy of Andrei Malaev-Babel.*

Baal's feast – such was Remizova's own existence during the period between the late 1950s and mid-1980s. Moreover, such was the life of all of the thinking, conscience-driven intelligentsia of that period.

1960s

Remizova's work in the 1940s and 1950s laid the foundations for her final masterpieces, created during the 1960s. During this decade, she wrote a new, original chapter in Russian theatrical 'Chekhoviana', by staging the Moscow premiere of Chekhov's *Platonov* (1960) and creating, in 1965, an ultimate theatrical version of Malyugin's *My Mocking Happiness*, a unique play based on Anton Chekhov's personal correspondence.

During the 1960s, Remizova also solidified her reputation as a comedic director, premiering, one by one, critically acclaimed box office blockbusters of Fredro's *Ladies and Hussars* (1960), Shaw's *The Millionairess* (1964) and Ostrovsky's *Enough Stupidity in Every Wise Man* (1968). At the heart of Remizova's productions of the 1960s was the duo of her new leading man, and one of Russia's finest actors, Yuri Yakovlev, and the inimitable Yuliya Borisova.

REMIZOVA IN PRACTICE

When working on plays by classical authors such as Hauptmann, Dostoyevsky, Chekhov, Gogol, Ostrovsky, Shaw and so forth, Remizova did not separate creators, as human beings, from their work. She carefully studied these authors' biographies, striving to acquire a feeling of admiration for them, as human beings, for their destinies and creativity. According to the German philosopher Rudolph Steiner, 'What was once a childlike veneration for persons becomes, later, a veneration for truth and knowledge.'[26] In a similar way, Remizova's study of an author's life helped her to permeate a deeper truth of their plays and to find herself, as a director, defending their positions and acquiring their point of view.

1970s and 1980s

During the decades of the 1970s and 1980s, Remizova remained active in her profession and directed highly successful Vakhtangov productions such as *Commendatore's Footsteps* by Vadim Korostylyov (1972). The premature closing of that performance, due to a political campaign orchestrated by some of her own actors, caused Remizova to switch her attention from the Vakhtangov Theatre to its celebrated school, the Shchukin Institute. On the Shchukin stage, she directed some of her best productions, including that of Gogol's *Gamblers* (1974) and Turgenev's *The Sponger* (1983).

Throughout the late 1970s to mid-1980s, Remizova saw her classic Vakhtangov productions gradually removed from the company's repertoire by the theatre's next artistic director Yevgeny Simonov. He was also responsible for closing, in previews, Remizova's final mainstage production of Hauptmann's *Festival of Peace* (1981). Remizova never recovered from that blow, psychologically or physically, although she remained personal friends with Simonov whom she had known since his infancy. She even defended him through a time when most of the troupe revolted against his leadership, causing his departure from the Vakhtangov in 1987. In the mid-1980s, Remizova co-founded the Vakhtangov Theatre's celebrated Small Stage, where in 1984 she directed her final production of *The Key to Slumbers* (loosely based on a play by Grigory Yagdfeld), featuring today's theatre stars Yevgeny Knyazev, Sergei Makovetsky and Yelena Sotnikova. Remizova is acknowledged today as a theatrical godmother to the Vakhtangov Theatre's most celebrated stars. Throughout the twentieth century, she was arguably the company's finest resident director, responsible for the formation of the theatre's famed troupe, one of the finest in Europe, and a creator of the theatre's classical repertoire.

8

Natalia Sats: A Soviet Life in the Theatre

Manon van de Water

Natalia Ilinichna Sats (1903–1993) has been the most influential woman in professional theatre for children and youth worldwide yet is perhaps the least well-known director in the Russian theatre world in general, certainly outside of Russia. Natalia Sats's life and work spanned the entire Soviet period, from the trials and tribulations of the 1917 Revolution to the demise of the Soviet Union in 1991, and she was familiar with the majority of directors discussed in this book at one point or another, personally and/ or professionally. Sats's life was devoted to theatre, in particular theatre for children and youth, and she firmly believed that children have the right to the highest of art forms, opera and ballet, a cultural education that she thought should be the prerogative of all children. Admired, feared, beloved and undefeatable, Natalia Sats worked for this right until her death in 1993 when she was still active as the artistic director of the last theatre she founded, the first professional musical theatre for children and youth devoted to opera and ballet.

Natalia Sats's passion for theatre was a product of both her upbringing and her subsequent artistic development in the context of the former Soviet Union.[1] Her father was Ilia Sats, who composed the music for the famous production of Maurice Maeterlinck's *Blue Bird*, directed by Konstantin Stanislavsky at the Moscow Art Theatre in 1908; her mother, Anna Shchastnaia, was a singer. In her autobiographies, Sats recalls listening with her sister to the compositions of her father and the singing of her mother that filled the house and the frequent visits of Sergei Rachmaninov, Stanislavsky, Vsevolod Meyerhold, Vera Komissarzhevskaya and Edward

Gordon Craig, among other notable artists of the time. A precocious child, she built up personal friendships with Yevgeny Vakhtangov and actors of the Moscow Art Theatre.[2] Although her father died of heart disease when she was eight, the company of these artists remained. Anna gave voice lessons to the actors of the Moscow Art Theatre and the Vakhtangov Studio. At the age of twelve, Natalia herself started giving piano lessons and contributed to the family income.[3] She soon found herself in the chaotic times of the Russian Revolution, an event she never denounced but rather saw as the start of her career. The chaos of the Russian Revolution and the subsequent Civil War offered unprecedented opportunities to ambitious youth like Natalia Sats, and Sats took full advantage, becoming a major force in the aesthetic education of the future Soviet citizen through the performing arts for the duration of the Soviet Union.

Sats wrote several autobiographies during her life, and although they do not comment extensively on politics or the Russian Revolution, when they do, it is in euphoric terms:

> I would be out of the house as soon as I woke up. It was such a joy to walk in a crowd that sang and rejoiced, to notice the first bright-green leaves of trees and watch the red flags flapping in the breeze. 'All power to the Soviets!', 'Art to the working people!' How novel those words were for us.[4]

Schools were suspended and Natalia was eager to work, so her mother used her contacts to send her to the Theatre and Music Section (Temusek) of the Moscow Soviet of Workers and Red Army Deputies which happened to be in need of someone to head the Children's Theatre Section.[5] Natalia Sats, as a mere fifteen-year-old, took her chances, and she never regretted it.[6]

While retrospective notions clearly position Soviet theatre for children and youth as an instrument of the totalitarian regime,[7] the euphoric optimism of Sats, as of many revolutionaries in those times, was simultaneously naive and genuine. Sats was convinced of her mission. She knew where to go and whom to talk to, and she was absolutely fearless. Part of this fearlessness may have been due to her childhood among the Moscow intelligentsia and the cultural elite, which was in favour of the Revolution and Marxist ideology at that time. Part of it was undoubtedly related to her strong personality. Part of it was sheer opportunism. She embraced the ideals of Marxism-Leninism, although she never was a party member.[8] Following her father's ideals, and the original mission of the Moscow Art Theatre, Sats genuinely believed in theatre for all though, not only the culturally elite. And she was willing to do anything, and endure a great deal, to make this ideal come true.

The remainder of this chapter will focus on two different periods of Sats's life and the directorial work she did and methods she employed: her early work in the 1920s with the Moscow Children's Theatre and her work at the Children's Musical Theatre in Moscow. Not all of this work

FIGURE 8.1 *Natalia Sats and Sergey Prokofiev during a rehearsal of* Peter and the Wolf *in 1936. By permission of Roksana Sats.*

can be considered innovative from a twenty-first-century perspective, but it was highly influential both inside the Soviet Union and worldwide, cited in many sources as the inspiration to found national professional theatres for young audiences: among others, in Japan, Europe (particularly Eastern Europe but from there to other European countries), and the United States.[9] Early theatre for children and youth in other countries often came out of education and social work and was by definition 'amateur'.[10] Sats, however, from the beginning eschewed any notions of children's theatre as second-class and emphasized professionalism and aesthetics in arts for young children (Figure 8.1).[11]

Early work

As director of the children's department of Temusek, Sats had taken charge of organizing a series of programmes for children in the eleven districts of Moscow, from theatre to music concerts to circus acts, all performed by established artists.[12] The ideological thought behind this was that all children, regardless of class or socio-economic background, should be able to see the best artists and performances for free – the first children in the world to be offered this opportunity.[13] The programme toured to different neighbourhoods all over Moscow, reaching out to children who in the period of 'economic dislocation'[14] could not come to the theatre without transportation or proper shoes. The dire infrastructure made touring to children very difficult, however, and the lack of plays, ballet or music appropriate for children became palpable. While the outreach performances were not stopped, Sats wanted to establish a theatre specifically for children in a special house. In October 1918, on the first anniversary of the October Revolution, the Children's Theatre of the Moscow Soviet, a government-supported children's theatre of puppets, ballet, shadow and marionettes, opened at 10 Mamonovsky Alley. It was the first state-supported professional theatre by adults for children with its own house in the world.[15] It consisted of two theatre spaces: one for puppets and one for marionettes. Nina Simonovich-Efimova, who was also working for the Temusek children's department, was in charge of the theatre space for puppets and shadow theatre.[16]

Meanwhile, the Moscow Soviet had decreed that once a week all tickets to the Bolshoi would be distributed free to children. Here, 'Aunt Natasha', as she was known among Moscow's children, spontaneously entered the stage in an attempt to help the young audience understand what went on in the ballet and alleviate the complaints of the artists against this unruly audience by trying to focus them on what was happening on stage. Inadvertently, Sats had stumbled on an idea that became a standard practice in her work and in many theatres for children and youth in Soviet Russia and Eastern Europe for many years to come.[17] Refined over the years, the introductions are described in the following exercise.

SATS IN PRACTICE

Audience preparation

- As you enter the stage, welcome the audience in the space.

- Alternatively, you can welcome them as they come in; often actors in costumes, whether they are in the play or not, fulfil this task in the bigger theatres; for small productions, you can build this into the production with the actors.

- When necessary explain the kind of production (opera, ballet, theatrical piece) – Sats maintains that the more the audience knows about the genre, the more they understand. For example, why does somebody all of a sudden start singing when they are sad? How does dance express feelings?

- Along with the above give some concrete ideas of what to focus on or how the story is told (through music and movement, text being sung, emotional expressions, movement, for example).

- Say something more about the style: is this a literal depiction, is it abstract, is it a fairy tale? Explain allegory and metaphor if applicable.
- When desired talk about audience etiquette:
    1. No getting up in middle of the performance unless absolutely necessary
    2. No disturbing other audience members
    3. No talking, eating or drinking
    4. No babies or very young children (the Children's Musical Theatre has a nursery room with care-givers who will watch the youngest children when the rest of the family enjoys the show)
- Explain what a shared experience means as opposed to watching something by yourself
- We applaud at end to thank the actors, director and technicians
- Depending on how much time you want to spend on this, it is also useful to explain that this is a collaborative event: while the actors are most visible, they are assisted by a director, designers, technicians, carpenters, costume constructors, ushers, janitors and so on. You can also save this for the end if you have a talk back or Q&A.

For Sats this was not disrespectful to the audience; nor did she see it as blatant didacticism. Rather, this was part and parcel of the audience's aesthetic education and a means to deepen the artistic experience.

Sats became acquainted with and gained the respect of Anatoly Lunacharsky, albeit distinctively not for the artistry in her productions. Historian Lenora Shpet states that Lunacharsky was appalled by the vulgar slapstick and the quality of the production he saw, *Max and Morits*, but was struck by the enthusiasm of both Sats and the performers: 'We have to use all that energy and love for the cause and create an experimental children's theatre.'[18]

Lunacharsky appointed a special committee to plan and organize a state-subsidized theatre for children and youth under the auspices of Narkompros, the Ministry of Enlightenment. Natalia Sats became one of the six members of the directorate of the theatre, which had Lunacharsky himself as permanent chair. The artistic committee included, among others, Stanislavsky. The theatre was to be housed on the premises of Sats's Children's Theatre of the Moscow Soviet,[19] which itself was to be absorbed into the new children's theatre. The rapidly emerging leader of the First State Theatre for Children,[20] however, was Henriette Pascar, a member of the directorate who was ideologically diametrically opposed to Sats. Sats left the directorate, and in 1923, Pascar was dismissed after she refused the concept of children's theatre as mass propaganda in the struggle for Communism.[21] Yuri Bondi, a student of Meyerhold, took over.

Meanwhile, Sats had founded a new theatre for children and youth of her own under the control of the Department of Education of the Moscow Soviet, a different department to Narkompros. The Moscow Theatre for Children opened in 1921, in temporary quarters, with a fairy-tale production, *The Pearl of Adalmina*. Sats and her partner (and later husband) Sergei Rozanov advocated a theatre for children that served the political goals of the new Soviet state, and because of a lack of plays, they favoured a repertory of adjusted fairy tales as the most appropriate material for children.[22] Each play had to convey an important political message or 'social idea'.[23] In *The Pearl of Adalmina*, this message is hard to miss. The play deals with a sensitive young princess who flees the cruelty and stupidity of the court to embrace a simpler and nobler life among 'the people'. 'Not everyone is sated, because not everyone works,' she tells the audience, and 'the country does not need a king; the people must rule the country'.[24]

For a short time period, Sats and Rozanov developed a philosophy of theatre for children, based on the teachings of Stanley Hall,[25] which subsequently led to a system that ultimately proved untenable in the new Soviet Society.[26] In 1924, they produced *Be Prepared!*, which 'for the first time featured Pioneers on the children's stage'.[27] This was a theatre of agitation and propaganda instead of politicized fairy tales. The new hero was the young Soviet Pioneer – always prepared – the 'child patriot of the new world order'.[28]

Be Prepared! was the first of a new genre called *igro-spektakl*, or play-production, in which the audience was invited to participate in several scenes. Besides active participation on stage, the audience was frequently urged by the actors to 'be prepared', to which the audience responded by shouting the Pioneer slogan '*vsegda gotov*' or 'always prepared'.[29]

SATS IN PRACTICE

Play-productions

The play-productions were staged according to the following corresponding rubrics:

> Material – contemporary life, work and struggle for socialism in the USSR.
> Characteristic style – constructivism.

> Dramatic form – play of a utopic character.
> Social idea – by tireless work and struggle we obtain socialism.
> Production form – play-production. A revolutionary feast.
> Decorative solutions – basically the expediency of machines: propellers, wheels, and movement.
> Music – revolutionary hymns, music of a heroic character.[30]
>
> Play-productions are something in between devised productions and written texts. As you see from the above, there is a clear structure, but within this structure, the director and especially actors need to improvise.
>
> Although the above is aligned with the struggle of obtaining socialism, the rubrics themselves could be adapted to the dramatization of social (justice) issues in the sociocultural and political context of the place where the production is generated.
>
> Try to fill in the rubrics above with more relevant and concrete material that applies to your situation. Develop your initial ideas by means of improvisation. If you feel comfortable, try to devise a mini-production (or full production if so desired) out of this.

Play-productions were taken over by other theatres (the travelling Moscow Theatre of the Young Spectator was for a while famous for them), and they remained popular in the Soviet theatre for children and youth until the early 1930s.

Sats and Rozanov continued to look for different modes of expression, though, experimenting with theatrical ways of communicating with their audience, which became a hallmark for the first decade of the Moscow Theatre for Children.[31] In 1927, they produced *The Negro Boy and the Monkey*, a pantomime for very young children, about the friendship between a black boy and a monkey who saves the boy from poisonous snakes. But the monkey is caught by 'bad white people' and taken to the circus. The boy, Nagua, looks all over the world and eventually ends up in Moscow, where he starts working in a chocolate factory. When he goes to the circus, he finds the monkey, who recognizes Nagua right away and jumps in his arms. Together they go back to Africa, where Nagua starts a Pioneer group in his own village. The narrative of this production is without any doubt extremely problematic for a contemporary audience, and the stereotypes beg to be addressed. From a non-narrative point of view, however, the production was a huge success, a final achievement of the 'synthetic production' the theatre had been looking for, combining music, dance, pantomime, acrobatics, animation and spoken word, although it was later also criticized as naive and scenographically formalistic, adrift from the general path laid out for a general Soviet theatre education.[32]

While the content of this production is subject to criticism, especially from a twenty-first-century perspective, the production style was indeed innovative for the time. Described in detail in *Novelly 1*, and in an abbreviated version, 'My Vocation', the production was one of the first that used animation and video as a theatrical device. This is also the chapter in which Sats states what it means for her to be a director *(rezhissyor)*. 'The education of a director begins with the study of human kind,' she states, 'the most baffling of creatures'.[33] She recalls the games of Ivan Turgenev and the exercises of the director Nikolai Gorchakov, who wrote one of the most widely used textbooks in Russia at the time, *Rezhissyorskiye uroki Stanislavskogo (Stanislavsky's Lessons for Directors)*.[34] This is one of the rare instances where Sats describes a specific exercise, which I have summarized and adapted in an exercise below.

SATS IN PRACTICE

Observe and imagine

As you are sitting on a bus, waiting in a doctor's office or having coffee on a terrace, look at the people around you.

Focus on one person and make up a biography of this person based on your observations. Observe the person's appearance, gestures, facial expressions, words, tone and pitch if you can hear them. Imagine the person's name, age, family circumstances, occupation, lifestyle, dreams and desires – based on your observations.

As you are getting comfortable with these observations try to expand the details and create a full life, including specific occurrences in the life of the individual you are observing. For example, you observe that the person is sad. Why would this person be sad? Has the person been fired? Has her beloved broken up with her? Has he lost a child due to leukaemia or kidnapping?

You can expand this further by taking on the personality you have created. Start slowly by walking like this person, thinking the person's thoughts, getting familiar with the person you created. As you get more comfortable with this, take on the character as you do shopping, cook, or do other activities that will get you more familiar with the character. Try to get out of your head and embody the character kinaesthetically and emotionally.

Natalia Sats did not so much envision these exercises as actor exercises but rather as ways to expand her own directorial imagination. She characterizes a director as someone 'who knows how to observe life',[35] something she trained in from a young age through the games and tasks her father gave her, and her natural inclination to organize, in particular theatrical games and plays.[36] The following quotation gives an indication of how she saw directing and herself as a director, as someone who had total control over all aspects of a production:

> The ability to fascinate others with a theatrical concept, to understand the personalities of the participant in a production, to assert your will despite the caprices of some, the tendency of others to quickly lose enthusiasm – how important these are for anyone who has decided to become a director!'[37]

From my readings by and about her and the interviews with people who have known her, Natalia Sats, as a director, looked at the big picture. In many ways, she was more a '*postanovshchicha*', a 'stager' focused on the mise-en-scène, combining all theatrical elements in one production, rather than a '*rezhissyor*' whose basic task is to work with actors.[38] Sats looked for a synthetic theatre, a theatre where many art forms blended together: 'literature, acting, mime, dance, music, and graphic expression – becoming the magnet of inspiration for a great diversity of artists'.[39]

At the time Sats envisioned *The Negro Boy*, many artists used film, mainly documentary, in a search for authenticity. Sats, working in children's theatre – which, it needs to be noted, had no examples or tradition to build on or against – envisioned cartoons as a way to reach the child audience while simultaneously incorporating the revolutionary artistic spirit that was demanded. Cartoon films, Sats believed, 'would broaden the possibilities of the stage without violating the basic artistic intention, as they would help to show quickly the changing scenes of nature and the indigenous background for some of the incidents'.[40] Sats describes

> a corner of the jungle, with lianas hanging, birds flying, elephants wandering about. A cartoon is projected onto the flat on the right, showing a thicket where our actors playing African children are hiding. They are lying in ambush, waiting for more animals to appear. At a signal from Nagua, the children start banging their tom-toms. The frightened animals scamper away (cartoon here). Nagua shoots at the hindmost doe but misses and starts in hot pursuit. A panorama of the forest in motion: Nagua is chasing the doe. At a certain moment, the actress playing Nagua disappears and the action is continued in the cartoon.[41]

Sats aims here to blend the way in which the cartoons are drawn with the scenery and to have the mannerisms and movement of the actress reflected identically in scenic and cartoon interpretation. *The Negro Boy* is a pantomime-dance to music with only a few words for the little boy.[42] Thus, she also worked closely with the composer Leonid Polovinkin, who had just graduated from the Moscow Conservatory and who would become her collaborator on many productions to follow. From this point on, we can clearly trace the particular regard she had for composers and musicians and her preference for music as the lead artistic element of a production.

By the end of the 1920s, state-supported theatre for children and youth was firmly established not only in Moscow but also in other cities throughout the Soviet Union.[43] The production practices reflected the general atmosphere of experimentation and innovation that was typical of the Russian theatre in the 1920s, encouraged by the New Economic Policy's spirit of freedom.[44] The plays evolved from fairy tales to politicized fairy tales to Marxist propaganda plays with the main objective of the ideological education of the young Soviet citizen, the leaders of tomorrow. The following decade would change all that. The increase in censorship, the doctrine of Socialist Realism, the condemnation of pedology[45] and formalism,[46] and Stalin's purges in the 1930s, which kept the whole intelligentsia, indeed the whole country, in their grip, tempered the enthusiasm, the energy and the experimentation that the Revolution and the 1920s had brought to all the arts, including theatre for children and youth.

Intermezzo

Although no one was really safe during the Purges of the 1930s, the arrest of Natalia Sats came at an unexpected moment. As all theatre and art, theatre for children and youth in the 1930s came under increased scrutiny and was to follow the doctrine of Socialist Realism introduced by Zhdanov in 1934.[47] In March 1936, the Central Committee of the Communist Party and the Council of People's Commissars established a new theatre in Moscow that was meant to be a model for the artistic, pedagogical and political functioning of Soviet theatres for young audiences.[48] The theatre was housed in the newly renovated theatre on Sverdlov Square (now Theatre Square), a theatre that formerly housed the Second Moscow Art Theatre, adjacent to the famous Maly and Bolshoi theatres. The theatre employed 375 people with an orchestra of twenty-eight.

Sats was named director of the theatre, which received the name Central Children's Theatre (*Tsentralnyi Detskii Teatr*). Although it was officially hailed as a new theatre,[49] 'the core consisted of the troupe of the Moscow Theatre for Children [Sats's theatre], taking along its earlier established tastes, principles, and traditions'.[50] Sats herself was convinced it was an endorsement of the practices of the Moscow Theatre for Children of which she was until then founder and artistic director.[51] Her tenure at the theatre was short-lived, although she was by all accounts successful, with her most well-known accomplishment the commissioning of *Peter and the Wolf* by Sergei Prokofiev.[52]

There are numerous accounts of why Sats was arrested in August 1937, but under Stalin's purges, the lack of a clear cause for arrest was not unusual and it may very well be that there never was an official charge, as Sats's daughter, Roksana Sats, maintained in an interview in 2013. Initially she was sent to a Siberian labour camp at Novo-Ivanovo. Later she was transferred to the Mariinsky camp in Siberia and in 1938 or 1939 to the Rybinsk camp in the Iaroslav province, not too far from Moscow. Although she had kept up her spirits by organizing theatrical events with her fellow prisoners throughout her exile, Rybinsk, which did not house political prisoners, gave her more freedom to put her talents to work. Among other endeavours, she organized a musical ensemble, 'the Jazz and Drama Group, directed by Natalia Sats', which included the warden, and she was allowed to tour to neighbouring camps.[53] In 1942, her sentence was over, but she was not allowed to return to Moscow. Instead, she was sent to work at the Opera in Alma Ata, Kazakhstan,[54] where, in September 1944, she received permission to found the Kazakh Theatre of the Young Spectator in an old movie house.[55] After more than a decade in Alma Ata and a brief stint in Saratov, she was finally allowed to return to Moscow.

Exoneration and the Children's Musical Theatre

When Sats was exonerated in 1957 during Khrushchev's Thaw, she was not given her job at the Central Children's Theatre back, as she should have been offered by law, but instead was appointed artistic director of the All-Union Touring Company. Although she laments this disappointment in her autobiographies, she remained officially loyal to the regime.

As expected, Sats did not sit still. She refused a pension, was appointed artistic director of the All-Union Touring Company, wrote a dissertation at the State Theatre Arts Institute (GITIS, or *Gosudarstvennyi Institut Teatralnogo Iskusstva*), published a book, *Children Come to the Theatre* (*Deti prikhodiat v teatr*; in effect, her dissertation), and became the head of the children's section of the Moscow *Estrada*.

Moreover, she fulfilled her dream in the decades that followed.[56] In 1963, she founded the first musical theatre for children in the world in Moscow, a theatre that was devoted to opera and later also ballet, with young students from theatre and music institutions in the company. The Children's Musical Theatre worked initially without its own building and from 1965 in a remodelled puppet theatre on 25th of October Street number 17, the former Slavianski Bazar.

The highpoint of the theatre was in 1979 when the specially designed and constructed Moscow State Children's Musical Theatre opened its doors.

Sats, now seventy-six, tightly supervised all aspects of the theatre's design and construction.⁵⁷ The theatre's emblem is a blue bird, holding a harp (Figure 8.2).

In this theatre, Sats realized her true theatrical passion, hints of which we find in her past accomplishments. The theatre's emblem was a deliberate ode to her father who composed the music for Stanislavsky's famous production of Maeterlinck's *Blue Bird*, in many histories hailed as the first production for children. From the moment Sats started to produce and direct for children, as shown above, it was music, opera and ballet that she thought most attractive, and beneficial, for her audience. In an ironic spin on her own critique of Pascar, she infused this in fairy tales, maintaining that 'fairy tale and truth are [for Sats] like sisters. The truth is inseparable from fairy tales'. Natalia Sats often repeated that 'the wings of fantasy cannot be separated from the life and work of the person'.⁵⁸ However, it was important for her that the stage version was not the same as the well-known fairy tale but that it would offer something new or illuminate the familiar and the ordinary in a new way.

The fairy-tale theme is continued inside this building. There is a bird cage with live birds you can see up close when you take a few stairs. There is a play corner. There is a beautiful room, panelled with wall-size, original *palech* (Russian lacquer art) paintings depicting Russian fairy tales. In the middle of the room stands a piano for children to play in the intermission. The buffet has natural light and plants. The smallest children can play in a staffed playroom while their older siblings go see the show. At every show fairy-tale characters greet the audience from a bridge that covers the entrance hall. In the intermission, a magician performs his tricks: 'A play in this theatre is a fairy tale in a fairy tale,' declared one of the first visitors.⁵⁹

FIGURE 8.2 *The building of the Moscow State Children's Musical Theatre, supervised by Sats, by permission of Roksana Sats.*

In a television interview, Sats notes:

> The fundamental function of art, it seems to me, is to instil in a person feelings of love and interest toward others. In this, art is stronger than anything else ... It is at times easier to reach a person's heart not only with words but also with music: the hero, his actions, his relationship to other people, the stage sets, costumes, help to better understand the language of the simultaneously played music. And music, in its turn, helps to feel more deeply the feelings of the characters, enhances with its power, which words could not express. I have come to this conclusion after long years of searching.[60]

Victor Victorov, Sats's collaborator since the 1960s on librettos and plays for the Musical Theatre, and author of *The Natalia Sats Children's Musical Theatre*, gives a good impression of Sats's directorial style through interviews with composers and actors, and letters cited. This brings me to the last 'exercise' (or, better yet, 'advice and lessons') Sats learned and lived by over her many years of directing.

SATS IN PRACTICE

Advice and lessons learned[61]

- Beauty when it offsets the intention cannot only be useless but also destructive.
- Simplicity is art's most intricate achievement.
- Every costume and all the details in the sets must have concrete functions and at the same time coincide with the play's content and the dynamic conception of the production.
- The decorative conception of the fairy tale must have a stylistic unity of colourfulness, fantasy and contemporaneity.
- The modern fairy tale must, in the staging, merge a fairy-tale-like colourfulness in a modern style.
- The director and the actor must be guided by one goal: to convey the musical idea through the proper image.
- It is not always body movement which expresses the dynamics of thought and emotion – they can be projected through the actor's musical intonation and state of being.

- Children's Theatre must be a theatre of great commitment, an educational and enlightening theatre and not a didactic one. Didacticism violates art for children.
- The presentation must be entertaining and instructive. We must not only stage the production as entertainment but also know why we produce it and what the young spectators will take away with them from the theatre.

For the next sixteen years, Sats remained the artistic director of the Children's Musical Theatre – throughout the Brezhnev period, into the period of *glasnost* and *perestroika*, and during the fall of the Soviet Union – until her death in 1993, when her husband, Viktor Provorov, took over the artistic direction. In 2000, the theatre was renamed the Natalia Sats Moscow State Children's Musical Theatre, and by 2013, the theatre, under the direction of Georgii Isaakian since 2010, identified itself in English as the Moscow State Opera and Ballet Theatre for Young Audiences Named after Natalia Sats.[62]

There is much more to be said about Natalia Sats, her remarkable life and her influence on theatre for children and youth in general, nationally and internationally. However, I would like to end this chapter with her own words.

In 1991, aged eighty-eight, she finished her last autobiography, *Life Is a Streaky Event (Zhizn – iavlenie polosatoe)*, in which she wrote everything she did not reveal before. These are her last words:

I am happy to live and work. Has 88 really arrived already?

When you have a clear goal in life and a passionate love for your work – it is not that bad. Believe me reader![63]

9

Mar Sulimov's School of Directing: A Case Study of the Production *Shoo, Death, Shoo!*

Sergei Tcherkasski

Mar Sulimov

Mar Vladimirovich Sulimov (1913–1994) – Russian theatre director, set designer, teacher and writer – was one of the leading masters of Leningrad–St Petersburg theatre pedagogy in the second half of the twentieth century. Throughout his career, Sulimov was the artistic director of theatres in Moscow, Leningrad, Petrozavodsk and Alma Ata, where he directed and designed over one hundred productions. His work gained serious critical acclaim and state prizes, but it was Sulimov's teaching at the St Petersburg State Theatre Arts Academy (at that time the Leningrad State Institute of Theatre, Music and Cinematography, abbreviated to LGITMiK) from the 1960s to the 1990s that secured his place in the history of the Russian school of theatre directing (Figure 9.1).

Sulimov wrote five books on director training. His book *Initiation to Directing*[1] brings together in a single volume nearly 600 pages of his major works that were published in the 1970s and 1980s.

Sulimov's writings cover two basic areas. The first, the methodology of the first and second years of director training, includes a detailed description and analysis of a variety of specific exercises for directors ('opening' exercises, etudes on paintings, etudes on poetry, etudes on prose, building a 'climactic' mise-en-scène, staging a fairy tale, exercises on the memory of physical actions and sensations). Sulimov also introduces the pedagogical

FIGURE 9.1 *Mar Sulimov in rehearsals for* Shoo, Death, Shoo! *(LGITMiK, 1983). Courtesy of Sergei Tcherkasski.*

concept of micro-performances and justifies the need for such an approach to initial, basic director training, arguing against the phased requirements of a traditional curriculum.

The second area of Sulimov's legacy is the detailed records (up to eighty or one hundred pages each) of his Action Analysis of four plays: *The Cherry Orchard* by Chekhov, *Truth – That's Fine, But Happiness Is Better* by Ostrovsky, and *Duck Hunting* and *Last Summer in Chulimsk* by Vampilov (a Russian classic of the twentieth century to be counted alongside Bulgakov, Erdman and Babel). These examples significantly clarify the basic principles of a director's analysis of dramatic material and the Method of Action Analysis.[2]

Another volume of Sulimov's legacy was published for his one hundredth anniversary. Called *Sulimov's School of Directing*,[3] it consists of his unpublished methodological papers and diaries alongside articles and research papers on his creative activity by more than forty authors – including Lev Dodin, Semyon Spivak, Sergei Tcherkasski and David Chambers. Both *Initiation to Directing* and *Sulimov's School of Directing* are in high demand with present-day students and faculty; thus Sulimov's methodology of director training continues to shape new generations of theatre makers.

Inside Sulimov's Studio: Directors perform a play

There is nothing unusual about directing students acting in their thesis play in Russian theatre schools. Both Stanislavsky and Meyerhold, reflecting their own path to directing, had insisted that a director should also be an actor and should understand the mechanisms and secrets of an actor's work and to some extent be in command of those skills. For Sulimov, who also appeared many times on stage as an actor and who believed that 'good directing first and foremost means inspiring good acting in your actors', an interest in developing the acting potential of future directors was natural. He argued that directing students should be able to act, and thus the curriculum of Sulimov's Studio regularly included the staging of a play with student-directors.

There is, however, an entire series of methodological problems in staging a production with a 'company of directors'. This chapter addresses these issues and reveals Sulimov's directing methodology using the production *Shoo, Death, Shoo!* as a case study.[4] The play by Lithuanian author Saulius Šaltenis was rehearsed and performed in 1983–1984 by Mar Sulimov's Directing Studio at the LGITMiK with students from the third enrolment (1980–1985). The author of this chapter was privileged to be one of those students. Much water has flowed under the bridge since then, but *Shoo, Death, Shoo!* is memorable not only to the audience and participants but also to the faculty of the LGITMiK. It seems that Sulimov's artistic work and rehearsal process had challenged many central issues of directing. As one of the faculty members commented 'the main quality of this production is its preciseness. It can be seen in the very choice of the play for the directors to act, in the genre of the production, in its challenging nature and finally – in the ability of the students of the Studio to do it justice'.[5]

In this chapter, we will try to retrace Sulimov's basic steps in working with this play. The documentary basis for this are notes from the *Diary* of Sulimov's Directing Studio (now in Sulimov's Archive at the St Petersburg State Theatre Library) and rehearsal notes taken by the author.[6]

Choosing the play

Sulimov, as always, began preparing in advance. In the middle of the second year, he proposed that the students begin searching for a play and by the third year the scales were leaning towards Lillian Hellman's play *The Little Foxes* – a play that could effectively cast the entire Studio, and had an interweaving of psychological dialogues, and a serious theme. It seemed as though a decision had been made. But suddenly Sulimov had changed his mind:

> Why is choosing a play to stage in the Studio so painstaking? – he explained his decision for us – Because I understand that the material we are going to rehearse needs to relate to *the theatre of tomorrow*. I can direct *The Little Foxes* very well, and the work we do will be very rewarding, but this material reflects yesterday. However, trying to mix genres, to mix Stanislavsky-based training with other approaches would relate to tomorrow's theatre. There's a paradox here: the theatre of today hasn't risen to Stanislavsky['s System], but Stanislavsky['s practice] is already limiting.[7] If you are kneeling and praying to him – nothing would have come out, but if you reject him entirely, it would have been even worse. We needed to find a play to try and join school with anti-school and some hooliganism![8]

That is how *Shoo, Death, Shoo!* was chosen – as a case for such 'hooliganism'. It is the story of a boy named Andrius from his early childhood till seventeen, the story of his heart's maturation.

The plot

The Shatas and Kaminkas families live in a small Lithuanian town – and are in a long-standing quarrel, which began when Kaminkas bought a cow from Grandfather Shatas, and it died the next day. Five-year-old Andrius Shatas wants to make friends with Luka Kaminkas but encounters not only the enmity of the two families but also Luka's taunts. To resolve the family quarrel, Andrius promises that 'in spite of everything'[9] he will buy Luka a cow. This dream goes on throughout the years – first Andrius collects pennies to buy the cow, and after ninth grade, he earns enough during the summer holidays to really buy a cow, and he presents it to Luka.

However Kaminkas, with the help of school's principal, forces his daughter to refuse this gift from 'the enemy'. When Luka, feeling guilty, comes to a night-time meeting with Andrius, Kaminkas roughly breaks it off and offends the feelings of boy and girl.

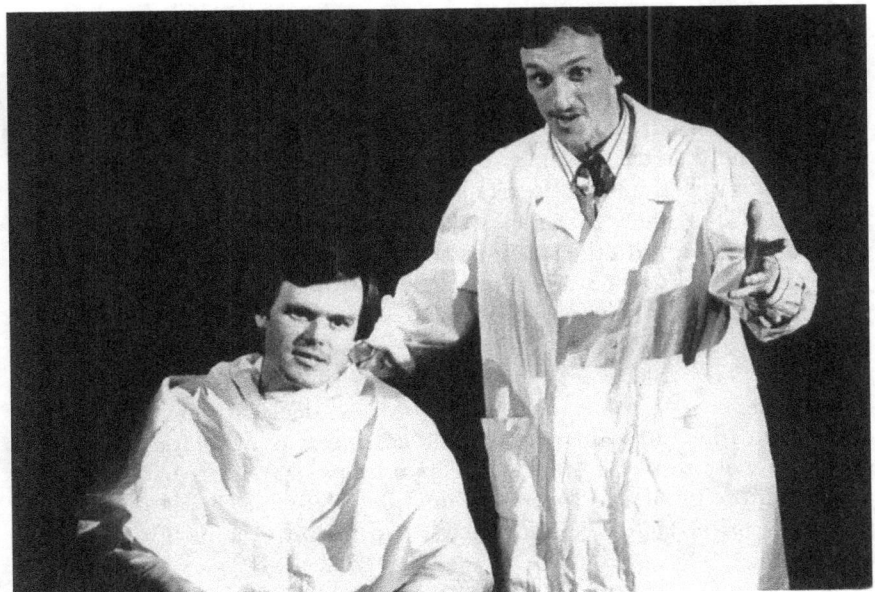

FIGURE 9.2 *Andrius (Andrei Maximov) and Barber Finkelstein (Yuri Spitcin). Shoo, Death, Shoo! (LGITMiK, 1984). Courtesy of Sergei Tcherkasski.*

Andrius's parents try to come to terms with the Kaminkas family and try to lead a cow into the neighbour's yard again, but Kaminkas kills the cow with a rifle shot. Shortly thereafter, he leaves town, taking Luka with him. Andrius, too, departs, leaving his parents at his childhood house to reconcile after his father's affair with the school teacher Meshkute and to wait idyllically for their new baby.

The play is written in the form of the protagonist's memories – and that is of crucial importance. Andrius recalls this whole 'funny and sad story about the cow' before leaving home, while sitting at shop of Finkelstein the barber, whose eyes are 'like a plateful of tears' (Figure 9.2).[10]

SULIMOV IN PRACTICE

The starting point for the play's Action Analysis

Reduce the play you are starting to work on to its event structure. Figure out the main events. Don't miss turning points of the plot. Try to develop a clear line of narration (that will lead you to understand the through-line of action). Get rid of minor detail. Imagine that you need to tell the plot for those who have never read the play.

Casting

Sulimov began work on the play with a pedagogical provocation: he asked the future actors of the production to cast themselves. Well, this was not the first time that the young directors assigned roles to somebody, but it was the first time they were interested in the outcome of this distribution so personally. They knew that they would act themselves and would have to spend a long time with the role they chose.

Soon there was a discussion of student proposals. It became clear that the main reasons for the students' desire to perform this or that role were rather typical ('I can't play Mother, as in my present state I do not want to suffer'; 'This role is very close to my life'; 'I want to try something I haven't played'). With all the sincerity of these declarations, the 'egotism' of the students' substantiation of the casting was evident. The 'actors' naturally were thinking about their own interests, rather than about the artistic integrity of the future production. Thus, after listening to the proposals of the 'actors', Sulimov returned them to the position of being directors:

> Casting contains the solution of your production. The casting of an actor can lead to a clear expression of a director's conception, or to its compromise. And Tovstonogov is right, insisting that double casting is impossible, at least in leading roles. In fact during rehearsals you – director and this very actor – create an individual, unique and inimitable score of the role. A role is created out of its creator, out of an actor. Here, an actor's expenditure of himself, his biological costs and his sincerity is fundamentally important. Therefore, in our art, courage and boldness to be honest are needed as much as talent. We cannot fire a gun with a curved barrel.
>
> However, in the theatre you'll constantly have to deal with statements like: 'I can play the lead well, because my husband left me, just like her'. The reasoning in playing a role by straight-line similarities with an actor's life is unacceptable. In the art of acting we are dealing with the restructuring, with the re-tuning of life experiences.
>
> There are also other types of argument in the fight for the role: 'I feel and understand this role so well! And that means I can play it'. Quite an erroneous argument! Here lies the distinction between the natures of the director and the actor, and the difference in their professional focus. The actor wants to play the *role* of Hamlet; the director stages the play *Hamlet* for the main point, thinking about what will speak to the audience in the *whole performance*.
>
> So beware of external circumstances that influence your decision in casting. Casting an actor for a part needs to be a chaste process and should only be available to the director. It launches the realization of a director's intent for the production.[11]

Of course, this was not the first time Sulimov discussed the principles of casting with the future directors. But the arguments of the teacher became particularly clear and effective on that day – when the students were alternating in their roles of directors and actors. It also brought up the issue of the director's ethical responsibility for the results of the casting. Sulimov strongly disagreed with the proposal of a student 'expanding his range' into a role that fundamentally does not coincide with his traits and abilities: 'Surely, creative growth for an actor is to expand the diversity of roles that he can perform. But a director should take risks with unusual casting only if you have good *proof* of the actor's potential. You mustn't put the actor up for failure just for the sake of experiment.'[12]

First impressions of the play

Discussion of the play itself began with an exchange of the directing students' impressions of the text. Sulimov asked them to recall the very first thoughts and feelings they had after reading *Shoo, Death, Shoo!*

They talked intensely and enthusiastically. But what did Sulimov identify as the most important, and what became cues for the director's further conversations with the actors about the future production? This can be understood from the phrases he underlined in the Studio's journal entry:

- The play is sad, and at the same time one can overcome the sadness.
- The play is fun, it should be played easily, but the spectators might get a strong emotional shock.
- It's a very kind play. The play shows that all people are good on the inside; you just have to reveal the goodness.
- The most painful moment still remains with me – when Luka is crying to her father, who trampled her happiness: 'You will never, ever go to heaven after this!'
- Even though the play is full of open theatricality, it is believable![13]

And there were questions:

- And what are we against in this play?
- Yes, what will be our *sverkhzadacha*,[14] our supertask?[15]

Here, Sulimov decisively interrupted the students. He always warned against hastily determining the director's supertask, knowing that the premature application of 'technique' can ruin the creative process. Now he reiterated:

The most important thing is to keep the impression from your first acquaintance with the play. Make it hold everything together; hammer it as a nail that will hold the future work. And stage the play for the sake of this first impression, for the sake of your first emotional burn. Because after the moment of the first encounter with the author's text we are easily influenced by our education, external thoughts and circumstances etc., but the first impression – that is an untainted response of our own heart in its purest form.[16]

Therefore, by asking the students to record their very first impressions of the play and their emotional response, Sulimov warned them against hasty conclusions and then drew their attention to the *study of the life* of the characters.

SULIMOV IN PRACTICE

First impressions of the play

Summarize your first impression of the play you are working on. Recall the very first thoughts and feelings that came after reading it. The main task is to put emotional response prior to director's techniques, even prior to Action Analysis, and then not to forget this emotional impulse that prompts your desire to direct this play. In a way, the task of Action Analysis is to prove that impulse, to find a technique to convey your 'touchy spots' to the audience.

The first talk about the play with the actors

Sulimov dedicated an entire month, fourteen classes, to an unhurried study of the play. It was a busy time spent comprehending the life of the characters, speculating about the nature of the author's individuality (the author's *nature of feelings*[17]), distinguishing the artistic structure of the play and attempting to bring the knowledge gained to *the system of the play*.

Only after that Sulimov announced the 'first' conversation about the play. He defined the genre of his next talk with the students exactly in that way. And the directing students again turned into actors. This is how Sulimov's policy speech on the play was documented in the Studio's *Diary* and my own notes:

So, we have a very peculiar play. And we must enter into it at an unusual angle, from some unexpected doorway. To determine its genre by some usual categories like fairy tale, parable, dramatic poem, means to limit it. Apparently all these genres are there, and only in their integrity they shape the unique style of the author's text.

The story is told in the form of the memories of the protagonist, so the author frees himself – and us! – from the logical sequence of events in the play. The logic and consistency in the play are very specific. After all, all these memories lead to the formation of a main character's new perception of the world, and that happens right before our eyes. And we, the audience, excitedly watch the accumulation of Andrius's emotional subtleties, his uneasy voyage in understanding his own soul and nature, and the growth of his ability for *humanology*.[18]

Let us think about the *nature* of our memories. They always consist of two components: specific events or life moments which serve as material for the memories, and the actual reason for the recollection. That is the basis of memories, always in a tendentious, biased position of a reminiscing person. Thus because the play consists of the hero's flashbacks, we are introduced to every character in fragments that are often contradictory. They are depicted not as live people in the process of their inner development but as characters' *debris*. Andrius sees himself either as an angel (in recollected scenes where, as he now feels, he has been wrongly offended), or as a bastard (in flashbacks that remind him of his shameful behaviour), at other times as a fool (when he remembers his lost happiness). And all these mixed images make up the whole Andrius. The others appear in his memories with the same motley, as if they are turning with different facets of their characters; thus each time we are seeing their subjective portraits, not their objective ones. Andrius recollects others with the same inconsistency with which he recollects himself, depending on *what* and *what for* he recalls this or that event.

Therefore, working on the play, we must respond to control key questions posed by the poetics of the piece itself. First, what *really happened*? Second, what Andrius *recollects* out of this (the touchy spot of each memory)? And third, *how* is he remembering it?

Memories are always emotionally coloured! And each of them is quite unlike the one before! Indeed, during the play the hero recalls a huge and important period of his life (coming of age, developing his own views on life and humanity). The nature of these memories is very different, depending on what age or slice of life he remembers. So, at five we believe in Santa Claus, and at fifteen – he no longer exists. And at five we live both in a fairy tale and in the real world simultaneously. And as we grow, the world becomes 'wonderless'.[19]

SULIMOV IN PRACTICE

Creating a 'novel of life'

Let us have a close look at Ranyevskaya's monologue 'Oh, my sins' from the second act of Chekhov's *The Cherry Orchard*. In twelve phrases, she expounds almost her whole life, or at least, its most significant events. In one of his books, Sulimov creates sequence of visions for each phrase.

For example, Ranyevskaya says, 'Right here on the river ... my boy drowned' and Sulimov questions:

> 'Need I suggest, that behind these words there is a whirlwind of visions, the acuteness of which cannot kill or even dull time, and whose creation entirely depends on the spiritual development and sensual experience of the director and the actress playing Ranyevskaya?'[20]
>
> How it was? Perhaps the boy, Grisha, asked her to go with him to the river, but HE [that is how, without naming him, Ranyevskaya always speaks about her lover], HE wanted to be alone with her, only with her, with her, wholly owned by him ... And she did not go with her son. Moreover, she drove him away. And went with HIM. Here is this room. Here, quickly drawn curtains, a locked door, a discarded garment ... And then, in that very moment, in his arms, there, in a crumpled bed, she heard an incomprehensible noise, running around in the house, screams ... And then – in a quickly thrown on dress she ran to the river, ... people on the shore, crowded ... here they saw her ... parted ... then she saw!
>
> This novel can and should be developed [by the director and an actress] in every possible way, to equip it with new details. And the more monstrous, the more merciless they will be, the better. It is necessary to get used to this novel, to make it an integral part of Ranyevskaya's life. Then it will turn out in what is written in Chekhov. And in this single phrase, there will be such a quantity of events, which would suffice for a detailed story.[21]

Sulimov's reflection in his policy speech reveals the basis for his choice of play with which he aimed to train the future directors. The main character not only remembered his life *as it happened* but tried to realize *what was happening* and assessed the events from his past in terms of his present spiritual experience. So the actors did not have to play life as we know it but to identify the *gist of the event* that took place earlier, now genre-interpreted through the hero's attitude. Such an approach underlines parallels between acting in this very production and the director's way of acting in the moments of *demonstration* in a rehearsal process (the director's 'demo acting'[22]).

Next, Sulimov stressed the importance of *genre shifts* in future performances:

> Andrius's memories begin with a dreaded black cat. And it is not clearly a cat but perhaps the horrible neighbour Kaminkas that cooks children in the boiler. And to whom Grandfather Shatas says 'Shoo!' when he is trying to defend his grandson Andrius who has a fever; oh, we can't remember ... Such an interweaving and combination of the real world with the imaginary world. The whole play is full of shifts and weaves of different layers – a fairy tale and fantasy and truth overlapping.
>
> Šaltenis's play registers Andrius's thought process. At times it is subordinated to logical analysis but it also makes sudden leaps. And this is natural indeed, sometimes we start remembering one thing, then our mind suddenly jumps to another thing. Therefore it is possible to interrupt the scene without ever finishing it. There is no need to follow a timeline – initial event, climax, resolution – you can start with some event and then everything jumps on to the 'wrong direction'.[23]

This is the very 'hooliganism' and 'anti-school' that Sulimov was trying to get his third-year students to understand. Sulimov was not afraid to sharpen the play's problems polemically by tuning the actors' way of thinking. Probably the teacher understood like nobody else the difficulty of finding a specific way of acting in this play (a *mode of existence*).[24] That is why he was attacking the actor's imagination to delete the possibilities of conventional artistic choices. The goal of the director's very first conversation with the actors was to entice them into the director's vision of the play, to make them share the director's love for the play.

SULIMOV IN PRACTICE

Creating a 'novel of life'

Imagine in detail crucial scenes from the past of the characters that determines their behaviour in the play. In Sulimov's words: 'You need to turn the play into a novel of life.'[25] Start not with thoughts about your future production or about play composition, not with answers to 'professional questions' – when? what? why? – but with the examination and imagining of the real life of the characters full of the smallest details. Study the life of the play with its minutiae.

After his detailed retracing of the through-line of the play, Sulimov returned to asking his students about their first impressions of *Shoo!* It turned out that the notes that had been taken were useful and became necessary for the new discussion. They became a kind of a tuning fork in researching the text of the play. Sulimov insisted on consistency in the initial stage of a director's work on a play:

> It is necessary to record the emotional burn that you had from reading the play and only then to analyse and investigate. If after a thorough study of the play – enriched with the knowledge of its mainspring and its minutiae – you arrive at your initial emotional response to the play, that's when you know that you have found truth.[26]

In the conclusion of his 'first talk with the actors', Sulimov repeated the issues that seemed particularly important in starting rehearsals:

> The *Mode of existence (Way of acting)*. The whole of this play is assembled from fragmental episodes that seem to be unrelated to each other. The message of the play appears from the comparison and confrontation of these fragments. Likewise, every character should be composed of fragments. Each scene gives room to discover and research only one side of the play's character. So you need to play one very distinct feature of the character in each episode, and at the end of the play, a set of these features will be summed up in the character.
>
> *The genre of the play* is a compound one. Different episodes are written by the playwright in different genres – you can see there psychological theatre and buffoonery, Chekhov and Maeterlinck. The main demand for this production is not verisimilitude, but verity, truth. A mix of acting styles, genres, and aesthetics is not eclecticism but the essence of our future performance.
>
> *The development of the play*. The play moves from fabulous childhood memories (with forgotten everyday details but the main emotional impulse strongly preserved) to reality when Andrius grows up and parts with childhood fantasies. In the beginning it's a fairy tale and circus, by the end almost like Chekhov (Chekhov, not a general realism).
>
> *Simultaneous* existence in many different genres! Andrius acts as the clown alongside the psychological theatre of the teacher Meshkute and his Father. You need to be brave and bold in your choices – if you are embarrassed while acting with this mix of genres – then it will not work. We have to stick to our artistic decisions.[27]

Sulimov's first talk as a director with the actor's company was fascinating for everybody. Rehearsals began enthusiastically. To begin, Sulimov had the students prepare the first couple of scenes of the play on their own.

> ### SULIMOV IN PRACTICE
>
> **Face of an author**
>
> Analyse the choice of facts that compile the given circumstances in plays by different authors. You will see that something which is important for one author has absolutely no meaning for another. For example, in Shakespeare's universe, it is either sunshine or tempest, but in Chekhov's world, it is drizzling rain or the stuffiness that predicts the rain which might come in a couple of hours that seriously influence character's behaviours. In *War and Peace*, Tolstoy describes an old oak with botanical preciseness, while you will hardly find any name of a tree in Dostoevsky's writing. So *the face of an author* (in Nemirovich-Danchenko's term) is seen in the choice of facts that compile the given circumstances.
>
> Analyse how the *face of the author* is visible in the details of given circumstances in a play you are working on.

First attempts

The first presentations of the scenes – as I can recollect even now – were really awful. Our classroom had never seen so much affectation and examples of show-off acting. Students freed from everyday logic were performing without any sense or taste. We sat quietly after the show, not knowing the reasons why we had failed. But Sulimov took the results rather stoically:

> Little has come of your rehearsals yet, and the first attempts have been very poor, but what else are we to expect? Therefore, the criterion of discussion is not whether it worked or it did not work. We have to ask ourselves: are we going in the right direction? And it is important not to give up after the first failures.
>
> I urged you to fantasize about the play uninhibitedly. So you were uninhibited, but reached the opposite result. Your freedom and artistic hooliganism are only *means* of expressing the *main theme*, the *essence* of the play. Yes, if you are loose and free it should allow the main theme of the play to emerge. But chatter should not obscure meaning. Today throughout the entire presentation I was not certain of what exactly was *happening*. I did not understand what my attention should be focused on. What *happens* to Andrius in every scenic episode – here is the question to which we must respond in each scene, in each improvisation.

FIGURE 9.3 *Andrius (Andrei Maximov) and Cow (Larisa Lelyanova). Shoo, Death, Shoo! (LGITMiK, 1984).* Courtesy of Sergei Tcherkasski.

Otherwise, all the looseness, and chatter becomes a staircase that leads to nowhere.

We mustn't focus on what is happening *in general*, but what is happening *to Andrius!* (Figure 9.3).[28]

Rehearsals

The play was rehearsed for over a year and it wasn't easy.[29] The declared way of acting – 'in the memories of the protagonist' – was sometimes captured in the rehearsals and sometimes lost again. The hardest thing was to find Andrius's own way of acting (his *mode of existence*). Soon it became clear that when Andrius was recollecting his past, he would play to the audience rather than to the other actors on stage. It was the audience that appeared as his main acting partner! So it was necessary to discover the nature of Andrius's indirect communication with the characters inside of his memories. It was also imperative to avoid everyday mise-en-scenes and the presentation of life in the form of the everyday. Often, despite the best efforts of the teachers-directors, the students would slip back into a 'regular' acting mode, and the needed paradoxicality that is inherent in the process of recollecting was lost time and again.

For example, in a scene where the Jesuitical boys had opened Andrius's eyes to his father's affair with the teacher, Sulimov comments on one student's performance:

> What I saw is how Andrius runs and bangs on the door of Meshkute's house, he is breathless here and now. On the contrary, in the play Andrius needs to recollect how he ran years ago without presenting it now. He needs to share this with the spectators. But how? Then he was motivated by anger and hatred, but now, as he is remembering his shameless intrusion he feels ashamed. How does this change your stage behaviour?[30]

The rehearsals led by acting teacher Anatoly Shvederski answered some of these questions. As an actor with a keen sense of form (years ago he had played Tybalt and was a wonderful character actor), with some of his 'demo acting', Shvederski managed to clarify each character's mode of existence.

Sulimov appreciated our efforts, but he immediately raised the bar as the students were already skilled actors with six months of rehearsals under their belts. After the dry run of the play, Sulimov summarized the main problems the performers were facing:

> What is not working here? First, Andrei [the student who plays Andrius] radically rebuilt the *nature* of Andrius's existence. Now it is evident that the entire play and its events are memories, and not a slice of life that took place here and now according to the laws of naturalistic theatre. But we talked about the *tendency* of memories, hence their distortion. Other characters play that alteration, but Andrei has not commented on it with his attitude or evaluations, etc. It is very important to establish the right partnership with the audience in this process of recollections. Right now contact with the audience has not been made and so Andrei cannot nourish his inner monologue from that. There should be a circle – your inner monologue pushes you to communicate with the audience, and communication with the spectator returns Andrius back to his stage relationships, and gives a new impulse for action, for memories. Andrius needs 'to discuss himself' with the audience.
>
> Second, Anatoly Samoylovich [Shvederski] gave the whole play an acute, sometimes paradoxical form. It's very good, regardless of the fact that some solutions are already lively and clear, others are still missing the target and need more work. But in any case, such vivid theatrical form, if it is devoid of genuine feeling, turns into a bad farce and unacceptable overplaying. For example, the scene where the teacher Meshkute is hanging around the Father's neck; *in reality* that is recollected by Andrius, there was no such scene and it could never have happened.

But both Father and Meshkute went so crazy with love that it produced exactly this very impression on Andrius who was completely stunned by their relations. Therefore, this improbable and grotesque scene should be played with *true* passion, i.e., it should exist under the laws of the psychological theatre's prissiness.

While acting any episode from Andrius's past we are allowed to emphasize only something that really happened. But in your acting we get exaggeration that was an end in itself, without any *truth* linked to the past events.

So in all hyperbolized scenes it is necessary first, to exaggerate only the *realities* of the recalled event – whether they were in overt or covert form, and secondly, to fill acute paradoxical form with *genuine* passions and feelings.

Third, many characters and facts are recalled by Andrius in a biased and distorted way, this way and that. Single characters might appear nasty and mean in one memory and quite bright in the other. So it is important not to lose your *perspective* of an actor who presents this character. It is necessary to clearly define what should remain in the spectator's perception as a final impression. Say Meshkute appears in flashbacks either as the lascivious cat, or as the suffering woman, etc. And what is your resulting attitude to her? What must she ultimately call for – deep sympathy or disgust, indignation? It is important not to miss that throughout your entire rehearsal work. This means that any scene needs somehow to bear a seed of the resulting attitude to this character.[31]

Obviously, Sulimov poses an increased level of complexity for his actors. Now, right before the first night, he focuses on the elements of the acting that were crucial for meaning making in the production. The fact that the director could afford such challenging tasks for his students characterizes their undoubted growth as actors during the half a year of rehearsals (Figure 9.4).

The premiere

The first performance of *Shoo, Death, Shoo!* directed by Mar Sulimov was played in December 1983 and was in repertoire for six months before the students graduated. It ran about twenty times. After the famous *Visible Song* at Tovstonogov's Studio (1965), *Shoo!* was, to my knowledge, the first performance by directing students to be so successful and long lived. What is the reason for the success of Sulimov's production? And most importantly, what was its impact on the professional development of students as future directors?

FIGURE 9.4 *Mother (Larisa Nitcenko) and Father (Alexandr Veselov). Shoo, Death, Shoo! (LGITMiK, 1984). Courtesy of Sergei Tcherkasski.*

Firstly, the answer lies in the methodological value of Sulimov's choice of play to work on with student-directors. The play by Šaltenis, which registers the process of memories, gave the students a unique opportunity to perform in diverse *modes of existence* – both in actor's mode and in director's mode. The laborious search for a mode of existence in this unusual dramaturgical material not only led to the creation of an interesting performance. The acting method used in the performances of *Shoo, Death, Shoo!* was similar to the mode of existence of a director in the process of 'demo acting' (I play *what*, not *how*), and that prepared the future directors for their coming encounters with professional actors. Not all directors have, as Stanislavsky said, 'the organism of an actor', the *external apparatus* of an actor. But the chosen play and the director's decision actively helped the students to develop their *inner acting potential* regardless of their actual abilities as an actor. This is probably the reason for the growth seen in the acting of *all* students involved in this production and for the final high-quality acting they displayed.

Noteworthy are the tactics of Sulimov in combining two pedagogical processes – *rehearsals with the actors* and *training the directors* – and his ability to have the students switch from one process to the other, alternating sessions where students were turned into co-directors of the play with those times when they did not have a minute to get out of their 'acting skin'. The production was not only a step forward in the development of the students as actors: they also gained valuable experience in various theatre disciplines – they arranged the music and set the lights, designed costumes, and even did a bit of carpentry. On the eve of their own work in professional theatre (after the first night of *Shoo!* students were out of the LGITMiK to direct their pre-diploma and diploma productions in the professional state companies), the *complex* tasks they had learned in the Studio's performance allowed them to be prepared for the creation of a production with *artistic integrity*.

Most curricula emphasize the need for the moral education of the student. Sulimov's rehearsals really developed soul. At one of the rehearsals, he proposed a working definition of the genre of the play – 'a heartfelt introspection'. He wanted not only the hero of the play but also the students to accumulate the ability to feel the pain of others: 'What does Andrius experience during the scene of the uneasy reconciliation of his Father and Mother? Compassion, sympathy, empathy. These feelings open the road to humaneness.'[32] Sulimov's moral lessons were perceived as more than just analysing a piece of playwriting.

The comments made by Sulimov after the premiere were also characteristic. After recognizing the success they had, Sulimov targeted the students to make a number of improvements:

> We have to have some further rehearsals not for the sake of performing, but for ourselves. The problem of organic behaviour on stage and believability of acting has been largely mastered since Stanislavsky. Nowadays these qualities can be seen in almost all graduates of theatre schools. The primary task of today's theatre is to find the *preciseness* in the character's psychology. We have to work on finding this *precision*. The grotesque, according to Stanislavsky, arises from the sharpening of the character's internal life that eventually leads to an escalation of the external form of their behaviour. But in our rehearsals we were often approaching the grotesque only through the search for an acute theatrical form. We need to keep finding the motivations for sharpening the inner psychological life of the characters to justify that form of open theatricality.[33]

Sulimov spoke at length, drawing students to new, exciting tasks, not all of which could or should have been solved in a school performance. However, a year of intensive rehearsals gave students a chance to listen anew to the wishes of their teacher before parting ways and entering the world of professional theatre. The experience of *Shoo!* became the basis for reflection and for the creative searches of each of the graduates of Sulimov's Studio. The process of rehearsing and acting in this production highlighted practically links between the Stanislavsky System and the genres of open theatricality, proved that the laws of creativity and the laws of nature in acting discovered by Stanislavsky are applicable to a variety of dramatic genres and aesthetics, and linked the technique of working with an actor to directing in epic theatre and a theatre of open theatricality.

Perhaps this is what Sulimov meant by saying at the beginning of the work that the directing student's thesis project *should reflect the theatre of the future.*[34]

10

Anatoly Efros's Principles of Acting and Directing: Psychological Truth, Active Analysis, Adaptations – 'Zigzags' and Thematic Modernity

James Thomas

Anatoly Efros (1925–1987) belongs to that special group of Russian artists and intellectuals who contributed to the era between the early 1950s and early 1960s known as 'The Thaw'. The name came from Ilya Ehrenberg's eponymous novel of 1954, comparing the atmosphere of the era to climatic change. Prompted by the succession of moderate leader Nikita Khrushchev after the death of Joseph Stalin in 1953, the Thaw era witnessed a recovery of cultural freedom after a prolonged period of chilling censorship. It awakened a desire to rediscover authentic Russian imagination instead of its Sovietized surrogate, to escape from Stalin's wearisome ideas and stereotypes in art and literature and to feel confident original creative work was possible once again. Anatoly Efros was one of the leading creative figures of the Thaw era. His life and work not only contributed to the hopes of that era but also left an important legacy (Figure 10.1).

FIGURE 10.1 *Anatoly Efros. Courtesy of the Anatoly Efros Archives.*

Early years

Anatoly Vasilyevich Efros (née Natan Isayevich) was born 3 July 1925 in Kharkov, a large city located in northeast Ukraine and an important centre of Jewish life. His parents worked at an aviation factory founded by family patriarch Isaac Vasilievich Efros, his father an aviation designer and his mother a translator of technical literature. In 1941, the Germans occupied Kharkov. As a teenager of Jewish heritage, Efros, his family and most of Kharkov's Jewish population evacuated 1,300 miles northeast to Perm, Russia, near the Ural Mountains. Young Efros worked there as a lathe operator at the proxy aviation factory until the end of the war.

Although his parents were not theatregoers, Efros said he always loved the theatre and enjoyed stories and books about Stanislavsky and the Moscow Art Theatre. After the end of the war in 1945, for some unknown reason, he did not go back to Kharkov with his parents, but instead ventured to Moscow to study acting. He auditioned for and was accepted at the acting studio of the Mossovet Theatre, which was established in 1923 and located a short distance northeast of Red Square. The Mossovet was led by Yuri Zavadsky, a direct student both of Stanislavsky and Yevgeny Vakhtangov, and it was here that Efros's direct contact with the MAT legacy began.

By 1946 Socialist Realism had been the norm for over a decade, and the practice of the Stanislavsky System had become hopelessly compromised. Soviet stages were monopolized by static compositions, clichéd characters, unimaginative scenery and oppressive propaganda. It was this rigidly orthodox environment that encouraged Efros to organize an unsanctioned theatre studio called 'The Realists' to study forms of acting different from the official line promoted by the government. Unfortunately, the cultural authorities simultaneously launched one of their periodic attacks against 'formalism, aestheticism and groups of bourgeois cosmopolitans', in other words, against disagreement in any form. Consequently, when Zavadsky found out about the Realists, he quashed the experiment before any political fallout could develop.[1] Zavadsky concluded that Efros's true aptitude was for directing, so he encouraged him to transfer to the directing programme at GITIS, ten minutes east of Red Square.[2]

GITIS was Moscow's leading theatre training institute at the time, and while Efros was there the MAT family tree continued to play an important role in his development. Nikolai Petrov, who studied under Vladimir Nemirovich-Danchenko, was head of the directing programme. Furthermore, Maria Knebel, Alexei Popov and Mikhail Tarkhanov – all students of Stanislavsky, Michael Chekhov, Yevgeny Vakhtangov and Vsevelod Meyerhold – were members of the same faculty. Maria Knebel's artistic influence on Efros was particularly significant (more about this below). Efros graduated from this extraordinary GITIS faculty in 1950.

By this time, the Communist Party had consolidated its authority over all the arts through the doctrine of Socialist Realism, which empowered the Soviets, in the service of this doctrine, to expropriate Stanislavsky because of the ostensible affinity of his principles with artistic Realism. The government established a committee to make sure Stanislavsky's writings conformed with Marx-Leninist dialectical materialism. Materialistic versions of Stanislavsky's teachings were then declared the official communist theatre aesthetic, while apolitical and unsuspecting Stanislavsky was canonized by the Soviets in the process. Drained of their original inspiration, Stanislavsky's principles were no longer an actor's personal work. From 1934 until the death of Stalin in 1953, many if not most Russian actors and directors lost respect for Stanislavsky and his (albeit bowdlerized) teachings – except Efros. From the start, he remained committed to Stanislavsky and what he learned from Stanislavsky's students.

Upon graduating from GITIS, Efros honed his skills at a succession of short engagements. In 1950, he directed plays with a touring theatre Knebel organized, travelling to provincial cities and sharing quarters in a railway carriage. In 1951, he directed a Soviet ideological play at the Ostrovsky Drama Theatre in Mikhailov, about 130 miles south of Moscow. In 1952, he obtained a position on the directing staff of the State Dramatic Theatre in Ryazan, an industrial city located 125 miles southeast of Moscow. He remained there for the next two years, directing *The Ardent Heart* by Alexander Ostrovsky and *Dog in the Manger* by Lope de Vega (following Stanislavsky's directing notes in each case), as well as a Russian Civil War history play, an anti-fascist play, an Estonian folk play, a comedy about modern Soviet life and a Byelorussian folk comedy. These three years at Moscow provincial theatres formed a gestation period for the aesthetic for which Efros was later celebrated.

EFROS IN PRACTICE

'Great artists don't always work only for themselves, they work for the future. Stanislavsky created such an art, and discussed it in such a way that no serious artistic person could ignore it [...]. Stanislavsky forever remains the great teacher.'[3]

Efros left no specific legacy of exercises as there is for Stanislavsky or Michael Chekhov. Rather, his books deal holistically with his approach to creating theatre, his artistic and ethical thoughts about the profession and his assessments of some of those with whom he worked or otherwise affected him. Recently made available in translation, Efros's books are instructive, readable, modern in sensibility and applicable to the realities of Anglo-American theatre.[4] From his books, it is possible to determine Efros's fundamental principles of rehearsal and practice as well as formulate relevant exercises to illustrate these principles. The principles consist of Psychological Truth in Acting, Active Analysis (comprising Mental Analysis and Etudes), Adaptations – 'Zigzags' and Thematic Modernity, which will be treated in succession throughout this chapter.

Psychological Truth in Acting

In view of Efros's disposition and training, it is no surprise his fundamental principle was Stanislavsky-based psychological truth. Today the term psychological truth has wide usage among actors and directors and just as many understandings. Nonetheless, each person's understanding of the term implies a way of thinking, whether aware of it or not. For Stanislavsky and Nemirovich-Danchenko, this way of thinking was quite specific: psychological truth is identified by correspondence of a character's actions with the innate individuality of the actor. Stanislavsky's term for this viewpoint was 'experiencing' (*perezhivanie*), which he explained as 'subconscious creation through the actor's conscious psychotechnique', contrasting it with other approaches in Chapter 2 of *An Actor's Work*.[5] For his part, Nemirovich-Danchenko explained experiencing this way:

> The actor of the old theatre acts either *emotion:* love, jealousy, hatred, joy, etc.; or *words,* underlining them, stressing each significant one; or a *situation,* laughable or dramatic; or a *mood,* or *physical self-consciousness.* In a word, inevitably during every instant of his presence on the stage he is *acting* something, *representing* something. Our demands on the actor are that he should *not act anything*; decidedly not a *thing;* neither feelings, nor moods, nor situations, nor words, nor styles, nor images. All this should come of itself *from the individuality of the actor, individuality liberated from stereotyped forms.*[6]

On the face of it, both Stanislavsky's expression and Nemirovich-Danchenko's explanation might appear to be vague and imprecise, yet there must be something observable and teachable about experiencing, otherwise there would be little hope of distinguishing it from other approaches found in Anglo-American acting, for example, the 'Spect-actor' of Augusto Boal,[7] the 'Alienation Effect' of Bertolt Brecht,[8] the 'Imaginary Body' of Michael Chekhov,[9] the 'Art as Vehicle' of Jerzy Grotowski,[10] the 'text-and-technique' of Michel Saint-Denis[11] or the 'emotional honesty' of Lee Strasberg.[12]

Exercises

1 Compare the approach to acting Stanislavsky teaches in Chapter 2 of *An Actor's Work* with those of Augusto Boal, Bertolt Brecht, Michael Chekhov, Jerzy Grotowski, Michel Saint-Denis and Lee Strasberg mentioned above.

2 What is the relationship of acting to its practitioners and to society implied with each approach?

Central Children's Theatre

After honing his craft in the provinces, in 1954, Efros became staff director, then leading director at Moscow's Central Children's Theatre (CCT), where he met up again with Maria Knebel, his mentor from GITIS. The Central Children's Theatre was established in 1936 from the remainders of MAT II and Stanislavsky's First and Second Studios.[13] It was located close to the legendary Bolshoi (Big) and Maly (Small) Theatres in an area of Moscow called Theatre Square, a short walk northeast of Red Square and the Kremlin. In 1950, Maria Knebel became Artistic Director there after her dismissal from MAT in an anti-Semitic purge of the company where she had been a member since 1921. For the past two decades, Soviet ideology had prohibited talk about spirit, subconscious or soul, forcing Knebel to talk about Stanislavsky's original principles only in ways that avoided too much notice. With the emergence of the Thaw era in 1954, 'the life of the human spirit' no longer needed to be kept secret, and Knebel could realize her lifelong mission of promoting Stanislavsky's original principles, most importantly, his groundbreaking, improvisation-based rehearsal method, Active Analysis. At CCT, Efros demonstrated that Stanislavsky's original principles, including Active Analysis, could succeed in the exacting conditions of the profession.

Young playwrights were drawn to CCT as well, since the creative freedom associated with children's theatre was a way of tiptoeing around some of the more rigid constraints of Socialist Realism. Working with Maria Knebel and thinking about Active Analysis, Efros developed an affinity for plays of everyday Russian life and authentic Russian culture. In due course, his work became a cultural magnet during the Thaw, when young people were searching for their place in a deadening environment that was the legacy of Stalinism. The 'Efros phenomenon', as it came to be known, began in 1954, with his production of Viktor Rozov's play *Good Luck!*, a comedy about the relations between parents and children and the search for a vocation in life. *Good Luck* was an amazing success with adolescents as well as their parents. Another defining moment was Efros's production of Alexander Khmelik's play *My Friend, Kolka!* (1958), in which justice triumphs when a high-spirited sixth-grader is wrongly accused of a misdemeanour. The play was so overwhelmingly popular that it is still performed throughout Russia. Unprecedented at CCT, Efros cast age-appropriate children from the theatre's affiliated acting studio instead of the young adults who customarily played such roles. Unprecedented as well was Efros's rejection of the fatal stage habits of Socialist Realism in favour of psychologically truthful acting, 'psychophysics' (psychology made visible through expressive movement), modernist scenery and a feeling of genuine contemporaneity. These features were to become the basis of Efros's characteristic aesthetic, empowering CCT to become one of the most popular theatres in Moscow if not the centre of modern theatre life in Russia.

EFROS IN PRACTICE

Active Analysis

'In life, everything is life. However, in art, it is analysis, analysis, construction, design.'[14]

As important as 'the life of the human spirit' was for Efros, it would not succeed for him without an exact basis, that is, without careful analysis. If analysis was not exact and beautiful, he believed even 'the life of the human spirit' would not help. Thus, Efros's second fundamental principle consists of Active Analysis, a groundbreaking analysis and rehearsal methodology developed by Stanislavsky in his final years. Active Analysis is a dialectical process linking a specific type of text analysis with improvised physical practice.[15] Efros learned about it from his GITIS mentor, Maria Knebel, whom Stanislavsky entrusted with teaching and promoting his final work.

As is well known, Stanislavsky and Nemirovich-Danchenko originated the practice of preliminary study of the play 'at the table' (*za stolom*), requiring 'enormous concentration, digging deep in the [text] and the actor's soul before going out on stage'.[16] Eventually, however, they came to differ about the role of table work in the rehearsal process. Nemirovich-Danchenko preferred 'to inspire the actors with the author's "internal image" of the characters at the beginning of rehearsals [at the table] and then proceed [with blocking, etc.] from this stable definition'. Stanislavsky, for his part, 'agreed with the need for preliminary work on the text with actors, [but] always emphasized the importance of the actor's imagination and psychology throughout the creative process'.[17] He developed Active Analysis with this principle in mind.

Active Analysis consists of two reciprocal stages of work. First is a special type of text analysis Stanislavsky simply called 'mental analysis', undertaken (more often by the director) prior to meeting with the actors.[18] Second is application of mental analysis through 'etudes'. Here we will deal with mental analysis; the next Efros in Practice section will deal with etudes.

Active Analysis: Mental Analysis

Because Stanislavsky believed plot was the most accessible means of understanding a play, mental analysis starts with close reading of the plot, specifically a play's 'events'. The term event here refers to occurrences that normally should not happen in the world of the play. For journalists, this kind of awareness amounts to a professional skill, using an aphorism as a reminder: 'Man bites dog' is an unusual, infrequent occurrence that is more likely to be reported by journalists as news than an ordinary everyday occurrence such as 'Dog bites man'. Events in plays are also unusual, infrequent occurrences, but with an important difference. Dramatic events are also first-time or last-time occurrences in the world of the play; they change the situation, bring about new ideas and feelings in the characters, changing their path in the play. For example, Polonius hides behind a curtain to eavesdrop on Hamlet and Ophelia, Nils Krogstad blackmails Nora Helmer (*A Doll's House*), Tom Wingfield invites Jim O'Connor to dinner (*The Glass Menagerie*), Shen Te accepts a gift of money from the gods (*The Good Person of Setzuan*), Colonel Vershinin arrives at the home of the Prozorov's (*Three Sisters*) and so on.

Exercises

1. Develop a Chain of External Events, that is, those major social interactions categorically necessary for the play's action. A social interaction may be understood as a meeting or gathering, plan or scheme, encounter with a person or group, an arrival or departure, a betrayal or disclosure, an acceptance or rejection and so forth. To be effective in rehearsal, such events should be formulated in the simplest possible terms comparable to the examples above, shorn of literary jargon or bookishness.

2. Study each event in the proposed chain to confirm each one both as an event in the sense explained here and indispensable. Indispensability can be tested by guessing how the play would change if a certain event were supposedly removed from the play.

Lenkom Theatre

In 1963, Efros was appointed Artistic Director at the Lenin Komsomol Theatre as an acknowledgement of his decade of success at CCT. The Lenkom, as it was nicknamed, had a checkered history. Komsomol is an acronym for Communist Youth League, and the official mission of this theatre was to produce plays supportive of Soviet ideology for young workers. Located close to Pushkin Square, one Metro stop north of Theatre Square and CCT, the building was originally a merchants' club designed and built for light entertainments (1909–1917); next it was turned into a political club (1918–1920), a Communist university (1920–1923) and a movie theatre (1923–1938). From 1938 to 1951, the Lenkom was led by MAT II alumnus Ivan Bersenev and was one of the most important theatres in Moscow. Since then, however, artistic directors had come and gone without leaving any traces in memory.

Only a year after Efros's appointment, Communist Party leaders ousted moderate leader Nikita Khrushchev and replaced him with conservative Leonid Brezhnev. This action set in motion the re-Stalinization of the USSR, leading to a prolonged reactionary period of negative economic, political and social outcomes called the 'Era of Stagnation'. Here was evidence that the government's policies were turning against the ideals of the Thaw; although for now, at least, Efros's encounter with the new regime's agenda still lay in the future.

At the Lenkom, Efros found a company dispirited from years of neglect and the absence of any unifying aesthetic. He revived their spirits by introducing the same aesthetic with which he had previously energized CCT. Namely, Stanislavsky-based psychological acting, a keen contemporary sensibility, animated staging and modernist production values. He started with new plays by Thaw-era writers Viktor Rozov, Edward Radzinsky, Alexei Arbuzov and Samuel Alyoshin. Their themes were just as up to date as before at CCT (namely, the desire to lead a good life in a ruthless social environment), but their implications were sharper now because the characters were no longer adolescents but young adults newly in charge of things, like Efros himself. Moscow's theatrical centre of gravity began to shift towards the Lenkom, freshly thriving under Efros's progressive leadership. On the other hand, the pressures of leading the Lenkom into uncharted territory took their toll on Efros's health, and in 1965 he suffered his first heart attack.

A significant moment in this cultural shift occurred in 1966 when Efros directed *The Seagull*, his first play by Anton Chekhov and the first historical play ever to be produced at the Lenkom.[19] Instead of the traditional lyrical approach to Chekhov created at the Moscow Art Theatre, Efros's interpretation was modern in tone and design, emphasizing the characters' openly spiteful interactions with one another and their openly indifferent betrayal of Treplev. The tone of anger and mutual hostility expressed a tough modernist sensibility, at that time the jurisdiction of Western European theatre. Efros's approach provoked serious opposition from traditionalists, especially the MAT. Nonetheless, he pushed ahead with his reformist aims, following up *The Seagull* with Mikhail Bulgakov's forbidden work, *Molière, or The Cabal of Hypocrites* (1967), concerning Molière's struggle with Louis XIV and the Church over *Tartuffe*.

The Seagull and *Molière* were successes with the public, but Efros's modernist approach to Chekhov and provocative choice of Bulgakov's critique of government censorship exasperated his post-Thaw superiors. Accordingly, after the premiere of *Molière*, Efros was dismissed as Artistic Director for 'ideological deficiencies'. He was proving to be too much of a tradition disrupter. He must have realized he would incur the displeasure of the authorities when he did not include the obligatory Soviet propaganda plays in the theatre's repertory. He also must have known there would be green-room problems when certain Lenkom actors were not selected for leading roles as before. A further serious problem for him was the resurgence of anti-Semitism in Soviet society at large, in the Moscow theatre community and in his own theatre company. Bearing in mind that Efros was a director and artist first and last, not an administrator or politician, in retrospect it was foreseeable that it would be beyond his capacity to deal with the partisan issues involved with running a theatre company under such circumstances.

EFROS IN PRACTICE

Active Analysis: Etudes

'The etude method is a super-practical thing. After psychophysical analysis of the text, everything must be so clear that it should be possible to go on stage immediately and improvise.'[20]

The next and most characteristic part of Active Analysis consists of etudes (sketches), comprising the applied, improvised component of the process. The essence of etudes is that after a certain amount of introductory study of the play with the actors at the table, the play is analysed actively 'on your feet', by means of etudes with improvised text. Active Analysis avoids protracted study of the play at the table in the orthodox manner of Nemirovich-Danchenko and most current Anglo-American theatre. Stanislavsky believed by using the actors' own words throughout this part of the process, their contact with the play would be psychophysical rather than merely intellectual, as it is at the table. Moreover, while intellectual knowledge of the play can be obtained from table study, etudes 'on your feet' enable this knowledge to be made concrete in the here and now.

Exercises

1. Study a selected play without reading according to roles. Directors should avoid too much intervention at this point so the actors' creative imaginations can be released as much as possible. After reaching a general understanding of the play in this manner, take on roles and begin the process of analysing short passages (let us call them minor events) from within a selected major event to prepare for etudes. The passages should be short so as not to overtax remembering. Each actor-character identifies his or her ideological goal (objective, task) in the passage. After that, etudes for the passage can begin, always using improvised dialogue and alternating with as many return trips to the table as may be needed to achieve the necessary accuracy. Here the director side-coaches as necessary to enable remembering and ensure the actors remain within the logic of the text.
2. How do you feel as an actor on stage in your first experience with etudes?
3. In what ways have the etudes either clarified or clouded the content and meaning of the selected passages?
4. Has the practice of text analysis changed in any way when returning to the table after performing an etude? How does it differ from text analysis in traditional table work?
5. How can etudes influence the prior mental analysis of the director?

Malaya Bronnaya Theatre

In 1967, after his dismissal from the Lenkom, Efros was bidden to join the directing staff of the Moscow Dramatic Theatre on Malaya Bronnaya Street (aka the Malaya Bronnaya Theatre), a twenty-minute walk east of the MAT. The choice of venue was significant. Originally this was the neighbourhood of the city's armour makers for whom it was named and by the nineteenth century it had evolved into the Jewish district of Moscow. In 1921, the Moscow State Jewish Theatre (GOSET) was established on that street under the direction of the famous Yiddish actor Solomon Mikhoels. Marc Chagall painted his celebrated murals for this theatre. GOSET was closed in 1949 owing to anti-Semitic oppression, after which it was turned over to an amateur group. Professional operation had resumed only two years before Efros arrived there.

At the Malaya Bronnaya, Efros began with *Three Sisters* (1967), another modernist interpretation of Chekhov, which offended traditionalists and was removed from the repertory. After this, Efros tried not to 'tweak the tiger's tail' any further, as the saying goes. From then on, he turned his attention to plays drawn from the established classical repertory. Released from leadership responsibilities, he could focus on developing his own aesthetic. His productions of *Romeo and Juliet* (1970), *Don Juan* (1973) by Molière, *Marriage* (1975) by Nikolai Gogol, *Othello* (1976) and Turgenev's *A Month in the Country* (1977) became classics of modern Russian theatre. He also began to publish his directorial explications and theatre reflections: *Repetitsiya-lyubov moya* (Rehearsal Is My Love, 1975), *Professia: Rezhissyor* (Occupation: Director, 1979) and *Prodolzheniye teatralnovo romana* (Theatre Novel Continued, 1985).[21]

Efros's standing with the authorities improved correspondingly and he began to be invited to direct at other theatres as well: the Mossovet Theatre (1969, 1974), Taganka Theatre (1975), Moscow Art Theatre (1981, 1982) and even at theatres outside the USSR (a rare privilege at the time), such as the Guthrie Theatre in Minneapolis (1978, 1979)[22] and Toen Theatre in Tokyo (1981–1982). His productions of *Marriage* and *A Month in the Country* received the Grand Prize at the Duisburg Theatre Festival. He also directed nine productions for Central Television, seven for All-Union Radio and four movies for Mosfilm. In 1975, at age 50, he suffered a second heart attack, but recovered quickly and continued to work as actively as before. An official sign of his political 'rehabilitation' occurred in 1976, when he was awarded the title of People's Artist of the USSR.

Then things reversed direction for him again. In 1978, a party factotum was added to the Malaya Bronnaya's management staff, and the working atmosphere there began to change for the worse. A full account of the theatrical, political and anti-Semitic manoeuvrings that followed would require an entire monograph. It is enough to say Efros found it increasingly difficult to work at the Malaya Bronnaya and in 1984 he resigned. By coincidence, this happened to be the same year Yuri Lyubimov was deprived of his Soviet citizenship and dismissed from his position as Artistic Director of the Taganka Theatre for publicly criticizing the Soviet Union while working abroad. Several well-known directors declined the open Taganka position because it was too risky. At that point Efros was offered the position and, despite the doubts of family and colleagues, he accepted the offer.

EFROS IN PRACTICE

Adaptations – 'Zigzags'

Besides Stanislavsky's well-known concept of objectives (i.e. to change someone for the better, to be helpful to someone, to seek romance from someone), important as well for Efros was Stanislavsky's concept of adaptations (i.e. apologetically, menacingly, wistfully). In the eponymous chapter of *An Actor's Work*, Stanislavsky explained adaptations as those 'mental and physical ingenuities people use to adjust their behaviour and so influence other people, which is their object[ive]'.[23] In other words, adaptations modify actions just as adverbs modify verbs. Efros's jargon for adaptations was 'zigzags', and he sought their greatest possible originality and unexpectedness in his work:

> Life is arranged so strangely – dialog is like a zigzag. But this is good. A straight line from one point to another is only good for a railroad.
>
> These zigzags should be distinctly visible and then it will be interesting, like life, like the complexity typical of life. This is not a diagram, this is flesh and as everyone knows, it is woven from contrasts.
>
> But more often, analysis is primitive and schematic: 'My objective is to ... ' and then the actor 'molds' himself directly towards this objective. Even a cat has hundreds of nuances. The question is to find them.
>
> There is meaning that is clear and open and there is what is concealed and essential. And this is where all the zigzags will come from: the more complex, concealed, latent meaning – this is the ideal.[24]

Efros's partiality for adaptations – 'zigzags' was not artificially laid on, but a logical outcome, he felt, of the peculiarly confused quality of the modern (Sovietized) personality. Revealed in rehearsals through Active Analysis, adaptations – 'zigzags' had the twofold outcome of releasing the innately modern temperaments of the actors and releasing new meanings in the plays themselves. It was this talent of Efros's that imprinted itself most on actors' sensibilities and audiences' memories.

Exercises

1. In *An Actor's Work*, read Chapters 3 ('Action', 'if', 'Given Circumstances'), 7 ('Bits and Tasks') and 11 ('An actor's adaptations and other elements, qualities, aptitudes and gifts'). Describe Stanislavsky's notions of action, tasks (objectives) and adaptations explained there. Discuss the interrelations among these notions.

2. Where etudes feel clichéd, repetitive or uninteresting, try changing a few of the more habitual adaptations. While intuitive adaptations are usually best, sometimes adaptations applied on purpose can reveal unnoticed meanings. For example, a character might well tease (action) someone teasingly (habitual adaptation), or instead, *angrily, jovially* or *ironically*; protect (action) someone protectively (habitual adaptation), or instead, *cordially, contemptibly* or *menacingly*; reject (action) someone decisively (habitual adaptation), or instead, *capriciously, indifferently* or *doubtfully*. Discuss any new meanings coming to light from this exercise.

Taganka Theatre

Founded in 1946, the Taganka Theatre is located southwest of Moscow centre in an Art Nouveau building on Taganka Square, across the street from the busy Taganka Metro station. It was one of the least attended theatres in Moscow until 1964, when Yuri Lyubimov, its new artistic director, brought his students from the Shchukin School of the Vakhtangov Theatre to reprise their graduation performance of Brecht's play, *The Good Person of Setzuan*. For the next twenty years, the Taganka was one of the most popular avant-garde theatres in the country. Devoted to the principles of Brecht and Vakhtangov, Lyubimov never used a front curtain and seldom used conventional scenery, rather preferring dynamic stage installations. In 1975, when Lyubimov was working abroad, Efros had directed a remarkable production of *The Cherry Orchard* there.[25] But when he accepted the leadership of the now leaderless Taganka in 1984, he was denounced by members of the Moscow theatre community for what they considered an attempt to undermine Lyubimov's reputation. Some Taganka actors rebelled by departing from the company, others showed their displeasure more underhandedly, through anti-Semitic behaviours, for example. Confident the Taganka actors would forget the past after a few successful productions, Efros began to work right away. He started with *The Lower Depths* (1984) by Maxim Gorky and Tennessee Williams's *A Lovely Sunday for a Picnic* (1985). In 1985, he led the company to the Belgrade International Theatre Festival, where *The Lower Depths* and a revival of *The Cherry Orchard* won the Grand Prize. In 1986, he directed a successful production of *The Misanthrope*. Efros seemed on his way to transforming the Taganka just as he had done with CCT, Lenkom and Malaya Bronnaya. Then, on 13 January 1987, he suffered a third, fatal, heart attack. His body was laid to rest in Novokuznetsk Cemetery on the eastern edge of Moscow. A pending production of *Hedda Gabler* remained unproduced.

EFROS IN PRACTICE

Thematic Modernity

Efros never sought to depict sociopolitical ideas direct from the stage as Bertolt Brecht did, nor did he engage in direct modernization of classic plays as Brecht also did. Nonetheless, his artistic vision was close to Brecht's because it was always focused on the present. This trait identifies Efros's principle of Thematic Modernity. Despite attempts at updating and context shifting, classics were then – and, one might add, still are – generally approached as story-telling dramas, with the portrayal of 'universal' human motives and actions being the only detectable purpose. By contrast, Efros explored how the core meanings of the classics could play out expressly in the present.

The first tour of Brecht's Berliner Ensemble to Moscow occurred in 1957, a year after his death. Russian audiences were perplexed by Brecht's non-realistic, non-psychological approach, but for Efros this approach was exciting in a new and unexpected way. His chief interest was in Brecht's ability to express the spirit of the present within the context of the past. He explored this line of thinking the very next year by directing Brecht's adaptation of the Joan-of-Arc story, *The Visions of Simone Machard*, at the Yermolova Theatre. A further stage of Efros's interest in this question occurred in 1964, when Yuri Lyubimov's production of Brecht's play, *The Good Person of Setzuan*, premiered at the Taganka Theatre.[26] Efros said of that experience:

> [The performance was] an absolutely special theatrical pleasure. [...] Earlier I thought that true aesthetic pleasure could be delivered to an

audience only through the subtlest psychological acting, but here they acted very roughly, representationally, at least if we were to judge it from the point of view of psychological acting. [...] I have read Brecht himself and read about him. And I saw the Berliner Ensemble [in Moscow in 1957], but perhaps for the first time Brecht 'reached' me. And, I believe, not only me.[27]

Brecht's aesthetic arose from the viewpoint of present-day *economics*, of course, while Efros's arose from present-day *psychology*. Thus, for him the Brechtian approach was exciting, but 'without sudden, deep, psychological illumination,' he said, 'without naturalness of feeling, without emotional fidelity to a role – even the most excellent acting can soon become tiresome'.[28] There was a personal issue at stake as well. 'At the Central Children's Theatre,' he said, 'it offended me when I was told my work was lovely, organic, pleasant directing. I always wanted to go for more sharpness.'[29] In this sharpness, Efros sought a correlation between Stanislavsky's psychological truth and Brecht's thematic modernity.[30]

Thematic modernity is innated in modern plays, but the question is not so simple in classic plays. Efros achieved his desired correlation by seeking out social implications not immediately obvious in classic plays, a search he accomplished with remarkable insight. In contrast to the traditional readings of *The Seagull, Romeo and Juliet, Othello* and *The Cherry Orchard*, for example, he perceived in them the implication that normal human life is dangerous if it is not perfectly aligned with a given social order. Consequently, he portrayed their protagonists as 'strangers in a strange land', so to speak, hunted down, excluded from society, even disposed of.[31] The implications for Soviet audiences were clear for those who chose to notice such things.

Exercises

Consider the question of thematic modernity from two viewpoints. First, by looking carefully at modernity in and of itself, sometimes referred to as the Zeitgeist or spirit of the times. Charles Baudelaire is credited with coining the term 'modernity' to designate the fleeting, ephemeral experience of life (especially in an urban metropolis) *and the inherent responsibility art has to capture that experience*. It stands to reason that mindfulness of modernity is no small matter for actors and directors. Second, by looking carefully at the traditional dramatic forms (comedy, tragedy, melodrama, tragicomedy, drama and farce), with the understanding that each form arose from and therefore implies a certain bond that transfers meaning between theatre and society.

1 Find historical and contemporary statements that attempt to explain modernity. Try to explain modernity in your own words.
2 Who are the essential figures and what are the essential material and non-material phenomena that express modernity?
3 What do you think the function of theatre should be in relation to modernity?
   a Theatre provides temporary relief from the pressures and distresses of modernity.
   b Theatre works to change the way modernity is viewed.
   c Theatre records and captures modernity.
   d Theatre beautifies the material aspects of modernity.
   e Theatre gives form and shape to modernity.
4 What are the traditional definitions of comedy, tragedy, melodrama, tragicomedy, drama and farce? Are these definitions in their accepted sense still effective today, or are they merely leftover literary-historical terms?
5 Select a classic play for study. What form does this play traditionally represent? In what way did that form reflect the society of its time? In its traditional form, is the play as effective today as when it was written?

How can a production of this play remain within its own framework while also taking into account modern living and thinking? How could a different form affect the play's meaning and conversely how could a different meaning affect the play's traditional form? What about the interpretation of the protagonist and antagonist? Does a modern protagonist always need to be sympathetic? An antagonist always unsympathetic?

Chronology of Efros's legacy in context

Two years after Efros's death, the Berlin Wall fell, communist regimes across Eastern Europe collapsed and in 1991 the USSR disbanded. In 1992, Moscow's Bakhrushin Theatre Museum organized an exhibition of his life and work. In 1993, the Russian Theatre Agency organized a conference in St Petersburg devoted to him. In 1994, the Russian Theatre Fund republished Efros's three books as a set, adding an assortment of his unpublished notes called *The Fourth Book* (*Chetvertaja Kniga*). Efros's standing continues to grow in this century. In 2000, forty-six actors, writers and critics contributed to *The Theatre of Anatoly Efros: Recollections and Articles* (*Teatr Anatolija Efrosa: vospominanija i stati*), and Vagrius Publishers re-issued selected passages from his books under the title *Anatoly Efros–Profession: Director* (*Anatolij Efros–Professija: Rezhissyor*). In the summer of 2005, Moscow television's Culture Channel observed the eightieth anniversary of his birth with a retrospective of his filmed plays, films, teleplays and a documentary of his life and work. English translations of his books were published in 2006, 2007 and 2009.[32] And in 2016, the Bakhrushin Theatre Museum presented a brand-new exhibition devoted to Efros's life and work.

11

Oleg Efremov: The Heir to Stanislavsky

Jesse Gardiner

Oleg Efremov was an actor's director who always put the actor at the centre of the production. In his view, the director's main objective was to facilitate the actor's art rather than to encumber it with stylized effects and devices. A disciple of the Stanislavsky System, Efremov believed in the superiority of theatrical realism over other styles of directing and subscribed to the Stanislavskian 'school of experiencing' (*shkola perezhivaniia*) according to which the actor creates the role anew for every performance. But like all followers of the System, Efremov interpreted it in his own way, emphasizing those elements that most suited his personal creative ethos and developing his own terminology and idiosyncratic practice. He encouraged his actors to reveal familiar emotional states in unexpected ways, evoking empathy in the auditorium and drawing each spectator into the creative process of the performance. Following Stanislavsky's (later) focus on physical action, he stressed the importance of breaking the role down into tasks and actions, and instructed his actors to recall personal experiences from their pasts in order to find the key to a truthful action. In terms of his broader world view, Efremov believed in the theatre's civic duty and strove to build a sense of unity between the ideals of the actor, director and writer in order to fulfil the social role required of the theatre by the public.

Biography

Oleg Nikolaevich Efremov was born in 1927 into a communal apartment off the famous Arbat Street in Moscow. During the Second World War, he moved with his parents to Vorkuta, inside the Arctic Circle, where his father was assigned to the managerial department of a forced labour camp (GULag). After returning to Moscow towards the end of the War, Efremov auditioned for the Moscow Art Theatre School Studio and was accepted as part of its 1945 cohort. It was here that Efremov became a devoted follower of the Stanislavsky System, which prioritizes truthful acting and the full incarnation of the role over stylization and cliché. The young Efremov and his classmates even signed an oath to Stanislavsky in their own blood! Efremov quickly made a name for himself as one of the more talented students at the MAT School Studio; however on graduating in 1948, Efremov, to his surprise, was not invited to join the main theatre troupe. Instead, he found work at the Moscow Central Children's Theatre which at that time had a particularly strong group of directors working for it, including Maria Knebel and Anatoly Efros. Efremov's first role at the Children's Theatre was the lead in Viktor Rozov's play *Her Friends* (1948). This was the start of a long and productive collaboration between Efremov and Rozov, who became known as one of the voices of the Thaw[1] generation and a breath of fresh air following the formulaic and didactic plays of the Stalinist era.

While pursuing his acting career at the Children's Theatre, Efremov was invited to return to the MAT School Studio to work as a junior teacher. It was through teaching at the School Studio that Efremov made his first steps as a director. In 1955, he staged Viktor Rozov's play *Good Luck* with a group of students at the School Studio. The success of this production led Efremov to set up a new theatre studio, under the auspices of the Moscow Art Theatre, with other recent graduates of the MAT School Studio. They decided to call the new studio the 'Sovremennik', meaning 'contemporary', signifying their desire to speak to a young, contemporary audience and revitalize the stagnant theatre scene. In April 1956, the Sovremennik Theatre Studio opened with a performance of Rozov's *Alive Forever* on a stage owned by the Moscow Art Theatre (see Figure 11.1). This was a watershed moment in Russian theatre – the Sovremennik was the first new theatre studio to open in Moscow for over twenty years.

Efremov wanted his new theatre studio to return to the true spirit of Stanislavsky and Nemirovich-Danchenko. He believed that the Moscow Art Theatre had lost its way as a result of its cosy relationship to the Soviet establishment and that artistic innovation and creativity had been sacrificed for the sake of political conformity. The Sovremennik Theatre Studio was set up to give a voice to the new post-war generation and to raise contemporary issues that concerned people in everyday life. This approach created problems for Efremov from the start: a number of his productions were banned by the Ministry of Culture for portraying Soviet society in too negative a light and the Sovremennik was threatened with closure. Throughout his career Efremov had a complicated relationship with the establishment. He joined the party immediately after Stalin died in 1953 and loosely identified with the Leninist school of thought which does

FIGURE 11.1 *Svetlana Mizeri and Oleg Efremov in* Alive Forever *at the Sovremennik Theatre Studio, 1956. Courtesy of the Moscow Sovremennik Theatre.*

not question the Revolution itself, only its perceived subversion afterwards under Stalin. In the 1960s and 1970s Efremov rose to a position of national prominence, winning many awards and enjoying a decent relationship with certain ministers, in particular Ekaterina Furtseva (Minister of Culture 1960–1974). In 1970 Furtseva invited Efremov to become the Chief Artistic Director of the Moscow Art Theatre.

By this point, the epicentre of the Moscow theatre scene had shifted and the young intelligentsia now flocked to the Sovremennik or the Taganka, rather than the Art Theatre. The famous home of Stanislavsky and Nemirovich-Danchenko was now a bloated, stagnating enterprise riven by internecine feuds and bureaucratic mismanagement. Efremov was determined to return the Moscow Art Theatre to its former glories and worked hard to change the culture within the troupe over the next fifteen years. However, he struggled to achieve meaningful reform in the face of opposition by the theatre's old guard. Eventually, he gave up trying to change the theatre as a whole and started to create a new troupe from within, inviting all those who shared his artistic vision to join him. In 1985 Mikhail Gorbachev was elected general secretary of the Communist Party and introduced the reforms of *perestroika* (restructuring) and *glasnost* (openness). Censorship ceased and theatres were able to stage plays that had been banned for over fifty years. Efremov seized the opportunity to push through his reforms and he split the Moscow Art Theatre into two troupes. Efremov took half the company to form the Chekhov Moscow Art Theatre based on Kamergerskii lane, while the other half, led by Tatiana Doronina, retained the name the Gorky Moscow Art Theatre and made its home just up the street on Tverskaia Boulevard.

Glasnost opened up new possibilities in terms of repertoire, but it also brought its own unique difficulties for Efremov, who for so long had found artistic purpose in exposing the hidden cracks in the regime. Now that everything was out in the open, Efremov and his generation were left feeling slightly redundant and directionless. The collapse of the Soviet Union saw Efremov return to the Russian classics, staging Chekhov's *The Cherry Orchard* (written in 1904) in 1989, Alexander Griboedov's *Woe from Wit* (1824) in 1992 and Alexander Pushkin's *Boris Godunov* (1825) in 1994. None of these productions was particularly successful, and a new generation of critics began to suggest that Efremov was on his way out. However, in 1997 he staged a production of Chekhov's *Three Sisters* at the Chekhov Moscow Art Theatre, completing a cycle of Chekhov productions that had begun with *Ivanov* in 1976. Efremov's *Three Sisters* was met with widespread acclaim in the press. The Soviet Union had disappeared but Russia was nevertheless still mired in economic difficulty and political corruption under the leadership of Boris Yeltsin. Efremov's directorial emphasis on the way life becomes trapped in cyclical repetitions resonated with spectators, many of whom saw their savings wiped out when the Russian Rouble defaulted a year later. Throughout his career, Efremov believed that the theatre had a duty to reveal life as it is and it was this sense of duty that concerned him in his final stage production, before he died in 2000 at the age of seventy-two.

Efremov's directorial technique

Following the teaching of Stanislavsky, Oleg Efremov saw the primary aim of any theatre production as the organic creation of 'the life of the human spirit of the role' (*zhizn chelovecheskogo dukha roli*).² Efremov believed that this was the very essence of theatre art, the guarantee of its vitality and the hardest type of art in general because it cannot be replaced by signs or semblances of truth.³ He claimed that the actor has one task: 'To live the life of a character on stage, to bring oneself to the feeling that "I am" (*Ia esm*) and that where there is truth, faith and "I am", inevitably there is genuine human **experiencing**' (*podlinnoe chelovecheskoe perezhivanie*).⁴ For the actor this means creating the role afresh during every performance, rather than falling back on rehearsed gestures, actions or stock methods of spoken delivery. The feeling of 'I am' requires the actor to be fully present in the moment of performance, to be open to moments of creative inspiration and to feel such a sense of kinship with the character that he or she is **transformed** (*perevoploshchennyi*) into it. Efremov believed that the authenticity of an actor's experiencing of the role defined the entire truthfulness of a theatre production. To ensure that a performance is sufficiently authentic, an actor should draw on his or her stock of lived experiences and impressions, psychological understanding, and world view.[5] This is often done through the use of what Stanislavsky called '**affective memory**' (*affektivnaia pamiat*), which is the ability to remember previous emotional states by recalling the physical sensations that accompanied them.

Like Stanislavsky, Efremov stressed the importance of being continuously aware of one's environment in order to add to one's supply of affective memories. He insisted that the work of the actor never ends; whether at home, on the bus, out with friends or at a restaurant, the actor should always maintain **awareness** (*vnimanie*) of what is going on around him or her in order to increase the store of memories at his or her disposal. Efremov extended this principle by encouraging his actors to go out into the world to gain real-life experience away from the stage. Often this would be related to a particular role or setting for a play: Efremov believed that one's own 'living impression' of real-life material is the stimulus to any creative work.[6] In preparation for a stage adaptation of Anatoly Kuznetsov's youth novel *Sequel to a Legend* (1958), Efremov took his troupe on a trip to the Siberian region in which the work is set in order to gather impressions and experience that the actors could draw on later. This is something that Stanislavsky also did with his actors at the Moscow Art Theatre, famously sending them to the Khitrov market in Moscow to study down-and-outs before staging Gorky's *The Lower Depths* (1902).

EFREMOV IN PRACTICE

Take your cast on a field trip to gain real-life experience that they can use to shape their performances. Arrange for your actors to shadow someone that shares the same profession as their character or to spend time observing a particular location or institution that features in your production to add to their stock of impressions and to increase the verisimilitude of the scene when performed.

Oleg Efremov remained an adherent of the Stanislavsky System throughout his career. Although he accepted the positive contribution made to theatre by those directors that adopted stylized forms and devices, such as Bertolt Brecht, he firmly believed that the 'school of experiencing' was the one true path in the theatre and was ill-disposed towards the 'school of **representation**' (*shkola predstavleniia*) in which the creation of the role happens only at rehearsal stage, after which the actor reproduces learned actions (verbal and physical) during the performance. Efremov appreciated directorial inventiveness and innovation, but he was sceptical of the use of device (*priem*) and cliché (*shtamp*) especially where these began to interfere with and overshadow the actor's truthful depiction of a character. He felt that stylized theatre lacked a meaningful connection with the audience and believed that it tried to make up for this through the use of dazzling spectacle and shocking devices. Instead, he insisted that a connection with the audience needs to be carefully constructed by the actors through **empathy** (*soperezhivanie*).

For Efremov, empathy meant taking an interest in the emotional reaction of the audience, an address to feeling, to the heart. He summed up this engagement with the audience as 'to the intellect via feeling' (*cherez chuvstvo k razumu*), which he argued was the true acting tradition of the Moscow Art Theatre.[7] Instead of a Brechtian appeal to the audience's rational thought via defamiliarization (*verfremdungseffekt*), Efremov believed in evoking the empathy of the audience so that the spectators would identify closely with the characters they watch on the stage. In this way, he argued, the spectator would be drawn into the creative process, able to affect the performance through his or her reaction and establish an interdependent link between actor and spectator, stage and auditorium, whereby each informs the other. One of Efremov's preferred techniques to steer actors away from cliché was to pronounce important lines in the script without any extra emphasis. He believed that deliberately embellishing significant moments oversimplified the performance and could create a false impression among the audience.[8] Delivering such lines in a prosaic fashion brought the performance closer to the patterns of real speech, he felt.

EFREMOV IN PRACTICE

When rehearsing significant moments in a play, encourage your actors to deliver their lines without any extra emphasis or embellishment. For example, if you were to take Hamlet's 'To be or not to be' soliloquy (*Hamlet* Act III, Scene I), the first line 'To be, or not to be, that is the question' should be delivered without heavy stress on any of the ictic syllables (be, not, be, is, quest-). This can help to avoid clichéd acting and enable the actor to find his or her own idiosyncratic method of delivery.

This mutual relationship between actor and spectator was rooted in what Efremov (via Stanislavsky) called the **'confessional'** (*ispovedalnyi*) principle. He considered this the most important quality of an actor: to express that which people experience but keep hidden in daily life. Efremov claimed that 'only the confessional principle in art enables the establishment of an electric arc between the actor and the auditorium, it is the essence of experiencing (*perezhivanie*), the essence of the Stanislavsky System'.[9] By tapping into the emotions and feelings that people keep locked away, the actor forms an emotional connection with the spectator that engages them in the performance. Of vital importance here, in Efremov's view, is the actor's own personal identity: he or she should know what it is they want to say to the audience when stepping out onto the stage. He observes: 'For me any actor is interesting to the extent that he can open himself up in confession. What do you want to say via the stage, what is your own personal theme?'[10] This personal theme or world view is what Stanislavsky described as the '**super-supertask**' (*sverkh-sverkhzadacha*). It is the perspective that conditions not only what the actor wants to convey to the audience but also the overriding goal of a production and indeed a theatre itself. Efremov saw the 'super-supertask' as the most important part of the Stanislavsky System because it provides the overall structure for everything else. The 'super-supertask' ties into a theatre's particular civic purpose and should be shared by all members of the collective.

Efremov believed that the director's role in a production is to provide the fertile space and conditions that facilitate the actors' creation of a truthful character. The actor is placed at the centre of the whole process, rather than being just one component of many to be manipulated by the director. He argued that 'the task of theatre is to investigate life through the actor – only the actor can penetrate the life of the human soul'.[11] To this end, he saw his role as training what he called '**actor-thinkers**' (*aktery-mysliteliia*) that are independent, creative focal points rather than elements of the director's grand vision. Undoubtedly, Efremov's long successful career as an actor influenced this outlook. He regularly acted major roles in his own productions and when trying to explain a point to an actor during rehearsal, he would often step into the role himself to show how he thought it should be played. Efremov believed that it was vital to give the actors space to express themselves and to feel in control of the mise-en-scène rather than feel subordinated to the director's arrangement of stylistic effects and devices.

Efremov often used Stanislavsky's distinction between a '**director of result**' (*rezhissyora rezultata*) and a '**director of root**' (*rezhissyora korniia*) to emphasize what he saw as the correct method followed by directors at the Moscow Art Theatre. A 'director of root', in Efremov's view, is one that develops the actor during the staging of a play, helping to reveal his or her individuality and ensuring that he or she relies on direct experiences of life to create the role. The director should be able to bring the actors with him in the creative process and 'unnoticeably nudge their creative searches onto the true path'.[12] It was very important for Efremov that the director's contribution should not become too forceful. His practice in rehearsal was to provide a general roadmap for the actors but to refrain from imposing strong ideas at the start. Only when the rehearsals had progressed significantly and the actors had been given the space to find their own interpretations of a role would he begin to reveal specific ideas and suggestions that they could adopt and bring into their work.

In Efremov's practice, the primary building block of the theatre is **action** (*deistvie*). Whereas the artist expresses his ideas through colours and lines and the musician through sounds, actors express themselves via action, he argued.[13] In his methodology, Efremov drew on Stanislavsky's **'method of physical actions'** (*metod fizicheskikh deistvii*), a technique developed towards the end of Stanislavsky's life in which the actor devises a sequence of physical actions that fit the **given circumstances** (*predlagaemye obstoiatelstva*) of the role. These physical actions are in turn linked to psychological feelings creating a 'unity of psychology and physiology'.[14] An action is the means by which an actor fulfils a particular **task** (*zadacha*) posed to his or her character by the play. For example, a task could be to obtain permission, to gain trust or to persuade someone to do something. These actions can then be linked together into what Stanislavsky called the **'through-line of action'** (*skvoznoe deistvie*) which unites all the different actions completed by the actor throughout the play.

Each individual actor has a 'through-line of action' that regulates his or her performance and there is also one for the play as a whole. By following the 'through-line of action', the actor is able to complete his or her **supertask** (*sverkhzadacha*), the sum of all the tasks they are set in the play, for example, Konstantin Treplev's supertask in Anton Chekhov's *The Seagull* could be to feel respected and loved. Efremov often used the term 'line of outer life' (*liniia vneshnei zhizni*) interchangeably with the 'through-line of action'. Explaining his method in conversation with the playwright Viktor Rozov, he noted: 'The most important thing in the theatre is to appropriately construct the line of outer life, specifically to carry out all the concrete tasks, hiding and preserving one's true inner emotional experience (*perezhivanie*), which is brought to the surface at any moment, possibly during a pause.'[15] The idea is that by carefully sequencing the outer actions necessary to fulfil the different tasks the actor creates the mechanism through which inner emotion and feeling can express itself at any moment.

One of the key techniques that Efremov used to help actors work out the correct action for each scene was the **etude**. In the System, etudes are improvised scenes performed by actors without recourse to the script. Etudes enable the actors to practise different variations of a scene, sometimes with dialogue and sometimes without, in order to work out the significant elements of a particular interaction. In Efremov's method, he conducted what he called **'evidence-etudes'** (*etiudy-dokazatelstva*), that is, etudes to discover evidence or information. These 'evidence-etudes' were used to help the actors work out the important tasks and motivations underlying a particular scene. When explaining how these etudes work, Efremov used the example of an actor being unable to carry out the relatively simple action of 'a meeting'. In this case, the director and actors would devise a number of different scenarios and circumstances related to the idea of 'a meeting' until the actor can find something in his or her memory that he or she can use as inspiration.[16] By running a number of different 'evidence-etudes' around the theme, the actor is given time to dig up something useful from his or her store of affective memories. Efremov felt that etudes should not be the starting point of a rehearsal, nor should the use of them become an end in itself. Rather they should be used in a targeted fashion whenever actors become stuck with a particular scene in order to clarify the fundamental tasks and actions therein.

EFREMOV IN PRACTICE

When rehearsing a difficult scene, ask each actor to break down their role into basic tasks and the actions required to fulfil them. Then get them to improvise an etude based on these actions without using any dialogue. As they do so, ask the actors to connect the actions they are performing with similar personal memories. For example, if the action is 'refusing a request', ask the actor to recall an occasion when they refused something in order to find the related emotional state. Once they have done this, repeat the etude but this time allow the actors to use their own improvised dialogue. Finally, you should return to rehearsing the scene with the script.

Etudes are useful ways of discovering the conflicts that underpin a scene, the point where an action meets a counteraction. The question 'where is the fundamental conflict?' became almost a catchphrase in Efremov's rehearsals. He would insist that a character can only become a living person when he or she embodies a specific conflict – this is the point at which he or she engages the spectator in empathy.[17] In 1976, Efremov staged a production of Chekhov's *Ivanov* at the Moscow Art Theatre. The role of Ivanov was played by Innokenty Smoktunovsky. Ivanov is a local government official who becomes caught up in a spiral of debt and infidelity until he finally commits suicide. Early on in rehearsals, Smoktunovsky struggled to achieve the right tone in his portrayal of the character. Efremov's advice was to avoid sweeping, broad-brush emotions and to focus instead on the internal conflicts gripping the character, in other words, rather than think of the character in terms of all-encompassing emotions such as 'depression' or 'paralysis', to focus on conflicts such as that between Ivanov's concern for his wife's condition and unwillingness/inability to pay for a trip to the Crimea to treat her illness, due to his debts.[18] This enabled Smoktunovsky to break the part down and find the key to enable a convincing performance. Another technique that Efremov used effectively in the rehearsals for *Ivanov* was to ask each actor to devise biographies for their character, extending before and after the given circumstances of the play text. By thinking up detailed biographies the actors could create a fuller, subtler character that seemed authentic to them, making the process of transformation into the role easier.

The essence of Efremov's directorial practice is to enable the actor to create a living person on the stage who invokes the empathy of the audience because of his or her truthful and confessional quality – it reveals to the spectator a feeling or emotional state that he or she recognizes but usually keeps hidden. Efremov used the term **'familiar surprises'** (*znakomye neozhidannosti*) to define this process. He argued that 'what is new in art is not something invented or unknown – it is that which is known to everyone, but which is found again through art'.[19] In his view, the art of the theatre is to surprise the spectator with that which he or she already knows; to convey this truth to the spectator in an unexpected or novel way. Efremov believed that in order to do this the actor must avoid all clichés, stock gestures and ready-made devices. The actor should also free himself or herself from any desire for success on the stage, otherwise they will play for applause and adulation rather than to create the necessary lifelike effect.

Efremov encouraged his actors to open themselves up to chance and contingency in rehearsals, to search for new innovative ways of performing the role, asking the question: And what if we do it the other way? What will emerge then? He called this practice **'reverse motion'** (*obratnyi khod*) and saw it as a vital means to combat cliché and to help the actors discover 'familiar surprises'.[20] In 1971 Efremov staged Maxim Gorky's *The Last Ones* at the Moscow Art Theatre, in one of his first productions as Chief Artistic Director, and he employed the technique of 'reverse motion' during rehearsals. He asked the actors to deliberately exaggerate their performance in scenes that were particularly sensitive or emotional, almost to the point of parody.[21] By getting the actors to explore different levels of emotion and degrees of sincerity, he was able to focus them back onto which feelings were genuine and which were false or clichéd.

EFREMOV IN PRACTICE

When rehearsing a particularly tense or emotional scene, ask the actors to play the scene as it is and then to repeat it, but this time in an overly exaggerated manner to the point of parody. For example, if the scene is 'saying a tearful goodbye', the actor might overplay their emotions, become hysterical, use extreme gestures or become overly physical with the person to whom they are bidding farewell. Returning back to the scene later, the actors should be able to better distinguish authentic emotion from exaggeration and cliché.

When Efremov set up the Sovremennik theatre studio in 1956 it was with the aim of restoring the artistic legacy of Stanislavsky and Nemirovich-Danchenko. But although the acting methodology followed by Efremov's collective was realist, in terms of set design the Sovremennik broke with the naturalistic tradition of the Art Theatre. Instead of painted backdrops and three-walled box sets, Efremov took a minimalist approach to design that stripped the stage down to basic items of furniture and stage flats, while creating the sense of specific locations primarily through lighting (see Figure 11.2). Efremov called this approach the '**spot-lights method**' (*metod svetovykh piaten*) because the acting space is delineated by lighting rather than walls, ceilings and doors.[22] Although this approach was partly a way of saving money in the early days of the studio, the 'spot-lights method' went on to become part of the Sovremennik's signature aesthetic and remained in use long after it had made the jump from studio to fully fledged theatre. Efremov argued that this type of design was important because it focused attention on the actors rather than the spaces they inhabited. By removing unnecessary detail on the set, the audience's attention would remain on the actors and the subtleties of their performance would be better perceived. It was a type of stage design that Efremov continued to use in his work at the Moscow Art Theatre, often in collaboration with the designer David Borovsky. In their 1976 production of *Ivanov*, Borovsky stripped the stage down to a wide-open space which emphasized Ivanov's isolation and loneliness. That is not to say, however, that Efremov did not also use naturalistic designs on the stage. He was a strong advocate of flexibility in terms of production style: the design and form should fit the demands of the particular play, rather than be applied rigidly in all contexts.

EFREMOV IN PRACTICE

During rehearsals why not experiment with a minimalist stage set-up by opening up the stage space and removing partition walls. Try stripping the set down to the minimum number of props and items of furniture necessary for the plot to function and use lighting spots to demarcate specific rooms or interior spaces. Doors can be indicated by self-standing door frames. The aim is to keep the attention focused on the actors rather than the detail around them.

As a young director, Efremov wanted to implement Stanislavsky's idea of the '**theatre house**' (*teatralnyi dom*) in which the actors would live and

FIGURE 11.2 Five Evenings *by Aleksandr Volodin at the Sovremennik Theatre Studio, 1959. Courtesy of the Moscow Sovremennik Theatre.*

eat together as a collective, making joint decisions on the selection of the repertoire and sharing responsibility for all the activities of the theatre. Although this proved hard to implement in practice, the idea of a theatre as a company of like-minded people, fully invested in a shared project remained central to Efremov's ethos as a director throughout his life. He saw the ensemble principle in theatre as vital: actors, directors and artists should speak in the same artistic language and pursue the same creative goals. When working on a production, Efremov believed in the importance of debate and discussion to ensure that the cast was moving together in the same direction. He would ask the actors to discuss the different supertasks of each character, before deciding on the overall supertask of the play. Efremov saw this as a crucial early stage in the rehearsal process to ensure that all the supertasks fitted into an overall scheme. As such, Efremov continuously strove to find a balance between giving actors the space to express their own individual creativity and ensuring that each personality was working in unison for the benefit of the ensemble. By being united in a shared goal (the super-supertask) a theatre collective could fulfil its social role to educate and inform. Efremov believed strongly that the theatre is a place of learning – not in a crude, didactic sense, but rather as a space that 'nurtures the possibility of self-education in people'.[23]

EFREMOV IN PRACTICE

Before starting to rehearse with the script, hold a round-table meeting and ask each member of the cast to break down their role into a series of separate tasks and write them down in a list. Discuss these tasks together and agree on an overall supertask for each character. Then join these supertasks together and ask the group to decide on one supertask that defines the play as a whole. The actors should keep both supertasks (individual and general) in mind when rehearsing and performing.

12

Interviews with Genrietta Ianovskaia

Manon van de Water

Genrietta Naumovna Ianovskaia[1] was born on 24 June 1940 in Leningrad (now St Petersburg) and studied with the director and teacher Georgy Tovstonogov as the only woman in a class of nine. Ianovskaia is relatively unknown outside Russia, and hardly anything has been published about her work and methods in English. As one of the very few female directors who gained notoriety after *glasnost* and *perestroika*, bringing the Moscow Tiuz, known in English as the Moscow New Generation Theatre, to the forefront of avant-garde theatre in Moscow, her place in this book is entirely deserved. This chapter relies mostly on original interviews with Ianovskaia as well as interviews published in Russian, and will illustrate her theatrical methods and philosophy which are interspersed throughout this chapter.

One of Ianovskaia's peers in Tovstonogov's course was Kama Ginkas, whom she married in 1964; they graduated in 1967. As will be illustrated here, they are a unique artistic pair, each with their own style and yet feeding off and inspiring each other.[2] Both Jewish and outspoken they were outcasts from the start in Soviet theatrical life.[3] As such, it was hard for them to be permanently connected to one theatre and find work in the cultural capitals of Moscow and Leningrad, since artistic directors were state appointed. Ianovskaia found a way in through the *tiuzes*, the theatres for the young spectator, albeit in the provinces.[4] Two years after graduation, Ianovskaia was appointed artistic director of the Krasnoyarsk Tiuz, the Krasnoyarsk Theatre of the Young Spectator, where she staged among others William Gibson's *The Miracle Worker* (1970) and Molière's *The Impostures of Scapin* (1971). It was a difficult time. On the one hand, Ianovskaia and

Ginkas finally had the freedom to more or less direct what they wanted. On the other hand, they lived under tough circumstances on the Yenisei river in Siberia, thousands of kilometres from the cultural capitals of Moscow and Leningrad. They rehearsed mornings and evenings, and if they had evening performances, they rehearsed after the performances were over. During breaks they ate and continued rehearsals and conversations. After rehearsals, they returned home through the frozen city and talked about the rehearsals. When actors showed up from the dormitory, Genrietta made tea and they continued talking and rehearsing. 'It was a Theatre. A Studio. All together in one', reminisces Ginkas.[5]

They returned to Leningrad in 1973. They staged a few productions but mostly they rehearsed scenes in their home with actors who were either unhappy with their directors or simply wanted to work with Ianovskaia and Ginkas. Ianovskaia and Ginkas considered them 'good workouts'.[6] They practised the lessons that they had learned from Tovstonogov.

IANOVSKAIA IN PRACTICE

Lessons from Tovstonogov[7]

Tovstonogov as directing teacher influenced many aspects of the directing techniques of Ianovskaia and Ginkas, although all three directors have their unique and specific style. The following are some lessons on directing Ianovskaia mentions in several interviews.[8]

1. You should build productions on blocks of action. Words do not tell the story of the play, actions do. This construction of actions in the play is the backbone of the entire production. Therefore start with finding these blocks of action in the play.

2. The director has a professional responsibility both to her actors and to her public. Never yell, but choose your comments wisely. A director must know her work, must realize that she is working with living material. If she does not, she leaves behind a generation of wounded actors who do not dare to enter the stage, caused by the ignorance of the director. The director owes the same responsibility and professionalism to the audience.[9]

3. Tovstonogov once said that it is always the director's fault: if you take an actor and he acts badly, it is your fault: either you did not teach him, or you did not take him off the part, or you did not mislead the spectator by covering for the artist .... That is a real director.[10]

The years of waiting did not embitter Ianovskaia and Ginkas. They hated Soviet life but they did not struggle with it; they simply ignored it. They believed in themselves, in their talent; they let their ideas and imagination flow freely and they waited. Ianovskaia remarks:

> Maybe if we would have been each alone, we would not have been able to bear it. But as it is ... each lived through the production of the other ... In the moments that he was dying, I just started to rage, to swear, to force him to do something. He wrote dramatizations, started to learn French, which he did not need at all, walked the dog ... When Kama understood that my end was in sight, he pulled me out. We created performances at home, built the scenery in our imaginations, just talked about theatre.[11]

Daniil Gink, their son, born in 1969, states it as follows: 'My parents were poor and in disfavour and I had to sleep in a suitcase.'[12]

In 1984 they moved to Moscow. Here Ianovskaia directed a production at the Mossovet Theatre in 1984 and at the Mayakovsky Theatre in 1987. In the same year, she was appointed Artistic Director of the Moscow Tiuz, where she already worked as a guest director, a move only made possible by *glasnost* and *perestroika*.[13] At the Moscow Tiuz, or as it is now known in English, the Moscow New Generation Theatre, her career took off.[14] It was not, however, without controversy.

Glasnost and *perestroika* had brought to the fore that theatre for children and youth by the end of the Soviet Union was in a terrible state. The repertory was stilted, the average age of the actor was forty-three and the mandatory ideological messages reinforced by the pedagogical sections of the *tiuzes* during compulsory field trips had given the once famous theatre for children and youth in Soviet Russia a negative image that was hard to overcome. It was not only the *tiuzes* fighting for their identity; all theatres were in limbo. If there was no ideology to adhere to, or to subvert through theatre semiotics, then what was the point? Many theatres needed to change direction and which direction to take was not immediately clear. The *tiuzes* in particular, as official ideological instruments of the regime to educate and acculturate the new Soviet citizen, had their feet swept from underneath them.[15]

The world of theatre for children and young people was aghast with the appointment of Ianovskaia as artistic director of the Moscow Tiuz. She was accused of not belonging in a theatre for children and youth, not caring about children or youth at all. In *Shto eto bylo? (What Was That?)* Ianovskaia explains her position thirty years later. What is most interesting about this is that her ideas are at the heart of theatre for children and youth as it is now mostly envisioned in the twenty-first century worldwide:[16]

> I do not understand what that is, 'children's theatre'. There is only one theatre – human ... I am very scared about what is going on in the mass media today. I am afraid of the invasion of cruelty. Therefore, I feel the

urgent need to stage plays for the youngest children. I am convinced that theatre should never scare children. That doesn't mean that you cannot talk with them about dramatic issues. It doesn't mean that you should never talk about serious things.[17]

In answer to whether *Dog's Heart*, her first production at the Moscow Tiuz, was an unusual choice for a *tiuz*, she says:

Who said that productions for youth only have to talk about school problems? .... The books that are mostly read [by youth 14–16 years old] are those that, in our perception, should be interesting to people of twenty and older. I believe that a statistically average 'young' spectator does not exist. With every spectator, from any age group, you always have to talk in the language of truth. That means the language of great literature.[18]

Among Ianovskaia's supporters were the people who considered her a gifted director who finally got a chance to put her talents to use and train her own company. Among her adversaries were those who saw her as an opportunist who would do anything to get a permanent position in Moscow. Letters for and against Ianovskaia were sent to the Ministry of Culture, even before she was appointed artistic director.

The productions described below, each from a different decade, illustrate Ianovskaia's directing methods.

In 1986 Ianovskaia started to rehearse *Dog's Heart*, an adaptation from the novel of the same name by Mikhail Bulgakov – a novel that was at that time still censored. *Dog's Heart* had a favourable albeit tumultuous reception and instantly made the theatre famous both nationally and abroad. Unquestionably, the production of this play adapted from Bulgakov was politically and ideologically charged. The playwright and novelist was a hero of the 1920s. His work was immensely popular but so controversial that it was all classified as forbidden by 1930. During the post-Stalin Thaw period, part of his work was finally published, but in limited editions, most of which disappeared directly into the black market. *Dog's Heart* was only published in Paris (in Russian – the '*Tamizdat*' – 'over-there-publishing') and was simply ignored in Russian anthologies, bibliographies and other writings about Bulgakov and his work.

The adaptation of *Dog's Heart* by A. Chervinskii quite religiously follows the novel.[19] Chervinskii basically took the dialogue and put it together in play format, a task that was facilitated by the original author, whose playwriting skills permeate the novel. Professor Preobrazhensky (a name derived from the Russian word for 'transformation') lives in a seven-room apartment (a luxury just after the Revolution), where he continues his sophisticated pre-revolutionary lifestyle and experiments with rejuvenation through brain transplantation. While the new house committee is after

Preobrazhensky's rooms, the professor picks up a dog from the street, has his assistant deliver a fresh corpse and transplants the hypophysis (the pituitary gland) of the deceased, an alcoholic and petty criminal, into the dog. The dog loses his tail, starts to talk and becomes human, taking the name of Poligraph Poligraphovich Sharikov (Sharik, 'ball', is the most common name for a dog in Russian). Unfortunately the 'new human being' turns into the most degenerate of proletarians: swearing, drinking, stalking women and eventually even denouncing the professor – his creator. When Sharikov points a gun at the professor, it is clear that the situation is out of control. The professor performs a counter-operation, and the investigators who come to search his house only find a barely talking dog, by the name of Sharikov.

The ideological metaphor of the play is easily seen. Sharikov stands for the proletariat, who used to live a dog's life but received a new identity through the operation – in effect, the Revolution. This turns the professor into Lenin, who takes nature into his own hands by promoting dog to human without realizing the consequences. In the light of *glasnost* and *perestroika* the play became as political and topical as can be, raising the question of responsibility: who is responsible, the professor-Lenin or Sharikov-proletariat?

Ianovskaia leaves the text intact, but sharpens the topicality and the attack on the old ideology by adding several theatrical features. *Dog's Heart*, like her later productions at the Moscow Tiuz, illustrates how she works with the designer.

IANOVSKAIA IN PRACTICE

Designer–director collaboration

For the vast majority of her productions except the productions for children, Ianovskaia works with designer Sergei Barkhin. Barkhin is a scenographer, which means that he does not only design the set but is, with the director, responsible for the production image as a whole, including set, costumes, lights and sounds. Barkhin does not merely interpret the ideas of the director but he responds with his own thoughts and impressions. This means an 'action reaction' between the designer and the director, a kind of dialectical relationship which ultimately results in synthesis. For example, in *Dog's Heart* Ianovskaia explained her concept and Barkhin said, 'I want to do Egypt.' This is not obvious and here the interplay with an imaginative director starts.

In this case the director responds, 'I wanted to do *Aïda*.' And that is when things begin to run on parallel tracks. *Aïda* and Egypt.[20]

> Figure 12.1 shows how this dialogue played out in the aesthetics of the production. Sharikov is surrounded by a chorus of four Egyptians. *Aïda* plays. Sharik Sharikov is ecstatic. He tries to imitate the Egyptians. The Egyptians are on a higher plane he will never be able to reach. Throughout the production we find this juxtaposition between Egypt, permeating the apartment of Preobrazhensky through his love for *Aïda*, and the proletarian life outside that Sharik Sharikov starts to embrace.
>
> Often the director's work is characterized as a collaboration between the director and the designers who are specialized in one aspect of the stage picture. I encourage young directors to find someone to collaborate with and try the dialectical method above, to see what comes out of this. It is a very good practice exercise.

In *Dog's Heart*, it also becomes clear where Ianovskaia differs from Tovstonogov's methods. Tovstonogov did not believe that it was necessary to have his own voice heard in a production. Starting with *Dog's Heart*, and very likely before that, Ianovskaia's stylized productions, her sharp expressive stage pictures, her penchant to insert poetry, characters or

FIGURE 12.1 Dog's Heart, *1987. Photo credit unknown. From the archive of the Moscow Tiuz.*

related texts or images into her production only to deepen its impact make her productions, in Laurence Senelick's words, 'tough and outspoken'.[21]

The following describes some stage pictures of *Dog's Heart*, which of course, as in the example exercise above, she arrived at in dialogue with Sergei Barkhin. It needs to be emphasized that Ianovskaia's productions can never be characterized as literal illustrations of a play text, they are always embellished with her imagination, based on the association of images that the text, or the context, or the conceptual idea, evokes.

The stage is covered with black pieces of paper, a metaphor from Bulgakov's novel *Teatralnyi roman* (translated as *Black Snow*) in which he writes that the Revolution altered everything so rigorously that even the snow turned black. The discrepancy between the professor's and the proletarian world is emphasized by contrasting the proletarian songs of the house committee with visual images of an Egyptian chorus from *Aïda* by Verdi. The professor is regularly visited by three 'uniformed' characters, the KGB, who are 'here to save you from importunate visitors' (for example, a Western imperialist offering to finance the professor's experiments), an image coming from the novel *Rokovye iaitsa* (*Fatal Eggs*) by Bulgakov. One of them hears the professor criticize Soviet society without interrupting him – a cynical comment on the unpredictability of action and consequences at the beginning of *Glasnost*.[22]

Ianovskaia's production of *Dog's Heart* did not end the internal discord in the Moscow Tiuz. In 1987 the Ministry of Culture had finally made up its mind about appointing Ianovskaia, handing her the power to act and decide in the capacity of artistic director. This led to a letter of protest signed by twenty-seven actors whose main concerns were the neglect of the children and the renunciation of their mission as a *tiuz*. Ianovskaia's loyal followers immediately protested the protest. A consensus was hard to achieve and the turmoil lasted for years. Ultimately, about half of the company left.

IANOVSKAIA IN PRACTICE

Finding metaphors

Ianovskaia always has something to say with her productions, and they are always contextualized, commenting on the past while linking to the present. She does this through images and metaphors that often hark back to one single overarching metaphor or question. In *Dog's Heart* this is a question about responsibility; in her following production, *Nightingale* (1988) it is the representation of past-present-future.

Pick a play or a play text that speaks to you.

Try to articulate why it speaks to you. Translate this into image(s) rather than words.

> Go back to the notion that a production is built on actions. What are these actions and how do they relate to the images you found?
> Is there a central image? Something that stands out?
> What does this central image convey? To you? To a potential audience?
> How do the other images fit into this?
> How does this lead to the overall tone of the production?
> Once you have this figured out for yourself you can start the dialogue with the scenographer/designers (see exercise above) and the preparation for the rehearsal process (see below).

Ianovskaia has changed her methods over the years. In her earlier work, she had everything thought out beforehand, every move, gesture, facial expression, tone. Now, she knows the direction of the scene, the overall production, she knows how it needs to sound, the overall tone. She spends a lot of time analysing the play. For her the most important things are the actions, not the words. This focus on actions is the main lead to alternative interpretations: 'Those who have eyes will see, those who have ears will hear', meaning that the tone of a word or sentence and the accompanying action gives the clue to interpretation, not the literal meaning of the words. This becomes very clear when you see one of Ianovskaia's productions: for example, *Goodbai Amerika!* which is a parody of a parody poem, *Mister Twister*, by Samuiil Marshak, originally written in 1933 and revised in 1952.[23]

Although Ianovskaia knows what she is after, she will not tell the actors. Instead she works very closely with them to *discover* the play. Her actors need to understand every move. Each actor is different and requires a different approach. But for each role Ianovskaia tries to find something absolutely unexpected, something the actor would not have thought of and cannot make up and she spends a lot of time on that. The actor needs an inner feeling, something that makes them act not like everyone else acted this piece, not cliché, but some other way. She wants to find the seed for the actor. The way she tries to get to this is through table reads with the actors.

IANOVSKAIA IN PRACTICE

Table reads

Ianovskaia typically holds very long 'table reads'. The actors are not allowed to play during these reads, only read. They take the scenes apart one by one: what happens, what is going on in the scene. Ianovskaia looks for the action verbs, for what she considers at the heart of the director's artistry. These analyses often turn into conversations, where it suddenly may jump out to the actor what she is after. Together they think, they talk, they search and at times the actors, especially those who worked with her before, ask her 'why don't you tell us! You already know!' But Ianovskaia considers it absolutely essential that *they* find it, while at the same time she finds it equally essential that she, the director, finds it for each role, because 'I know it is hidden somewhere, I know it is somewhere'.[24]

To find the unexpected is a starting point for Ianovskaia in her directing, even if the spectator, used as they are to the clichés from past productions, may not agree. Her main way of getting to this is asking questions and discussing actions.

Rather than relying solely on a rational analysis of the play, try to explore with your actors to 'find the unexpected'. What is happening? Why? What is the character doing? What are the contradictions? Why? What else?

The above is clear in her production of Ostrovsky's *The Storm* (1997), where she subverts the traditional interpretation, through action, theatrical devices, and in this case the insertion of a mute character. Ostrovsky's *The Storm*, a metaphor in and of itself of a threatening thunderstorm, plays in the world of the nineteenth-century merchant class. The young Katerina is married to Tikhon and lives in the house of the dominant Marfa Kabanova, Tikhon's mother. When Tikhon is away, she falls in love in with Boris, the visiting nephew of a rich merchant. Unable to deal with her feelings she drowns herself when Boris leaves. The revisionist production focuses less on Katerina's doomed love than on the atmosphere that facilitated her tragedy, as the title in fact indicates. Ianovskaia, with designer Sergei Barkhin, creates a place where, in the words of John Freedman, 'dreams collide with brute force', a world in which 'intellect, gentleness and insanity go hand in hand, and crude intimidation is the keeper of order'.[25]

This was the second attempt by Ianovskaia to stage the production. On the first try she could not get the casting right, nor the location of the play. 'I wanted to stage the production in a warehouse or an abandoned factory', she said.[26] The current production takes place in the theatre, but it might as well be a factory or warehouse. The stage and auditorium are backstage, behind a brick wall. Stage and audience, eighty people at most, are divided by a tin trough set into real dirt over the entire width of the stage: the river Volga. A rain machine hangs high up in the flies. Scaffolding on the sides and back have thunder sheets which are operated by the 'storm men' who watch the play unfold, change the props and deliver silent commentary. Russian nesting dolls and other 'folk' ornaments are scattered around. Among the thirty-five productions of Ostrovsky's plays at the time of the premiere,[27] this production stands out, because of both its unusual interpretation and its highly theatrical and suggestive set.

The production is filled with signifiers, or, as Davydova puts it, 'everything breathes meaning'.[28] Thus, the 'Russian' costumes Ostrovsky indicates in his play acquire in this production a slightly Soviet look. The closed, vertical set – where even high up in the flies there seems no way out, and where the river Volga is set off by two mirror doors stage right and left, one of which eventually leads Katerina to her grave – gives the impression that the play unfolds in a large *Kommunalka* (Soviet communal apartment) rather than a small village.[29] These signifiers and their inevitable varied interpretation and perception cause the most 'controversy' in the many, predominantly favourable, reviews (Figure 12.2).

With *The Storm* Ianovskaia created once again a production that was critically acclaimed, yet also a source of ideological debate. Does Ianovskaia in *The Storm* 'debunk' national myths by focusing on the archetypes of 'our' national consciousness?[30] Or is she presenting the classic play free from the 'nauseating' traditional Soviet teachings?[31] Does Ianovskaia challenge the Soviet notion of Katerina as 'a ray of light in the dark tsardom'[32] or does she highlight it by her interpretation of Katerina as innocent, pure, without 'protesting pathos, or poetic musings'?[33] As she has done in previous productions, Ianovskaia evokes with this production a debate that has its roots in preconceptions and assumptions. She challenges preconceived notions through theatrical signs and signifiers, offering a simultaneously highly intellectual and highly emotional production. It is the cultural-based context that supplies the meaning in this production, at least for the (Soviet) Russian audience. Ianovskaia attacks the revolutionary legends of her youth; in *The Storm* she challenges the Soviet textbook interpretation of the play. Minaev remarks that Ianovskaia's production is not so much the play *The Storm* as a critical paper on the play.[34] Despite all this, though, the production won several awards and was praised for its artistic merits: Ianovskaia received the 'Crystal Turandot' and 'The Seagull' awards for best director of the season. The actress Iuliia Svezhakova was awarded the 'Crystal Turandot' for best debut as Katerina, and the '*Komsomolskaia Pravda*' award for best dramatic role of the season. Era Ziganshina received the Stanislavsky award for her role as Kabanova. *The Storm* was one of the highlights of the Golden Mask Awards of 1998, for which it received nominations in four categories (but surprisingly did not win in any).

Ianovskaia's productions are undeniably 'director's theatre'. Among the reviews of her production there are always some remarks on the sometimes overbearing presence of the director's hand. Iuliia Svezhakova comments on her success as Katerina in *The Storm*: 'My success in the role of Katerina is completely her [Ianovskaia's] achievement. When they ask me: who is your [Katerina]? I answer: it's Genrietta Ianovskaia.'[35]

FIGURE 12.2 The Storm, *1997. Katerina, just before she drowns herself. Photo credit unknown. From the archive of the Moscow Tiuz.*

IANOVSKAIA IN PRACTICE

Rehearsal process

It does not matter to Ianovskaia whether she works with young or seasoned actors. She works equally seriously with all, using different ways. She trusts her actors and has a very clear head about the extent of her role as a director: 'A time comes when the actor must get inside the role and the director must get out of the show.'[36]

Rehearsals are to work with the artists You cannot convey these things by words. You can only convey your ideas by means of rehearsal, through the tone, the gesture, the glance, the joke, the silence. This reveals the genre, which Tovstonogov considered as the perspective formed between the surface of real life and the author's view. Chekhov is an author, and the director is an author. Therefore that perspective, the feel of the genre, has to be present from the start in the way the rehearsals are conducted. Ianovskaia adds:

> I like it most when they laugh during rehearsals. Quite often, from the very beginning, it looks like we are just wasting time during rehearsals, I chat with them, we are talking about this and that – that they are laying tiles in the streets, whatever. Because I really care that the actors feel liberated. They have to understand that they can do anything stupid. I love it when they ask any type of question: stupid or complex. Any. I love questions. Because it means there is a little impasse. And the actor needs to absolutely know that little impasse to come to life.
>
> Once a director who staged a show for us came and complained that the actors were misbehaving. That they asked futile questions on purpose. 'Look, I said to her, go turn off the light, and she asked me why?' So I [Ianosvskaia] asked him 'Why? Because she wants to create secret atmosphere at home, or because her eyes hurt, or because someone is coming and she wants to look pretty in the dimmed light?' There is an enormous variety of possibilities why she wants to turn off the light. And the artist needs to understand, he is not a log who is just going to turn off the light. If the actor asks me something I am happy, and we are trying to find out together why. We try to clear it up and we find out why ... I am trained internally to explain every move. The actors need to know every movement from A to Z and Why. With the help of a very clear consciousness we are trying to call up the subconscious. That means we analyse what that is and consciously build a line to call it up. You understand, that is a superior rehearsal. It succeeds very rarely. If you see that it does not work for an artist you start changing it again and talk about whatever comes into mind, you fish, you think about devices on how to cover that what he cannot do, offer him to find other ways. I always tell the actors that a production is not a composition of scenes. A production is a monologue of a group of people. I and you. It is our joint monologue. Therefore, before they enter their scene they listen to the scene before, to get into this monologue in the rhythm that they either have to break or continue.[37]

This long anecdote is at the same time an exercise for the director. Do you work with your actors or do you dictate? Do you treat them as human beings or your clay? There is a philosophical difference in these approaches that influences the way you make the productions. Ianovskaia employs both methods: she knows what she wants but she wants it from the actors.

Take some small scenes and see if you can work with your actors in a similar way, having done the preparation in the exercises above. Talk with them, let them explore, ask why and see what comes to the surface.

Despite the success with theatre for young and older adults the Moscow Tiuz keeps staging productions for children on a regular basis, directed by Ianovskaia, guest artists and, on occasion, Kama Ginkas. They take their audience very seriously, as taught by their teacher Tovstonogov. They maintain that if they find their work interesting, the audience will be with them. They are not looking for easy laughs or easy cries; they are making theatre for those who thank them because they feel taken seriously and capable of understanding. Moreover, that does not have to be the audience as a monolithic whole. Each audience member draws their own impressions.[38] In 2009 Ianovskaia directed *The Wolf and the Seven Goats*, which at the time of writing (2017) is still on the repertory.[39] It is a delightful and quirky show, which reveals Ianovskaia's directing techniques just as much as any other of her productions.

IANOVSKAIA IN PRACTICE

Working for a young audience

Regarding my question about the differences in working for young and adult audiences, Ianovskaia remarks: I work the same with productions for children as for adults. Because I think up what I find interesting, I think it up for myself. I understand that if you make a production for very small children then you have to have several points of view. One is, I cannot scare him. He should not be scared that the wolf eats the little goats. He has to expect it and understand it but he cannot be scared by it. That is one. Second, what makes directors often very happy at children's theatre shows, is very bad with us. If an artist tells me 'that' [see below] happened at our show I tell him that they played very badly. A person in the audience must not assume that he can steer the production. Whether he is little or big. When he enters the organism of theatre, theatre is a total power, it devours you, it hears you, you hear it, but it tells you what it wants to say and you cannot change the flow of the action. You cannot yell: 'Do not go to the left – there is a wolf!' If he does that, that means that you have given him the right to do that, it means you worked so he could do that. I do not want that.

We played *The Wolf and the Seven Goats*, it was the first performance and all of the sudden a boy from the audience yells: 'Wolf, don't go away. I'm going to pee and then I'll be back.' Now that suits me, he was in despair, he had to go there and here was this! That is great!⁴⁰

Although we often separate directing for young audiences from directing for adults, it is great practice for any director to try his or her hand on a production for children. When doing so, keep in mind the caveats mentioned above. Also avoid the mindset of taking theatre for young audiences as 'second hand' theatre or a stepping stone to the 'real' theatre or 'theatre but not theatre'.

Whether for children or adults, Ianovskaia wants to make theatre that has its own thought, its own emotion, its own relationship with the world – in conversation with the audience. There can be an exchange about different views of the world. But the production, as conceived by the director and the actors, cannot be interrupted.

Ianovskaia's latest production is *The Balding Cupid* (2016), which very much shows the directing methods and techniques she mentions in the interview excerpts above.⁴¹

The play by Yevgeny Popov,⁴² originally titled *The Balding Boy*, takes place in the 1970s, in a country that is not there anymore, in a wooden apartment complex, inhabited by people who could be 'your' parents. It is a comedy about love, Chekhov-style, or better still: 'what is love?'⁴³ According to Kama Ginkas it plays in Krasnoyarsk, at the time when the Soviets had cultivated a common lifestyle. It is about people who are thrown out of life, 'who keep themselves busy with something, but primarily drink, get into jail, shoot, love, and get married. The life of people who do not acknowledge that their lives have been castrated long ago, that there is no real life. They are satisfied with the little bit they have.'⁴⁴

Here, too, the collaboration with designer Sergei Barkhin is clear, as he not so much illustrates as tells the world in the stage pictures. A two-storey barrack, made of aluminium painted to look like wood, crosses the stage into the auditorium. On the opposite side is a smaller identical house, leaving a narrow alley upstage, closed off, as it were, by a beaten motorcycle. At a water pump centre stage the inhabitants meet. The struggle of communal housing is emphasized by who uses the outhouse connected to the smaller building. This is a comedy, but in Ginkas's words it deals with 'the love of talented people who try to use their talents but it does not work out. A horrible comedy. A horrible Soviet comedy' (Figure 12.3).[45]

Again Ianovskaia says something about the present, while staging the past. Olga Zavalishina concludes her review:

> Genrietta Ianovskaia's production paints not only a picture of the changing past, it talks about our times. About the contemporary world at the edges of big cities, where, just like in Popov's play, people live, and also want love, happiness, but they cannot even find the strength to pass the threshold. And what to do about that is not clear at all.[46]

Russia has a tradition of repertory theatre which for anyone interested in Russian theatre is a blessing. Productions stay on the repertory for years, often decades. Even the *Blue Bird* by Maurice Maeterlinck can still be seen occasionally in Stanislavsky's original 1908 mise-en-scène at the Gorky Moscow Art Theatre. This also means that these productions need to be kept alive. Ianovskaia tells the following to her actors on regular occasions:

> I tell my actors that on stage they have to give themselves sincerely. I tell them the time that you sincerely live on stage will not count against your life. That means you will live long. ... A production is played hundreds of

FIGURE 12.3 The Balding Cupid, 2016. *Lisa Krivitskaia (Mariia Lugavaia)*. Photo credit unknown. From the archives of the Moscow Tiuz.

times for many years, we just closed *Ivanov*, which was on the repertoire since 1993, *The Storm* was closed not long ago, and sometimes you have to blow new life into it. And then I go for 5 minutes before the show. I say 'I want to remind you of one thing: for some it is the first time they hear this, but some people I want to remind. They say that when a person dies, a picture of his life passes by in front of his eyes. And it may just be the case that in front of his eyes your face slips by. And if so, that minute needs to be worthy, it needs to show a worthy face.' I always try to connect them to the world. To go beyond the frame of the production.[47]

Genrietta Ianovskaia is one of the last active directors, trained in the Soviet tradition, to stage productions straddling the old Soviet world and contemporary Russia. She uses her art to make an impact, to state a point, through action on stage, collaboration with the designer, coaching of her actors. As such she is one of the most influential Russian directors of the last fifty years.

Conclusion

Amy Skinner

This volume draws to a close in two parts: a conclusion and a postscript. The former returns to the book's starting point by re-emphasizing the ongoing value of twentieth-century Russian theatre for today's theatre makers and by exploring the nature and function of theatrical influence across cultures and eras. The intention is not to trace the lineages of specific practitioners, but instead to shift focus from individual directors to a broader view of Russian and Soviet theatre making, identifying themes that emerge in these diverse approaches to practice. In the second section, the Postscript, I provide an annotated bibliography for each of the twelve directors discussed in this volume. The purpose is to guide readers who are looking to engage further with any of these practitioners by offering a series of English-language access points to the documentation and analysis of their practice. Taken together, the conclusion and postscript continue the work of the 'In Practice' exercises in each chapter, inviting the reader into a continued, embodied exploration of Russia's directors in the rehearsal room.

Principles from practice: Identifying themes

Work on this volume proceeds from two premises. The first is that the practitioners discussed here have much to offer to contemporary theatre makers, and that exploration of their practice is, as Andrei Malaev-Babel puts it in his chapter on Vakhtangov, 'essential for anyone who seriously approaches the field of theatre'. The second premise is the conviction that embodied experiences of practice are essential in understanding and engaging with the work of Russia's directors. Each chapter here has framed one practitioner through these premises, and each makes the significance of the individual practitioners abundantly clear: their work has had wide-reaching implications, shaping contemporary understanding of theatre as a discipline in all its diversity, from acting to mise-en-scène, puppetry to performance for young audiences. Their deeply embedded commitment to directing as a practical act with a developed and essential theoretical basis allows today's readers access to a range of staging examples, pedagogical exercises and theoretical treatises which speak directly to the foundational questions of theatre making, from the relationship with the spectator to the nature of acting, the conceptualization of character, the shaping of theatrical space and the art form's sociopolitical implications.

Tracing the individual legacies and lineages of each of the directors discussed here is beyond the scope of this conclusion. As practices occurring in a different time and place, these legacies are mobile and contested. The complexities associated with cross-cultural transmission are enhanced in the case of Russia, and particularly Soviet Russia: the Iron Curtain, and the biases associated with the Soviet Union, have complicated transmission routes between Russia and the West.[1] In many instances, access to these directors' practices are mediated via written accounts, photographic images, archives and hearsay; direct contact with practitioners or primary source material is equally open to multiple interpretations. Ideas are shared, altered, misunderstood or revised. Origins are lost or rewritten. The result is a rich and complex field of transmissions and translations, in which instances of direct and acknowledged influence only tell part of the story. Where these do exist, however, they indicate an enduring interest in Russian practice in the West. Practitioners like Peter Sellars, Katie Mitchell and Declan Donellan celebrate the Russian influences that are embedded in their theatre making and training experiences.[2] Some British conservatories are offering teaching in Russia for their students,[3] and recent commemorative events for the 1917 Revolution included reference to the role of theatre making in the early Soviet era.[4] The establishment of two research networks since 2010 focused on cultural exchange between Russia and the West, and the ongoing work of the Stanislavski Centre at Rose Bruford College indicates that contemporary interest in Russian theatre exists in the academy, as well as in the spheres of theatre training and professional practice.[5]

Individual legacies are an essential part of Russia's theatrical influence in the West, and in the case of some practitioners (for example, Stanislavsky) it seems almost redundant to note their profile and significance.[6] However, as indicated in the Introduction to this volume, not all of the practitioners discussed here have enjoyed this level of recognition outside of Russia. The complexities of transmission mean that whether or not a director has an established following or profile in the West is not necessarily indicative of the importance, and potential utility, of their practice for contemporary theatre makers. The mechanics of transmission mean that focusing on individual practitioner legacies will always be an exclusive and partial act. As such, rather than these extant legacies, this conclusion opts to look forward, considering aspects of Russian theatre practice that emerge in this volume and have the potential to contribute to current and future discussions on directing. To this end, four directing principles have been identified, each of which frames a set of approaches to an aspect of theatre making (rehearsal, space, imagination and interaction). These are far from comprehensive; however, they capture something of a wider 'flavour' of twentieth-century Russian theatre directing, drawing attention to priorities beyond acting and spectatorship (a preoccupation with which has been taken, to some extent, as a given in this context).

Principle one: Approaching rehearsal

The titles of Efros's books *The Craft of Rehearsal* and *The Joy of Rehearsal* capture something of the respect with which the directors in this volume approached the rehearsal process. In some instances lasting for months or even years, and located within a system of long-established theatre companies, the rehearsal processes of the practitioners discussed here are largely exploratory and driven by exercises based on the director's extended methodology. The value of the final outcome is related to the value of the process, and the development of the actor's understanding is as essential as blocking or mise-en-scène. Many of the practical exercises suggested in this volume advocate a range of rehearsal activities that include improvisation, the use of the etude (or 'study') and different methods of textual analysis (many related to the Stanislavskian model of analytical division into tasks and objectives). Chekhov and Tairov emphasize improvisation as a tool for engaging with the text or developing the actor's technique. James Thomas's chapter on Efros discusses the nature of improvised etudes as a rehearsal tool within Active Analysis, but Meyerhold, Vakhtangov and others also engaged with study-based rehearsal processes. Ianovskaia's long table reads are intended to give the actor time to make discoveries in a collective setting and Tcherkasski's chapter on Sulimov illustrates how the rehearsal process can become a training ground for directing pedagogy. Remizova's guidance to Malaev-Babel to '[not] be in a hurry to solidify blockings' perhaps encapsulates this attitude towards the rehearsal process as one of collective, creative discovery.

Principle two: Approaching space

The centrality of theatrical space as a facet of the director's role is frequently highlighted in this volume. In his advice to Ianovskaia and Ginkas, quoted by Manon van de Water in Chapter 12, Georgy Tovstonogov reminds the director that 'words do not tell the story of the play, actions do'. The facilitation of an environment in which the actor can realize these actions, and which communicates directly with the spectator, is essential to much of the directing practice discussed here. Maria Shevtsova explores Stanislavsky's generation of performance space in terms of the mood which it generates, and recommends that the reader think of setting as 'not just a static backdrop against which the actors sit [...], but [as] an environment to help them to act, and their characters to interact with each other'. Meyerhold's use of the visual arts indicates a consistent exploration of stage space which draws on practice in other disciplines, an approach echoed in Tairov's work on the musicality of space. Spatial metaphors are also an important aspect of the rehearsal process; for example, in Chekhov's spatialization of key elements in the play's narrative or structure. Although the collaborative relationship with the stage designer is a vital aspect for many of the theatres in this volume (see the chapters on Efremov or Ianovskaia for specific examples), the conceptualization of space also forms a foundation of the director's own role, and the work of these practitioners suggests that stage direction is often a fundamentally scenographic process.

Principle three: Approaching imagination

Many of the practitioners in this volume highlight the centrality of imagination in the director's process. Imagination is approached less as a natural gift and more as a tool which must be regularly sharpened through exercises and practice. Stanislavsky's discipline of visualization in the preparation of his director's scores is one way in which the director's ability to imagine facilitates the rehearsal process. Sats's 'observe and imagine' task gives the director a specific tool for developing imaginative thinking through the dramaturgical devices of narrative and character. The notion of the 'imaginary audience', proposed by Vakhtangov, demonstrates the importance of imagination for the director during all stages of the rehearsal process. Other rehearsal techniques develop the actor's imagination, for example, through improvisation or character exercises (Chekhov's landscape task or Sulimov's 'novel of life') or through the atmosphere generated in the rehearsal room (for example, Remizova's commitment to the empowerment of actors). Simonovich-Efimova's exercises for puppeteers shift imagination into the realm of object manipulation, combining highly skilled physicality with the ability to generate an imaginative response in the spectator.

Principle four: Approaching interactions

The directors discussed in this volume are often closely inter-related, not only in terms of the themes in their practice, but also in their working relationships. Cross references and aesthetic lineages break out between the chapters included here, drawing attention to the interconnectedness of the directors' practices. Some of these connections are integral to the practitioners' biographies: they are teachers and pupils, former actors, graduates of schools of training and schools of thought. Other connections are ideological: adoptions, expansions or rejections of another practitioners' ideas. Taken together, these form a network of practice which underwrites the development of the individual's aesthetic. Remizova's status as Vakhtangov's protégé, Efremov's association of his practice with a revival of Stanislavsky or Meyerhold's vocal dislike of Tairov are all examples of this network in action.[7] The network of practice implies that Russian theatre directing emerged through, and existed in, dialogue. Through their work onstage and in theoretical treatises, practitioners engaged in an ongoing conversation about the nature and purpose of performance. It is difficult to see the work of these directors existing in isolation; each director's aesthetic contributed to a wider conversation on questions of theatrical purpose, style and function.

These four principles provide contextualization for the individual directors' methods, framing their concerns in relation to the wider field of practice that developed in twentieth-century Russian theatre. The combination of individual methods and thematic principles gives some indication of potential areas of influence for these directors on contemporary theatre making; however, how historical theatre practice is accessed and used in today's rehearsal settings is closely tied to the way in which the relationship between historical and contemporary practice is conceptualized. To conclude this volume, I would like to offer a model for the conceptualization of this relationship in Meyerhold's theory of the biomechanical *otkaz*. By understanding twentieth-century Russian theatre as providing an '*otkaz* moment' for the contemporary director, it is possible to engage with the necessity of historical approaches in the development of current and future theatre practice.

Valuing the past: The *otkaz* moment

The *otkaz* is the first element of the acting cycle, a system of movement analysis developed in the early 1920s by Meyerhold in response to the Taylorist work cycle.[8] Commonly translated into English as the 'refusal', the *otkaz* precedes the cycle's main movement or *posil*, which in turn gives way to the *tochka* – Russian for 'full stop' – to complete the tripartite structure.[9] Through division into these sections, Meyerhold provided the actor with a model for the analysis and execution of all onstage movement, in the director's own words, from 'intention' to 'realization' to 'reaction'.[10] For an actor training in Meyerhold's system of biomechanics, effectiveness in performance was associated with mastery of the acting cycle and the rules of movement that it implied.

Meyerhold's *otkaz* is a useful way to conceptualize the value of twentieth-century Russian theatre for the contemporary theatre maker. Based on the principle of refusal, the *otkaz* is a movement against the final desired action. Any biomechanical movement (*posil*) must be preceded by the act of refusal contained in the *otkaz*: to step forward, the actor must first withdraw the leg backwards; to shake hands, the actor must first pull the arm back behind the body. Jonathan Pitches describes the *otkaz* as 'a kind of gestural prologue', a moment of preparation for movement, which in practice also lends emphasis to the *posil* and momentum to the movement sequence.[11] This emphasis gives the *otkaz* its specifically theatricality quality: it is a tool aimed not only at the actor, but also at the spectator. The refusal highlights the *posil*, preparing the spectator to watch the movement as much as the actor to perform it.

Engagement with the historical theatre offers the contemporary theatre maker an *otkaz* moment. This is first a breathing space: withdrawal to the theatre of the past provides an opportunity for reflection. It is also an act of emphasis, drawing attention to elements of the director's own practice through the lens of past experience. The act of withdrawing to the historical theatre to explore past productions, developing thinking or creative work, gives distance and directs the attention of the theatre maker towards what is particularly important or valuable in their own practice. In addition, the *otkaz* is a model of progress and champions stepping back to move forwards, consciously and deliberately moving away from the goal in order to approach it in a more strategic and effective way. Anna Seymour notes that:

> In the process of otkaz, we see an embodied theatrical structure whereby it is recognized that in order to move forward it is necessary first to go back to gather control.[12]

The metaphor of gathering is a particularly relevant one in this context: gathering information, ideas, practices and images from the historical theatre becomes a way for the contemporary theatre maker to understand aspects of their own practice. The *otkaz*'s stepping back is seen as an active and intentional process. There is nothing nostalgic about it: the act of refusal is functional and forward-focused. In the same way, as David Chambers notes, our relationship with the theatre of the past should not be about theatrical nostalgia: instead, it is about gaining momentum for the future.[13]

The *otkaz* moment also challenges the myth of 'relevance'. The identification of past directing practice as 'still relevant' implies that the historical theatre is beholden to the contemporary theatre practitioner for validation: the historical is seen as nothing more than a facet of the contemporary. The relationship between *otkaz* and *posil* again provides a helpful model: the *otkaz* is connected to, but different from, the *posil*. There is no need for these two movements to be continuous; indeed, in biomechanical training, they are often associated with separate rhythmic beats counted aloud by the trainer. In the same way, there is no need for the historical theatre to offer practice which is identical to, directly related to or obviously 'relevant' to the style or content of that practised by the contemporary director. The withdrawal of the *otkaz*, in this instance, need not be seen only as a withdrawal backwards in time, but also as a refusal of prevailing style, personal preference or theatrical aesthetic. The step back does not rely on the accepted influence of a particular practitioner, or on established areas of 'relevance'. Instead, it is the opportunity to engage with difference and distance in order to promote new ways of thinking about one's own practice.

This volume began with David Chambers's belief that historical theatre makers can offer 'inspired guidance to the theatre of the future'.[14] It is, of course, impossible to do anything more than speculate on the form or direction of tomorrow's theatre. One thing, however, is clear: in their practice, their theoretical writing, their commitment to directing pedagogy and their innovative approaches to theatre making, the directors of the twentieth-century Russian theatre provide the contemporary practitioner with a wealth of *otkaz* moments. Whatever the future theatre holds, their status as some of directing's most 'inspired guides' is assured.

Postscript: Where to Next?

Amy Skinner

Each of the chapters in this volume has provided an insight into the aesthetic and working practice of one of Russia's theatre directors. The chapters are closely focused on elements of each director's practice, providing in some instances an overview and in others a more detailed analysis of one aspect of their approach. Either way, each director offers a wealth of knowledge and inspiration beyond what can be contained in these pages. For many of the directors discussed here, there is limited material available in English; for others – Stanislavsky, for example – the material available is so extensive that it is difficult to know where to start, particularly when looking specifically for sources with a directing, rather than exclusively acting or actor training, perspective. In this postscript, I would like to offer some guidance on where further information about each director can be found. The lists below have been complied in consultation with the authors of each chapter. They are divided into primary material (that written by the director), secondary material and commentaries, and, if appropriate, digital or online resources. All material recommended is in the English language, and names of translators are given.

In addition to the specific recommendations for each director below, you will also find that many of the theatre companies referenced in this volume still exist and have easily accessible websites, for example, the Moscow Art Theatre (www.mxat.ru), the Meyerhold Centre (www.meyerhold.ru), the Vakhantgov Theatre (www.vakhtangov.ru), the Sovremennik (sovremennik.ru) and the Moscow Theatre of the Young Spectator (moscowtyz.ru). These websites provide interesting visual material and offer some insight into how the ideas of the earlier practitioners in this volume are being used today. If you are seeking original Russian language documents related to the practitioners, some archive material can be found on the website of RGALI (*Rossiiskii Gosudarstvennyi Arkhiv Literatury i Iskusstva* or The

Russian State Archive of Literature and Art), which has an English language interface (www.rgali.ru). These archives are searchable, with some material available online in digitized form.

KONSTANTIN STANISLAVSKY

Stanislavsky's writing in translation

Balukhaty, S. D. *The Seagull Produced by Stanislavsky*, translated by David Magarshack. London: David Dobson Ltd, 1952. This volume contains Stanislavsky's director's score for *The Seagull*.

Commentaries on Stanislavsky's direction

Gorchakov, Nikolai M. *Stanislavsky Directs*, translated by Miriam Goldina. New York: Limelight Editions, 1985.

Innes, Christopher and Maria Shevtsova. *The Cambridge Introduction to Theatre Directing*. Cambridge: Cambridge University Press, 2013, especially pages 62–76.

Stroyeva, N. M. 'Three Sisters at the MAT', in *Re: Direction: A Theoretical and Practical Guide*, edited by Rebecca Schneider and Gabrielle Cody 40–48, Abingdon and New York: Routledge, 2003.

Torpokov, Vasily Osipovich. *Stanislavski in Rehearsal: The Final Years*, translated by Christine Edwards. New York and London: Routledge, 1998.

VSEVOLOD MEYERHOLD

Meyerhold's writing in translation

Braun, Edward (ed. and trans.). *Meyerhold on Theatre*. London and New York: Bloomsbury Methuen Drama, 1969, 2016. Part six, 'The Government Inspector', includes notes from Meyerhold's rehearsal process on this production and gives a clear insight into his approach.

Gladkov, Aleksandr. *Meyerhold Speaks, Meyerhold Rehearses*, translated by Alma Law. Amsterdam: Harwood Academic Press, 1997. This volume includes Gladkov's notes on Meyerhold in rehearsal.

Commentaries on Meyerhold's direction

Rudnitsky, Konstantin. *Meyerhold the Director*, translated by George Petrov. Ann Arbor, MI: Ardis, 1981.

NINA SIMONOVICH-EFIMOVA

Simonovich-Efimova's writing in translation

Simonovich-Efimova, Nina. *Adventures of a Russian Puppet Theatre*, translated by Elena Mitcoff. Birmingham, MI: Puppetry Imprints, 1935. Facsimile version reprinted in 2012 by Martino Fine Books.

Simonovich-Efimova, Nina. 'Notes on Hand Puppets', translated by Elena Mitcoff, *Puppetry: A Yearbook of Puppets and Marionettes* 1 (1930): 55–58.

Simonovich-Efimova, Nina. 'Petrushka Gets Sick', translated by Dassia N. Posner, *Puppetry International* 16 (Fall 2004): 29–31.

Commentaries on Simonovich-Efimova's direction

Posner, Dassia N. 'Life-Death and Disobedient Obedience: Russian Modernist Redefinitions of the Puppet', in *The Routledge Companion to Puppetry and Material Performance*, edited by Dassia N. Posner, Claudia Orenstein, and John Bell, 130–143. London: Routledge, 2014.

Yablonskaya, Miuda N. *Women Artists of Russia's New Age, 1900–1935*, edited and translated by Anthony Parton. New York: Rizzoli International Publications, 1990.

YEVGENY VAKHTANGOV

Vakhtangov's writing in translation

Vakhtangov, Yevgeny. *The Vakhtangov Sourcebook*, edited, translated and introduced by Andrei Malaev-Babel. London: Routledge, 2011.

Commentaries on Vakhtangov's direction

Gorchakov, N. *The Vakhtangov School of Stage Art*. Moscow: Foreign Languages Publishing House, 1959.

Malaev-Babel, A. *Yevgeny Vakhtangov: A Critical Portrait*. London and New York: Routledge, 2012.

Yzraely, Y. *Vakhtangov Directing 'The Dybbuk'*. PhD thesis, Carnegie-Mellon University's Department of Drama, 1970.

ALEXANDER TAIROV

Tairov's writing in translation

Tairov, Alexander. *Notes of a Director*, translated by William Kulke. Miami: Miami University Press, 1969.

Commentaries on Tairov's direction

Worrall, Nick. *Modernism to Realism on the Soviet Stage: Tairov – Vakhtangov – Okhlopkov*. Cambridge: Cambridge University Press, 2008.

MICHAEL CHEKHOV

Chekhov's writing in translation

Chekhov, Michael. *To the Actor*. London: Routledge, 2002.

Commentaries on Chekhov's direction

Autant-Mathieu, Marie-Christine and Yana Meerzon (eds.). *The Routledge Companion to Michael Chekhov*. Abingdon: Routledge, 2015.

Digital resources

Digital Theatre masterclasses in Chekhov's technique by the American Michael Chekhov Association (MICHA), https://www.digitaltheatreplus.com/education/collections/micha-michael-chekhov-association

ALEXANDRA REMIZOVA

Commentaries on Remizova's direction

Malaev-Babel, A. 'Aleksandra Remizova: An "Actors' Director"', in *Women, Collective Creation, and Devised Performance*, edited by K. Syssoyeva and S. Proudfit, 81–97. New York: Palgrave Macmillan, 2016.

Digital resources

Television version of Remizova's 1955 production of Mamin-Sibiryak's *Gold*, filmed 1977: http://www.dailymotion.com/video/x2t40qe

Television version of Remizova's 1958 production of Dostoyevsky's *The Idiot*, adapted for the stage by Yuri Olesha, filmed 1979: https://www.youtube.com/watch?v=a1wZxktjlCI

Television version of Remizova's 1960 production of Fredro's *Ladies and Husars*, filmed 1976: Part 1 https://www.youtube.com/watch?v=YGSJRvvgryo, Part 2 https://www.youtube.com/watch?v=0AlRFvmBopY

Television version of Remizova's 1964 production of Shaw's *The Millionairess*, filmed 1974: https://www.youtube.com/watch?v=Vxi4YNfAz4E

Television version of Remizova's 1968 production of Ostrovsky's *Enough Stupidity in Every Wise Man*, filmed 1971: Part 1 https://www.youtube.com/watch?v=YMSZn_DJ5D8, Part 2 https://www.youtube.com/watch?v=Ks-5PHe5P00

NATALIA SATS

Sats's writing in translation

Sats, Natalia. *Sketches from My Life*. Moscow: Raduga, 1985.

Commentaries on Sats's direction

Victorov, Victor. *The Natalia Sats Children's Musical Theatre*. Moscow: Raduga, 1986.

van de Water, Manon. 'Raising the Soviet Citizen: Natalia Sats's Revolutionary Theatre for Children and Youth, 1917–1932', in *Nationalism and Youth in Theatre and Performance*, edited by Angela Schweigart-Gallagher and Victoria Pettersen Lantz, 85–99. London: Routledge, 2014.

Digital resources

The website of The Moscow State Opera and Ballet Theatre Named After Natalia Sats: http://teatr-sats.ru

MAR SULIMOV

Sulimov's writing in translation and commentary

Tcherkasski, Sergei. 'Inside Sulimov's Studio: Directors Perform a Play'. *Stanislavski Studies: Practice, Legacy, and Contemporary Theater* 2, no. 2 (2014): 4–25. This article contains translations and images, as well as commentary.

ANATOLY EFROS

Efros's writing in translation

Efros, Anatoly. *Beyond Rehearsal*, translated by James Thomas. New York: Peter Lang, 2009.

Efros, Anatoly. *The Craft of Rehearsal*, translated by James Thomas. New York: Peter Lang, 2007.

Efros, Anatoly. *The Joy of Rehearsal*, translated by James Thomas. New York: Peter Lang, 2006, 2011.

Commentaries on Efros's direction

Dixon, Ross. 'Slaughtering Sacred Seagulls: An Analysis of Anatoly Efros's Production of *The Seagull* at the Lenkom Theatre in 1967'. *Irish Slavonic Studies* 21 (2001): 49–73.

Shevtsova, Maria. *The Theatre Practice of Anatoly Efros, a Contemporary Soviet Director*. Devon, England: Department of Theatre Dartington College of Arts, 1978.

Digital resources

Efros, Anatoly. 'Dmitiry Krymov Laboratory', http://eng.efros.org/people/efros_anatolii_vasilevich/

OLEG EFREMOV

Commentaries on Efremov's direction

Smeliansky, Anatoly. *Oleg Yefremov: Masters of Soviet Art*, translated by Mikhail Nikolsky. Moscow: Novosti Press Agency Publishing House, 1988.

GENRIETTA IANOVSKAIA

Commentaries on Ianovskaia's direction

van de Water, Manon. 'Mister Twister Mister Twister or Goodbye America!: The Interdependence of Meanings and Material Conditions'. *Essays in Theatre/Études Théâtrales* 16, no. 1 (1997): 85–93.

van de Water, Manon. *Moscow Theatres for Young People: A Cultural History of Ideological Coercion and Artistic Innovation, 1917–2000*. New York: Palgrave Macmillan, 2006.

Digital resources

The website of the Moscow Tiuz; http://moscowtyz.ru/en/about-theatre

NOTES

Note on Transliteration and Russian Terms

1 Konstantin Rudnitsky, *Russian and Soviet Theatre: Tradition and the Avant-Garde*, trans. Roxane Permar (London: Thames and Hudson, 2000).

Introduction

1 David Chambers, 'Reconstructing Revizor: An Introduction to "After Penza"', *Theater* 28, no. 2 (1998): 60.
2 Stanislavsky, quoted in Joshua Logan, 'Foreword', in *The Stanislavski System: The Professional Training of an Actor*, ed. Sonia Moore (New York: Penguin Books, 1984), xvi.
3 Robert Leach, 'Russian Theatre in World Theatre', in *A History of Russian Theatre*, eds. Robert Leach and Victor Borovsky (Cambridge: Cambridge University Press, 1999).
4 Ibid., 2.
5 Ibid.
6 See, for example, Jonathan Pitches (ed.), *Russians in Britain: British Theatre and the Russian Tradition of Actor Training* (Abingdon: Routledge, 2012).
7 See Norris Houghton, *Moscow Rehearsals* (London: George Allen and Unwin, 1938) and André Van Gyseghem, *Theatre in Soviet Russia* (London: Faber and Faber, 1943). The State Meyerhold Theatre, or *Gosudarstvennyi Teatr imeni Vs. Meierkholda*, was abbreviated to GosTIM. Prior to being granted State Theatre status, it was known simply as the TIM: Meyerhold Theatre or *Teatr imeni Vs. Meierkholda*.
8 For more detailed analysis of the relationship between Russian theatre and Soviet policy, see, for example, Leach and Borovsky, *A History of Russian Theatre*; Nikolai Gorchakov, *The Theater in Soviet Russia*, trans. E. Lehrman (New York: Columbia University Press, 1957); Robert Leach, *Revolutionary Theatre* (London: Routledge, 1994); Rudnitsky, *Russian and Soviet Theatre*; Anatoly Smeliansky, *The Russian Theatre after Stalin*, trans. Patrick Miles (Cambridge: Cambridge University Press, 1999).
9 Gorchakov, *The Theater in Soviet Russia*, 108.

10 Edward Braun, *Meyerhold: A Revolution in Theatre* (London: Methuen, 1998), 152. Lunacharksy was head of Narkompros (*Narodnyi komissariat prosveshcheniya*, or People's Commissariat for Enlightenment).

11 Aleksandr Gladkov, *Meyerhold Speaks, Meyerhold Rehearses*, trans. Alma Law (Amsterdam: Harwood Academic Press, 1997), 93.

12 Rudnitsky, *Russian and Soviet Theatre*, 45.

13 John Freedman, *Silence's Roar: The Life and Drama of Nikolai Erdman* (Ontario: Mosaic Press, 1992), 58. Lenin's NEP (*Novaya Ekonomicheskaya Politika*, or New Economic Policy) was introduced in 1921 to boost the Soviet economy by allowing elements of capitalist trade.

14 Marc Slonim, *Russian Theater from the Empire to the Soviets* (London: Methuen, 1961), 307.

15 Birgit Beumers, 'The "thaw" and after: 1953–1986', in Leach and Borovsky, *A History of Russian Theatre*, 372. *Zastoi* (stagnation) is used to refer to the political, economic and social stagnation which took place during the Brezhnev era.

16 Anatoly Smeliansky, 'Russian Theatre in the Post-communist Era', in Leach and Borovsky, *A History of Russian Theatre*, 384.

17 Quoted in Rudnitsky, *Russian and Soviet Theatre*, 41.

18 Among those not included in this volume are Lev Dodin, Nikolai Evreinov, Yury Lyubimov and Nikolai Okhlopkov. Many others could be added to this list. Further information on these directors is available. See, for example: Maria Shevtsova, *Lev Dodin and the Maly Drama Theatre: Process to Performance* (London: Routledge, 2004); Sharon Marie Carnicke, *The Theatrical Instinct: Nikolai Evreinov and the Russian Theatre of the Early Twentieth Century* (New York: Peter Lang, 1989); Spencer Golub, *Evreinov: The Theatre of Paradox and Transformation* (Ann Arbor, MI: UMI Research Press, 1984); Birgit Beumers, *Yury Lyubimov: At the Taganka theatre (1964–1994)* (Amsterdam: Hardwood Academic Press, 1997); Nick Worrall, *Modernism to Realism on the Soviet Stage: Tairov, Vakhtangov, Okhlopkov* (Cambridge: Cambridge University Press, 2008).

19 It is essential to read the directors discussed here in context. In some instances, our historical and critical distance allows us to critique their choices: the openly propagandist nature of some of the theatre made in the early 1920s can feel uncomfortable to a modern viewer, as can some of the choices of texts from the perspectives of gender or race. In these instances, the chapter authors have been careful to highlight the complexity of these decisions from a contemporary perspective.

Chapter 1

1 I am indebted to the Leverhulme Trust Research Award for giving me the opportunity to undertake research necessary for this chapter.

2 Konstantin Stanislavsky, *My Life in Art*, trans. and ed. Jean Benedetti (London and New York: Routledge, 2008), 89–158.

3   Ibid., 158–164.
4   Letter to Nemirovich-Danchenko of 10 September 1898, *Stanislavsky – A Life in Letters*, selected, trans. and ed. Laurence Senelick (London and New York: Routledge, 2014), 110.
5   Quoted in Olga Radishcheva, *Stanislavsky i Nemirovich-Danchenko: istoriya teatralnykh otnosheny, 1897–1908* (*Stanislavsky and Nemirovich-Danchenko: A History of Theatre Relations, 1897–1908*) (Moscow: Artist. Director. Theatre, 1997), 61. Translations from sources cited in Russian here and below are mine.
6   S. D. Balukhaty, *The Seagull Produced by Stanislavsky*, trans. David Magarshack (London: David Dobson Ltd, 1952), 55.
7   Gorky's *Meshchanye* has been translated variously into English as *The Petty Bourgeois, Small People* and *The Philistines*.
8   For development of this vital point, see my section on Stanislavsky in Christopher Innes and Maria Shevtsova, *The Cambridge Introduction to Theatre Directing* (Cambridge: Cambridge University Press, 2013), 62–76.
9   K. L. Rudnitsky, *Russkoye rezhissyorskoye iskusstvo, 1898–1917* (*The Russian Art of Directing, 1898–1917*) (Moscow: GITIS, 2014), 102.
10 Quoted ibid., 102.
11 Stanislavsky, *My Life in Art*, 113–116.
12 Quoted in Radishcheva, *Stanislavsky*, 269.
13 Ibid. Radishcheva's commentary.
14 Ibid., 62.
15 Laurence Senelick, *The Chekhov Theatre: A Century of the Plays in Performance* (Cambridge: Cambridge University Press, 1997), 43.
16 For complementary material, see my other examples from *The Seagull* and more detailed commentary than is possible here in *The Cambridge Introduction to Theatre Directing*, 68–74.
17 Note that Stanislavsky starts from '1' on every page, whereas Magarshack's translation (as cited above and used here because the non-Russian reader can access it) numbers them consecutively for each act. I have deleted 'Miss' from 'Arkadina' but have otherwise kept the translation intact.
18 Balukhaty, *The Seagull*, 234–237.
19 Deduced from observations scattered throughout Radishcheva's book, several based on testimonies and memoires.
20 *Moskovsky Khudozhestvenny Teatr v russkoy teatralnoy kritike, 1898–1905* (*The Moscow Art Theatre in Russian Theatre Criticism*) (Moscow: Artist. Director. Theatre, 2005), 402.
21 Konstantin Stanislavsky, *Rezhissyorskiye ekzemplyary K. S. Stanislavskogo, Tom 3, 1901–1904* (*K. S. Stanislavsky's Production Plans, Vol. 3, 1901–1904*) (Moscow: Iskusstvo, 1983), 348–349.
22 This view, *grosso modo*, appears in M. N. Stroyeva, *Rezhissyorskiye iskaniya Stanislavskogo, 1898–1917* (*Stanislavsky's Directorial Search, 1898–1917*) (Moscow: Nauka, 1973), 91–93.

23 Quoted ibid., 112.
24 *Rezhissyorskiye ekzemplyary K. S. Stanislavskogo, Tom 4, 1902–1905 (K. S. Stanislavsky's Production Plans, Vol 4, 1902–1905)* (Moscow: Iskusstvo, 1986), 466–467, including quotations from Stanislavsky's plan.
25 Ibid., 484–485.
26 Jean Benedetti, selected, ed. and trans., *The Moscow Art Theatre Letters* (London: Methuen Drama, 1991), 140–141.
27 Quoted in Stroyeva, *Rezhissyorskiye iskaniya*, 113.
28 See my forthcoming book *Rediscovering Stanislavsky*, Cambridge University Press.

Chapter 2

1 Details of Meyerhold's final days and his arrest and execution can be found in Edward Braun, 'Meyerhold: The Final Act', *New Theatre Quarterly* 9 (1993): 3–15 and Laurence Senelick, 'The Making of a Martyr: The Legend of Meyerhold's Last Public Appearance', *Theatre Research International* 22 (2003): 157–168.
2 Meyerhold, cited in Gladkov, *Meyerhold Speaks*, 116.
3 Edward Braun, *Meyerhold on Theatre* (London and New York: Bloomsbury, Methuen Drama, 2016), 19.
4 Robert Leach, *Vsevolod Meyerhold* (Cambridge: Cambridge University Press, 1989), 13.
5 Meyerhold, in Gladkov, *Meyerhold Speaks*, 93.
6 Ibid., 91.
7 David Bradby and David Williams, *Director's Theatre* (London: Macmillan, 1988), 14. Meyerhold uses two diagrams to express this difference, which can be found in Bradby and Williams or in their original context in Meyerhold's essay 'First Attempts at a Stylized Theatre', in Braun, *Meyerhold on Theatre*, 59.
8 Meyerhold, in Braun, *Meyerhold on Theatre*, 150. It is important to note that Meyerhold was not above the use of hyperbole to make his points: this apparent rejection of language should be contextualized, particularly as it was written when his interest in the commedia dell'arte was at its peak. Although Meyerhold was never a slave to the playwright's words, and would frequently edit and rewrite play texts to suit his purposes, language remained central to his productions.
9 Meyerhold, in Gladkov, *Meyerhold Speaks*, 37.
10 Patrice Pavis, *Contemporary Mise en Scène: Staging Theatre Today*, trans. Joel Anderson. (Abingdon/New York: Routledge, 2013), 4.
11 Houghton, *Moscow Rehearsals*, 117. Houghton uses an alternative transliteration of Meyerhold's name.
12 Meyerhold in Gladkov, *Meyerhold Speaks*, 134.

13 Ibid., 126.
14 Houghton, *Moscow Rehearsals*, 126.
15 Meyerhold, in Braun, *Meyerhold on Theatre*, 31.
16 See, for example, Marjorie Hoover, *Meyerhold and His Set Designers* (New York: Peter Lang, 1988); Alla Mikhailova, *Meyerhold and Set Designers*, trans. E. Bessmertnaya (Moscow: Galart, 1995); Amy Skinner, *Meyerhold and the Cubists* (Bristol and Chicago: Intellect and University of Chicago Press, 2015).
17 Mikhailova, *Meyerhold and Set Designers*, 51.
18 Houghton, *Moscow Rehearsals*, 131.
19 Gladkov, *Meyerhold Speaks*, 166.
20 Ibid., 51.
21 Acts I and II of *The Bedbug* had different designers: the Kukryniksy designed Act I in their characteristic caricature style; Alexander Rodchenko created a constructivist vision of the future for Act II.
22 Kukryniksy, 'V rabote nad "Klopom"', in *Vstrechi s Meierkhol'dom*, ed. L. D. Vendrovskaya (Moscow: Vserossiiskoe Teatral'noe Obshchestvo, 1967), 386. English translation by Natalia Vinokurova.
23 Mikhailova, *Meyerhold and Set Designers*, 51.
24 Ibid., 64.
25 Ibid., 65.
26 Jane Collins and Arnold Aronson, 'Drawing and Design', *Theatre and Performance Design* 3, nos. 1–2 (2017): 1.
27 Olga Feigelman, 'Molodye khudozhniki na spektakliakh Meierkhol'da', in *Tvorcheskoe Nasledie V. E. Meierkhol'da*, eds. L. D. Vendrovskaya and A. V. Fevral'skii (Moscow: Vserossiikoe Teatral'noe Obshchestvo, 1978), 458. Translation by Natalia Vinokurova.
28 Ibid.
29 Leach, *Vsevolod Meyerhold*, 86.
30 Meyerhold, in Braun, *Meyerhold on Theatre*, 83.
31 Walter Crane, *Line and Form* (London: G. Bell and Sons, 1900), 23.
32 Nick Worrall, 'Meyerhold directs Gogol's *Government Inspector*', *Theatre Quarterly* 2, no. 7 (1972): 81.
33 Ibid.
34 Nikolai Tarabukin 'Kompozitsiya izobrazitelnoi storony spektaklya "Revizor"', in *N. M. Tarabukin o V. E. Meierkhol'de*, ed. O. M. Feldman (Moscow: OGI, 1998), 18. English translation by Natalia Vinokurova.
35 Nikolai Tarabukin, 'Analiz kompozitsii "Gore umu" v postanovke Vs. Meierkhol'da', in *N. M. Tarabukin o V. E. Meierkhol'de*, ed. O. M. Feldman (Moscow: OGI, 1998), 86. English translation by Natalia Vinokurova.
36 Ibid., 84.
37 Gladkov, *Meyerhold Speaks*, 124.
38 Tarabukin, 'Analiz kompozitsii "Gore umu"', 92.

Chapter 3

This chapter is adapted and expanded from Dassia N. Posner, 'Sculpture in Motion: Nina Simonovich-Efimova and the Petrushka Theatre', in *Women in the Arts in the Belle Epoque: Essays on Influential Artists, Writers and Performers* ©, ed. Paul Fryer (by permission of McFarland & Company, Inc, 2012), Box 611, Jefferson NC 28640. www.mcfarlandpub.com. Some sections also build upon Dassia N. Posner, 'Life-Death and Disobedient Obedience: Russian Modernist Redefinitions of the Puppet,' in *The Routledge Companion to Puppetry and Material Performance*, eds. Dassia N. Posner, Claudia Orenstein and John Bell (London: Routledge, 2014). Translations from Russian are my own unless reproduced from an English-language source.

1. Nina Simonovich-Efimova, *Zapiski petrushechnika i stat'i o teatre kukol*, ed. N. Zhizhina (Leningrad: Iskusstvo, 1980), 144. Reprinted from Nina Simonovich-Efimova, *Zapiski petrushechnika* (Moscow: Gosudarstvennoe izdatel'stvo, 1925).

2. Simonovich-Efimova is commonly abbreviated to Efimova in English translations of her work.

3. Adrian Efimov, 'Dvizhushchaisia skul'ptura', in *Chto zhe takoe teatr kukol?* ed. N. V. Filina (Moscow: STD, 1990), 80.

4. Nina Simonovich-Efimova. 'Kukol'nyi teatr khudozhnikov' Typescript, 1940, 1. Efimov collection, GATsTK (Obraztsov State Central Academic Puppet Theatre Museum Archive), Moscow.

5. Adrian Efimov, '*Macbeth* at the Puppet Theatre of Nina and Ivan Jefimov'. Typescript in English (Moscow: June 1964), 1. Efimov collection, GATsTK, Moscow.

6. Miuda Yablonskaya, *Women Artists of Russia's New Age, 1900–1935*, ed. and trans. Anthony Parton (New York: Rizzoli International Publications, 1990), 201.

7. Simonovich-Efimova, *Zapiski petrushechnika*, (Moscow: Gosudarstvennoe izdatel'stvo, 1925). Simonovich-Efimova's book was reissued with additional materials in 1980 as *Zapiski petrushechnika i stat'i o teatre kukol*, ed. N. Zhizhina; intro. Anna Nekrylova; foreword by Natalia Sats (Leningrad: Iskusstvo, 1980). All citations are from the 1980 edition. The English version – Nina Efimova, *Adventures of a Russian Puppet Theatre*, trans. Elena Mitcoff (Birmingham, MI: Puppetry Imprints, 1935) – is an adaptation rather than a translation. Although it significantly influenced US puppetry, the English edition does not capture the full depth of Efimova's thinking.

8. Henryk Jurkowski, *A History of European Puppetry*. Vol. 2, *The Twentieth Century*, ed. in collaboration with Penny Francis (Lewiston: Edwin Mellen Press, 1998), 1–2.

9. A *balagan* is a temporary wooden booth theatre that was constructed at Russian fairgrounds during the eighteenth and nineteenth centuries, especially during the Shrovetide and Easter week festivals. Theatrical performances in these booth theatres were one of the fairground's main attractions; 'to frequent the *balagans*' became a colloquial term for going to the fairground

itself. These theatres ranged in size: some housed spectacular pantomimes and large audiences, while others were small puppet booths containing a single puppeteer. The title of Alexander Blok's play *Balaganchik*, famously directed by Vsevolod Meyerhold in 1906, refers to a little *balagan*, a puppet show booth.

10 See Dassia N. Posner, *The Director's Prism: E. T. A. Hoffmann and the Russian Theatrical Avant-Garde* (Evanston, IL: Northwestern University Press, 2016).

11 Vsevelod Meyerhold, 'The Fairground Booth', in *Meyerhold on Theatre*, ed. and trans. Edward Braun (New York: Hill & Wang, 1969), 129.

12 Iulia Slonimskaia, 'Marionetka', Apollon 3 (March 1916): 1–42.

13 Yablonskaya, *Women Artists*, 202.

14 Nekrylova, Introduction to *Zapiski petrushechnika*, 8.

15 Yablonskaya, *Women Artists*, 202.

16 Nekrylova, Introduction to *Zapiski petrushechnika*, 27.

17 Yablonskaya, *Women Artists*, 203.

18 John E. Bowlt, *The Silver Age: Russian Art of the Early Twentieth Century and the 'World of Art' Group* (Newtonville, MA: Oriental Research Partners, 1982), 87.

19 See Catriona Kelly's detailed discussion of the popular Petrushka tradition in *Petrushka: The Russian Carnival Puppet Theatre* (Cambridge: Cambridge University Press, 1990).

20 Alexander Gref and Elena Slonimskaya, 'Petrushka's Voice', in *Routledge Companion to Puppetry and Material Performance*, 73.

21 Simonovich-Efimova, *Zapiski petrushechnika*, 119.

22 Simonovich-Efimova, 'Kukol'nyi teatr', 3.

23 Revised from Nina Simonovich-Efimova, 'Petrushka Gets Sick', trans. Dassia N. Posner, *Puppetry International* 16 (Fall 2004): 29–31.

24 John E. Bowlt, 'Cabaret in Russia', *Canadian-American Slavic Studies* 19, no. 4 (Winter 1985): 451–452.

25 Nekrylova, Introduction to *Zapiski petrushechnika*, 7.

26 Bartram, 'Kukol'nyi teatr', in *Izbrannye stat'i. Vospominaniia o khudozhnike* (Moscow: Sovetskii khudozhnik, 1979), 24.

27 Nataliia Sats, Forward to *Zapiski petrushechnika*, 33.

28 Nekrylova, Introduction to *Zapiski petrushechnika*, 9.

29 Simonovich-Efimova, 'Kukol'nyi teatr', 3.

30 Nina Simonovich-Efimova, *Katalog vystavki. Zhivopis'. Grafika. Teatr. Keramika* (Moscow: Sov. Khudozhnik, 1968), 16.

31 N. I. Smirnova, *Sovetskii teatr kukol, 1918–1932* (Moscow: Izdatel'stvo Akademii nauk SSSR, 1963), 120.

32 Alternate names for this theatre include the Puppet Studio on Mamonovsky Alley and the Sats Children's Theatre of the Moscow Soviet. 10 Mamonovsky Alley has since hosted various children's theatres, including the Theatre for Young Spectators (*Teatr iunykh zritelei*). Manon van de Water, *Moscow*

Theatres for Young People: A Cultural History of Ideological Coercion and Artistic Innovation, 1917–2000 (New York: Palgrave Macmillan, 2006), 246.

33 Bartram, 'Kukol'nyi teatr', 26.
34 Simonovich-Efimova, *Zapiski petrushechnika*, 214.
35 Smirnova, *Sovetskii teatr kukol*, 121.
36 Nekrylova, Introduction to *Zapiski petrushechnika*, 9. Smirnova notes that the 'Puppet Studio' on Mamonovsky Alley reopened sporadically in 1919 and 1920 but without the Efimovs. Smirnova, *Sovetskii teatr kukol*, 122. After the puppet division was transferred to the Kamerny Theatre in 1920, the First State Theatre for Children opened at Mamonovsky Alley. Van de Water, *Moscow Theatres for Young People*, 45 and N. Kostrova, 'Pervye sovetskie kukol'niki', in *Chto zhe takoe teatr kukol?* ed. N. V. Filina (Moscow: STD, 1990), 90–91.
37 Miuda N. Yablonskaya, *Women Artists of Russia's New Age, 1900–1935*, ed. and trans. Anthony Parton (New York: Rizzoli International Publications, 1990), 206. The Efimovs created forty-two new shows between 1916 and 1936 but only three between 1936 and 1948, the year Simonovich-Efimova died. See 'Repertuar khudozhnikov N. Ia. Simonovich-Efimovoi i I. S. Efimova v kukol'nom i tenevom teatrakh'. Typescript with handwritten additions, n.d., 2 pp. Efimov collection, GATsTK, Moscow.
38 Simonovich-Efimova, 'Kukol'nyi teatr', 3.
39 Nina Simonovich-Efimova, 'O Petrushke', *Vestnik teatra* 34 (23–28 September 1919): 6–8.
40 Simonovich-Efimova, *Zapiski petrushechnika*, 43–44.
41 Efimov, 'Dvizhushchaisia skul'ptura', 80.
42 George and her son Maurice Sand began their puppetry experiments in a domestic setting and were among the first in France to establish an artistic puppet theatre. Although Simonovich-Efimova never experimented with the commedia dell'arte themes that captivated the Sands, both idealized glove puppets and experimented with rod puppets. See George Sand, *The Snow Man*, trans. Virginia Vaughan (Boston: Roberts Brothers, 1871), 161–162.
43 Simonovich-Efimova contrasts gendered pronouns in Russian. Simonovich-Efimova, *Zapiski petrushechnika*, 49–50.
44 Simonovich-Efimova, 'O Petrushke', 8.
45 Simonovich-Efimova, *Zapiski petrushechnika*, 43.
46 Ibid., 132.
47 Ibid.
48 Ibid., 133.
49 Simonovich-Efimova, 'O Petrushke', 7.
50 Nekrylova, Introduction to *Zapiski petrushechnika*, 7.
51 Ibid., 24.
52 Efimov, '*Macbeth*', 5.
53 Ibid.

54 Ibid., 9–10.
55 Rebecca Cunningham, 'The Russian Women Artist Designers of the Avant-Garde', *TD&T* 34, no. 2 (1998): 38–52.
56 Jurkowski, *A History of European Puppetry*, 32; Kostrova, 'Pervye sovetskie kukol'niki', 90–91.
57 Nina Simonovich-Efimova, 'Ocherki zhizni i tvorchestva I. S. Efimova', in *Ob iskusstve i khudozhnikakh*, eds. A. B. Matveeva and Adrian Efimov (Moscow: Sovetskii khudozhnik, 1977), 35.
58 Jane Taylor (ed.), *Handspring Puppet Company* (Parkwood, South Africa: David Krut, 2009), 168.

Chapter 4

1 Y. Vakhtangov, *The Vakhtangov Sourcebook*, ed. A. Malaev-Babel (London and New York: Routledge, 2011a), 128.
2 K. Stanislavsky, 'Nadpis' na portrete' (*Inscription on a Portrait*), in *Yevgeny Vakhtangov*, eds. Vendrovskaya and Kaptereva (Moscow: VTO, 1984), 429.
3 G. Tovstonogov, *Zerkalo stseny* (*Mirrow of the Stage*), vol. 1 (Leningrad: Iskusstvo, 1984), 183.
4 Vakhtangov's own Studio changed names several times before it became the State Academic Vakhtangov Theatre in 1926. To avoid confusion, we will refer to it as the Vakhtangov Studio in this chapter.
5 Vakhtangov's *Princess Turandot* had several subsequent revivals; the accurate count of its performances has now been lost.
6 Vakhtangov, quoted in N. Gorchakov, *Rezhissyorskiye uroki Vakhtangova* (*Vakhtangov's Directorial Lessons*) (Moscow: Iskusstvo, 1957), 43.
7 See Y. Smirnov-Nesvitsky, *Yevgeny Vakhtangov* (Leningrad: Iskusstvo, 1987), 179–180; N. Smirnova, *Yevgeny Vakhtangov* (Moscow: Znaniye, 1982), 10.
8 N. Volkov, *Vakhtangov* (Moscow: Korabl', 1922), 20.
9 V. Ivanov, *Russkiye Sezony Teatra Gabima* (*The Russian Seasons of the Habima Theatre*) (Moscow: Artist. Rezhissyor. Teatr, 1999), 96; V. Ivanov, 'Ot sostavitelya' (*From the Editor*), in *Yevgeny Vakhtangov, Dokumenty i svidetel'stva* (*Yevgeny Vakhtangov, Documents and Evidence*), ed. Vl. Ivanov, vol. 1 (Moscow: INDRIK, 2011), 14.
10 P. Markov, 'Printsessa Turandot i sovremennyi teatr' (*Princess Turandot and the Contemporary Theater*), in *Printsessa Turandot* (*Princess Turandot*) (Moscow-Petrograd: Gosudarstvennoie Izdatel'stvo, 1923), 49–50.
11 In 1919, for example, twelve of Vakhtangov's most talented students, including Yury Zavadsky, separated from his Studio, leaving Vakhtangov devastated. Some of them, Zavadsky included, later returned to Vakhtangov.
12 Vakhtangov, *The Vakhtangov Sourcebook*, 131.
13 Ibid., 111.

14 Vakhtangov asked his students to picture the process of character study as a triangle where an actor gradually moves from its side to its apex.
15 Vakhtangov, *The Vakhtangov Sourcebook*, 105.
16 B. Zakhava, *Vakhtangov i ego studia* (*Vakhtangov and His Studio*), 3rd edn. (Moscow: Arsis Books, 2010), 234.
17 M. Chekhov, *The Path of the Actor* (London and New York: Routledge, 2005), 70.
18 Ibid., 68.
19 Vakhtangov, *The Vakhtangov Sourcebook*, 106–107.
20 Zakhava, *Vakhtangov i ego studia*, 272.
21 According to Vakhtangov (*The Vakhtangov Sourcebook*, 112), an actor can radiate their thoughts and emotions, while Michael Chekhov (*To the Actor* (London and New York: Routledge, 2002), 40) also speaks of radiated movements. Vakhtangov associated radiation with *prana*, or life force, that is drawn from nature and other sources and is radiated by the actor from two inner centres: that of thought (the head) and that of emotion (solar plexus). From these two centres, it is conducted through the human body, stimulating emotions, movements, thoughts and speeches.
22 Vakhtangov, *The Vakhtangov Sourcebook*, 89.
23 Ibid., 99.
24 Chekhov, *To the Actor*, 146.
25 Ibid., 146–147.
26 Vakhtangov, *The Vakhtangov Sourcebook*, 156.
27 Yevgeny Vakhtangov, *Yevgeny Vakhtangov, Dokumenty i svidetel'stva* (*Yevgeny Vakhtangov, Documents and Evidence*), ed. V. Ivanov, vol. 2 (Moscow: INDRIK, 2011b), 456.
28 Stanislavsky, quoted in Gorchakov, *Rezhissyorskiye*, 183–184.

Chapter 5

1 Dasha Krijanskaia, 'Alexander Tairov (1885–1950)', in *Fifty Key Theatre Directors*, eds. Shomit Mitter and Maria Shevtsova (Abingdon: Routledge, 2005), 37.
2 Quoted in Innes and Shevtsova, *The Cambridge Introduction to Theatre Directing*, 87.
3 Hallie Flanagan, *Shifting Scenes of the Modern European Theatre* (London: George Harrap, 1929), 146.
4 Worrall, *Modernism to Realism*, 18.
5 Alexander Tairov, *Notes of a Director*, trans. William Kulke (Oxford, OH: Miami University Press, 1969), 92–93.
6 Konstantin Stanislavsky, 'Letter to Herbert Graf 11 October 1927', in *Stanislavsky: A Life in Letters*, ed. Laurence Senelick (Abingdon: Routledge, 2014), 493.

7 Gladkov, *Meyerhold Speaks*, 97.
8 Aleksandr Tairov, 'Hocus-pocus in the Science of Theatrical Art' (1922), in *The Soviet Theater: A Documentary History*, eds. Laurence Senelick and Sergei Ostrovsky (New Haven, CT: Yale University Press, 2014), 176.
9 Yevgeny Vakhtangov, 'From a Diary' (26 March 1921), in *The Soviet Theater*, eds. Senelick and Ostrovsky, 136.
10 Tairov, *Notes of a Director*, 51.
11 Oliver Sayler, *The Russian Theatre under the Revolution* (London: Brentano's, 1923), 137.
12 Aleksandr Tairov, 'The Kamerny Theatre' (1933), in *The Soviet Theater*, eds. Senelick and Ostrovsky, 409.
13 Quoted in Dassia Posner, 'Performance as Polemic: Tairov's 1920 Princess Brambilla', *Theatre Survey* 51, no. 1 (May 2010): 34.
14 'Kronika', *Izvestia* (1924) in *The Soviet Theater*, eds. Senelick and Ostrovsky, 182–183.
15 Ibid.
16 Krijanskaia, 'Alexander Tairov', 37.
17 Tairov, *Notes of a Director*, 91.
18 Ibid.
19 Rudnitsky, *Russian and Soviet Theatre*, 18.
20 Laurence Senelick, 'Salome in Russia', *Nineteenth Century Theatre Research* 12, no. 1 (1984): 94.
21 Sayler, *The Russian Theatre under the Revolution*, 160–161.
22 Tairov, *Notes of a Director*, 82.
23 Nancy Van Baer, 'Design and Movement in the Theatre of the Russian Avant-Garde', in *Theatre in Revolution: Russian Avant-Garde Stage Design*, ed. Nancy Van Baer (London: Thames and Hudson, 1991), 42.
24 Tairov, *Notes of a Director*, 120. Emphasis his.
25 Thomas Joseph Torda, 'Tairov's Phaedra: Monumental Mythological Tragedy', *The Drama Review* 29, no. 4 (1985): 78.
26 Ibid.
27 John Bowlt and Nina D. Lobanov-Rostovsky, *Encyclopaedia of Russian Stage Design: 1880–1930: volume II* (Woodbridge: Antique Collectors' Club, 2013), 380.
28 Rudnitsky, *Russian and Soviet Theatre*, 237.
29 Walter Benjamin, 'Moscow Diary [Extract] (1926)', in *The Soviet Theater*, eds. Senelick and Ostrovsky, 286.
30 Tairov, *Notes of a Director*, 110.
31 Ibid.
32 Ibid., 100.

33 Edward Gordon Craig, *On the Art of Theatre* (Abingdon: Routledge, 2009 [1911]), 28–29.
34 Tairov, *Notes of a Director*, 76.
35 Rudnitsky, *Russian and Soviet Theatre*, 15.
36 Worrall, *Modernism to Realism*, 33, 35.
37 Tairov, *Notes of a Director*, 82.
38 Ibid., 88.
39 Ibid.
40 Krijanskaia, 'Alexander Tairov', 39.
41 Worrall, *Modernism to Realism*, 18.
42 Torda, 'Tairov's Phaedra', 80.
43 Cited in Torda, 'Tairov's Phaedra', 77.
44 Tairov, *Notes of a Director*, 78.
45 Posner, 'Performance as Polemic', 48.
46 Ibid., 56.
47 Thomas Joseph Torda, 'Tairov's Princess Brambilla: A Fantastic, Phantasmagoric "Capriccio" at the Moscow Kamerny Theatre', *Theatre Journal* 32, no. 4 (December 1980): 498.
48 Tairov, *Notes of a Director*, 77.
49 Ibid., 109.
50 Ibid., 110.
51 Georgii Kovalenko, 'The Constructivist Stage', in *Theatre in Revolution*, ed. Baer, 152.
52 Horst Frenz, 'Alexander Tairov and the 1930 World Tour of the Kamerny Theatre', in *Studies in Theatre and Drama: Essays in Honor of Hubert Heffner*, ed. Oscar Brockett (The Hague: Mouton, 1972), 177.
53 Flanagan, *Shifting Scenes*, 152.
54 Julia Listengarten, 'Problematics of Theatrical Negotiations: Directing, Scenography and State Ideology', in *Directors and Designers*, ed. Christine White (Chicago: Chicago University Press, 2009), 133.
55 Rudnitsky, *Russian and Soviet Theatre*, 136.
56 Edward Braun reads the set design of these two productions in parallel. Braun, *Meyerhold: A Revolution in Theatre*, 195.
57 Listengarten, 'Problematics of Theatrical Negotiations', 126.
58 Rudnitsky, *Russian and Soviet Theatre*, 154–155.
59 Lucas Harriman, 'The Russian Betrayal of G. K. Chesterton's The Man Who Was Thursday', *Comparative Literature* 62, no. 1 (2010): 44.
60 Tairov, *Notes of a Director*, 97.
61 Ibid., 101.
62 Ibid., 112.

63 Aleksandr Tairov, 'Interview about *Giroflé-Girofla* (10 October 1922)', in *The Soviet Theater*, eds. Senelick and Ostrovsky, 175.
64 Rudnitsky, *Russian and Soviet Theatre*, 148–149.
65 Tairov, *Notes of a Director*, 103.
66 Ibid., 141.
67 Ibid., 142.
68 Rudnitsky, *Russian and Soviet Theatre*, 149.
69 Anatoly Lunacharsky, 'Theater and Revolutionary Russia' (1922), in *The Soviet Theater*, eds. Senelick and Ostrovsky, 171. Lunacharsky, like so many of his governmental colleagues, changed his mind about Tairov's theatre at various points. He particularly admired *Phaedre*.
70 See Baer, *Theatre in Revolution*, 189, for a more detailed plot description.
71 Alexsandr Tairov, '*The Optimistic Tragedy* (1932)', in *The Soviet Theater*, eds. Senelick and Ostrovsky, 340.
72 Alisa Koonen, 'Stranitsy zhizni (1975)', in *The Soviet Theater*, eds. Senelick and Ostrovsky, 339.
73 Cited in Gregor Aronson, 'The Tragedy of the Cosmopolite Tairov', *The Russian Review* 11, no. 3 (June 1952): 153.
74 Cited in ibid., 155.
75 Van Baer, *Theatre in Revolution*, 54.
76 Worrall, *Modernism to Realism*, 57.
77 Boris Golubovsky, 'Bol'shie malen'kie teatry' (1998), in *The Soviet Theater*, eds. Senelick and Ostrovsky, 338.
78 Y. A. Golovashenko, *Rezhissyorskoe iskusstvo Tairova* (Moscow: Iskusstvo, 1970), cited in J. B. Priestley, *Maggie Gale* (London: Routledge, 2008), 147.
79 Katherine Weinstein, 'Towards a Theatre of Creative Imagination', *Eugene O'Neill Review* (May 1998): 162.
80 Eugene O'Neill, letter to *New York Herald*, 30 June 1930, in *The Unknown O'Neill: Unpublished or Unfamiliar Writings of Eugene O'Neill*, Eugene O'Neill (New Haven, CT: Yale University Press, 1988), 418.
81 Rudnitsky, *Russian and Soviet Theatre*, 196.
82 Tairov, *Notes of a Director*, 80.
83 Torda, '*Tairov's Princess Brambilla*', 491.
84 Tairov, *Notes of a Director*, 143.

Chapter 6

1 See, for example, John E. Bowlt (ed.), *Russian Avant-Garde Theatre: War, Revolution and Design* (London: Nick Hern, 2014), 17.
2 See Liisa Byckling, 'Michael Chekhov's Work as a Director', in *The Routledge Companion to Michael Chekhov*, eds. Marie-Christine Autant-Mathieu and

Yana Meerzon (Abingdon: Routledge, 2015), 21–39, and Alma H. Law, 'Chekhov's Russian Hamlet (1924)', *TDR: The Drama Review* 27, no. 3 (1983): 34–45.

3   This collection is held for the Dartington Hall Trust at the South West Heritage Centre in Exeter.

4   For clear and detailed introductions to his work, with a strong focus on acting, see Chekhov's own book *To the Actor* (London and New York, Routledge, 2002) and Franc Chamberlain, *Michael Chekhov* (London: Routledge, 2004).

5   Chekhov, *To the Actor*, li.

6   Ibid.

7   Rudolf Steiner (1861–1925) was an Austrian philosopher, who founded the esoteric, spiritual movement of Anthroposophy in the early twentieth century. The Anthroposophists believe that the spiritual realm is an objective phenomenon and practise meditation to develop their capacity to observe and understand it.

8   The General Political Agency was a forerunner of the KGB (the acronym by which the Russian Committee for State Security was known, which was the Soviet Union's main security agency from 1954 onwards).

9   Chekhov, *The Path of the Actor* (London and New York: Routledge, 2005), 136.

10 Ibid., 219.

11 Emanuel Levy, *The Habima, Israel's National Theater 1917–1977: A Study of Cultural Nationalism* (New York: Columbia University Press, 1979), 107.

12 For more information on Chekhov's work at Dartington, see Tom Cornford, 'A New Kind of Conversation: Michael Chekhov's Turn to the Crafts', *Theatre, Dance and Performance Training* 4, no. 2 (2013): 189–203 and Tom Cornford, 'The English Theatre Studios of Michael Chekhov and Michel Saint-Denis 1935–1965', PhD thesis, University of Warwick, 2012, http://webcat.warwick.ac.uk/record=b2684505~S1 (accessed 12 September 2017), 33–123.

13 A script and production score can be found (under the title *Revisor*) in Charles Leonard (ed.), *Michael Chekhov's To the Director and Playwright* (New York: Harper and Row, 1963), 111–329.

14 Quoted in Deirdre Hurst du Prey's Teaching Notes for classes at the Michael Chekhov Studio, New York; Michael Chekhov Theatre Studio Deirdre Hurst du Prey Archive, MC/S9/2.

15 Chekhov, *To the Actor*, 94.

16 Leonard, *Michael Chekhov's To the Director and Playwright*, 45.

17 *Michael Chekhov on Theatre and the Art of Acting* (CD, The Working Arts Library, 2005), Disc 1.

18 *Michael Chekhov on Theatre*, Disc 1.

19 Tom Cornford, 'Michael Chekhov: The Spiritual Realm and Invisible Body', in *Theatre and Ghosts: Materiality, Performance and Modernity*, eds. Mary Luckhurst and Emilie Morin (Basingstoke: Palgrave Macmillan, 2014), 179.

20 Quoted in Cornford, 'A New Kind of Conversation', 195.

21 Transcription of class dated 16 October 1936, Michael Chekhov Theatre Studio Deirdre Hurst du Prey Archive, MC/S1/A/1.

22 Chekhov, *To the Actor*, 48–49.
23 Quoted in Cornford, 'Michael Chekhov: The Spiritual Realm and the Invisible Body', 195.
24 Michael Chekhov, *Lessons for Teachers of His Acting Technique*, ed. Deirdre Hurst du Prey (Ottawa: Dovehouse Editions, 2000), 71.
25 Chekhov, *To the Actor*, 99.
26 Chekhov, *To the Actor*, 104.
27 Rudolf Steiner, 'Understanding the Spiritual World (Part One)' (18 April 1914), in 'The Presence of the Dead on the Spiritual Path', http://wn.rsarchive.org/Lectures/GA154/English/AP1990/19140418p01.html (accessed 3 October 2017).
28 Law, 'Chekhov's Russian Hamlet', 35.
29 Michael Chekhov, *On the Technique of Acting* (New York: Harper Collins, 1991), 89.
30 Ibid.
31 Tikhonovich, quoted in Law, 'Chekhov's Russian Hamlet', 35.
32 Law, 'Chekhov's Russian Hamlet', 35.
33 Andrei Kirillov and Franc Chamberlain (eds.), 'Rehearsal Protocols for *Hamlet* by William Shakespeare at the Second Moscow Art Theatre', *Theatre, Dance and Performance Training* 4, no. 2 (2013): 243.
34 Ibid., 247.
35 Michael Chekhov, *The Chekhov Theatre Studio* (London: The Curwen Press, 1936), 18.
36 Julie Sanders, *Adaptation and Appropriation* (Abingdon: Routledge, 2016), 53.
37 For more information, see Chamberlain, *Michael Chekhov*, 83–104.
38 Chekhov, *The Chekhov Theatre Studio*, 16.
39 Chamberlain, *Michael Chekhov*, 91–103.
40 Chekhov, *To the Actor*, 13.
41 Transcription of class dated 22 October 1937, MC/S1/A/3.
42 Transcription of class dated 8 November 1936, MC/S1/A/1.
43 Transcription of class dated 12 October 1937, MC/S1/A/3.
44 Chekhov, *To the Actor*, 36.
45 Ibid., 16.
46 Ibid., 12.
47 Transcription of class dated 11 December 1936, MC/S1/A/1.

Chapter 7

1 Natalia Sats of the Moscow Theatre for Children may be considered an exception (see Chapter 8), as could Nina Simonovich-Efimova's work with puppets (see Chapter 3). Nevertheless, Remizova remains the one and only case in the Russian theatre for adults.

2   Her longest-running production (Fredro's *Ladies and Husars*) performed to sold-out houses for over a quarter of a century.
3   Russian title: '*Sviatynya braka*' (*Holy Matrimony*).
4   An incessant door buzzer sound, in the middle of the night, stayed in the national psyche for decades.
5   Unpublished interview with Remizova, on her process, dated 13 January 1959, p. 4. The typescript, with Remizova's corrections, is kept in the Remizova family archive in Moscow.
6   Ibid., 2.
7   Ibid., 5.
8   It was, of course, ironic that Remizova's comeback after being charged with 'cosmopolitanism' was yet again with a play based on a work by a foreign author.
9   P. Ivanov, 'K voprosu tvorcheskoi vzyskatel'nosti' (*On the matter of creative strictness*), *Vechernyaya Moskva* 14 January (1953): 4.
10 V. Hugo, *Les Miserables* trans. Charles E. Wilbour (Ware: Wordsworth Editions, 1994), xiv.
11 K. Stanislavsky, *Sobranie sochinenii v vos'mi tomakh* (*Collected Works in Eight Volumes*), vol. 4 (Moscow: Iskusstvo, 1957), 453.
12 A. Matskin, 'Opravdaniye groteska' (*Justification of Grotesque*), *Teatr* October (1955): 65.
13 Ibid., 63.
14 Ibid., 69.
15 Unpublished 1959 interview, p. 9.
16 L. Grossman, 'Roman-tragediya' (*Tragic Novel*), *Vechernyaya Moskva* 6 May (1958): 4.
17 N. Berkovsky, Literatura i teatr (*Literature and Theatre*) (Moscow: Iskusstvo, 1969), 578–589.
18 Dostoyevsky's letter to Apollon Maikov, 12 January 1868, quoted in Konstantin K. Mochulsky, *Dostoevsky: His Life and Work* (Princeton, NJ: Princeton University Press, 1967), 344.
19 This is confirmed by several critics; see Y. Golovashenko, *Klassika na stsene* (*Classical Works Onstage*) (Moscow: Iskusstvo, 1964); T. Chebotarskaya, 'Geroi Dostoyevskogo v romane i na stsene' ('Dostoyevsky Characters in His Novel and Onstage'), *Moskovskaya Pravda* 29 May (1958): 3.
20 Cherbotarskaya, 'Geroi', 3.
21 Golovashenko, *Klassika*, 165.
22 Ibid., 164.
23 Ibid., 165.
24 Grossman, 'Roman-tragediya', 4.
25 Cherbotarskaya, 'Geroi', 3.
26 R. Steiner, *Knowledge of the Higher Worlds: How Is It Achieved?* (Forest Row: Rudolf Steiner Press, 2011), 12.

Chapter 8

1. Part of the biographical information on Sats is taken from Manon van de Water, 'Raising the Soviet Citizen: Natalia Sats's Revolutionary Theatre for Children and Youth, 1917–1932', in *Nationalism and Youth in Theatre and Performance*, eds. Angela Sweigart-Gallagher and Victoria Pettersen Lantz (London: Routledge, 2014), 85–99.

2. Most of the works on Sats or featuring Sats in Russian or English have been authored by herself. She wrote several autobiographies, among them *Zhizn' – iavlenie polosatoe* (Moskva: Novosti, 1991), *Deti prikhodiat v teatr* (Moskva: Iskusstvo, 1961), *Vsegda s toboi* (Moskva: Detskaia Literatura, 1965) and *Novelly moei zhizni*, vols. 1 and 2 (Moskva: Iskusstvo, 1979, 1984). Of the two volumes of *Novelly*, a compilation has been translated into English, as *Sketches from My Life* (Moskva: Raduga, 1985). Parts of these biographies overlap, and some areas are rich in detailed descriptions, but large segments of her life are also brushed over, and of course the material is a product of memory and forgetting and has to be interpreted with a certain scepticism. For ease of cross-referencing for the English reader, where possible the quotes are from *Sketches from My Life* in the original translation. All other translations are mine.

3. Natalia Sats had one younger sister, Nina, with whom she was very close. Nina was robbed and murdered near Evpatoria on the Black Sea in the early 1920s when she was twenty years old. Sats, *Sketches from My Life*, English translation of revised Russian text, 92–93.

4. Ibid., 61.

5. Ibid., 61–62.

6. Ibid., 259.

7. See, for example, van de Water *Moscow Theatres for Young People*.

8. Galina Kolosova, interview by author, 24 September 2013.

9. See, for example, Michelle Solberg, 'The Global Post-war Youth Crisis and Contemporary Theatre for Young Audiences in Japan' (PhD diss., University of Wisconsin–Madison, 2013), 102–104, 108; Daisaku Ikeda, 'Natalia Sats – Triumph of the Human Spirit', *SGI Quarterly*, http://www.sgiquarterly.org/global2006Jan-1.html (accessed 25 February 2018); Winifred Ward, *Theatre for Children*, rev. edn. (Anchorage: Kentucky, 1950), 19–29, 125; Lowell Swortzell (ed.), *Six Plays for Young People from the Federal Theatre Project (1936–1939)* (New York: Greenwood, 1986), 8–10; and Wolfgang Schneider and Gerd Taube (eds.), *Kinder- und Jugendtheater in Russland* (Tübingen: Gunter Narr Verlag, 2003), vii.

10. Winifred Ward, the 'mother' of children's theatre in the United States, bluntly states that 'Drama for Children in other [non-Russian] European countries has not been notable'. Ward, *Theatre for Children*, 20.

11. Sats was both doubtful of the qualifications of child actors and strongly objected to the exploitation of children as actors. Natalia Sats, *Nash Put': Moskovskii Teatr dlia Detei i ego zritel'* (Moskva: Moskovskii Oblastnoi Otdel Narodnogo Obrazovaniia, 1932), 4.

12 Sats, *Deti prichodiat v teatr*, 35–39; Sats, *Sketches from My Life*, 64–68.
13 Sats, *Nash Put'*, 5.
14 Economic dislocation generally refers to the state where economic conditions have changed to the point that the jobs people held no longer exist leading to high unemployment and displacement of workers from the work environment and means of earning income. Economic Displacement in 1917 and in Lenin's 'Resolution on Measures to Cope with Economic Dislocation' referred more specifically to the Marxist notion of the need for proletarian ownership of factories. For more specifics, see Bolshevik.info.
15 Sats, *Nash Put'*, 5. I am very aware that 'first' is a big claim. However, decades of international research in Theatre for Young Audiences (TYA) has not rendered any evidence that refutes this claim.
16 Lenora Shpet, *Sovetskii teatr dlia detei: Stranitsy istorii 1918–1945* (Moskva: Iskusstvo, 1971), 25–27. For more on Simonovich-Efimova, see Chapter 3.
17 Introductions like this are to this day a hallmark of the Natalia Sats Musical Theatre, where every opera and ballet performance is currently (2013) introduced by Natalia Sats's daughter, Roksana Sats.
18 Quoted in Shpet, *Sovetskii*, 45.
19 10 Mamonovsky Alley, later 10 Sadovsky Alley, and now 10 Mamonovsky Alley once again. The theatre has been housing theatres for young audiences since the ballet and puppet theatre first moved there in 1918. From 1941 until this day, it is the home of the Moscow TIUZ (Mtiuz), the Moscow Theatre of the Young Spectator, in English now known as the New Generation Theatre. The Mtiuz became the vanguard of 'Perestroika Theatre' and one of the most innovative 'art' theatres in Moscow in the 1990s (see Chapter 12).
20 Sats points out, rightly, that 'First' is a misnomer since her 1918 Children's Theatre of the Moscow Soviet was technically 'first'. Sats, *Nash Put'*, 7.
21 George E. Shail, 'The Leningrad Theatre of Young Spectators' (Diss., New York University, 1980), 683.
22 Sats, *Nash Put'*, 10–24.
23 Shpet, *Sovetskii*, 65.
24 Quoted in ibid., 66.
25 Hall emphasized the 'dramatic instinct' of children, theorizing that children acquire values and ideas of modern civilization by instinctive play. Basically, they replicate the activities of primitive people in the evolution from the simple to the complex. Following these theories, Sats and Rozanov developed stories about animals, nomads, tribal life and so forth, which they tried to incorporate into plays about the culture of the folk art of people in many lands and places. Eventually Sats and Rozanov abandoned the concept, considering it too limited and too rooted in folk and fairy tales, a genre that became increasingly suspect.
26 For more on Hall's theories, see Richard Courtney, *Play, Drama, and Thought: The Intellectual Background to Dramatic Education* (London: Cassell, 1968), 36–38; 66–67.
27 Shpet, *Sovetskii*, 72.

28 Shail, 'The Leningrad Theatre', 67. The Pioneers was a Soviet youth organization for children ages 10 to 15, founded in 1922. The official uniform of the Pioneers was a white shirt or blouse with a red handkerchief; the official slogan was *'vsegda gotov'* (always prepared).
29 Gene Sosin, 'Children's Theatre and Drama in the Soviet Union (1917–1953)' (Diss., Columbia University, Ann Arbor: UMI, 1958), 78.
30 Shpet, *Sovetskii*, 73.
31 Ibid., 74.
32 Ibid.; see also Boris Wolfson, 'Juggernaut in Drag', in *Russian Children's Literature and Culture*, eds. Marina Balina and Larissa Rudova (New York: Routledge, 2008), 177–179. *The Negro Boy and the Monkey* was taken back up by Natalia Sats in her Musical Theatre and was still on the repertoire in 1994.
33 Natalia Sats, 'My Vocation', in *Theatre for Young Audiences*, ed. Nellie McCaslin (New York: Longman, 1978), 109.
34 Moscow: Iskusstvo, 1951.
35 Ibid., 110.
36 Ibid., 110–111.
37 Ibid., 111.
38 In Russia to this day you can find both roles as well as the überrole of *Rezhissyor-postanovshchik*, which would be more akin to artistic director. The director is also the producer; there is no distinction made between those two functions.
39 Sats, 'My Vocation', 112.
40 Ibid.
41 Sats, *Sketches from My Life*, 112.
42 By the 1930s, it had become customary that boy roles would be played by petit female actors in drag (and in Nagua's case in blackface too). This custom, called the *'aktrisa-travesty'* (travesty actress) endured until years after *glasnost* and *perestroika*. See also Wolfson, 'Juggernaut in Drag', 186–188.
43 By 1930 there were twenty theatres for children and youth, by 1932 forty-two, and in 1940, just before the Second World War, there were more than seventy state-subsidized theatres for young audiences in the Soviet Union. Shail, 'The Leningrad Theatre', 84–85, 681.
44 During the New Economic Policy, which lasted from 1921 to 1927, a partial return to private enterprise was allowed, especially in farming and private industry. This instigated a feeling of freedom, which led to many daring, avant-garde experimentations and innovations in theatre, art and literature. As this chapter indicates, this was not limited to theatres for adults – students of Stanislavsky, Meyerhold, Vakhtangov and others also experimented in children's theatre.
45 'Pedology' was the official term for the scientific study of heredity and environment as factors in child development and relied heavily on quantitative study. By the mid-1930s, the belief in determination through heredity and

environment, as well as quantitative 'fact' studies in general, was considered to be anti-Marxist because it refuted the idea of dialectics, progress and chance inherent in the ideology of Marxism-Leninism.

46 The term 'formalism', or 'bourgeois formalism', originally pointed to art that relied on form instead of social content, but soon it became 'a catch phrase for any form of artistic experimentation antithetical to official support for the realistic representation of life and reality in all the arts'. Shail, 'The Leningrad Theatre', 520.

47 For more details, see van de Water, *Moscow Theatres for Young People*, 52–60.

48 Shail, 'The Leningrad Theatre', 534, 768.

49 *Komsomolskaia Pravda*, quoted in Shpet, *Sovetskii*, 221.

50 Ibid.

51 Sats, *Deti prichodiat v teatr*, 279–284.

52 *Peter and the Wolf* premiered 5 May 1936. For a rare glimpse of Natalia Sats on video, and a documentary on *Peter and the Wolf*, see *Peter and the Wolf*, vcr., narrated by Natalia Sats with documentary, 1986 (Albany: Suny, 1990).

53 Sats, *Sketches from My Life*, 273–283.

54 While this may seem strange it was not. In the early 1930s Natalia Sats was invited by Otto Klemperer to direct Verdi's *Falstaff* at the Kroll Opera in Berlin, and both Verdi's *Falstaff* and Mozart's *Marriage of Figaro* at the Teatro Colón in Buenos Aires in the early 1930s. She was 29 at the time, and 'there had been never any female operatic directors in Europe'. In her autobiographies, she maintains that it was her love for children that made her go back to producing theatre and music for children time and again. Sats, *Sketches from My Life*, 149–165, 180–204.

55 Ibid., 310–14; 323–27.

56 Sats's daughter Roksana Sats states in the preface to *Nataliia Sats v zerkale i otrazheniiakh* (2013) (*Natalia Sats in images and reflections*) (printed in 2014 by the theatre): '"It seems to me that my whole life, some unknown path led me to this, the most important thing," wrote [Natalia Sats]. This most important thing is the creation of the first and to this day only professional theatre of opera and ballet for children in the world, which now carries her name' (6).

57 Her spacious office was placed above the artists' entrance so she could keep an eye on who was coming and going.

58 Viktor Viktorov, *Nataliia Sats i detskii musikal'nyi teatr* (Moscow: Kompositor, 1993), 44. The English translation by Miriam Morton is published as Victor Victorov, *The Natalia Sats Children's Musical Theatre* (Moscow: Raduga, 1986). Like Sats's translated biographies (*Novelly* I and II), the Russian and English versions are not identical. Citations from the Russian edition are documented as Viktorov with a K, and the translations are mine.

59 Viktorov, *Nataliia Sats i detskii*, 44.

60 Quoted in Victorov, *The Natalia Sats*, 53–54.

61 Adapted from Victor Victorov's notes at the Artistic Councils of the Children's Musical Theatre, 136–139.

62 While the theatre had, as all theatres in Russia, a difficult time in the 1990s, it has fully recovered. At this point, it has its own symphony orchestra (over 100 musicians), opera (75 singers) and ballet (60 dancers) companies, as well as its own professional chorus. http://teatr-sats.ru (accessed 1 February 2017).

63 Sats, *Zhizn'*, 588.

Chapter 9

1 Mar Sulimov, *Priglashenie v rezhissuru (Initiation to Directing)* (St Petersburg: St Petersburg University Publishing House, 2004).

2 The term '*Metod deistvennogo analiza*' (*Method of Action Analysis*) was introduced into Russian theatre practice in the late 1950s and early 1960s by Maria Knebel (in her teaching and her book *About the Method of Action Analysis of Play and the Role*, Moscow, 1961), who had summarized Stanislavsky's lessons in directing she received in the 1930s. The technically correct and more helpful English translation of this term is 'the Method of Analysis through Action' or 'the Method of Analysis by means of Action'. In English-language literature, this method is commonly called Action Analysis or often, but not correctly, Active Analysis. This chapter will use Action Analysis and Analysis through Action interchangeably. Main exponents of Action Analysis are Maria Knebel, her disciple Anatoly Efros and Alexander Polamishev in Moscow and Georgy Tovstongov and Mar Sulimov in Leningrad–St Petersburg, each of which has left fundamental books with their own interpretation of Action Analysis (sometimes even with different terminology). The correlation of the Method of Physical Actions (corrupted in the practice of Mikhail Kedrov and reinterpreted in the work of Jerzy Grotowski) and the Etude Method with the Method of Action Analysis is a separate problem also interpreted differently.

3 Sergei Tcherkasski (ed.), *Rezhissyorskaya shkola Sulimova (Sulimov's School of Directing)* (St Petersburg: SPbGATI, 2013).

4 Saulius Šaltenis, *Brys, Smert', Brys!* A play in two acts (Moscow: VAAP, 1977).

5 Boris Muraviev, speech during the discussion about the production *Shoo, Death, Shoo!* An excerpt from the director's department meeting protocol, 12 December 1983 // M. V. Sulimov's Archive at the St Petersburg State Theatre Library. ORiRK, F. 54.

6 All further quotations from Sulimov are taken from *Our Diary*, the journal of Sulimov's Studio. Notebook 9. 1–70; Notebook 10. 78–80; Notebook 11. 28a–28g, 31–37 // M. V. Sulimov's Archive at the St Petersburg State Theatre Library. ORiRK, F. 54; and notes taken by the author from rehearsals with Prof. Mar Sulimov in 1982–1984 (S. Tcherkasski Archive).

7 Sulimov underlined more than once that it is crucial to make a difference between the Stanislavsky System as a system of actor training that goes out of laws of nature and thus is universal and objective, and the aesthetic of Stanislavsky's own directing practice at the Moscow Art Theatre of the first decades of the twentieth century.

8 Sulimov's Studio, *Our Diary*.

9   Šaltenis, *Brys, Smert', Brys!*, 7.
10 Ibid., 4.
11 Sulimov's Studio, *Our Diary*.
12 Ibid.
13 Ibid.
14 *Sverkhzadacha* – a term of the Stanislavsky System – translated as *supertask* (Konstantin Stanislavski, *An Actor's Work*, trans. J. Benedetti (London: Routledge, 2008)) and *superobjective* (Constantin Stanislavski, *An Actor Prepares*, trans. E. R. Hapgood (London: Geoffrey Bles, 1936)). The supertask/superobjective of a playwright is the theme, the inner meaning of the play, the reason why it was written. The supertask/superobjective of a director is the reason why this play is staged today, in the way it is staged.
15 Sulimov's Studio, *Our Diary*.
16 Ibid.
17 *The nature of feelings (priroda chuvstv)* is another term from Stanislavsky-based vocabulary; it describes an author's or a character's mode of perception of life. The nature of feelings is closely connected with what Nemirovich-Danchenko called *the face of the author*.
18 *Humanology* is a neologism coined in Russian many years ago to describe the study of the human. Sulimov usually insists that 'the art of directing is the art of *humanology*', thus underlining that theatre is first of all the *study* of the human, not entertainment, and directing is first of all connected with the deep analysis of the human soul and only secondly – with the staging of the production.
19 Sulimov's Studio, *Our Diary*; Sergei Tcherkasski, Notes from Prof. Sulimov's rehearsals.
20 Mar Sulimov, *Posvyashenie v rezhissuru (Initiation to Directing)* (St Petersburg: St Petersburg University Publishing House, 2004), 340.
21 Ibid., 339–340.
22 When during the rehearsal a director acts some bit of the scene, or moments of the part or a character's behaviour to explain it for an actor more clearly, he usually presents not *how* to act but *what* to act; in other words, he performs the main intention, not the actual behaviour. That is the main difference between actor's acting and director's acting – the first needs to experience the part, the latter is somewhat presenting it. Furthermore, parallels with psychological acting vs. *die Verfremdung* and Stanislavsky vs. Brecht might be seen here. Many Russian directors, Stanislavsky and Meyerhold among them, were especially known for their inspiring demonstrations during rehearsals.
23 Sulimov's Studio, *Our Diary*.
24 *Mode of existence (sposob sushestvovania)* is a term from the Stanislavsky-based vocabulary that describes a particular way of living through the role. For example, an encounter with an event requires different ways of evaluating it and consequent character behaviour even inside the similar genres; thus fear of punishment needs to be performed differently, with its own mode of existence, in comedies by Molière or Gogol.

25 This phrase, initially coined by Tovstonogov, was repeated by Sulimov hundreds of times. See Tcherkasski, Notes from Prof. Sulimov's classes 1980–1985.
26 Sulimov's Studio, *Our Diary*.
27 Ibid.
28 Ibid.
29 To be clear, rehearsals of *Shoo, Death, Shoo!* was not the only work students were doing during this period. They were also continuing their training in other subjects (voice and speech, dance, movement, lectures in literature, theatre history and art history) as well as fulfilling the directing programme's curriculum including the staging of one-act plays.
30 Sulimov's Studio, *Our Diary*.
31 Ibid.
32 Ibid.
33 Ibid.
34 An early, unabridged version of this chapter first appeared as Sergei Tcherkasski, 'Inside Sulimov's Studio: Directors Perform a Play', *Stanislavski Studies* 2, no. 2 (2014): 4–46. http://www.tandfonline.com/doi/abs/10.1080/20567790.2014.11419722, reprinted by permission of Taylor & Francis Ltd, http://www.tandfonline.com. A more detailed account of Sulimov's work on *Shoo, Death, Shoo!* and the principles of Action Analysis might be found there.

Chapter 10

1 Zavadsky had to be particularly careful. Earlier he had served a term of internal exile at Rostov-on-Don.
2 GITIS (*Gosudarstvennyi institut teatralnogo iskusstva*) is the State Institute of Theatrical Art.
3 Anatoly Efros, *The Craft of Rehearsal*, trans. James Thomas (New York: Peter Lang, 2007), 60.
4 Anatoly Efros, *The Joy of Rehearsal*, trans. James Thomas (New York: Peter Lang, 2006); *The Craft of Rehearsal*, trans. James Thomas (New York: Peter Lang, 2007); *Beyond Rehearsal*, trans. James Thomas (New York: Peter Lang, 2009).
5 Konstantin Stanislavski, 'The Stage as Art and Stock-in-Trade', in *An Actor's Work*, trans. Jean Benedetti (New York: Routledge, 2008), 18.
6 Vladimir Nemirovich-Danchenko, *My Life in the Russian Theatre*, trans. John Cournos (New York: Theatre Arts Books, 2000), 160 (italics added).
7 Augusto Boal, *Theatre of the Oppressed*, trans. Charles A. McBride (New York: Theatre Communications Group, 1993), 36–72.
8 Bertolt Brecht, *Brecht on Theatre: The Development of an Aesthetic*, trans. John Willett (New York: Hill and Wang, 1977), 179–208.
9 Chekhov, *To the Actor*, 21–34.

10 Jerzy Grotowski, *Towards a Poor Theatre*, trans. Eugenio Barba (New York: Routledge, 2002), 1–17.
11 Michael Saint-Denis, *Training for the Theatre* (New York: Theatre Arts, 1982), 79–99.
12 Lee Strasberg, *A Dream of Passion: The Development of the Method* (New York: Little-Brown, 1987), 123–174.
13 'In 1912, K. S. Stanislavsky and L. A. Sulerzhitskii founded the First Studio of the Moscow Art Theater to train young actors in the Stanislavsky method. Opened in 1913, the studio was reorganized as the second Moscow Art Theater in 1924. The Second Studio of the Moscow Art Theater was founded in 1916 by the stage director V. L. Mchedelov. Actors and actresses trained in this studio, including A. K. Tarasova, K. N. Elanskaia, O. N. Androvskaia, N. P. Khmelev, and M. M. Ianshin, joined the Moscow Art Theater in 1924. In 1920, the Vakhtangov Studio was reorganized as the Third Studio of the Moscow Art Theater (opened 1921), which later became the Evg. Vakhtangov Theater. The Fourth Studio of the Moscow Art Theater was formed in 1921 from a group of actors of the Moscow Art Theater. Headed by G. S. Burdzhalov, V. V. Luzhskii, and E. M. Raevskaia, the studio became a theater in 1924 and was named the Realistic Theater in 1927'; *The Great Soviet Encyclopedia*, 3rd edn. S.v. 'Studios of the Moscow Art Theater'. Retrieved 29 June 2017 from http://encyclopedia2.thefreedictionary.com/Studios+of+the+Moscow+Art+Theater
14 Efros, *The Craft of Rehearsal*, 58.
15 James Thomas, *A Director's Guide to Stanislavsky's Active Analysis* (London: Bloomsbury, 2006).
16 Nicholas Rzhevsky, *The Modern Russian Theatre: A Literary and Cultural History* (London: M. E. Sharpe, 2009), 39.
17 Ibid.
18 See James Thomas, 'Action Analysis', in *Script Analysis for Actors, Directors and Designers*, 5th edn. (New York: Focal Press, 2014), 1–40.
19 Ros Dixon, 'Slaughtering Sacred Seagulls: Anatolii Efros's Production of *The Seagull* at the Lenkom in 1966', *Irish Slavonic Studies* 21 (2000): 49–73.
20 Efros, *The Joy of Rehearsal*, 42–43.
21 Efros, *The Joy of Rehearsal; The Craft of Rehearsal; Beyond Rehearsal*.
22 Efros's revivals of *Marriage* and *Molière* at Minneapolis's Guthrie Theatre so impressed the Board of Directors as to offer him the position of Artistic Director, which he declined.
23 Stanislavski, *An Actor's Work*, 258–272.
24 Efros, *The Joy of Rehearsal*, 197.
25 See Maria Shevtsova, 'Anatolij Efros Directs Chekhov's *The Cherry Orchard* and Gogol's *Marriage*', *Theatre Quarterly* 7, no. 26 (1977): 34–46.
26 See Beumers, *Yuri Lyubimov*.
27 Efros, *The Joy of Rehearsal*, 104–105.
28 Ibid., 87.

29 Anatoly Efros, *Chaika (The Seagull)* (St Petersburg: Baltiskiye Sezon, 2010), 333.
30 Efros, *The Joy of Rehearsal*, 86–87.
31 Treplev was not just an avant-garde playwright but also an intruder in a world where he did not belong: 'A deadly struggle between the settled world and the man in a torn jacket' (Efros, *Chaika*, 459). Romeo and Juliet were not just teenagers in love but also 'the flowers of the nation. They walked in the mud [...] like white doves among a flock of crows' (Efros, *The Joy of Rehearsal*, 25). Othello was a 'stranger' not just because he was black but also 'for the fact that he is better than [Iago's society], cleverer, purer, more complex; for the fact that he knows much, is capable of love, and is capable of being open-hearted' (Efros, *The Joy of Rehearsal*, 117). Concerning his 1975 production of *The Cherry Orchard* at the Taganka Theatre, Efros said, 'A dying tribe of eccentrics. A small, helpless, unfortunate flock. *But at the Taganka, it will not be sentimental.* In the center, on a patch of ground, is a garden, a stone cemetery marker, and even a chair – a complete still life of their past and present life. A strongbox of their life. They often sit there, all of them, *as though waiting for an ambush*' (Efros, *The Craft of Rehearsal*, 63, italics added).
32 See note 3.

Chapter 11

1 The period following Stalin's death in 1953, during which censorship was somewhat relaxed and opportunities for open discussion increased, is known as the Thaw, after the eponymous novella by Ilya Ehrenburg written in 1954. The Thaw actually consisted of a series of small thaws and reactionary freezes that lasted until Nikita Khrushchev was deposed from power in 1964.
2 Oleg Efremov, 'Moi Stanislavskii', *Sovremennaia dramaturgiia* 3 (1983): 266.
3 Ibid., 267.
4 Oleg Efremov, 'Maski, my vas uznaem!', *Nedelia* 1 (January 1967): 12.
5 Oleg Efremov, 'Kino i teatr – puti vzaimodeistviia', *Iskusstvo kino* 6 (1982): 344–355.
6 Oleg Efremov, 'Kogda mne zadaiut vopros: kak voznik vash teatr, kakova ego programma' (1965), cited in *Oleg Efremov nastoiashchii stroitel' teatra*, ed. Lidiia Bogova (Moscow: Zerba E, 2011), 162–186.
7 Efremov, 'Moi Stanislavskii', 270.
8 Anatoly Smeliansky, *Oleg Yefremov: Masters of Soviet Art* (Moscow: Novosti Press Agency Publishing House, 1988), 21.
9 N. Volianskaia, 'V tvorcheskoi laboratorii Rezhissyora', *Teatr* 10 (1973): 51.
10 Ibid., 51.
11 Oleg Efremov, 'Vozvrashchenie', *Sovetskaia kul'tura* 14 June 1988.
12 Oleg Efremov, 'Uroki velikogo mastera', *Novyi mir* 1 (1977): 261–266.
13 Efremov, 'Kogda mne zadaiut vopros', 182.

14 Ibid.
15 'Teatr "Sovremennika". Stenogramma ot 26 Iiunia 1956, besedy V. S. Rozova i O. N. Efremova o p'ese "Vechno zhivye" i ee postanovke v studii pri MKhATe', RGALI f. 3152, op. 4, d. 1.
16 Efremov, 'Kogda mne zadaiut vopros', 176.
17 Oleg Efremov, 'Bol'she vsego ustaesh' ot otvetstvennosti', in *Rezhissyorskii teatr'. Razgovory pod zanaves veka* (Moscow, 1999), 141–154.
18 Galina Brodskaia, 'Literaturnaia zapis'', in *Oleg Efremov o teatre i o sebe*, ed. Anatoly Smeliansky (Moscow: Moskovskii khudozhestvennyi teatr, 1997), 133–138.
19 Efremov, 'Kogda mne zadaiut vopros', 179.
20 Ibid., 180.
21 Smeliansky, *Oleg Efremov o teatre i o sebe*, 69.
22 'Teatr "Sovremennika". Stenogramma ot 26 Iiunia 1956', RGALI f. 3152, op. 4, d. 1.
23 Oleg Efremov, 'Nachnem s sebia', *Sovremennaia dramaturgiia* 3 (1986): 223–234.

Chapter 12

1 The Moscow Tiuz has a very comprehensive website where you can find, among other information, a short biography of Genrietta Ianovskaia as well as a comprehensive list of her productions and awards in Russian and English. Because of space limits I will not repeat this here. http://moscowtyz.ru (accessed 25 February 2018).
2 It needs to be noted that much more has been written in English about Kama Ginkas, which is rather typical.
3 Their circle of students and emerging artists included the poet Joseph Brodsky, who typically would barge into their communal apartment at 7.00 am and awaken them with poetry recitations. See John Freedman and Kama Ginkas, *Provoking Theater: Kama Ginkas Directs* (Hanover: Smith and Kraus, 2003), chapter 10.
4 The *Tiuz, Teatr Iunogo Zritelia* or Theatre of the Young Spectator was founded shortly after the Revolution as the first professional state-supported theatre for young audiences in the world. Starting in Moscow and Leningrad *tiuzes* soon spread to other cities throughout the Soviet Union. Often, although not always, the theatres were indicated by the name of the city and tiuz, like the Moscow Tiuz or Mtiuz, the Lentiuz etc. After the Second World War the socialist republics often had two *tiuzes*, the Russian-speaking tiuz and the local-language tiuz.
5 In Freedman and Ginkas, *Provoking Theater*, 157.
6 Ibid., 215.

7   Georgy Tovstonogov (1915–1989) had his debut at the theatre in 1949 with *Somewhere in Siberia* in his native town Tbilisi. There he staged some productions for the Russian Tiuz before he came to Moscow and started directing at the Central Children's Theatre. Aleksandra Gozenpud calls Tovstonogov's arrival at the Central Children's Theatre a 'turning point … the first step on the ladder he would climb in the coming years'. She asserts that thanks to the two productions he staged at the Central Children's Theatre, Tovstonogov was discovered in Moscow and Leningrad, where he directed at the Leninsky Komsomol Theatre from 1950 to 1956 and was ultimately awarded the artistic leadership of the Bolshoi Drama Theatre in Leningrad. Aleksandra Gozenpud, *Tsentral'nii detskii teatr 1936–1961* (Moskva: Nauka, 1967), 56. According to Anatoly Smeliansky, Tovstonogov turned the Bolshoi Drama Company into 'the strongest Russian company of the post-Stalin period'. Smeliansky, *The Russian Theatre after Stalin*, 13.

8   Unless otherwise noted, director-notes come from my interview with Ianovskaia on 31 May 2016; all translations from this interview, and at other places when not noted, are mine.

9   *Shto eto bylo? Rasgovory s Natal'ei Kaz'minoi i bez nee* (*What Was That? Conversations with Nataliia Kazmina and without Her*), Kama Ginkas i Genrietta Ianovskaia (Moskva: Artist. Rezhissyor. Teatr, 2014). This book project, basically a conversation with Ginkas and Ianovskaia conducted over several years was started with critic Nataliia Kazmina, who passed away unexpectedly in 2011. Ginkas and Ianovskaia finished the book, hence the title. The citations here come from excerpts of the book which can be found, in Russian, on the internet: https://yandex.ru/search/?text=Наталья%20Кузьмина%20%22Что%20это%20было%3F%22%20Кама%20Гинкас%20Генриетта%20Яновская&lr=103392&rnd=51110

10 Genrietta Ianovskaia, Personal Interview, 31 May 2016.

11 *Shto eto bylo? Rasgovory s Natal'ei Kaz'minoi i bez nee*, Kama Ginkas i Genrietta Ianovskaia: http://iamaglika.livejournal.com/72809.html (accessed 16 February 2018).

12 Daniil Gink, in John Freedman, *Moscow Performances 1991–1996* (Amsterdam: Harwood, 1997), 215.

13 The Ministry of Culture was in charge of appointing artistic directors, although the theatres, especially when *perestroika* progressed, could express their preference. Located at 10 Mamonovsky Alley, the Moscow Tiuz is in the same space in which Natalia Sats started her puppet and marionette theatre in 1918.

14 Kama Ginkas remained a freelance director but increasingly made use of the actors and space of the Mtiuz.

15 For more on the theatres for children and youth in Soviet Russia and beyond, see van de Water, *Moscow Theatres for Young People*.

16 See the mission of ASSITEJ, the International Association of Theatre for Children and Youth, founded in 1965, with current national centres and networks in over 100 countries. Soviet Russia and the Eastern Bloc countries were, at its inception, a driving force and a model for the international organization. The twenty-first century has brought a major shift within the

17 Ekaterina Eremina, '*Roman c teatrom*', 28 April 2015, http://kultprosvet.by/roman-s-teatrom-kultprosvet/ (accessed 16 February 2018).

18 Quoted in V. Vakhramov, 'Luchshie spektakli v peredi', *Vecherniaia Moskva* 4 September 1987.

19 Nicholas Rzhevsky adapted and translated the novella in English as *Dog Heart* (New York: Slavic Cultural Center Press, 1998); Michael Glenny translated Chervinskii's adaptation as *Heart of a Dog* in his anthology *Stars in the Morning Sky* (London: Hern, 1998). I have translated the title as *Dog's Heart*, following the original (*sobache serdtse* instead of *serdtse sobaki*) and translations in other languages (Dutch *Hondehart*, German *Hundeherz*).

20 Freedman and Ginkas, *Provoking Theater*, 63.

21 Laurence Senelick, *Historical Dictionary of Russian Theatre* (Lanham, MD: Scarecrow, 2007), 159. In her production of Tennessee Williams's *A Streetcar Named Desire*, for another example, Ianovskaia inserted a non-existing scene, Stella and Blanche, holding their breath, start the last of their unsold legacy – a windup toy. A model estate 'Dream' with white columns and soft light behind the venetian windows rotates on a mahogany stand under the soft sound of bells. Elena D'iakova, '*Vyshedshie iz odnogo baraka*', *Novaia Gazeta* 16 May 2016, https://www.novayagazeta.ru/articles/2016/05/16/68617-vyshedshie-iz-odnogo-baraka (accessed 16 February 2018).

22 For a more detailed description of this production including excerpts of reviews, see van de Water, *Moscow Theatres for Young People*, 141–147; for the changes in the Moscow Tiuz in general with *glasnost* and *perestroika* and the fall of the Soviet Union, see Chapters 4, 6, 7 and 9.

23 For a detailed description see Manon van de Water, 'Mister Twister or Goodbye America!: The Interdependence of Meanings and Material Conditions', *Essays in Theatre/Études Théâtrales* 16, no. 1 (1997): 85–93.

24 Genrietta Ianovskaia, Personal Interview, 31 May 2016.

25 John Freedman, *Moscow Performances II: The 1996–1997 Season* (Amsterdam: Harwood, 1998), 48, 46.

26 Quoted in Roman Dolzhanskii, '*Vtoroi pokhod na "Grozu"*', *Kommersant'-daily* 14 February 1997.

27 As in the 1920s new contemporary plays were rare in 1990s Russia. Thus, many theatres reached back to the classics. Ostrovsky was particularly popular.

28 Marina Davydova, '*Za zerkal'noi dver'iu*', *Nezavisimaia gazeta* 18 March 1997.

29 Ibid.

30 N. Agisheva, '*Elektrichestvo ili Bozh'ia kara*', *Moskovskie novosti* 9–16 March 1997.

31 Natal'ia Krymova, '*Te zhe razgovory, te zhe liudi....* ', Archives Mtiuz.

32 Dina Goder, '*Zabud'te pro "luch sveta v temnom tsarstvo"*', *Itogi* 4 March 1997.

33 Mariia Zaionts, '*Luch sveta v svetlom tsarstve*', *Obshchaia gazeta* 20–26 February 1997.

34 Boris Minaev, '*Genrietta Ianovskaia: ot "Sobach'ego serdtsa" – do "Grozy"*', *Ogonek* 25 (June 1997): 52–54. More precisely, the critique would be on a paper by the critic Dmitrii Pisarev, which was studied in the Soviet schools next to the perfunctory interpretation by Dobroliubov (the famous words 'ray of light in the dark tsardom' cited in most, if not all, Russian reviews come from Dobroliubov).

35 N. Kaminskaia, '*Vnachale byla Katerina*', *Kul'tura* 30 December 1997.

36 Freedman and Ginkas, *Provoking Theater*, 130.

37 Personal Interview, 31 May 2016.

38 This is a persistent problem in TYA – Theatre for Young Audiences – to this day, that productions for young people, unlike productions for adults, are evaluated based on if the audience 'liked' it. It is also a reason for the lack of scholarship in TYA, a phenomenon the International TYA Research Network, founded in 2006 and now a network of ASSITEJ, attempts to challenge. https://ityarn.wordpress.com

39 See (in Russian) a short clip: https://www.youtube.com/watch?v=0ampalVDdv8 (accessed 16 February 2018).

40 Personal Interview, 31 May 2016.

41 For a short clip with interviews and stage images (in Russian), see https://www.youtube.com/watch?v=RksTuSzI4nI (accessed 16 February 2018).

42 Yevgeny Anatolevich Popov (1946–) was suppressed under the Soviets in the 1970s. Popov was part of an underground publishing almanak, *Metropol*, together with, among others, Anna Akhmadulina and Vassilii Pavlovich Aksenov.

43 http://moscowtyz.ru/pleshivyy-amurpremera (accessed 16 February 2018).

44 Kama Ginkas, Personal Interview, 31 May 2016.

45 Ginkas, Personal Interview.

46 http://moscowtyz.ru/olga-zavalishina-pleshivyy-amur (accessed 16 February 2018).

47 Personal Interview, 31 May 2016.

Conclusion

1 I have written about issues of transmission and Russian theatre practice in more detail elsewhere; see Amy Skinner, 'Riding the Waves: Uncovering Biomechanics in Britain', in *Russians in Britain: British Theatre and the Russian Tradition of Actor Training*, ed. Jonathan Pitches (London and New York: Routledge, 2012), 86–109.

2 For more on this, see Jonathan Pitches, 'Conclusion: A Common Theatre History? The Russian Tradition in Britain Today: Katie Mitchell, Declan Donnellan and Michael Boyd', in *Russians in Britain: British Theatre and the*

Russian Tradition of Actor Training, ed. Jonathan Pitches (London and New York: Routledge, 2012), 192–210. A *Guardian* newspaper article on Sellars mentions the director's 'love for the Russian theatre which [...] colour[ed] his work for decades'. https://www.theguardian.com/music/2000/may/20/classicalmusicandopera (accessed 21 October 2018).

3 The MA/MFA in Theatre Directing at the East 15 conservatoire, for example, offers modules at GITIS; see http://www.east15.ac.uk/courses/mamfa-theatre-directing/ (accessed 17 May 2018).

4 My own article on theatre and revolution was commissioned to illustrate the significance of performance in 1917; see Amy Skinner, 'Spotlights and Searchlights: Theatre and the Russian Revolution', *Culture Matters*, 4 January 2018, http://culturematters.org.uk/index.php/arts/theatre/item/2705-spotlights-and-searchlights-theatre-and-the-russian-revolution (accessed 18 May 2018).

5 The Russian-Anglo Research Network was founded in 2011; see https://anglorussiannetwork.wordpress.com/ (accessed 16 May 2018). The Russian Theatre Research Network was founded in 2012; see Amy Skinner, 'An introduction to the Russian Theatre Research Network', *Stanislavski Studies* 3, no. 1 (2015): 31–34.

6 This is not to say that Stanislavsky's legacy is either straightforward or uncontested, but simply that his name and some aspects of his practice (although often partial or misunderstood) are widely acknowledged.

7 Meyerhold claimed that there was 'no theatre more opposed and alien to [him] than the Kamerny [...] between us and the Kamerny there is an abyss'. In Aleksandr Gladkov, *Meyerhold Speaks, Meyerhold Rehearses*, edited and translated by Alma Law (Amsterdam: Harwood Academic Press, 1997), 97.

8 Frederick Winslow Taylor's work concerns efficiency and economy in a work setting and proposes the physical mastery of certain tools by the worker in order to improve productivity. More on biomechanics can be found in Alma Law and Mel Gordon, *Meyerhold, Eisenstein and Biomechanics* (Jefferson: McFarland, 2012). More on Meyerhold's use of Taylorism can be found in Mel Gordon, 'Meyerhold's Biomechanics', *TDR: The Drama Review* 18, no. 3 (1974): 73–88.

9 Although these terms can be translated, biomechanical terminology is most commonly used in Russian in the rehearsal or training room. As such, I use the Russian terms here, rather than their English translations.

10 Meyerhold, in Braun, *Meyerhold on Theatre*, 247.

11 Jonathan Pitches, *Vsevolod Meyerhold* (London and New York: Routledge, 2003), 55.

12 Anna Seymour, quoted in Phil Jones, *Drama as Therapy, Vol. 1: Theory, Practice and Research*, 2nd edn. (London and New York: Routledge, 2007), 235. Seymour applies this understanding of the *otkaz* in her work in dramatherapy.

13 Chambers, 'Reconstructing Revizor', 60.

14 Ibid.

BIBLIOGRAPHY

Abramov, A. 'Vsye moi synovia'. *Vechernyaya Moskva*, 3 December 1948: 4.
Agisheva, N. 'Elektrichevstvo ili Bozh'ia kara'. *Moskovskie novosti*, 9–16 March 1997.
'Anatoly Efros'. Dmitry Krymov Laboratory, http://eng.efros.org/people/efros_anatolii_vasilevich/ (accessed 31 May 2017).
Aronson, Gregor. 'The Tragedy of the Cosmopolite Tairov'. *The Russian Review* 11, no. 3 (June 1952): 148–156.
Baer, Nancy van Norman. *Theatre in Revolution: Russian Avant-Garde Stage Design*. London: Thames and Hudson, 1991.
Balukhaty, S. D. *The Seagull Produced by Stanislavsky*, translated by David Magarshack. London: David Dobson Ltd, 1952.
Bartram, N. D. 'Kukol'nyi Teatr'. In *Izbrannye stat'i. Vospominaniia o khudozhnike*, 17–35. Moscow: Sovetskii Khudozhnik, 1979.
Berkovsky, N. *Literatura i teatr*. Moscow: Iskusstvo, 1969.
Beumers, Birgit. 'The "Thaw" and After: 1953–1986'. In *A History of Russian Theatre*, edited by Robert Leach and Victor Borovsky, 358–381. Cambridge: Cambridge University Press, 1999.
Beumers, Birgit. *Yury Lyubimov: At the Taganka Theatre (1964–1994)*. Amsterdam: Hardwood Academic Press, 1997.
Bowlt, John E. 'Cabaret in Russia'. *Canadian-American Slavic Studies* 19, no. 4 (Winter 1985): 443–463.
Bowlt, John E. *The Silver Age: Russian Art of the Early Twentieth Century and the 'World of Art' Group*, 2nd edn. Newtonville, MA: Oriental Research Partners, 1982.
Bowlt, John E. (ed.). *Russian Avant-Garde Theatre: War, Revolution and Design*. London: Nick Hern, 2014.
Bowlt, John and Nina D. Lobanov-Rostovsky. *Encyclopaedia of Russian Stage Design: 1880–1930: Volume II*. Woodbridge: Antique Collectors' Club, 2013.
Bradby, David and David Williams. *Director's Theatre*. London: Macmillan, 1988.
Braun, Edward. *Meyerhold: A Revolution in Theatre*. London: Methuen, 1998.
Braun, Edward. *Meyerhold on Theatre*. London and New York: Bloomsbury, Methuen Drama, 2016.
Braun, Edward. *Meyerhold on Theatre*. New York: Hill & Wang, 1969.
Braun, Edward. 'Meyerhold: The Final Act'. *New Theatre Quarterly* 9 (1993): 3–15.
Brockett, Oscar (ed.). *Studies in Theatre and Drama: Essays in Honor of Hubert Heffner*. The Hague: Mouton, 1972.
Brodskaia, Galina. 'Literaturnaia zapis''. In *Oleg Efremov o teatre i o sebe*, edited by Anatoly Smeliansky, 133–138. Moscow: Moskovskii khudozhestvennyi teatr, 1997.

Bulgakov, Mikhail. *Dog Heart*, translated by Nicholas Rzhevsky. New York: Slavic Cultural Center Press, 1998.
Bulgakov, Mikhail. *Heart of a Dog*, adapted by A. Chervinskii, translated by Michael Glenny. In *Stars in the Morning Sky*. London: Hern, 1998.
Byckling, Liisa. 'Michael Chekhov's Work as a Director'. In *The Routledge Companion to Michael Chekhov*, edited by Marie-Christine Autant-Mathieu and Yana Meerzon, 21–39. Abingdon: Routledge, 2015.
Carnicke, Sharon Marie. *The Theatrical Instinct: Nikolai Evreinov and the Russian Theatre of the Early Twentieth Century*. New York: Peter Lang, 1989.
Chamberlain, Franc. *Michael Chekhov*. London: Routledge, 2004.
Chambers, David. 'Reconstructing Revizor: An Introduction to "After Penza"'. *Theater* 28, no. 2 (1998): 56–60.
Chebotarskaya, T. 'Geroi Dostoyevskogo v romane i na stsene'. *Moskovskaya Pravda*, 29 May 1958: 3.
Chekhov, Michael. *Lessons for Teachers of His Acting Technique*, edited by Deirdre Hurst du Prey. Ottawa: Dovehouse Editions, 2000.
Chekhov, Michael. *On the Technique of Acting*. New York: Harper Collins, 1991.
Chekhov, Michael. *The Chekhov Theatre Studio*. London: The Curwen Press, 1936.
Chekhov, Michael. *The Path of the Actor*. London and New York: Routledge, 2005.
Chekhov, Michael. *To the Actor*. London and New York: Routledge, 2002.
Clayton, J. Douglas. *Pierrot in Petrograd: The Commedia dell'Arte/Balagan in Twentieth-Century Russian Theatre and Drama*. Montréal; Kingston: McGill-Queen's University Press, 1993.
Collins, Jane and Arnold Aronson. 'Drawing and Design'. *Theatre and Performance Design* 3, nos. 1–2 (2017): 1–3.
Cornford, Tom. 'A New Kind of Conversation: Michael Chekhov's Turn to the Crafts'. *Theatre, Dance and Performance Training* 4, no. 2 (2013): 189–203.
Cornford, Tom. 'Michael Chekhov: The Spiritual Realm and Invisible Body'. In *Theatre and Ghosts: Materiality, Performance and Modernity*, edited by Mary Luckhurst and Emilie Morin, 178–196. Basingstoke: Palgrave Macmillan, 2014.
Cornford, Tom. 'The English Theatre Studios of Michael Chekhov and Michel Saint-Denis 1935–1965'. PhD thesis, University of Warwick, 2012, http://webcat.warwick.ac.uk/record=b2684505~S1 (accessed 12 September 2017).
Courtney, Richard. *Play, Drama, and Thought: The Intellectual Background to Dramatic Education*. London: Cassell, 1968.
Craig, Edward Gordon. *On the Art of Theatre*. Abingdon: Routledge, 2009, 1911.
Crane, Walter. *Line and Form*. London: G. Bell and Sons, 1900.
Cunningham, Rebecca. 'The Russian Women Artist Designers of the Avant-Garde'. *TD&T* 34, no. 2 (1998): 38–52.
Davydova, Marina. 'Za zerkal'noi dver'iu'. *Nezavisimaia gazeta*, 18 March 1997.
D'iakova, Elena. 'Vyshedshie iz odnogo baraka'. *Novaia Gazeta*, 16 May 2016, https://www.novayagazeta.ru/articles/2016/05/16/68617-vyshedshie-iz-odnogo-baraka (accessed 16 February 2018).
Dixon, Ross. 'Slaughtering Sacred Seagulls: An Analysis of Anatoly Efros's Production of *The Seagull* at the Lenkom Theatre in 1967'. *Irish Slavonic Studies* 21 (2001): 49–74.
Dolzhanskii, Roman. 'Vtoroi pokhod na "Grozu"'. *Kommersant'-daily*, 14 February 1997.

Efimov, Adrian. 'Dvizhushchaisia skul'ptura'. In *Chto zhe takoe teatr kukol?* edited by N. V. Filina, 74–88. Moscow: STD, 1990.
Efimov, Adrian. '*Macbeth* at the Puppet Theatre of Nina and Ivan Jefimov'. Typescript in English translation. Moscow: June 1964, 1–13. Efimov collection, Obraztsov State Central Academic Puppet Theatre Museum Archive (GATsTK), Moscow.
Efimova, Nina. *Adventures of a Russian Puppet Theatre. Including Its Discoveries in Making and Performing with Hand-Puppets, Rod-Puppets and Shadow-Figures, Now Disclosed for All*, translated by Elena Mitcoff. Birmingham, MI: Puppetry Imprints, 1935.
Efremov, Oleg. 'Bol'she vsego ustaesh' ot otvetstvennosti'. In *Rezhissyorskii teatr: Razgovory pod zanaves veka*, 141–154. Moscow: Moskovskii khudozhestvennyi teatr, 1999.
Efremov, Oleg. 'Kino i teatr – puti vzaimodeistviia'. *Iskusstvo kino*, 6 (1982): 344–355.
Efremov, Oleg. 'Kogda mne zadaiut vopros: kak voznik vash teatr, kakova ego programma' (1965). In *Oleg Efremov nastoiashchii stroitel' teatra*, edited by Lidiia Bogova, 162–186. Moscow: Zerba E, 2011.
Efremov, Oleg. 'Maski, my vas uznaem!' *Nedelia*, 1 January 1967.
Efremov, Oleg. 'Moi Stanislavskii'. *Sovremennaia dramaturgiia* 3 (1983): 265–270.
Efremov, Oleg. 'Nachnem s Sebia'. *Sovremennaia dramaturgia* 3 (1986): 223–234.
Efremov, Oleg. 'Uroki velikogo mastera'. *Novyi mir* 1 (1977): 261–266.
Efremov, Oleg. 'Vozvrashchenie'. *Sovetskaia kul'tura*, 14 June 1988.
Efros, Anatoly. *Beyond Rehearsal*, translated by James Thomas. New York: Peter Lang, 2009.
Efros, Anatoly. 'Directing Victor Rozov's Plays: The 'Thaw' and the Young Audience'. In *Through the Magic Curtain: Theatre for Children, Adolescents and Youth in the U.S.S.R.: 27 Authoritative Essays*, translated by Miriam Morton. Kentucky: Anchorage Press, 1979.
Efros, Anatoly. 'Energy, Enervation, and the Mathematics of Intrigue: Anatoly Efros in Conversation with Spencer Golub'. *Theatre Quarterly* 7, no. 26 (1977): 28–33.
Efros, Anatoly. *The Craft of Rehearsal*, translated by James Thomas. New York: Peter Lang, 2007.
Efros, Anatoly. *The Joy of Rehearsal*, translated by James Thomas. New York: Peter Lang, 2006, 2011.
Efros, Anatoly. 'What Is Hecuba to Them? Nikolai Gogol's *Marriage* at the Guthrie Theatre', translated by James Thomas. *Theatre Topics* 3, no. 2 (1993): 177–195.
Eremina, Ekatrina. 'Roman c Teatrom', 28 April 2015, http://kultprosvet.by/roman-s-teatrom-kultprosvet/ (accessed 16 February 2018).
Feigelman, Olga. 'Molodye khudozhniki na spektakliakh Meierkhol'da'. In *Tvorcheskoe Nasledie V. E. Meierkhol'da*, edited by L. D. Vendrovskaya and A. V. Fevral'skii, 454–465. Moscow: Vserossiikoe Teatralnoe Obshchestvo, 1978.
Feldman, O. M. (ed.). *N. M. Tarabukin o V. E. Meierkhol'de*. Moscow: OGI, 1998.
Filina, N. V. (ed.). *Chto zhe takoe teatr kukol?: Sbornik statei*. Moscow: STD, 1990.
Flanagan, Hallie. *Shifting Scenes of the Modern European Theatre*. London: George Harrap, 1929.
Freedman, John. *Moscow Performances 1991–1996*. Amsterdam: Harwood, 1997.
Freedman, John. *Moscow Performances II: The 1996–1997 Season*. Amsterdam: Harwood, 1998.

Freedman, John. *Silence's Roar: The Life and Drama of Nikolai Erdman*. Ontario: Mosaic Press, 1992.
Freedman, John and Kama Ginkas. *Provoking Theater: Kama Ginkas Directs*. Hanover: Smith and Kraus, 2003.
Gale, Maggie. *J.B. Priestley*. London: Routledge, 2008.
Ginkas, Kama and Genrietta Ianovskaia. *Shto eto bylo? Rasgovory s Natal'ei Kaz'minoi i bez nee*. Moskva: Artist. Rezhissyor. Teatr, 2014.
Gladkov, Aleksandr. *Meyerhold Speaks, Meyerhold Rehearses*, edited and translated by Alma Law. Amsterdam: Harwood Academic Press, 1997.
Glenny, Michael. *Stars in the Morning Sky*. London: Hern, 1998.
Goder, Dina. 'Zabud'te pro "luch sveta v temnom tsarstvo"'. *Itogi*, 4 March 1997.
Golovashenko, Y. *Klassika na stsene*. Moscow: Iskusstvo, 1964.
Golub, Spencer. *Evreinov: The Theatre of Paradox and Transformation*. Ann Arbor, MI: UMI Research Press, 1984.
Gorchakov, Nikolai. *Rezhissyorskiye uroki Stanislavskogo*. Moscow: Iskusstvo, 1951.
Gorchakov, Nikolai. *Rezhissyorskiye uroki Vakhtangova*. Moscow: Iskusstvo, 1957.
Gorchakov, Nikolai. *The Theater in Soviet Russia*, translated by E. Lehrman. New York: Columbia University Press, 1957.
Gordon, Mel. 'Meyerhold's Biomechanics'. *TDR: The Drama Review* 18, no. 3 (1974): 73–88.
Gozenpud, Aleksandra. *Tsentral'nii detskii teatr 1936–1961*. Moskva: Nauka, 1967.
Gref, Alexander and Elena Slonimskaya. 'Petrushka's Voice'. In *The Routledge Companion to Puppetry and Material Performance*, edited by Dassia N. Posner, Claudia Orenstein, and John Bell, 69–75. London: Routledge, 2014.
Grinvald, Y. 'Vsye moi synovia'. *Moskovskiy Bolshevik* 290, no. 8736 (1948): 3.
Grossman, L. 'Roman-tragediya'. *Vechernyaya Moskva*, 6 May 1958: 4.
Harriman, Lucas. 'The Russian Betrayal of G.K. Chesterton's The Man Who Was Thursday'. *Comparative Literature* 62, no. 1 (2010): 41–54.
Hoover, Marjorie. *Meyerhold and His Set Designers*. New York: Peter Lang, 1988.
Houghton, Norris. *Moscow Rehearsals*. London: George Allen and Unwin, 1938.
Hugo, V. *Les Miserables*, translated by Charles E. Wilbour. Ware: Wordsworth Editions, 1994.
Ikeda, Daisaku. 'Natalia Sats – Triumph of the Human Spirit'. *SGI Quarterly*, http://www.sgiquarterly.org/global2006Jan-1.html (accessed 1 May 2018).
Innes, Christopher and Maria Shevtsova. *The Cambridge Introduction to Theatre Directing*. Cambridge: Cambridge University Press, 2013.
Ivanov, P. 'K voprosu tvorcheskoi vzyskatel'nosti'. *Vechernyaya Moskva*, 14 January 1953: 4.
Ivanov, V. 'Ot sostavitelya'. In *Yevgeny Vakhtangov, Dokumenty i svidetel'stva*, vol. 1, edited by Vl. Ivanov. Moscow: INDRIK, 2011.
Ivanov, V. *Russkiye sezony teatra Gabima*. Moscow: Artist. Rezhissyor. Teatr, 1999.
Jones, Phil. *Drama as Therapy, Vol. 1: Theory, Practice and Research*, 2nd edn. London and New York: Routledge, 2007.
Jurkowski, Henryk. *A History of European Puppetry, Vol. 2: The Twentieth Century*, edited in collaboration with Penny Francis. Lewiston, Queenston, Lampeter: Edwin Mellen Press, 1998.

Kaminskaia, N. 'Vnachale byla Katerina'. *Kul'tura*, 30 December 1997.
Kazanskaya, A. 'Vospominanya o Gritsenko'. In *Vakhtangovets Nikolai Gritsenko*, edited by M. Malikova, 27–29. Moscow: Teatralis, 2011.
Kelly, Catriona. *Petrushka: The Russian Carnival Puppet Theatre*. Cambridge: Cambridge University Press, 1990.
Kirillov, Andrei and Franc Chamberlain (eds.). 'Rehearsal Protocols for *Hamlet* by William Shakespeare at the Second Moscow Art Theatre'. *Theatre, Dance and Performance Training* 4, no. 2 (2013): 243–279.
Kostrova, N. 'Pervye sovetskie kukol'niki'. In *Chto zhe takoe teatr kukol?* edited by N. V. Filina, 88–105. Moscow: STD, 1990.
Kukryniksy. 'V rabote nad "Klopom"'. In *Vstrechi s Meierkhol'dom*, edited by L. D. Vendrovskaya, 382–386. Moscow: Vserossiiskoe Teatral'noe Obshchestvo, 1967.
Law, Alma. 'Chekhov's Russian Hamlet (1924)'. *TDR: The Drama Review* 27, no. 3 (1983): 34–45.
Law, Alma and Mel Gordon. *Meyerhold, Eisenstein and Biomechanics*. Jefferson: McFarland, 2012.
Leach, Robert. *Revolutionary Theatre*. London: Routledge, 1994.
Leach, Robert. 'Russian Theatre in World Theatre'. In *A History of Russian Theatre*, edited by Robert Leach and Victor Borovsky, 1–5. Cambridge: Cambridge University Press, 1999.
Leach, Robert. *Vsevolod Meyerhold*. Cambridge: Cambridge University Press, 1989.
Leach, Robert and Victor Borovsky (eds). *A History of Russian Theatre*. Cambridge: Cambridge University Press, 1999.
Leonard, Charles (ed.). *Michael Chekhov's to the Director and Playwright*. New York: Harper and Row, 1963.
Levy, Emanuel. *The Habima, Israel's National Theater 1917–1977: A Study of Cultural Nationalism*. New York: Columbia University Press, 1979.
Markov, P. 'Printsessa Turandot i sovremennyi teatr'. In *Printsessa Turandot*. Moscow-Petrograd: Gosudarstvennoie Izdatel'stvo, 1923.
Matskin, A. 'Opravdaniye groteska'. *Teatr*, October 1955: 60–68.
Michael Chekhov on Theatre and the Art of Acting. CD, The Working Arts Library, 2005. Disc 1.
Mikhailova, Alla. *Meyerhold and Set Designers*, translated by E. Bessmertnaya. Moscow: Galart, 1995.
Minaev, Boris. 'Genrietta Ianovskaia: ot "Sobach'ego serdtsa"—do "Grozy"'. *Ogonek*, 25 June 1997: 52–54.
Mitter, Shomit and Maria Shevtsova. *Fifty Key Theatre Directors*. Abingdon: Routledge, 2005.
Moore, Sonia. *The Stanislavsky System: The Professional Training of an Actor*. New York: Penguin Books, 1984.
Nataliia Sats v zerkale i otrazheniiakh (2013). The Natalia Sats Musical Theatre for Children, 2014.
Nekrylova, Anna F. Introduction *to Zapiski petrushechnika i stat'i o teatre kukol*, edited by N. A. Zhizhina, 5–32. Leningrad: Iskusstvo, 1980.
Obraztsov, Sergei. *My Profession*. Amsterdam: Fredonia Books, 2001.
O'Mahoney, John. 'The Mighty Munchkin'. *The Guardian*, 20 May 2000, https://www.theguardian.com/music/2000/may/20/classicalmusicandopera (accessed 17 May 2018).

O'Neill, Eugene. *The Unknown O'Neill: Unpublished or Unfamiliar Writings of Eugene O'Neill*. New Haven, CT: Yale University Press, 1988.

Pavis, Patrice. *Contemporary Mise en Scène: Staging Theatre Today*, translated by Joel Anderson. Abingdon and New York: Routledge, 2013.

Petrov, N. *Rezhissyor chitayet p'esu*. Leningrad: State Fiction Publishers, 1934.

Pitches, Jonathan. 'Conclusion: a Common Theatre History? The Russian Tradition in Britain Today: Katie Mitchell, Declan Donnellan and Michael Boyd'. In *Russians in Britain: British Theatre and the Russian Tradition of Actor Training*, edited by Jonathan Pitches, 192–210. London and New York: Routledge, 2012.

Pitches, Jonathan. *Vsevolod Meyerhold*. London and New York: Routledge, 2003.

Pitches, Jonathan (ed.). *Russians in Britain: British Theatre and the Russian Tradition of Actor Training*. Abingdon: Routledge, 2012.

Posner, Dassia N. 'Life-Death and Disobedient Obedience: Russian Modernist Redefinitions of the Puppet'. In *The Routledge Companion to Puppetry and Material Performance*, edited by Dassia N. Posner, Claudia Orenstein and John Bell, 130–143. London: Routledge, 2014.

Posner, Dassia N. 'Performance as Polemic: Tairov's 1920 Princess Brambilla'. *Theatre Survey* 51, no. 1 (May 2010): 33–64.

Posner, Dassia N. 'Sculpture in Motion: Nina Simonovich-Efimova and the Petrushka Theatre'. In *Women in the Arts in the Belle Epoque: Essays on Influential Artists, Writers and Performers*, edited by Paul Fryer. Jefferson, NC: McFarland, 2012.

Posner, Dassia N. *The Director's Prism: E. T. A. Hoffmann and the Russian Theatrical Avant-Garde*. Evanston: Northwestern University Press, 2016.

Radishcheva, Olga. *Stanislavsky i Nemirovich-Danchenko: istoriya teatralnykh otnosheny, 1897–1908*. Moscow: Artist. Rezhissyor. Teatr, 1997.

'Repertuar khudozhnikov N. Ia. Simonovich-Efimovoi i I. S. Efimova v kukol'nom i tenevom teatrakh.' Typescript with handwritten additions, n.d., 2 pp. Efimov collection, Obraztsov State Central Academic Puppet Theatre Museum Archive (GATsTK), Moscow.

Rudnitsky, Konstantin. *Russian and Soviet Theatre: Tradition and the Avant-Garde*, translated by Roxane Permar. London: Thames and Hudson, 2000.

Rudnitsky, Konstantin. *Russkoye rezhissyorskoye iskusstvo, 1898–1917*. Moscow: GITIS, 2014.

Rzhevsky, Nicholas. *Dog Heart*. New York: Slavic Cultural Center Press, 1998.

Šaltenis, Saulius. *Brys, Smert', Brys! A Play in Two Acts*, translated by Edward Radzinskii. Moscow: VAAP, 1977.

Sand, George. *The Snow Man: A Novel*, translated by Virginia Vaughan. Boston: Roberts Brothers, 1871.

Sanders, Julie. *Adaptation and Appropriation*. Abingdon: Routledge, 2016.

Sats, Nataliia. *Deti prichodiat v teatr*. Moskva: Iskusstvo, 1961.

Sats, Nataliia. Foreword to *Zapiski petrushechnika i stat'i o teatre kukol*, edited by N. A. Zhizhina, 33–38. Leningrad: Iskusstvo, 1980.

Sats, Nataliia. *Nash Put': Moskovskii Teatr dlia Detei i ego zritel'*. Moskva: Moskovskii Oblastnoi Otdel Narodnogo Obrazovaniia, 1932.

Sats, Nataliia. *Novelly moei zhizni*, vols. 1 and 2. Moskva: Iskusstvo, 1979, 1984.

Sats, Nataliia. *Sketches from My Life*. English translation of revised Russian text. Moskva: Raduga, 1985.

Sats, Nataliia. 'My Vocation'. In *Theatre for Young Audiences*, edited by Nellie McCaslin, 109–116. New York: Longman, 1978.
Sats, Nataliia. *Vsegda s toboi*. Moskva: Detskaia Literatura, 1965.
Sats, Nataliia. *Zhizn' – iavlenie polosatoe*. Moskva: Novosti, 1991.
Sayler, Oliver. *The Russian Theatre under the Revolution*. London: Brentano's, 1923.
Schneider, Wolfgang and Gerd Taube (eds.). *Kinder- und Jugendtheater in Russland*. Tübingen: Gunter Narr Verlag, 2003.
Senelick, Laurence. *Historical Dictionary of Russian Theatre*. Lanham, MD: Scarecrow, 2007.
Senelick, Laurence. 'Salome in Russia'. *Nineteenth Century Theatre Research* 12, no. 1 (1984): 93.
Senelick, Laurence. *Stanislavsky: A Life in Letters*. London and New York: Routledge, 2014.
Senelick, Laurence. *The Chekhov Theatre: A Century of the Plays in Performance*. Cambridge: Cambridge University Press, 1997.
Senelick, Laurence. 'The Making of a Martyr: The Legend of Meyerhold's Last Public Appearance'. *Theatre Research International* 22 (2003): 157–168.
Senelick, Laurence and Sergei Ostrovsky. *The Soviet Theater: A Documentary History*. New Haven, CT: Yale University Press, 2014.
Shail, George E. 'The Leningrad Theatre of Young Spectators'. Dissertation, New York University, 1980.
Shevtsova, Maria. 'Anatolij Efros Directs Chekhov's *The Cherry Orchard* and Gogol's *Marriage*'. *Theatre Quarterly* 7, no. 26 (1977): 34–46.
Shevtsova, Maria. *Lev Dodin and the Maly Drama Theatre: Process to Performance*. London: Routledge, 2004.
Shevtsova, Maria. *The Theatre Practice of Anatoly Efros, a Contemporary Soviet Director*. Devon: Department of Theatre Dartington College of Arts, 1978.
Shpet, Lenora. *Sovetskii teatr dlia detei: Stranitsy istorii 1918–1945*. Moskva: Iskusstvo, 1971.
Simonovich-Efimova, Nina Ia. *Katalog vystavki. Zhivopis'. Grafika. Teatr. Keramika*. Moscow: Sov. Khudozhnik, 1968.
Simonovich-Efimova, Nina Ia. 'Kukol'nyi teatr khudozhnikov'. Typescript, 1940, 4 pp. Efimov collection, Obraztsov State Central Academic Puppet Theatre Museum Archive (GATsTK), Moscow.
Simonovich-Efimova, Nina Ia. 'Ocherki zhizni i tvorchestva I. S. Efimova'. In *Ob iskusstve i khudozhnikakh*, edited by A. B. Matveeva and Adrian Efimov, 30–39. Moscow: Sovetskii khudozhnik, 1977.
Simonovich-Efimova, Nina Ia. 'O Petrushke'. *Vestnik teatra* 34 (23–28 September 1919): 6–8.
Simonovich-Efimova, Nina Ia. 'Petrushka Gets Sick', translated by Dassia N. Posner. *Puppetry International* 16 (Fall 2004): 29–31.
Simonovich-Efimova, Nina Ia. *Zapiski petrushechnika*. Moscow: Gosudarstvennoe izdatel'stvo, 1925.
Simonovich-Efimova, Nina Ia. *Zapiski petrushechnika i stat'i o teatre kukol*, edited by N. A. Zhizhina. Leningrad: Iskusstvo, 1980.
Skinner, Amy. 'An Introduction to the Russian Theatre Research Network'. *Stanislavski Studies* 3, no. 1 (2015): 31–34.
Skinner, Amy. *Meyerhold and the Cubists*. Bristol: Intellect and Chicago: University of Chicago Press, 2015.

Skinner, Amy. 'Riding the Waves: Uncovering Biomechanics in Britain'. In *Russians in Britain: British Theatre and the Russian Tradition of Actor Training*, edited by Jonathan Pitches, 86–109. London and New York: Routledge, 2012.

Skinner, Amy. 'Spotlights and Searchlights: Theatre and the Russian Revolution'. *Culture Matters*, 4 January 2018, http://culturematters.org.uk/index.php/arts/theatre/item/2705-spotlights-and-searchlights-theatre-and-the-russian-revolution (accessed 18 May 2018).

Slonim, Marc. *Russian Theater from the Empire to the Soviets*. London: Methuen, 1961.

Slonimskaia, Iulia. 'Marionetka'. *Apollon*, 3 March 1916: 1–42.

Smeliansky, Anatoly. *Oleg Efremov o teatre i o sebe*. Moscow: Moskovskii khudozhestvennyi teatr, 1997.

Smeliansky, Anatoly. *Oleg Yefremov: Masters of Soviet Art*. Moscow: Novosti Press Agency Publishing House, 1988.

Smeliansky, Anatoly. 'Russian Theatre in the Post-communist Era'. In *A History of Russian Theatre*, edited by Robert Leach and Victor Borovsky, 382–406. Cambridge: Cambridge University Press, 1999.

Smeliansky, Anatoly. *The Russian Theatre after Stalin*, translated by Patrick Miles. Cambridge: Cambridge University Press, 1999.

Smirnova, N. I. *Sovetskii teatr kukol 1918–1932*. Moscow: Izdatel'stvo akademii nauk SSSR, 1963.

Smirnova, N. I. *Yevgeny Vakhtangov*. Moscow: Znaniye, 1982.

Smirnov-Nesvitsky, Y. *Yevgeny Vakhtangov*. Leningrad: Iskusstvo, 1987.

Solberg, Michelle. 'The Global Post-War Youth Crisis and Contemporary Theatre for Young Audiences in Japan'. PhD thesis, University of Wisconsin–Madison, 2013.

Sosin, Gene. 'Children's Theatre and Drama in the Soviet Union (1917–1953)'. Dissertation, Columbia University, 1958.

Stanislavski, K. S. *An Actor Prepares*, translated by Elizabeth Reynolds Hapgood. London: Geoffrey Bles, 1937.

Stanislavski, K. S. *An Actor's Work*, translated by Jean Benedetti. London: Routledge, 2008.

Stanislavsky, Konstantin. *My Life in Art*, edited and translated by Jean Benedetti. London and New York: Routledge, 2008.

Stanislavsky, Konstantin. 'Nadpis' na portrete'. In *Yevgeny Vakhtangov*, edited by L. Vendrovskaya and G. Kaptereva. Moscow: VTO, 1984.

Stanislavsky, Konstantin. 'Neskolko mislei po povdu rezhissyorskogo fakulteta'. In *Sobranie sochinenii* (8 vols), vol. 6, 288. Moscow: Iskusstvo, 1959.

Stanislavsky, Konstantin. *Rezhissyorskiye ekzemplyary K. S. Stanislavskogo, Tom 3, 1901–1904*. Moscow: Iskusstvo, 1983.

Stanislavsky, Konstantin. *Rezhissyorskiye ekzemplyary K. S. Stanislavskogo, Tom 4, 1902–1905*. Moscow: Iskusstvo, 1986.

Stanislavsky, Konstantin. *Sobranie sochinenii v vos'mi tomakh*, vol. 4. Moscow: Iskusstvo, 1957.

Steiner, Rudolf. *Knowledge of the Higher Worlds: How Is It Achieved?* Forest Row: Rudolf Steiner Press, 2011.

Steiner, Rudolf. 'Understanding the Spiritual World (Part One)' (18 April 1914), in 'The Presence of the Dead on the Spiritual Path', http://wn.rsarchive.org/Lectures/GA154/English/AP1990/19140418p01.html (accessed 3 October 2017).

Stroyeva, M. N. *Rezhissyorskiye iskaniya Stanislavskogo, 1898–1917 (Stanislavsky's Directorial Search, 1898–1917)*. Moscow: Nauka, 1973.
Sulimov, Mar. *Our Diary*, journal of Sulimov's Directing Studio. Notebook 9. 1–70; Notebook 10. 78–80; Notebook 11. 28a–28g, 31–37 // M. V. Sulimov's Archive at the St Petersburg State Theatre Library. OR and RK, F. 54.
Sulimov, Mar. *Posvyashenie v rezhissuru*. St Petersburg: St Petersburg University Publishing House, 2004, http://teatr-lib.ru/Library/Sulimov/dir/ (accessed 1 May 2018).
Swortzell, Lowell (ed.). *Six Plays for Young People from the Federal Theatre Project (1936–1939)*. New York: Greenwood, 1986.
Tairov, Alexander. *Notes of a Director*, translated by William Kulke. Oxford, OH: Miami University Press, 1969.
Taylor, Jane (ed.). *Handspring Puppet Company*. Parkwood, South Africa: David Krut, 2009.
Tcherkasski, Sergei. 'Forward – to Early Stanislavsky! or Reconstruction of Actor Training at the First Studio of the Moscow Art Theatre'. *Stanislavski Studies: Practice, Legacy, and Contemporary Theater* 5, no. 1 (2017): 85–110, http://www.tandfonline.com/doi/full/10.1080/20567790.2017.1298347 (accessed 1 May 2018)
Tcherkasski, Sergei. 'Inside Sulimov's Studio: Directors Perform a Play'. *Stanislavski Studies* 2, no. 2 (2014): 4–46, http://www.tandfonline.com/doi/abs/10.1080/20567790.2014.11419722 (accessed 1 May 2018).
Tcherkasski, Sergei (ed.). *Rezhissyorskaya shkola Sylimova*. St Petersburg: St Petersburg State Theatre Arts Academy, 2013.
Teatr 'Sovremennika'. Stenogramma ot 26 Iiunia 1956, besedy V. S. Rozova i O. N. Efremova o p'ese 'Vechno zhivye' i ee postanovke v studii pri MKhATe', RGALI f. 3152, op. 4, d. 1.
Torda, Thomas Joseph. 'Tairov's Phaedra: Monumental Mythological Tragedy'. *TDR: The Drama Review* 29, no. 4 (1985): 76–90.
Torda, Thomas Joseph. 'Tairov's Princess Brambilla: A Fantastic, Phantasmagoric "Capriccio" at the Moscow Kamerny Theatre'. *Theatre Journal* 32, no. 4 (December 1980): 488–498.
Tovstonogov, G. *Zerkalo stseny*, vol. 1. Leningrad: Iskusstvo, 1984.
Vakhramov, V. 'Luchshie spektakli v peredi'. *Vecherniaia Moskva*, 4 September 1987.
Vakhtangov, Y. *The Vakhtangov Sourcebook*, edited by A. Malaev-Babel. London and New York: Routledge, 2011.
Vakhtangov, Y. *Yevgeny Vakhtangov, Dokumenty i svidetel'stva*, vol. 2, edited by V. Ivanov. Moscow: INDRIK, 2011.
van de Water, Manon. *Moscow Theatres for Young People: A Cultural History of Ideological Coercion and Artistic Innovation, 1917–2000*. New York: Palgrave Macmillan, 2006.
van de Water, Manon. 'Mister Twister or Goodbye America!: The Interdependence of Meanings and Material Conditions'. *Essays in Theatre/Études Théâtrales* 16, no. 1 (1997): 85–93.
van de Water, Manon. 'Raising the Soviet Citizen: Natalia Sats's Revolutionary Theatre for Children and Youth, 1917–1932'. In *Nationalism and Youth in Theatre and Performance*, edited by Angela Schweigart-Gallagher and Victoria Pettersen Lantz, 85–99. London: Routledge, 2014.

Van Gyseghem, André. *Theatre in Soviet Russia*. London: Faber and Faber, 1943.
Viktorov, Viktor. *Nataliia Sats i detskii musikal'nyi teatr*. Moscow: Kompositor, 1993. Translated by Miriam Morton as Victor Victorov, *The Natalia Sats Children's Musical Theatre*. Moscow: Raduga, 1986.
Vinogradov, Yuri, Olga Radishcheva, and Ekaterina Shingareva (selected and ed.). *Moskovsky Khudozhestvenny Teatr v russkoy teatral'noy kritike, 1898-1905*. Moscow: Artist. Director. Theatre, 2005.
Volianskaia, N. 'V tvorcheskoi laboratorii rezhissyora'. *Teatr* 10 (1973): 32–51.
Volkov, N. *Vakhtangov*, Moscow: Korabl', 1922.
Von Kleist, Heinrich. 'On the Marionette Theatre', translated by Thomas G. Neumiller. *TDR: The Drama Review* 16, no. 3 (September 1972): 22–26.
Ward, Winnifred. *Theatre for Children*, rev. edn. Kentucky: Anchorage, 1950.
White, Christine (ed.). *Directors and Designers*. Chicago: Chicago University Press, 2009.
Wolfson, Boris. 'Juggernaut in Drag'. In *Russian Children's Literature and Culture*, edited by Marina Balina and Larissa Rudova, 173–191. New York: Routledge, 2008.
Worrall, Nick. 'Meyerhold Directs Gogol's *Government Inspector*'. *Theatre Quarterly* 2, no. 7 (1972): 75–95.
Worrall, Nick. *Modernism to Realism on the Soviet Stage: Tairov – Vakhtangov – Okhlopkov*. Cambridge: Cambridge University Press, 2008.
Yablonskaya, Miuda N. *Women Artists of Russia's New Age, 1900–1935*, edited and translated by Anthony Parton. New York: Rizzoli International Publications, 1990.
Zaionts, Mariia. 'Luch sveta v svetlom tsarstve'. *Obshchaia gazeta*, 20–26 February 1997.
Zakhava, B. *Vakhtangov i ego studia*, 3rd edn. Moscow: Arsis Books, 2010.

INDEX

Note: Productions and literary works are listed respectively under their playwrights' and authors' name where known.

Abrikosov, Andrei 118
abstract art 29, 60, 105, 131
acrobatics 84, 85, 133
action (*deistvie*) 186
Active Analysis 9, 11, 164, 165, 166–8, 170, 172, 211, 243 n.2
actor
  and audience 31, 71–7, 89–90, 179–91, 201
  casting 146–7
  and character 95–107, 155–6, 170, 244 n.22
  -creator 84, 95–107
  director 15–19, 26, 139, 146, 159, 184
  genius 68–71
  individuality 61–77, 123, 146, 157, 164
  master- 81–2, 84
  and visual arts 27–42
actor-thinkers (*aktery-mysliteliia*) 185
actor training 79, 96, 98, 213, 217, 243 n.7
Adashev School 66
Affective Memory (*affektivnaia pamiat*) 183, 187
agitprop 89
Aïda plays 197–9
Akhmadulina, Anna 251 n.42
Akimov, Nikolai
  production of *Doit-on le dire? (Should we tell?)* (Labiche) 112
Aksenov, VassiliiPavlovich 251 n.42
'*aktrisa-travesty*'
  (travesty actress) 241 n.42
AleksandrinskyTheatre 13
alienation 66, 91–2, 165, 252 n.7

All-Union Radio 171
All-Union Touring Company 137
Alyoshin, Samuel 169
Andropov, Yury 6
Androvskaia, O. N. 246 n.13
animation 133–4
Annensky, Innokenty
  Famira Kifared (See under Tairov, Alexander)
An-sky, S.
  Dybbuk, The (See under Vakhtangov, Yevgeny)
Anthroposophy 96, 102, 236 n.7
aphorism 167
Arbuzov, Alexei 169
art
  Meyerhold's view 31–3
  Michael Chekhov's four qualities 104–7, 165
  Sats's view 139–40
  Tairov's view 81
Art as Vehicle 165
Artaud, Antonin 64
art forms 7, 9, 27, 47, 58, 127, 135, 210
artistic director (*Rezhissyor-postanovshchik*) 112, 117, 121, 125, 127, 136, 137, 140, 141, 165, 168–9, 172, 173, 181, 188, 193, 195–6, 199, 241 n.38, 249 n.13
ASSITEJ 249 n.16, 251 n.38
atmosphere, performance and 16, 23, 26, 37, 61, 82, 85, 90, 99–101, 105, 107, 120, 136, 161, 171, 201, 204, 212
audience
  and actor relationship 31, 71–7, 89–90, 179–91, 201

and director 9, 29–30, 40, 42, 73, 89–90, 100, 146, 154, 184–5, 194
etiquette 131
imaginary 73–4, 93, 212
memories 173
preparation 10, 130–1
and stage 89–90
young 127–40, 193–208, 210, 240 n.19, 241 n.43, 248 n.4, 251 n.38
authenticity 65, 91, 135, 161, 166, 183, 188
avant-garde 2, 4, 5, 27, 28, 51, 61, 69, 82, 173, 193
awareness (*vnimanie*) 163, 167, 183

Babel, Isaac 115, 142
backdrop 82, 87, 189, 212
Bakhrushin Theatre Museum 176, 177
balagan (temporary wooden booth theatre) 45, 228–9 n.9
ballet 85, 86, 127, 130, 137, 138, 140, 240 n.17, 240 n.19, 242 n.56, 243 n.62
Barba, Eugenio 63
Barkhin, Sergei 11, 197, 199, 201, 206
Baudelaire, Charles 175
Beaumarchais, Pierre
  Marriage of Figaro, The (*See under* Stanislavsky, Konstantin)
beauty 25, 64, 75, 81, 86, 87, 89, 104, 106, 113, 139
Beethoven 88
beginnings 99, 105–6, 107, 118
Belgrade International Theatre Festival 174
Benjamin, Walter 83
Berliner Ensemble 174, 175
Bersenev, Ivan 10, 168
Beumers, Birgit 6
Bezin, Ivan 35, 36
Blok, Alexander 4
  Balaganchik (*See* Meyerhold, Vsevolod Emilevich)
Boal, Augusto 165
Boccaccio
  Decameron 58
body language 15, 21
body paint 84
Boleslavsky, Richard 64, 66

Bolshevism 4
Bolshoi Theatre 136, 249 n.7
Bondi, Yuri 132
Boner, Georgette 97
Borisova, Yuliya 113, 118, 119, 122–3
Borovsky, David 189
box office 17, 124
Bradby, David 29, 226 n.7
Braun, Edward 4, 28
Brecht, Bertolt 26, 63, 66, 76, 91, 165, 173, 174–5, 183, 184, 244 n.22
  Visions of Simone Machard, The (*See under* Efros, Anatoly)
Brezhnev, Leonid 6, 140, 168
bridge (metaphor) 40, 41
British acting conservatories 210
Briusov, Valery
  Phaedra (*See under* Tairov, Alexander)
Broadway 97, 104
Brodsky, Joseph 248 n.3
Brook, Peter 2, 63
Bulgakov, Mikhail 142
  Cabal of Hypocrites, The (*See under* Efros, Anatoly)
  Dog's Heart (*See under* Ianovskaia, Genrietta)
  Molière (*See under* Efros, Anatoly)
  Rokovyeiaitsa (*Fatal Eggs*) 199
  Teatralnyi roman (*Black Snow*) 199
Burdzhalov, G. S. 246 n.13

capitalism 80, 87, 91–2, 113, 224 n.13
catharsis 90
censorship 5–6, 115, 136, 161, 169, 181–2, 196, 247 n.1
Central Children's Theatre (CCT) 136, 137, 165–6, 175, 180, 249 n.7
Central Committee of the Communist Party 90, 136
Central Television 171
Chagall, Marc 64, 171
Chambers, David 1, 143, 214, 215
character
  actor- 95–107, 155–6, 170, 244 n.22
  creation 74
  essence 69
  features 45

mode of existence 151, 152, 154, 155, 157, 244 n.24
national 116–17
sketches 36, 123
structure 70, 76
characterization 9, 35, 74, 75–6, 81, 84–6, 88
Cheban, Alexander 101
Chekhov, Anton 13–14, 62, 113, 124, 169, 186
  Cherry Orchard, The (*See under* Efremov, Oleg)
  Ivanov (*See under* Efremov, Oleg)
  Platonov (*See under* Remizova, Alexandra)
  Seagull, The (*See under* Efros, Anatoly; Stanislavsky, Konstantin)
  Three Sisters (*See under* Efros, Anatoly)
  Wedding, The (*See* Vakhtangov, Yevgeny)
Chekhov, Michael 64, 125, 163, 165
  acting/directing techniques 98–107, 165
  life and career 96–8
  productions
    Cricket on the Hearth, The (Dickens) 97
    Deluge, The 105
    Golden Steed, The (Rainis) 104–5
    Government Inspector, The (Gogol) 97, 98, 100
    Hamlet (Shakespeare) 97, 101, 102–3
    King Lear (Shakespeare) 97, 101–2
    Possessed, The (Dostoyevsky) 97, 103–4
    Sorochinsky Fair (Mussorgsky) 98
    Troublemaker-Doublemaker 98
    Twelfth Night (Shakespeare) 97
  on Vakhtangov 69–70, 73–4
Chekhov Moscow Art Theatre 182
Chekhov Theatre Studio 96, 97, 98, 236 n.21
Chernenko, Konstantin 6
Chervinskii, A.

Dog's Heart (Bulgakov) 196–7
Chesterton, G. K.
  Man Who Was Thursday, The (*See under* Tairov, Alexander)
Children's Musical Theatre. *See* Moscow State Children's Musical Theatre
children's theatre school 8, 10, 43–60, 82, 127–40, 151, 165–8, 175, 180, 193–208
Chopin 88
choreography 23, 57, 81, 88
Chronegk, Ludwig 17
circus 129, 133, 152
Civil War 3, 45, 52, 111, 128, 164
classics 10, 17, 75, 90, 103, 110, 114, 125, 142, 171, 174, 175, 176, 182, 202, 250 n.27
class warfare 81
cliché (*shtamp*) 13, 163, 173, 180, 184, 188, 200, 201
climax 25, 107, 141, 151
clowning 85, 152
Cocteau, Jean 91
collectivism/collectivization 5, 81
colour 15, 36, 55, 82, 93, 100–1, 139, 149, 186
comedy 13, 85, 112, 164, 166, 175, 176, 206, 207
commedia dell'arte 28, 75–6, 86, 226 n.8, 230 n.42
communism 37, 75, 103, 132
Communist Party 90, 113–14, 121, 136, 163, 168, 181
compositional schema 37–9
confessional (*ispovedalnyi*) principle 184–5, 188
consistency 149, 152
constructivism 9, 33, 39, 74, 75, 81, 86–8, 89, 132, 227 n.21
Cornford, Tom 9–10, 95–107
corps-de-théâtre 82
cosmopolitanism 117, 163, 238 n.8
costumes 36, 68, 75, 84, 88, 130–1, 139, 158, 197, 202
Council of People's Commissars 136
court drama 86
Craig, Edward Gordon 33–4, 46, 63, 66, 84, 127–8

Crane, Walter 36–7
Crystal Turandot award 202
cubist productions 60, 82, 85–6, 87
Culture Channel 177
curtain 48, 51, 70, 96, 150, 167, 173, 210
cuts, of text 15

Dalcrozeeurhythmics 56
dance 43, 57, 58, 60, 72, 89, 130, 133, 135
dead performance 100
defamiliarization (*verfremdungseffekt*) 26, 184
Demidov, Nikolai 62, 64
demo acting 151, 155, 157
de-Stalinization 6
device (*priem*) 184, 185, 188, 201, 204, 212
Diaghilev, Sergei 91
Dickens, Charles 103
  Cricket on the Hearth, The (See under Chekhov, Michael)
director, role of. See also *individual directors*
  characterization 84–6
  collaboration 81–4, 99, 179, 197–8
  constructivism 86–8
  definitions 44, 79
  essential skills 31
  training/lessons/exercises 134, 141–59
  use of line 39–41
director of result (*rezhissyorarezultata*) 185
director of root (*rezhissyorakorniia*) 185
distancing technique 26
division of labour 14
Dobuzhinsky, Mstislav 98
Dodin, Lev 143, 224 n.18
Donnellan, Declan 2, 210
Doronina, Tatiana 182
Dostoyevsky, Fyodor 103, 125
  Idiot, The (See under Remizova, Alexandra)
  Possessed, The (See under Chekhov, Michael)
double competence 33–6
dramatic forms 175
dramatic instinct, of children 240 n.25
dramaturgy 5, 14, 24, 103, 157, 212
drawing/sketching skills 33–6
Dugin, Vyacheslav 118
Duisburg Theatre Festival 171
dynamism 9, 22, 38, 39–40, 62, 68, 80, 82–3, 86, 100, 104, 139, 173
ease, quality of 104, 105–6
economic dislocation 129, 240 n.14

Efimov, Adrian 43
Efimov, Ivan 45
Efremov, Oleg 179–91
  awards 181
  biography 179–82
  directorial technique 182–91
  productions
    Boris Godunov (Pushkin) 182
    Cherry Orchard, The (Chekhov, Anton) 182
    Ivanov (Chekhov, Anton) 187–8
    Last Ones, The (Gorky) 188
    Lower Depths, The (Gorky) 183
    Sequel to a Legend (Kuznetsov) 183
    Woe from Wit (Griboedov) 182
Efros, Anatoly 161–77
  awards 171, 174
  at Central Children's Theatre (CCT) 165–8
  directing principles 164–5
  legacy 176–7
  at Lenkom Theatre 168–70
  at Malaya Bronnaya Theatre 171–3
  productions
    Ardent Heart, The (Ostrovsky) 164
    Cabal of Hypocrites, The (Bulgakov) 169
    Cherry Orchard, The (Chekhov, Anton) 173, 174, 175
    Dog in the Manger (Lope de Vega) 164
    Don Juan (Molière) 171
    Good Luck! (Rozov) 166
    Good Person of Setzuan (Brecht) 173, 174–5
    Hedda Gabler (Ibsen) 174
    Lovely Sunday for a Picnic, A (Williams) 174

Lower Depths, The (Gorky) 174
Marriage (Gogol) 171
Misanthrope, The (Molière) 174
Molière (Bulgakov) 169
Month in the Country, A
 (Turgenev) 171
My Friend, Kolka! (Khmelik)
 166
Othello (Shakespeare) 171, 175
Romeo and Juliet (Shakespeare)
 171, 175
Seagull, The (Chekhov, Anton)
 169, 175
Three Sisters (Chekhov, Anton)
 171
Visions of Simone Machard, The
 (Brecht) 174
psychological truth in acting 164–5
publications
 Anatoly Efros–Profession:
 Director 177
 Craft of Rehearsal, The 211
 Fourth Book, The
 (*ChetvertajaKniga*) 176
 Joy of Rehearsal, The 211
 Repetitsiya-lyubovmoya
 (Rehearsal Is My Love) 171
 at Taganka Theatre 173–6
Efros, Isaac Vasilievich 162
Ehrenburg, Ilya 6, 161, 247 n.1
Einstein, Albert 64
Elanskaia, K. N. 246 n.13
Elmhirst, Dorothy Whitney 97
Elmhirst, Leonard 97
emotional experience (*perezhivanie*)
 131, 186
emotional honesty 165
empathy 92, 158, 179, 184, 187, 188
Enchanted Pear Tree, The (Simonovich-
 Efimova) 58
endings 99, 105–6, 107, 118
entirety 67–8, 70, 104, 106–7
Erdman, Nikolai 5, 142
 Suicide, The 5
etudes 11, 18, 141, 164, 167, 170–1,
 173, 186–7, 211, 243 n.2
evidence-etudes
 (*etiudy-dokazatelstva*) 186–7
Evreinov, Nikolai 224 n.18

experimentation 2, 5, 27, 136, 241
 n.44, 242 n.46
expressionism 74, 91, 92
Exter, Alexandra 60, 82, 88

fables 51
face of the author 153, 244 n.17
facial expression 57, 72, 134, 200
fairy tales 52, 76, 131, 132, 136, 138–9,
 141, 149, 151, 152, 240 n.25
familiar surprises (*znakomye
 neozhidannosti*) 188
fantastical plays 85
Fantastic Realism 7, 9, 66, 67, 74–7
farce 21, 155, 175, 176
fascism 97, 103, 113, 115, 164
fashion designers 75
Federal Theatre Project 79–80
Feigelman, Olga 35
fencing 85
fine arts 31, 32, 47
First World War 45, 112
Five Year Plans 5
Flanagan, Hallie 80, 87
flashback 149, 156
folk tales 104–5, 164
form 4–8, 10, 22, 27, 30, 33, 34, 36,
 40, 41, 45, 55, 58, 59, 67, 80,
 83, 104–5, 106, 107, 133, 145,
 148, 155, 158, 163, 175, 176,
 189
formalism 41, 120, 133, 136, 163,
 242 n.46
Forterre, Henri 88
Fredro, Aleksander
 Ladies and Hussars (*See under*
 Remizova, Alexandra)
Freedman, John 201
freedom of movement 86
Free Theatre 79
freeze-frame 41
Frenz, Horst 87
Furtseva, Ekaterina 181
futurism 75, 87

Gardiner, Jesse 11, 179–91
Garin, Erast 35
General Political Agency 96, 236 n.8
genius 68–9, 123

genre 14, 130, 132, 143, 144, 148–51, 152, 158, 159, 203–4, 240 n.25, 244 n.24
geometric designs 82, 83, 85, 87, 93
gesture 15
    Chekhov's technique 99–100, 104–5
    Ianovskaia's approach 203
    and movement 71, 83, 86
    puppet 54–9
    rhythm and 64
    Tairov's technique 83
    Vakhtangov's approach 72, 102
Gibson, William
    Miracle Worker, The (See under Ianovskaia, Genrietta)
Ginkas, Kama 193, 194, 195, 206, 207, 211, 248 n.2, 249 n.9, 249 n.14
GITIS 137, 163–4, 165, 167
given circumstances (*predlagaemye obstoiatelstva*) 70, 153, 173, 186, 188
Gladkov, Aleksandr 32
glance 203
glasnost (openness) 6, 11, 140, 181, 182, 193, 195, 197, 199, 241 n.42, 250 n.22
Glazunov, Osvald 114, 115
Glenny, Michael
    Heart of a Dog 250 n.19
    Stars in the Morning Sky 250 n.19
glove-and-rod puppets 51
glove puppets 47, 48, 51, 52, 55, 58, 230 n.42
Goethe, Johann Wolfgang von 114
Gogol, Nikolai 125
    Gamblers (See under Remizova, Alexandra)
    Government Inspector, The (See under Chekhov, Michael; Meyerhold, Vsevolod Emilevich)
    Marriage (See under Efros, Anatoly)
Golden Mask Awards 202
Golovashenko, Y. 122
Golovin, Alexander 33
Golubovsky, Boris 91
Gorbachev, Mikhail 6, 181

Gorchakov, Nikolai 4, 134
Gordon, Mel 252 n.8
Gorky, Maxim 64
    Children of the Sun 15
    Last Ones, The (See under Efremov, Oleg)
    Lower Depths, The (See under Efros, Anatoly)
    Petty Bourgeois, The (*Meshchanye*) 15, 24–5, 225 n.7
Gorky Moscow Art Theatre 182, 207
Goryaev, Vitaly 35
Gozenpud, Aleksandra 249 n.7
Gozzi, Count Carlo
    Princess Turandot (See under Vakhtangov, Yevgeny)
graphic expression 135
Grave, Alexander 118
Greek theatre 85–6, 90, 116
Griboedov, Alexander
    Woe from Wit (See under Efremov, Oleg)
Griboyedovprize 13
Gritsenko, Nikolai 119, 122–3
Grossman, Leonid 122
grotesque 28, 63, 74, 76, 118, 120, 156, 158
Grotowski, Jerzy 63, 64, 165, 243 n.2
Guardian newspaper 252 n.2
GULag 180
Guthrie Theatre 171
gymnastics 84, 85
Gyseghem, André van 3

Habima Theatre (National Theatre of Israel) 64, 97
Hall, Stanley 132
Handspring Puppet Company 60
Harriman, Lucas 87
Hauptmann, Gerhart 14
    Festival of Peace (See under Remizova, Alexandra)
    Before Sunset (See under Remizova, Alexandra)
Hellenistic art 85–6
Hellman, Lillian
    Little Foxes, The (See under Sulimov, Mar)
historical plays 169

Hitler, Adolf 115
Hoffman, E. T. A.
　Princess Brambilla (*See under*
　　Tairov, Alexander)
Hollywood 98
Houghton, Norris 3, 30, 31, 32
Hugo, Victor
　Les Miserables (*See under*
　　Remizova, Alexandra)
humanology 149, 244 n.18
hyper-realism 89

Ianovskaia, Genrietta 8, 193–208
　awards 202
　children's theatre shows 205–6
　productions
　　Balding Cupid, The 206–7
　　Dog's Heart (Bulgakov) 196–9
　　Goodbai Amerika! 200
　　Impostures of Scapin, The
　　　(Molière) 193
　　Miracle Worker, The (Gibson)
　　　193
　　Nightingale 199
　　Storm, The (Ostrovsky) 201–2
　　Wolf and the Seven Goats, The
　　　205–6
Ianshin, M. M. 246 n.13
Ibsen, Henrik
　Hedda Gabler (*See under* Efros,
　　Anatoly)
　Pillars of Society, The 18
igro-spektakl. See play-productions
images, power/function of 31–3
Imaginary Body 99, 165
Imperial Theatres 5, 33
impressionism 74, 87
improvisation 57, 61, 64, 73, 86, 92,
　105–6, 133, 153, 166–7, 170,
　186, 187, 211, 212
industrialization 5
in-house training programme 84–6
inner justification 9, 61, 66
innovation 5, 11, 14, 27–9, 45, 47, 54,
　58, 82, 136, 180, 184, 241 n.44
'intellect via feeling' (*cherezchuvstvo k
　razumu*) 184
inter-artistic collaboration 79
Isaakian, Georgii 140

Jazz and Drama Group 137
joke 89, 203
juggling 56, 76, 85

Kalidasa
　Sakuntala (*See under* Tairov,
　　Alexander)
KamernyTheatre 60, 79–82, 86, 90,
　230 n.36, 252 n.7
Kazakh Theatre of the Young
　Spectator 137
Kazmina, Nataliia 249 n.9
Kedrov, Mikhail 243 n.2
Khmelev, N. P. 246 n.13
Khmelik, Alexander
　My Friend, Kolka! (*See under* Efros,
　　Anatoly)
Khrushchev, Nikita 6, 121–2, 137, 161,
　168, 247 n.1
kinaesthetics 83
Klemperer, Otto 242 n.54
Knebel, Maria 163–4, 165
　*About the Method of Action Analysis
　　of Play and the Role* 243 n.2
Knyazev, Yevgeny 125
Koltsov, Mikhail 115
Komissarzhevskaya, Vera 79, 127
Komsomolskaia Pravda award 202
Koonen, Alisa 60, 79, 81–2, 90
Korostylyov, Vadim
　Commendatore's Footsteps (*See
　　under* Remizova, Alexandra)
Korovina, Yelena 118
Kovalenko, Georgii 87
Krasnoyarsk Theatre of the Young
　Spectator 193
Krylov, Anna 51–2, 228 n.7
Krylov, Ivan 51
Krylov, Porfiri 32
Kugel, Aleksandr 16
Kupriyanov, Mikhail 32
Kuznetsov, Anatoly
　Sequel to a Legend (*See under*
　　Efremov, Oleg)

Labiche, Eugene
　Doit-on le dire? (*Should we tell?*)
　　(*See under* Akimov, Nikolai)
Lamanova, Nadezhda 75

Las Palmas Theatre 98
Law, Alma 102, 252 n.8
Leach, Robert 28
  History of Russian Theatre, A 2
Lecoq, Charles
  Giroflé-Girolfa (*See under* Tairov, Alexander)
Léger, Ferdnand 91
Lelyanova, Larisa 154
Lenin, Vladimir 3, 5, 128, 224 n.13, 240 n.14
Leningrad Comedy Theatre 112
Leningrad Music Hall 112
Leningrad State Institute of Theatre, Music and Cinematography (LGITMiK). *See* St Petersburg State Theatre Arts Academy
Leninsky Komsomol Theatre 249 n.7
Lesgaftexercises 56
Lessing, Gotthold Ephraim 114
Le Théâtre Tchekoff 97
light 15, 33, 37, 55, 57, 87, 101, 158, 189, 197, 204
line
  and associative meaning 36–7
  basic element of visual art 36–7
  and compositional schema 37–9
  improvisation and quality of ease 105–6
  and movement 39–41
linearity 92–3
'line of outer life' (*liniia vneshnei zhizni*) 186
Listengarten, Julia 87
Lope de Vega
  Dog in the Manger (*See under* Efros, Anatoly)
Loscialpo, Flavia 34
Lugavaia, Mariia 207
Lunacharsky, Anatoly 4, 5, 81, 89, 131
Luzhskii, V. V. 246 n.13
Lyceum Theatre 97
Lyubimov, Yuri 172, 173, 174, 224 n.18

Maeterlinck, Maurice
  Blue Bird (*See under* Stanislavsky, Konstantin)
  Miracle of St. Anthony, The (*See under* Vakhtangov, Yevgeny)

Makovetsky, Sergei 125
Malaev-Babel, Andrei 7, 9, 10, 61–77, 109–25, 209, 211
Maly theatre 136
Malyugin, Leonid
  My Mocking Happiness (*See under* Remizova, Alexandra)
Mamet, David 63
Mamin-Sibiryak, Dmitry
  Gold (*See under* Remizova, Alexandra)
Mammalian, Rouben 64
Mamonovsky Alley Theatre 52, 130, 230 n.36
Manet, Édouard 36
Mansurova, Tsitsiliya 115, 118
marionette 45–6, 52, 54–5, 60, 84, 86, 130
Markov, Pavel 65
Marshak, Samuiil
  Mister Twister 200
Marxism 128, 136, 240, 242 n.45
Marxism-Leninism 128, 242 n.45
mask 43, 75–6, 86, 92
Matskin, Aleksandr 120–1
Maximov, Andrei 145, 154
Mayakovsky, Vladimir 4, 32
  Bedbug, The 32
Mayakovsky Theatre 195
McColl, Ewan 2
Mchedelov, V. L. 246 n.13
McPharlin, Paul 60
melodrama 20, 21, 114, 120, 175, 176
memory, nature of 32, 141, 149, 155, 156, 168, 183, 187, 239 n.2
mental analysis 11, 164, 167–8, 170
metaphors 6, 11, 40, 46, 60, 101, 131, 197, 199–200, 201, 212, 214
method of action analysis (*metoddeistvennogoanaliza*) 243 n.2
method of physical actions (*metodfizicheskikhdeistvii*) 18, 186, 243 n.2
Meyerhold, Vsevolod Emilevich 1, 2, 4, 19, 127, 163
  art of 'looking at pictures' 31–3
  birth and education 28

'Courses of Instruction in the Art of Theatre Production' 34
criticism of 80
directing and theatrical practices 27–42, 87, 143
drawing/sketching skills 33–6
'First Attempts at a Stylized Theatre' 226 n.7
innovation and interdisciplinarity 27–9, 41–2
mise-en-scène 29–31
'Naturalistic Theatre and the Theatre of Mood, The' 31
persecution and arrest 28
productions
  Balaganchik (Blok) 229 n.9
  Death of Tarelkin, The 39
  Don Juan 30
  Government Inspector, The 30, 35, 36
  Lady of the Camelias, The 31, 36
  Lake Lyul 39, 87
  Magnanimous Cuckold, The 39
  Roar China! 39–40
  Second Commander, The 36, 37, 38
  Semyon Kotko (Prokofiev) 28
  Sister Beatrice 36
  Thirty-Three Fainting Fits 30
  Woe to Wit 38
use of line 36–41
Vakhtangov on 62
visual art techniques 36–41
Michael Chekhov Theatre Studio Deirdre Hurst du Prey Archive 96
micro-performances 142
Mikhailova, Alla 32–4
Mikhoels, Solomon 171
military communism 75
Miller, Arthur
  All My Sons (See under Remizova, Alexandra)
mimesis 82
Ministry of Culture 180, 196, 199, 249 n.13
mirror, as tool 57, 58
mirror-performance 18
mise-en-scène 9, 27–42, 49, 135, 141, 154, 185, 207, 210, 211

Mitchell, Katie 2, 210
Mobile Theatre 51–4, 79
mode of existence 151, 152, 154, 155, 157, 244 n.24
Molière
  Impostures of Scapin, The (See under Ianovskaia, Genrietta)
  Misanthrope, The (See under Efros, Anatoly)
monologue 25, 111, 150, 155, 204
mood 14, 16, 23, 24, 26, 37, 73, 165, 212
Morton, Miriam 242 n.58
Moscow Art Theatre (MAT) 3, 11, 13, 15–18, 23–6, 64, 66, 84, 96–7, 99, 101, 111, 127–8, 136, 162, 169, 171, 180–5, 187–9, 207, 217, 243 n.7, 246 n.13
  First Studio 64, 66, 96, 111, 246 n.13
  Second Studio 136, 165, 168, 246 n.13
  Third Studio 111, 246 n.13
Moscow Association of Artists 47, 51
Moscow Conservatory 135
Moscow Philharmonic School 13
Moscow Satire Theatre 58
Moscow Soviet of Workers and Red Army Deputies 128
Moscow State Children's Musical Theatre 128–9, 132, 136–40
Moscow State Jewish Theatre (GOSET) 171
Mosfilm 171
Mossovet Theatre 163, 171, 195
motif 86, 88
movement 9, 15, 23, 29, 32, 35–41, 43–4, 52, 54–9, 71–3, 80, 83, 86, 88, 92, 99, 102, 104, 105, 122, 130, 133, 135, 139, 166, 204, 213–14, 232 n.21, 245 n.29
Mozart
  Marriage of Figaro (See under Sats, Natalia Ilinichna)
music 19, 22–3, 50–1, 56, 58, 76, 84–8, 101, 116, 127–8, 129–30, 133, 135–40, 158, 186, 212, 242 n.54
Mussorgsky
  Sorochinsky Fair (See under Chekhov, Michael)

Narkompros (Ministry of Education and Culture) 52, 96–7, 132
Natalia Sats Children's Musical Theatre, The. *See* Moscow State Children's Musical Theatre
naturalism 7, 28, 62, 74, 80, 82, 84, 86, 89, 92, 121, 155, 189
nature of feelings (*prirodachuvstv*) 148, 244 n.17
Nekrylova, Anna 51, 52
Nemirovich-Danchenko, Vladimir 3, 10, 13–19, 21, 25, 26, 28, 63, 66, 99, 153, 163, 164–5, 167, 170, 180–1, 189, 244 n.17
NEP (New Economic Policy) 5, 136, 224 n.13, 241 n.44
new theatre art 97, 98
Nitcenko, Larisa 157

objectives, concept of 9, 73, 100, 136, 149, 172–3, 179, 211, 236 n.7, 243 n.7, 244 n.14
Obraztsov, Sergei 60
October Revolution 45, 51–2, 130
Okhlopkov, Nikolai 89, 224 n.18
Olesha, Yuri 122
O'Neill, Eugene
  All God's Chillun Got Wings (*See under* Tairov, Alexander)
  Desire under the Elms (*See under* Tairov, Alexander)
  Hairy Ape, The (*See under* Tairov, Alexander)
opera 28, 98, 127, 130, 137, 138, 140, 240, 242 n.56, 243 n.62
ostraneniye 26
Ostrovsky, Alexander 125
  Ardent Heart (*See under* Efros, Anatoly; Stanislavsky, Konstantin)
  Enough Stupidity in Every Wise Man (*See under* Remizova, Alexandra)
  Storm, The (*See under* Ianovskaia, Genrietta)
  Truth – That's Fine, But Happiness Is Better (*See under* Sulimov, Mar
Ostrovsky Drama Theatre 164
'*otkaz* moment' 213–15, 252 n.12

Ouspenskaya, Maria 66
outline 35, 37, 59, 67

painting 27, 32, 34, 36, 47, 52, 60, 74, 116, 120, 141
palech paintings (Russian lacquer art) 138
pantomime 32, 133, 135, 229 n.9
parody 188, 200
Pascar, Henriette 132, 138
Pavis, Patrice 29, 30
pedology 136, 241–2 n.45
People's Artist of the USSR award 80, 171
perestroika (rebuilding) 6, 11, 140, 181, 193, 195, 197, 240 n.19, 241 n.42, 249 n.13, 250 n.22
Petrov, Nikolai 163
Petrushka theatre 43–60
petrushki (puppet) 51, 55, 60
phantasmagoria 86
Pisarev, Dmitrii 251 n.34
pitch 134
Pitches, Jonathan 214
play-productions 132–3
point of view 66, 76, 98, 125, 133, 175
Polamishev, Alexander 243 n.2
polarity 2, 99, 102, 104–6
political freedom 81
Polovinkin, Leonid 135
Popov, Alexei 163
Popov, Yevgeny 251 n.42
  Balding Boy, The 206–7
Posner, Dassia N. 7, 9, 43–60
post-impressionism 87
prana (life force) 232 n.21
precision 15, 18, 56, 158
pretext 61
Prey, Deirdre Hurst du 96, 97
  'Actor is the Theatre, The' 98–9
Priestley, J. B.
  An Inspector Calls (*See under* Tairov, Alexander)
professionalism 8, 28, 34, 45, 46, 47, 52, 63, 97, 127, 129, 130, 146, 151, 156, 157, 158, 167, 171, 194, 210, 242 n.56, 248 n.4
Prokofiev, Sergei 28, 129, 136
Proletkult 4–5

propaganda plays 4, 10, 132, 136, 163, 169
props 37, 83, 84, 189
proscenium 48, 89
prose 17, 24, 141
Provorov, Viktor 140
prozodezhda (Meyerholdian costume) 75
psychological acting 10, 169, 175, 244 n.22
Psychological Gesture 70
psychology 27, 29, 158, 166, 167, 175, 186
psychophysics 73, 166, 170
psychotechnique 165
Pulcinella 48
Punch and Judy show 48
Puppeteers of America 60
Puppetry Yearbook (McPharlin) 60
puppet theatre/puppetry
   materials and design innovations 58–9
   mobile theatre 51–4
   origin and development 43–7
   Petrushka/Petrushki tradition 43–60
   puppet as a living being 54–5, 59–60
   puppeteers contrasted with actors/pianist 55–6
   techniques 56–9
   theoretical and practical foundation 54–9
   using bare hands as puppets 60
Purges 5–6, 113, 115, 121, 136–7
Pushkin, Alexander
   Boris Godunov (*See under* Efremov, Oleg)

Rachmaninov, Sergei 98, 127
Racine, Jean 86
radio 112, 171
Radzinsky, Edward 169
Raevskaia, E. M. 246 n.13
Rainis, Janis
   Golden Steed, The (*See under* Chekhov, Michael)
realism 2, 5, 7, 9, 74, 80, 82, 87, 89, 92, 117, 152, 179, 189
Realists, The 163

real time 21
rehearsals
   drawings and sketches 31–6
   Efremov's approach 183–90
   Efros's approach 164, 167–8, 171, 172
   Ianovskaia's approach 194, 200, 203–5
   Meyerhold's approach 29–30, 32–6
   Michael Chekhov's approach 95, 98, 101, 103–7
   pedagogical processes 152, 154–9
   Remizova's approach 109, 111, 115, 121, 123–4
   Sats's approach 129
   Simonovich-Efimova's approach 57
   Stanislavsky's approach 18, 21–2, 26
   Sulimov's approach 142–3, 146, 151–8
   Vakhtangov's approach 61, 64–5, 68, 71–3
Reinhart, Max 63
Rembrandt 32
Remizova, Alexandra 7, 65
   biography 111–13
   'Chekhoviana' 124
   interview 116
   productions
      All My Sons (Miller) 112–13, 117
      Before Sunset (Hauptmann) 112, 114–16
      Commendatore's Footsteps (Korostylyov) 125
      Enough Stupidity in Every Wise Man (Ostrovsky) 113, 124
      Festival of Peace (Hauptmann) 125
      Gamblers (Gogol) 125
      Gold (Mamin-Sibiryak) 112–13, 119–21
      Idiot, The (Dostoyevsky) 114, 121–4
      Key to Slumbers, The (Yagdfeld) 125
      Ladies and Hussars (Fredro) 113, 124
      Les Miserables (Hugo) 112, 117–18

Marriage, The (Simukov) 112
Millionairess, The (Shaw) 113, 124
My Mocking Happiness (Malyugin) 113, 124
Platonov (Chekhov, Anton) 113, 124
Sponger, The (Turgenev) 125
rehearsal techniques 109
Renaissance 36
repetitions 15, 37, 50, 182
representational theatre 67, 74
reverse motion (*obratnyikhod*) 188
rezhissyor. See director
RGALI 34, 217–18
rhythm 22, 39, 50–1, 56, 64, 75, 85, 86, 88, 92, 101, 204, 214
ritual 64
Rodchenko, Alexander 227 n.1
rod puppet design 46, 51, 58, 230 n.42
Roksanova, Maria 14
romanticism 5, 24
Rovina, Hannah 64
Rozanov, Sergei 132–3, 240 n.25
Rozov, Viktor 169
  Alive Forever 180
  Good Luck 180
Rudnitsky, Konstantin 4, 82
Russian-Anglo Research Network 252 n.5
Russian Revolution 3, 4–5, 28, 37, 66, 128
Russian theatre
  elemental process 6–7
  historical/political context 3–7
  influence on contemporary Western theatre 1–3
Russian Theatre Agency 175
Russian Theatre Fund 176
Russian Theatre Research Network 252 n.5
Rzhevsky, Nicholas
  Dog Heart (Bulgakov) 250 n.19

Saint-Denis, Michel 165
Šaltenis, Saulius
  Shoo, Death, Shoo! (*See under* Sulimov, Mar)
Samoylovich, Anatoly 155

Sand, George 54–5, 230 n.42
Sand, Maurice 230 n.42
Sanders, Julie 103
satire 5, 58, 86
Sats, Ilia 127, 128
Sats, Natalia Ilinichna 52, 127–40
  advice and lessons 139–40
  arrest of 137
  life and early work 127–36
  productions
    Be Prepared! 132
    Falstaff (Verdi) 242 n.54
    Marriage of Figaro (Mozart) 242 n.54
    Negro Boy and the Monkey, The 133, 135
    Pearl of Adalmina, The 132
    Peter and the Wolf 129, 136, 242 n.52
  publications
    Children Come to the Theatre (*Detiprikhodiat v teatr*) 137
    Life Is a Streaky Event (*Zhizn – iavlenie polosatoe*) 140
    Sketches from My Life 239 nn.2–3
  under Stalin's purges 136–7
Sats, Nina 239 n.3
Sats, Roksana 137, 138, 240 n.17
Sayler, Oliver 80, 82
scenery 34, 135, 163, 166, 173, 195
scenography 11, 27, 87, 133, 197, 200, 212
'school of experiencing' (*shkola perezhivaniia*) 179, 183
'school of representation' (*shkola predstavleniia*) 183–4
Schopenhauer, Arthur 31, 32
sculpture 27, 74
Seagull award 202
Second World War 113, 179, 241 n.43, 248 n.4
Sellars, Peter 2, 210, 252 n.2
Senelick, Laurence 82, 199
  Streetcar Named Desire, A (Williams) 250 n.21
Seymour, Anna 214
shadow theatre 37, 45–7, 51–4, 58–9, 130, 183

Shalevich, Vyacheslav 121
Shalomytova, Antonia 88
shape 33, 37, 39, 82, 83, 176
Shaw, George Bernard 64, 125
   Millionairess, The (*See under* Remizova, Alexandra)
   St Joan (*See under* Tairov, Alexander)
Shchastnaia, Anna 127, 128
Shchukin Institute 64, 125
Shdanoff, George 97, 103
Shestakov, Viktor 87
Shevtsova, Maria 7, 13–26, 211–12
Shikhmatov, Leonid 115
Shklovsky, Viktor 7
Shpet, Lenora 131
Shvederski, Anatoly 155
silence 22, 203
Simonov, Ruben 112, 117
Simonov, Yevgeny 125
Simonovich-Efimova, Nina 7
   adaptations
      Enchanted Pear Tree, The (Boccaccio) 58
      Macbeth (Shakespeare) 58–9
   lifelong goal 54
   mobile theatre performances 51–4
   Petrushka Gets Sick 48–9, 55
   Petrushka theatre 43–60
   publications
      'About Petrushka' 54, 58
      Notes of a Petrushka Player 54, 56–7
   theory and practice 54–9
   Thirteen Writers 58
Simov, Viktor 19
Simukov, Aleksey
   Marriage, The (*See under* Remizova, Alexandra)
Skinner, Amy 1–11, 27–42, 209–15
slapstick 48, 131
Slonim, Marc 5
Smeliansky, Anatoly 6, 249 n.7
Smoktunovsky, Innokenty 187
Smyshlyaev, Valentin 10, 101, 102, 103
Socialist Realism 5–6, 7, 54, 80, 96, 136, 163, 166
Society of Art and Literature 13, 17
Sokolov, Nikolai 32

Sokolov, Vladimir 60
soliloquy 31, 184
Sotnikova, Yelena 125
sound effects 15–16, 22, 50, 56, 186, 197
Soviet Television 120–1
Soviet Union, collapse of 113–14, 127, 140, 176, 182, 195, 250 n.22
Soviet Writers' Congress 5
Sovremennik Theatre Studio 180, 181, 189, 190
spectator. *See* audience
Spitcin, Yuri 145
Spivak, Semyon 143
spot-lights method (*metod svetovykh piaten*) 189
stage design/set design 14, 16, 32, 34, 37, 39, 81–8, 91–2, 139, 173, 189, 212
Stagnation Era (*zastoi*) 6, 122, 168, 224 n.15
Stalin, Joseph 5–6, 28, 80, 113, 115, 121–2, 136–7, 161, 163, 166, 168, 180–1, 196, 247 n.1
stance 15
Stanislavsky, Konstantin 2, 7, 8–9, 51
   directing and theatrical practices 13–26, 67, 143, 144, 166, 179
   emotional realism 87
   naturalism 28
   productions
      Ardent Heart (Ostrovsky) 63, 164
      Blue Bird (Maeterlinck) 127, 138, 207
      Marriage of Figaro, The (Beaumarchais) 63
      Seagull, The (Chekhov, Anton) 13–15, 19–21
      Sunken Bell, The 14
      Three Sisters, The (Chekhov, Anton) 14, 15–16
      Uncle Vanya (Chekhov, Anton) 14, 15, 16, 17
   psychological truth 164–5
Stanislavsky award 202
Stanislavsky State Opera Theatre, Moscow 28
State Academic Vakhtangov Theatre 64, 66

State Meyerhold Theatre (GosTIM) 3, 223 n.7
Steiner, Rudolf 96, 102, 125, 236 n.7
Stenberg Brothers 83, 91–2
story lines 14, 48
St Petersburg State Theatre Arts Academy 141, 143
Straight, Beatrice 97, 146, 172
Strasberg, Lee 63, 165
Strindberg, August
  Erick XIV (*See under* Vakhtangov, Yevgeny)
Stroyeva, Marianna 16
structural realism 87
stylization 87, 180
'subconscious perception and subconscious expression' 64, 67–9
subtext 15
Sulerzhitsky, Leopold 66
Sulimov, Mar 141–59, 243 n.2
  Action Analysis
    Cherry Orchard, The (Chekhov, Anton) 142, 150
    Duck Hunting (Vampilov) 142
    Last Summer in Chulimsk (Vampilov) 142
    Truth – That's Fine, But Happiness Is Better (Ostrovsky) 142
  directing methodology 143–59
  Initiation to Directing 141–2, 143
  legacy 141–3
  productions
    Little Foxes, The (Hellman) 144
    Shoo, Death, Shoo! (Šaltenis) 143, 144–59, 245 n.29, 245 n.34
    Visible Song 156
  Studio's *Diary* 148–9
  Sulimov's School of Directing 143
Sundgaard, Arnold 98
super-supertask (*sverkh-sverkhzadacha*) 185, 186, 190
surrealism 74
surveillance 6
Suvorin Theatre School 96
Svezhakova, Iuliia 202
swazzle 48
symbolism 28, 34, 63, 70, 74, 83, 85, 92

synthetic production 9, 44, 68, 80, 84, 86, 133, 135
System, The 11, 61–2, 66, 76, 96, 144, 159, 163, 179, 180, 183, 185, 186, 243 n.7, 244 n.14

table reads 200–1, 211
Tagore, Rabindranath 64
Tairov, Alexander 8, 60, 79–93
  actor–audience relationship 89–90
  characterization 84–6
  collaboration 81–4
  constructivism 86–8
  criticism of 80–1, 90
  Notes of a Director 80
  as People's Artist of the USSR 80
  pressure from Soviet authorities 80–1, 90
  productions
    All God's Chillun Got Wings (O'Neill) 91
    Desire under the Elms (O'Neill) 83, 91
    FamiraKifared (Annensky) 85, 88
    Giroflé-Girolfa (Lecoq) 88, 89
    Hairy Ape, The (O'Neill) 91–2
    Inspector Calls, An (Priestley) 91
    Machinal (Treadwell) 91
    Man Who Was Thursday, The (Chesterton) 80, 87–8
    Optimistic Tragedy, The (Vishnevsky) 80, 90, 91, 92
    Phaedra (Briusov) 83, 86
    Princess Brambilla (Hoffman) 86, 92
    Sakuntala (Kalidasa) 84
    Salome (Wilde) 82–3, 88
    St Joan (Shaw) 91
    Threepenny Opera, The (Brecht) 91
  promotion of Western plays 90–2
Tarabukin, Nikolai 37–9, 41
Tarasova, A. K. 246 n.13
Tarkhanov, Mikhail 163
task (*zadacha*) 9, 17, 26, 83, 85, 87, 88, 104, 130, 134–5, 148, 158, 170, 173, 179, 182, 185, 186, 187, 190–1, 211
Tatarinov, Vladimir 101

Taylor, Frederick Winslow 213, 252 n.8
Tcherkasski, Sergei 10, 141–59, 211
television 112, 113, 120, 139, 171, 177
text-and-technique 165
Thaw era 6, 10, 121, 137, 161, 166, 168–9, 180, 196, 247 n.1
Theatre for Young Audiences (TYA) 240 n.15
theatre house (*teatralnyidom*) 189–90
Theatre of the Moscow Soviet of Workers, Soldier, and Peasant Deputies 52
Theatre Square (Sverdlov Square) 136, 165, 168
thematic modernity 164, 174–6
theme 22, 30, 34, 37, 38, 39, 41, 46, 79, 114, 117, 138, 144, 153, 169, 185, 187, 209–15
Thomas, James 161–77, 211
thrillers 87
through-line 114, 145, 151–2
through-line of action (*skvoznoedeistvie*) 186
time, and aesthetic 80
Toen Theatre 171
Tolstoy, Alexei 14
Tolstoy, Lev 66
tone 13, 16, 18, 20, 25–6, 85, 134, 169, 187, 200, 203
Torda, Thomas Joseph 86
Tovstonogov, Georgy 63, 193, 243 n.2, 249 n.7
Tovstonogov Studio 156
tragedy 85, 90, 91, 103, 115, 175, 176, 201
tragicomedy 175, 176
transformation (*perevoploshchennyi*) 182–183
transition 7, 73, 101, 102, 105–6
transnational aesthetics 79
Treadwell, Sophie
   Machinal (See under Tairov, Alexander)
Treplev, Konstantin 247 n.31
   Seagull, The (Chekhov, Anton) 186
triplicity 102, 104
tropes 86
Trotsky, Leon 5

Tsar Fyodor Ioannich (Tolstoy) 14
Turgenev, Ivan
   Sponger, The (See under Remizova, Alexandra)

Ulyanov, Mikhail 113

Vakhtangov, Yevgeny 7, 61–77, 128, 163
   'All Saints' Notes' 67
   biography 66–7
   Fantastic Realism 66, 74–7
   influence 63–6
   instantaneous grasp of character 69–74
   and Meyerhold, comparison with 62, 68, 75
   principles 173
   productions
      Dybbuk, The (An-sky) 64, 67
      Erick XIV (Strindberg) 64, 67, 69–70, 102, 104–5
      Miracle of St. Anthony, The (Maeterlinck) 111
      Princess Turandot (Gozzi) 64, 65–6, 67, 74–7, 111
      Wedding, The (Chekhov, Michael) 64, 111
   subconscious and creativity 67–9
   theatrical uniform/costumes 75
   'Two Final Talks with Students' 67
Vakhtangov Studios 63–4, 66, 75–7, 111–12, 128
Vakhtangov Theatre 64, 111–12
Vakhtangov Theatre Institute (Shchukin School) 113
Vakidin, Victor 35
Vampilov, Alexander
   Duck Hunting (See under Sulimov, Mar
   Last Summer in Chulimsk (See under Sulimov, Mar)
van de Water, Manon 10, 11, 127–40, 193–208
Velásquez, Diego 36
verbs 172, 201
Verdi, Giuseppe
   Aïda 198

Falstaff (*See under* Sats, Natalia Ilinichna)
Veselov, Alexandr 157
Vesnin, Alexander 82–3, 86, 87
Victorov, Victor 139–40
　Natalia Sats Children's Musical Theatre, The 139
video 134
vignettes 16
virtuosity 55, 76
Vishnevsky, Vsevolod
　Optimistic Tragedy, The (*See under* Tairov, Alexander)
visual communication 32
visual effects 15
voice training 84, 85, 128
Volodin, Aleksandr 190

Warden, Claire 8, 9, 79–93
Wilde, Oscar
　Salome (*See under* Tairov, Alexander)
Williams, David 29, 226 n.7
Williams, Tennessee
　Lovely Sunday for a Picnic, A (*See under* Efros, Anatoly)

Streetcar Named Desire, A (*See under* Senelick, Laurence)
World of Art group 33, 46
worldview 47, 60, 179, 183, 185
Worrall, Nick 37
Worth of Life, The (Nemirovich-Danchenko) 13

Yagdfeld, Grigory
　Key to Slumbers, The (*See under* Remizova, Alexandra)
Yakovlev, Yuri 113
Yakulov, Georgy 92
Yeltsin, Boris 6, 182
Yermolova Theatre 174
yoga 70

Zakhava, Boris 69, 71
zastoi. *See* Stagnation Era
Zavadsky, Yuri 65, 112, 163, 231 n.11
Zavalishina, Olga 207
Zeitgeist 175
Ziganshina, Era 202
zigzags (adaptations) 164, 172–3

www.ingramcontent.com/pod-product-compliance
Lightning Source LLC
Chambersburg PA
CBHW052214300426
44115CB00011B/1686